A Chapter A Day

Keeps me on the Lord's way

READING THROUGH THE

New Testament

IN A YEAR

by David E. Sproule, II

A Chapter A Day: Keeps Me on the Lord's Way

David Sproule
4067 Leo Lane
Palm Beach Gardens, FL 33410

ISBN: 9798364941183

Helpful Information
About Using This Book

(You will want to read this!)

The Need for Personal Bible Study

This book is designed to help YOU walk through the New Testament and to build your knowledge-based faith in the exciting truths found therein. Rather than reading multiple chapters each day, the focus of this study tool is on one chapter per day.

Take your time as you read each chapter. Consider carefully and personally what is being said. Put yourself in the setting. Imagine that it was written to you (for it was!). When it comes to Bible study, you will truly "get out" what you "put in."

Suggested Resources for Using This Study Tool

It would be most beneficial to use a reference Bible that has marginal notes, footnotes or center-column references that refer the reader to other Bible passages—such as the location of Old Testament quotations and cross-references to similar passages. This study tool does not provide those reference points which would be found in most reference Bibles.

Be cautious with "Study Bibles" that offer commentary in addition to simple cross-references. Recognize the difference between the words from God and the words from man, and always put the words of man to the test using the words of God (Acts 17:11).

Use a good, reliable translation, such as: King James Version, New King James Version, American Standard Version, New American Standard Bible, English Standard Version. This study tool utilizes the New King James Version in most of its quotes and word excerpts.

Secure some Pigma ink Micron pens for marking your Bible. The fine tips and the bleed-resistant, fade-resistant ink will prove invaluable to you for years to come. Use a ruler or small plastic edge or card for underlining and drawing lines to keep everything straight and crisp.

Component #1 of This Study: The Reading Schedule

In order to read through the New Testament in one year, all you need to read is five chapters per week. This study tool divides those chapters into weekly sections and provides study helps for all seven days of the week. The full daily reading schedule can be found in Appendix B.

Component #2 of This Study: The "Helpful Notes"

There are three "Helpful Notes" provided for each New Testament chapter. These are designed to provide insight into certain elements of the chapter, in order to make it more understandable or to highlight certain words or phrases for deeper study.

Component #3 of This Study: The Review Questions

There are three Review Questions provided for each New Testament chapter. These are designed to have simple answers that are fairly easy to find while reading the chapter. In this way, even children can naturally be part of your daily Bible study. There should be adequate room to write the answers to the questions right here in the book.

Component #4: "Verse for Meditation and Prayer"

There is a key verse from each chapter provided for each day. Spend time reading over that verse several times (five to ten times), focusing on each word and committing the thought of it (if not the very words) to memory. Try reading it out loud. Then, before you conclude your daily study, pray to God and pray through that verse with Him.

Component #5 of This Study: "Mark Your Bible"

Day 6 of every Bible study week is called "Mark Your Bible." This section contains dozens (from 30 to over 70) possible notes that you may want to mark in your Bible—including words to underline or circle, words or phrases to connect within the chapter, word definitions, cross-references to other Bible passages, explanations of Bible words, phrases or teachings, etc. Truly there is more on the "Mark Your Bible" pages than you may be able to digest and mark in one day. How can you handle this?

> Suggestion #1 for "Mark Your Bible": Don't wait until Day 6 to look at those pages. As you read through your daily chapter, look ahead to the marking pages for that chapter. There will likely be some explanatory notes that will be helpful for your study that day.

Suggestion #2 for "Mark Your Bible": You may choose to go ahead and mark your Bible on the days that you are actually reading through the chapter (with some or all of the suggested markings).

Suggestion #3 for "Mark Your Bible": You may choose to use both Day 6 and Day 7 (the "Day of Reflection") to mark your Bible, spreading it over two days.

Suggestion #4 for "Mark Your Bible": There are likely some parts of the "Helpful Notes" for each chapter that you may find worthwhile to also mark in your Bible.

Suggestion #5 for "Mark Your Bible": Find the method that works for you. This is not a rigid system. Marking your Bible should be an enjoyable and learning exercise, which will prove to be beneficial to you for years to come.

Component #8 of This Study: "Day of Reflection"

Sometimes it is nice to pause and ponder. The "Day of Reflection" is designed to intentionally take time to consider what you read during the week, what application you need to make, what helped you draw closer to Jesus, what further study you may want to make at a future time. Even if you don't actually write anything down on these days, take the time to stop and reflect.

Component #7 of This Study: Introduction to N.T. Books

There is some very brief introductory information for each book of the New Testament in Appendix A. You may find some of this helpful to write near the title of each book in your Bible.

Component #8 of This Study: "The Index"

As you study each chapter each day, check the index for words, phrases or concepts that may be addressed and explained elsewhere in the book. There is likely some helpful information contained in the "Helpful Notes" or "Mark Your Bible" section elsewhere in this book that would benefit your study of your daily chapter. Use the index a lot.

Also, as you study through this book, if you find a useful note of information, look back at the index to ensure that you will be able to easily find it again later. If you don't see it in the index, write your own words and page numbers back there to easily reference in future study.

Not Enough?

If you want more than one chapter per day, try reading the same chapter over again but from different translations. Reading the same section of Scripture from multiple, reliable translations can help the text to come alive even more and the difference in translations can sometimes help to explain certain words, phrases and passages. Recommended translations include: King James Version, New King James Version, American Standard Version, New American Standard Bible, English Standard Version.

Sources

Many sources were consulted in compiling the information in this book, including notes from the author's own margins. In order to maintain the readability and simplicity of the pages of this book, specific sources were not cited for word definitions and geographical or historical data. The author does not claim to be an expert in any of these areas. The following sources were used in preparing this book:

Balz, Horst and Gerhard Schneider. *Exegetical Dictionary of the New Testament (3 vols).* Grand Rapids: Eerdmans, 1991.

(BDAG) Bauer, Walter, F.W. Danker, William F. Arndt, and F. Wilbur Gingrich. *A Greek-English Lexicon of the New Testament and other Early Christian Literature.* 3rd ed. Chicago: U Chicago P, 2000.

Mounce, William D. *Mounce's Complete Expository Dictionary of Old & New Testament Words.* Grand Rapids: Zondervan, 2006.

Pfeiffer, Charles F., Howard F. Vos and John Rea. *Wycliffe Bible Dictionary.* Peabody, MA: Hendrickson, 1975.

Renn, Stephen D. (ed). *Expository Dictionary of Bible Words.* Peabody, MA: Hendrickson, 2005.

Robertson, A.T. *Word Pictures in the New Testament (6 vols).* Nashville: Broadman, 1960.

Silva, Moises, J.D. Douglas and Merrill C. Tenney. *Zondervan Illustrated Bible Dictionary.* Grand Rapids: Zondervan, 2011.

Spicq, Ceslas. *Theological Lexicon of the New Testament (3 vols).* Peabody, MA: Hendrickson, 1994.

Thayer, Joseph Henry. *Thayer's Greek-English Lexicon of the New Testament.* Peabody, MA: Hendrickson, 1896.

Vine, W.E. *Vine's Complete Expository Dictionary of Old and New Testament Words.* Nashville: Nelson, 1996.

Table of Contents

Table of Contents

Week 1

January 1-7

January 1	Read Matthew 1
January 2	Read Matthew 2
January 3	Read Matthew 3
January 4	Read Matthew 4
January 5	Read Matthew 5
January 6	Mark Your Bible
January 7	Day of Reflection

Prayer for this week:

"Heavenly Father, help me to truly set aside time to study Your Word this week!"

January 1 Week 1, Day 1

Matthew 1

Helpful Notes: ** See Brief Introduction to Matthew on page 631.*

1. **Begot** = The Greek word *gennao* means "to cause something to come into existence through procreation; to become the parent of; to bring forth"; thus, the term denotes direct descent and it is not used of Jesus in verse 16; the names on this list are limited to those who were in the direct line of Jesus, and other offspring are not mentioned for that reason.
2. **Betrothed** = The Jewish betrothal was much more binding than a modern engagement; the betrothal to be married typically lasted 10-12 months, and the couple was considered to be "husband" (1:19) and "wife" (1:20); unfaithfulness by either party was deemed to be adultery; ending the relationship before the official marriage required a certificate of divorcement.
3. **Virgin** = Jesus was miraculously conceived of the Holy Spirit; the virgin was told, "The Holy Spirit will come upon you, and the power of the Highest will overshadow you; therefore," He would be "called the Son of God" (Luke 1:35); Jesus could not have retained His deity on earth otherwise; Mary was a virgin upon Jesus' birth, but she and Joseph had other children later (Mark 6:3).

1. Who are the five women mentioned (four by name) in the genealogy of Jesus?

2. What do we learn about the heart and true character of Joseph, the earthly father of Jesus?

3. Who prophesied in the Old Testament that Jesus would be born of a virgin?

Verse for Meditation and Prayer: **Matthew 1:21**

"And she will bring forth a Son, and you shall call His name JESUS, for He will save His people from their sins."

Matthew 2

Helpful Notes:

1. **Herod the King** = This was Herod the Great, who was appointed as "The King of the Jews" under Roman rule and finally conquered Palestine in 37 B.C.; Herod began reconstruction of the temple in Jerusalem and it wasn't finished until around 62-64 A.D. (cf. John 2:20); other Herods in the New Testament were his descendants.
2. **Wise Men/Magi** = These were considered to be priests or philosophers (with a devotion to astrology) from east of the Euphrates, perhaps in Persia; they traveled for weeks for the sole purpose of falling down prostrate before the Child Jesus; the legend of "The Three Kings" is just that—legend, as their number is not specified.
3. **Fulfilled** = Matthew wrote especially for a Jewish audience, so he focused quite a bit on Jesus fulfilling Old Testament prophecies; twelve times in the book, Matthew used the word "fulfill" in connection with Jesus and an O.T. prophecy; the Greek word *pleroo* means "to fulfill, to complete, to carry out to the full"; He had to fulfill "all things that are written by the prophets concerning the Son of Man" (Luke 18:31), in order to prove Himself to be the Messiah; there were 332 specific prophecies made and fulfilled.

1. In what city (be specific) was Jesus born, in fulfillment of prophecy (Micah 5:2)?

2. What celestial phenomenon did God create to lead the wise men to Jesus?

3. What did the wise men do (emotionally and physically) when they found the Child Jesus?

Verse for Meditation and Prayer: **Matthew 2:10**

"When they saw the star, they rejoiced with exceedingly great joy."

January 3 Week 1, Day 3

Matthew 3

Helpful Notes:

1. **Pharisees** = This Jewish sect originated during the intertestamental period; they were the largest sect in Jesus' day, numbering around 6,000; Paul said they were "the strictest sect" (Acts 26:5), as they demanded strict adherence to their oral law and traditions, emphasizing that more than the law of God itself; they were the radical legalists among the Jews, who flaunted their religion (Matt. 6:1-18).
2. **Sadducees** = They also originated during the intertestamental period; they held only to the Pentateuch, while the Pharisees held mainly to their traditions; they were the aristocrats and politicians among the Jews, inclined to support Greek ways; they were materialists, who did not believe in the resurrection, the immortality of the soul, angels or spirits; the Sadducees were the majority party in the Sanhedrin and the theological liberals among the Jews.
3. **Righteousness** = Simply stated, it is the quality of being or doing that which is right, and in this case, right in the eyes of God; one is made right with God by submitting to and obeying His commands; Psalm 119:172 says, "All your commandments are righteousness"; Jesus needed to be baptized in order to be right in the eyes of God.

1. What message was John preaching everywhere he went?

2. Why would John try to prevent Jesus from being baptized?

3. In what way were all three members of the Godhead present at Jesus' baptism?

Verse for Meditation and Prayer: **Matthew 3:15**

"But Jesus answered and said to him, 'Permit it to be so now, for thus it is fitting for us to fulfill all righteousness.'"

Matthew 4

Helpful Notes:

1. **Satan** = The Greek word simply means "adversary"; the Greek word for "devil" *(diabolos)* means "slanderer, accuser"; he is the arch-enemy of God and God's people, as he incites people to evil and to sin against God; his eternal destiny of "everlasting fire" is prepared (Matt. 25:41) and reserved (Jude 6), where he will be "tormented day and night forever and ever" (Rev. 20:10).
2. **Repent** = Repentance is a change of mind that leads to a change of action; it is not merely remorse or sorrow, as those fall short of an actual change of mind (Matt. 27:3; John 17:12; Acts 2:37); but godly remorse or sorrow can lead to repentance (2 Cor. 7:10), as one reflects upon the goodness of God (Rom. 2:4); repentance is necessary to be converted (Acts 3:19), and it must be followed by fruits, showing that genuine repentance has taken place.
3. **Galilee** = This is the northern region of Palestine, above the region of Samaria; Jesus was raised in Nazareth, which is Galilee, and He spent much of His ministry in Galilee, as the Jews in Jerusalem turned hostile toward Him; Jesus made Capernaum (on the northern edge of the Sea of Galilee) to be His new hometown.

1. What did Jesus do in response to every temptation of the devil?

2. After Jesus called them, how long did it take Peter, Andrew, James and John to leave their livelihood and start following Him?

3. What good news did Jesus go about preaching among the Jews and Gentiles in Galilee? (What was He preaching "the gospel of"? Remember that "gospel" means "good news.")

Verse for Meditation and Prayer: **Matthew 4:4**

"Man shall not live by bread alone, but by every word that proceeds from the mouth of God."

January 5 Week 1, Day 5

Matthew 5

Helpful Notes:

1. **Blessed** = The word "blessed" comes from the Greek word *makarios,* which is best understood as "happy, fortunate, privileged," with the nature of that which is the highest good based on a right relationship with God; this happiness or joy is not determined or affected by outside circumstances, but it recognizes a certain privilege as a recipient of Divine favor.
2. **Inherit the earth** = All things belong to our God (Psa. 24:1) and He will richly supply all of our needs on this earth (Matt. 6:33; Phil. 4:19); God's people enjoy an abundance of blessings (physical and spiritual) in this life; while our citizenship is in heaven (Phil. 3:20) and we await our inheritance there when this earth is destroyed (1 Pet. 1:4; 2 Pet. 3:10), we are blessed to be part of Christ's kingdom on earth now (Col. 1:13; John 3:3-5); heaven will not be on earth.
3. **Love** = The Greek word for "love" your enemies is *agapao;* the word emphasizes an unselfish, unconditional, self-sacrificing disposition toward others that desires what is best for them and takes action in their best interest; this "love" is known by the actions it takes—as is most evidenced in the actions God took toward us.

1. How can we possibly rejoice and be exceedingly glad when people mistreat us because we are Christians?

2. What supreme example for us to follow does Jesus use for loving our enemies?

3. While a murderer will be in danger of the judgment, who else does Jesus say will be in danger?

Verse for Meditation and Prayer: **Matthew 5:16**

"Let your light so shine before men, that they may see your good works and glorify your Father in heaven."

Mark Your Bible

1. **Matthew 1:1**—Jesus is the fulfillment of O.T. promises: the Seed promised to Abraham (Gen. 22:18), the King promised to David (2 Sam. 7:12-16).
2. **Matthew 1:1**—Matthew provides a legal genealogy, which traces Jesus from Abraham through Joseph, to prove His pure Jewish heritage. Legal genealogies do not always convey exact father-son connections.
3. **Matthew 1:3, 5, 6**—Genealogies did not usually contain the names of women, but leading up to Mary, four women are listed and three of them had obvious sexual blemishes in their records. But Jesus was going to forgive all of that.
4. **Matthew 1:5**—The inclusion of Rahab in the genealogy of Jesus shows the mercy and excellency of God! Thus, she is not called "Rahab the harlot" (as she often is), but simply "Rahab."
5. **Matthew 1:16**—"Of whom" is a feminine, singular pronoun, which points to Mary (of whom Jesus was born) and not Joseph.
6. **Matthew 1:16**—Jesus is "the Christ" (N.T. word for "Messiah," John 1:41), which means "the anointed one"; He is the coming One promised in the Old Testament, and He fulfilled all 332 prophecies made about the Messiah/Christ.
7. **Matthew 1:21**—Jesus means, "Jehovah is salvation."
8. **Matthew 2:1**—Judea was in the southern region of Palestine between the Jordan River and Mediterranean Sea. Samaria and Galilee were to the north.
9. **Matthew 2:1, 5-6**—There was more than one Bethlehem in Palestine. If Jesus had been born in the Bethlehem in Zebulun, He would not have been the Christ.
10. **Matthew 2:2, 8, 11**— The word "worship" is from *proskuneo* (literally, "to kiss towards"), meaning "to prostrate oneself before, to do reverence to."

(continued on next page)

Mark Your Bible

11. **Matthew 2:7, 16**—Herod tried to estimate how old the Child might be, and determined Jesus could have been as old as 2 years of age.
12. **Matthew 2:11**—The masculine, singular pronoun "Him" indicates that they did not worship Mary.
13. **Matthew 2:22**—This is the only mention of Herod the Great's son, Archelaus. He ruled over Judea, Samaria and Idumea for a short time after his father's death. When he was removed, Rome appointed procurators/governors instead (starting in A.D. 6).
14. **Matthew 3:3**—John prepared the way for <u>Jesus</u>. Isaiah 40:3 prophesied that John ("the voice") would prepare the way for <u>Jehovah</u> (LORD). Therefore, Jesus is Jehovah.
15. **Matthew 3:10-12**—"Fire" is the last word in all three verses. It is the same fire (hell fire) in all verses, including the promise that Jesus would baptize in fire.
16. **Matthew 3:11**—The baptism of the Holy Spirit and the baptism of fire are distinct from each other (Acts 1:5; Matt. 13:50).
17. **Matthew 3:14**—The purpose of baptism (John's baptism and Christ's baptism of the Great Commission) is in order to obtain (i.e., "for") the remission of sins. The fact that John "tried to prevent" (imperfect tense emphasizes repeated refusal) the sinless Jesus from being baptized affirms that John knew its purpose.
18. **Matthew 3:16**—The fact that Jesus "came up from the water" helps to establish that baptism involves immersion in water.
19. **Matthew 3:16-17**—The three members of the Godhead could be independently identified at the baptism of Jesus.
20. **Matthew 4:1**—Jesus was tempted in the same ways and with the same devices of the devil that all people from the beginning have been tempted (1 John 2:15-17; Heb. 4:15; Gen. 3:6).
21. **Matthew 4:1, 3, 5, 8, 10, 11**—Underline the words "the devil" (4 uses), "the tempter" and "Satan," and connect them with a line.

Mark Your Bible

22. **Matthew 4:3**—"The tempter" is actually a present tense verb denoting "the ever-tempting one." It is not just a noun of identification but a verb characterizing his constant activity.
23. **Matthew 4:4, 7, 10**—"It is written" is in the Greek perfect tense, emphasizing that what God had written in the past remained just as true and authoritative today.
24. **Matthew 4:17**—The phrase "at hand" means "to draw near, to approach." The kingdom was only three years away (established in Acts 2).
25. **Matthew 4:18**—The Sea of Galilee played a significant and regular part in the life of Jesus. It was 13 miles long and 7 miles wide, and it was 695 feet below sea level.
26. **Matthew 5:5**—As God's faithful children, God's richest blessings in this life are ours on this earth now, but Jesus was not teaching that heaven would be on earth for eternity.
27. **Matthew 5:17**—In fulfilling the Law, Jesus fulfilled all prophecies of the coming Messiah and He obeyed perfectly its requirements. In so doing, He took it out of the way (Eph. 2:14-15; Col. 2:14).
28. **Matthew 5:18**—A jot is the smallest letter in the Hebrew alphabet and a tittle is the smallest stroke of the pen that distinguishes one letter from another. God's Word is sacred and precisely accurate in its minutest detail.
29. **Matthew 5:22**—The Greek word for "hell" is *gehenna*. Of the 12 times it is used in the Greek New Testament, Jesus used it 11 times. The most loving man who ever lived—Jesus—taught more on hell than anyone else in the Bible.
30. **Matthew 5:28**—A continuing, longing gaze that lusts for a woman's body in sinful. It is not the actual equivalent of physical adultery (which is the sexual act itself), but it engages the heart in sin.
31. **Matthew 5:32**—The Greek word for "except" means "apart from, saving for," which emphasizes that this is the one and only exception and there is not another.

January 7

Week 1, Day 7

Day of Reflection

Take time today to reflect on the five chapters that you read this week. You may choose to read all five chapters again, in one sitting, or certain parts of them. Take time today to answer at least one of these questions below. You may or may not write anything down—you can choose to write or simply reflect.

1. What personal application do I need to make from the chapters I have read this week?

2. How can these five chapters help draw me closer to Jesus?

3. What words, phrases or verses in these chapters do I want to go back and study more in depth?

4. What questions do I have about what I have read this week on which I need to do some further Biblical research?

Week 2

January 8-14

January 8	Read Matthew 6
January 9	Read Matthew 7
January 10	Read Matthew 8
January 11	Read Matthew 9
January 12	Read Matthew 10
January 13	Mark Your Bible
January 14	Day of Reflection

Prayer for this week:

"Heavenly Father, help me to enjoy studying from Your Word this week!"

January 8 Week 2, Day 1

Matthew 6

Helpful Notes:

1. **Hypocrites** = The Greek word for "hypocrite" was used for "an actor or pretender," in the sense that one was a "play-actor or role-player"; they were not being "real," but they were being "fake," like an actor on stage speaking behind different masks; the individuals of whom Jesus spoke professed beliefs or opinions that they did not hold, in order to conceal their real feelings or motives; hypocrites say one thing and do another, laying expectations on others that they do not do themselves.
2. **Hallowed** = This word, used to address the Father in prayer, is a verb—a passive imperative in the third person singular; it means "to treat as holy and sacred, consecrate, reverence, sanctify"; obviously God is already holy and sanctified, but He expects to be addressed and approached with that understanding and desire; it is the very opposite of common or ordinary.
3. **Mammon** = The English word "mammon" comes from the Greek word used here, *mamonas;* it is "wealth, riches, material possessions," but more than that, the word signifies "that which is trusted or treasured"; the possession of wealth and riches is not the problem, but when one's trust is in his property, it is not in Christ.

1. In order for the Father to forgive our trespasses, what did Jesus say we must do to others?

2. How can God, others and even ourselves know where our heart is?

3. In order to stop worrying, what did Jesus say to look at and why did He point them out?

Verse for Meditation and Prayer: **Matthew 6:33**

"But seek first the kingdom of God and His righteousness, and all these things shall be added to you."

January 9 Week 2, Day 2

Matthew 7

Helpful Notes:

1. **Narrow** = The Greek word *stenos* means "strait (not to be confused with 'straight'), confined, restricted, compressed, difficult to navigate"; it was used of a narrow passage between high rocks or a particularly tight place; Jesus used this word to describe the entrance into eternal life, and He places this in sharp contrast with the wide, roomy, effortless path that leads to eternal destruction; every person on earth is on one of these two paths.
2. **Scribes** = These were the so-called "scholars" who interpreted the law, sometimes hand-copied the law, and most often taught the law publicly; they were called "lawyers" and "teachers of the law," and were very influential due to the high respect Jews had for their knowledge of the law; they considered themselves the protectors of the oral traditions of the Jews; most of them were Pharisees and many of them were members of the Sanhedrin.
3. **False prophets** = Jesus warned about teachers who sound good and look good but are not teachers of true doctrine; every teacher must be checked, to ensure that what is being taught is truly what the Bible teaches; while some today suggest we should "not judge" others in their teaching, Jesus commands just the opposite.

1. Instead of teaching not to judge at all, how does Jesus say we will be judged when we do judge others?

2. What will Jesus say to those who claim to be following Him but are not actually doing His will?

3. Unlike all others, with what did Jesus teach that others could not (and did not), which astonished His hearers?

Verse for Meditation and Prayer: **Matthew 7:21**

"Not everyone who says to Me, 'Lord, Lord,' shall enter the kingdom of heaven, but he who does the will of My Father in heaven."

Matthew 8

Helpful Notes:

1. **Leprosy, priest** = Leprosy was a horribly dreaded disease in Bible times, that involved a contagious, scaly condition that required those inflicted to separate themselves from civilization (leprosy of the ancient world is not the same as modern-day Hansen's disease); under the Law of Moses, the priests diagnosed one inflicted with leprosy and were the only ones who could diagnose one as cured and allow him or her back among the people (Lev. 13-14).
2. **Centurion** = This was a commander of one hundred soldiers in the Roman army, which also identified him as a Gentile; interestingly, most of the centurions mentioned in the N.T. are presented in a favorable light (Matt. 8:5-13; 27:54; Acts 10:1-2; 27:43).
3. **Gadarenes/Gerasenes** = These are the names of the inhabitants of Gadara/Gerasa; these areas likely overlapped, with Gadara considered the chief city of the area and Gerasa referring to a larger area; Gadara was located about 6 miles southeast of the southern end of the Sea of Galilee, as part of Decapolis; the area was predominantly non-Jewish; this is the only mention in the N.T.

1. What relative did Peter have, which helps to prove that he was not the first Pope?

2. Rather than live in a stately mansion with all the splendor of a king, what did Jesus say about where He lived?

3. When Jesus rebuked His disciples and the storm, what did the storm immediately do?

Verse for Meditation and Prayer: **Matthew 8:11**

"And I say to you that many will come from east and west, and sit down with Abraham, Isaac, and Jacob in the kingdom of heaven."

January 11 Week 2, Day 4

Matthew 9

<u>Helpful Notes:</u>

1. **His own city** = During His ministry, Jesus made Capernaum His home base (Matt. 4:12-16); Capernaum was on the northern edge of the Sea of Galilee, west of the mouth of the Jordan River; it appears to have been a town of considerable size in the days of Christ, and the gospels record many events in this city; however, Jesus pronounced a woe of destruction because the people there did not follow Him (Matt. 11:23-24).
2. **Publican** = This is a term used in the older translations for a "tax collector"; tax collectors were hated by the Jews and viewed as traitors, compromisers, oppressors and apostates, working to perpetuate Roman rule (a pagan power) over them; tax collectors usually demanded more taxes than were required in order to enrich themselves; it's intriguing that Jesus chose a tax collector to be one of His apostles and an author of a N.T. book.
3. **Sinners** = This was a common designation of the Pharisees for all who did not observe the tradition of the elders, especially their self-imposed rules of purification; these people were not welcome in the synagogues; the term is applied to particularly disreputable people like prostitutes.

1. When the Pharisees maintained their elite, arrogant, judgmental attitude, what did Jesus say they needed to learn?
2. Why was Jesus moved with compassion for the people?
3. In the great harvest field of souls wanting and needing to be saved, what does the Lord of harvest need?

Verse for Meditation and Prayer: **<u>Matthew 9:38</u>**

"Therefore pray the Lord of the harvest to send out laborers into His harvest."

January 12 Week 2, Day 5

Matthew 10

Helpful Notes:

1. **Disciple** = The Greek word for disciple, *mathetes*, is found over 250 times in the N.T., and it refers to "a learner, pupil, one who follows the teachings of another"; the term most often refers to the followers of Jesus, in general, and it sometimes refers to the twelve apostles specifically; disciples of Christ were given a special name by the Lord in the book of Acts: "Christians" (Acts 11:26).
2. **Destroy** = This is not extinction or annihilation; the Greek word *apollumi* means "ruin, loss, not of being, but of well-being," which is descriptive of the eternal and conscious torment (Matt. 25:46; Luke 16:19-31) that one experiences when separated from God upon one's banishment in hell (2 Thess. 1:9); the same Greek word is used of "lost" sheep (Matt. 10:6), "lost" son (Luke 15:24), and of the disciples "perishing" with hunger (Luke 15:17) or in a storm (Luke 8:24)—it certainly does not entail going "out of existence."
3. **Hell** = Jesus taught that this is a real place where fires of torment burn for eternity and there will be eternal, conscious punishment of the wicked (Matt. 25:46); the Greek word *gehenna* had its origin in "the Valley of Hinnom" outside Jerusalem, where babies were sacrificed to the god Molech, and eventually it became the city dump, where the fire was continually burning; it was a horrendous place that involved perpetual suffering and weeping.

1. What did Jesus tell the apostles to do when people would "not receive you nor hear your words"?

2. What promise is made for those who confess Christ?

3. Since the message of the gospel would be so exclusive and sharp, what did Jesus say would happen to some families?

Verse for Meditation and Prayer: **Matthew 10:28**

"And do not fear those who kill the body but cannot kill the soul. But rather fear Him who is able to destroy both soul and body in hell."

Mark Your Bible

1. **Matthew 6:1, 5, 16**—The expressions "to be seen" and "that they may appear" denote the purpose of the actions and involves a performance designed to gain attention, admiration and accolades.
2. **Matthew 6:2, 5, 16**—The expression "have their reward" indicates they have "fully received" all the reward they will ever get.
3. **Matthew 6:7**—Praying the same thing multiple times is not wrong (Matt. 26:44; 2 Cor. 12:8). But when saying the same thing (i.e., repetitions) is done idly (like certain religions, even counting how many of the same prayers are said), Jesus condemned such.
4. **Matthew 6:8, 32**—Connect these two verses: Your Father knows all that you need. Underline those words.
5. **Matthew 6:9**—Our prayers are to be directed to and addressed to our "Father" in heaven (cf. John 15:16; 16:23).
6. **Matthew 6:10**—The kingdom of God did come in Acts 2 and Christ is reigning now as King (Col. 1:13; Rev. 1:9). The kingdom is the church (Matt. 16:18-19). There will be an eternal reign of Christ in His heavenly kingdom (2 Tim. 4:18), but that will not be on earth.
7. **Matthew 6:12**—Circle the word "as." God's forgiveness of our sins is contingent upon ("as," a comparative adverb) our forgiveness of others (cf. 6:14-15).
8. **Matthew 6:25, 27, 31, 34**—"Worry" literally means "to draw in different directions, divide the mind, split up inside, distract." Worry is at its core a thought process driven by and into anxiety. A Christian must endeavor to stop worry from invading his mind.
9. **Matthew 6:33**—Proper priorities must be set in life. Christ will accept no place less than first. "Seek" is a present tense imperative, indicating continuous, ongoing obligation (not optional).
10. **Matthew 7:1**—Jesus is not condemning all judging, for He expects us (1) to be able to identify "dogs" and "hogs" (7:6), (2) to inspect and differentiate fruits (7:20), and (3) He commands us to "judge with righteous judgment" (John 7:24).

(continued on next page)

Mark Your Bible

11. **Matthew 7:2**—Jesus affirms that the standard or measurement by which you judge others will be used to judge you. Therefore, use the Bible (Acts 17:11; 1 Thess. 5:21-22), for all will be judged by it (John 12:48).
12. **Matthew 7:7**—"Ask, seek, knock" are in the Greek present tense, emphasizing to keep on doing this continually. See also James 4:2.
13. **Matthew 7:11**—Not only does our heavenly Father "know" what we need (6:8, 32), but He will continually "give good things" to His children who "keep on asking" (present tense) Him (cf. Jas. 1:17).
14. **Matthew 7:12**—"Do also to them" is a Greek present tense imperative, denoting sustained activity as commanded by God. It is not a "one-time thing" or "when-it's-convenient thing." It is an "all-the-time-as-Jesus-wants-me-to thing." The Golden Rule has and will change relationships in homes, nations, workplaces and churches.
15. **Matthew 7:21**—Belief and calling on Jesus as Lord are not sufficient for salvation (cf. Luke 6:46). Underline this key verse.
16. **Matthew 7:22-23**—"Many" sincerely religious people will be condemned to hell for doing what they felt was right but was not actually authorized by God. Circle the word "many" in verse 22 and the word "many" in verse 13 and draw a line to connect them.
17. **Matthew 7:24, 26**—The difference between a "wise" person and a "foolish" person is that the wise "does" what Jesus says and the foolish "does not do" what Jesus says.
18. **Matthew 7:28**—The word "astonished" is in the Greek imperfect tense, emphasizing an ongoing amazement at Jesus' teaching.
19. **Matthew 8:10**—Interestingly, Jesus praises the "great faith" of two individuals during His ministry and they were both Gentiles (cf. 15:28).
20. **Matthew 8:11-12**—Jesus predicts that many Gentiles would be saved but most Jews (who should have received His kingdom, for it was theirs for the taking) would be lost.

Mark Your Bible

21. **Matthew 8:11**—This implies that there will be recognition after death.
22. **Matthew 8:14**—The N.T. emphasizes more than once that Peter was married (cf. 1 Cor. 9:5), which does not coincide with modern religious dogma that claims Peter to be the first pope (and celibate).
23. **Matthew 8:21**—Many things in life are not intrinsically wrong until they take priority over Christ and serving Him.
24. **Matthew 8:26**—Jesus frequently denounced His disciples' lack of faith (cf. 14:31; 16:8). Even in the very presence of Christ Himself, their "little faith" was evident but not acceptable.
25. **Matthew 9:2**—True faith is evident through action (Jas. 2:18).
26. **Matthew 9:6**—Jesus had the power to forgive anyone of any sin without any conditions (including the thief on the cross).
27. **Matthew 9:13**—Without genuine concern for people, going through the motions of serving the Lord is worthless.
28. **Matthew 9:13**—Of course, all are sinners. The difference is in those who know it (i.e., acknowledge that they are "sinners") and those who ignore it (i.e., perceive themselves to be "the righteous").
29. **Matthew 9:34**—They did not deny that a miracle had actually been done, and that should have jarred them (see 12:22-32).
30. **Matthew 10:3**—"Lebbaeus, whose surname was Thaddaeus" is another name for Judas the son of James (Luke 6:16; Acts 1:13; John 14:22).
31. **Matthew 10:14**—The Jews considered even dust from the Gentiles to be polluted and unholy. If a Jew rejected the apostles, they were to be treated as a heathen Gentile and to renounce further contact.
32. **Matthew 10:19-20**—This promise was to the apostles specifically and is not made to man today. We have the Bible.
33. **Matthew 10:26, 28, 31**—Underline and connect "do not fear."
34. **Matthew 10:28**—Jesus distinguishes between the soul and the body. The soul is eternal, the body is temporary.

Day of Reflection

Take time today to reflect on the five chapters that you read this week. You may choose to read all five chapters again, in one sitting, or certain parts of them. Take time today to answer at least one of these questions below. You may or may not write anything down—you can choose to write or simply reflect.

1. What personal application do I need to make from the chapters I have read this week?

2. How can these five chapters help draw me closer to Jesus?

3. What words, phrases or verses in these chapters do I want to go back and study more in depth?

4. What questions do I have about what I have read this week on which I need to do some further Biblical research?

Week 3

January 15-21

January 15	Read Matthew 11
January 16	Read Matthew 12
January 17	Read Matthew 13
January 18	Read Matthew 14
January 19	Read Matthew 15
January 20	Mark Your Bible
January 21	Day of Reflection

Prayer for this week:

"Heavenly Father,
thank You for giving me the Bible!"

Matthew 11

Helpful Notes:

1. **Hades** = There is a major difference between "hell" and "Hades," which is not reflected in the KJV (see "Helpful Notes" on Matthew 10 for "Hell"); "Hades" (the N.T. equivalent of the O.T. "Sheol") is the intermediate state of the dead, where the spirits/souls of the righteous (in Paradise) and the wicked (in torments) await the resurrection at Christ's return; the two separate regions of Hades can be seen in Luke 16:19-31, Acts 2:27, 31, etc.; at Christ's return, Hades will deliver up the spirits therein to appear in judgment before Christ (Rev. 1:18; 20:11-14).
2. **Yoke** = The word indicates labor and service, and it was used to expedite the bearing of burdens; one may think that Christ even using the word "yoke" would involve a heavy burden, but He said that His yoke is "easy" and "light," for (1) it is fitted to our greatest needs, (2) Jesus helps us with it [for there are two sides to share in a yoke] and (3) our love motivates us (1 John 5:3).
3. **Meek** = The Greek word *praus* (adjective) or *prautes* (noun) is used to describe the perfect combination of strength and gentleness, in which one's power, strength and temper are kept under control by one's spirit (and by one's submission to God); simply stated, meekness involves "strength under control," and is perfectly possessed and demonstrated in the life of Christ.

1. How did Jesus describe the character of John the Baptist?

2. Why was Jesus rebuking the cities where He had been preaching?

3. What is it about the invitation of Jesus in Matthew 11:28-30 that is so appealing and comforting?

Verse for Meditation and Prayer: **Matthew 11:28**

"Come to Me, all you who labor and are heavy laden, and I will give you rest."

Matthew 12

Helpful Notes:

1. **Beelzebub** = This was a name from ancient idolatry (perhaps of a Philistine deity) that was applied by the Jews to the power of Satan ("the ruler of the demons"); the Jews disparagingly aligned this term with Jesus, when He was casting out demons—a woefully inconsistent argument which Jesus refuted easily.
2. **Demons** = These were unclean, evil, malevolent spirits (not "devils"), who were permitted by God in the days of Jesus and the apostles to inhabit some people (under the control of "the prince of demons," the devil); this temporary (i.e., limited to this period of time only) possession was no doubt for the purpose of demonstrating the superior power of God over the devil; demon possession would (and did) cease when the miraculous powers ceased and Divine revelation was complete (Zech. 13:1-2; 1 Cor. 13:8-13).
3. **Sign** = The Greek word *semeion* generically applied to a "distinguishing mark whereby something is known"; the word was often applied to miracles to emphasize the proof that a miracle demonstrated of the Divine power behind it for the purpose of demonstrating the Divine authority of the one performing it.

1. The Pharisees made up their own laws and traditions about the Sabbath, but whose laws of the Sabbath were actually binding?

2. Rather than casting out demons by the power of the devil, by whose power did Jesus cast out demons?

3. In a spiritual sense, who did Jesus say are His mother and brother and sister?

Verse for Meditation and Prayer: **Matthew 12:35**

"A good man out of the good treasure of his heart brings forth good things, and an evil man out of the evil treasure brings forth evil things."

January 17

Week 3, Day 3

Matthew 13

Helpful Notes:

1. **Kingdom of heaven** = Matthew is the only writer to use this expression (and he uses it 32 times); he uses this interchangeably with the more common "kingdom of God" (used by other N.T. writers) five times; the O.T. prophets foretold of a coming kingdom, which "the God of heaven" would "set up" (Dan. 2:44) and over which the Messiah King would rule; Christ's kingdom is His church (Matt. 16:18-19), which was set up in Acts 2.
2. **Parable** = The Greek *parabole* literally means "a placing beside," denoting placing one thing beside another thing for comparison; in telling parables, Jesus laid a story next to a valuable lesson He wanted to teach in order to prove His point; a parable, then, is an earthly story with a heavenly meaning, designed to reveal truth (to those searching) and conceal truth (from dishonest hearts).
3. **Tares** = In the parable, the tares are "the sons of the wicked ones," who have been sown by the devil; it is possible that these are referring to bad seeds in the kingdom/church, who have fallen away from the Lord and yielded to the devil's influence; however, since Jesus says, "the field is the world," the tares more likely represent the wicked followers of the devil, who are living right alongside the righteous followers of Christ in the world, "practicing" (present tense) evil; when He returns, Jesus will cast them into hell.

1. How does Jesus use a small mustard seed to illustrate the growth of His kingdom/church?
2. In the parables of the tares and the dragnet, how does Jesus describe hell?
3. When a disciple teaches about the kingdom of heaven, Jesus said he is like a "householder" bringing "out of his" what?

Verse for Meditation and Prayer: **Matthew 13:44**

"Again, the kingdom of heaven is like treasure hidden in a field, which a man found and hid; and for joy over it he goes and sells all that he has and buys that field."

January 18 — Week 3, Day 4

Matthew 14

Helpful Notes:

1. **Herod the tetrarch** = This is Herod Antipas, a son of Herod the Great (Matt. 2), who was tetrarch of Galilee and Perea after his father's death; he divorced the daughter of Aretas, an Arab king, to marry his niece, Herodias, who had deserted her husband (Herod's brother, Philip); he is the Herod before whom Jesus appeared on trial in Luke 23:6-12, and he is the uncle of Herod Agrippa I, who murdered the apostle James (Acts 12:1-24).
2. **Prophet** = Generally, this is a spokesman, one who speaks forth or openly, especially doing so for another; specifically of John, he was a person inspired to proclaim or reveal the mind or counsel of God; while a prophet would sometimes foretell the future (as did some O.T. prophets), the word itself does not demand that meaning; a prophet spoke of things (as revealed by God to him) that could not have been naturally known—of past, present or future.
3. **Fourth watch** = The ancient Jews divided the night hours (between sunset and sunrise) into three watches (see Judges 7:19); the Romans divided the night hours into four equal periods; the fourth watch would have been 3:00-6:00 a.m.

1. Twice in this chapter, it says that Jesus went away to a place "by Himself." What can we learn from that?

2. How was it possible that Peter himself could walk upon the water and why then did he sink?

3. What does that word "immediately" (used three times in verses 22-33) tell us about the response of Jesus to His people?

Verse for Meditation and Prayer: **Matthew 14:33**

"Then those who were in the boat came and worshiped Him, saying, 'Truly You are the Son of God.'"

January 19 Week 3, Day 5

Matthew 15

Helpful Notes:

1. **Tradition** = The Greek word for "tradition" simply refers to "instruction that has been handed down"; the Jews had oral teachings that were handed down (and to which they held firmly), which involved human laws and practices that "transgressed" the law of God, for they went beyond what "is written" (Matt. 15:3; Col. 2:8; 1 Cor. 4:6; 2 John 9); traditions of men must never be elevated to the place of sacred law, and sacred law must never be reduced to the level of human tradition (Matt. 15:8-9; Mark 7:1-13).
2. **Heart** = The word "heart" is mostly used in Scripture in a figurative sense to denote the inner person, seat of emotions and center of all mental functions, from which flows all thoughts, passions and desires, leading one to act in accordance therewith; the term is often used in ways that we might think of using the word "soul" or "mind"; since "out of the heart" proceeds good or evil, we must always guard our heart, as to what we allow in and out of it.
3. **Tyre and Sidon** = These are cities of Phoenicia on the Mediterranean coast (about as far north as Jesus traveled); Jesus entered Gentile territory for the first time in His ministry when He visited these cities.

1. When men bind their own traditions, what effect does that have on the law/commandments of God?

2. What will happen to every doctrine and religion (i.e., "every plant") that God has "not planted"?

3. When teachers who are blind to the truth lead people who are blind to the truth, where will they end up?

Verse for Meditation and Prayer: **Matthew 15:8**

*"These people draw near to Me with their mouth,
And honor Me with their lips, But their heart is far from Me."*

Mark Your Bible

1. **Matthew 11:5**—All of these things were fulfillment of O.T. Scripture and expected of the coming Messiah (Isa. 29:18; 35:4-6; 61:1).
2. **Matthew 11:9**—John the Baptist was "more than" an ordinary prophet, for he was the herald of the Messiah Himself (Matt. 3:10-12), he was supernaturally conceived (Luke 1:7, 13, 24), and he was the subject of O.T. prophecy (Isa. 40:3; Mal. 3:1; 4:4-6).
3. **Matthew 11:11**—Everyone in the kingdom would be greater than John because each of them would have a greater knowledge of Christ and His eternal scheme of redemption and they would have the full abundance of spiritual blessings (Eph. 1:3; 3:3-4).
4. **Matthew 11:14**—John fulfilled the prophecies that Malachi made about Elijah, who would come before Christ (Mal. 3:1; 4:5-6; Matt. 17:10-13).
5. **Matthew 11:18-19**—This was NOT teaching that Jesus was a glutton or that Jesus drank wine. This was a mocking accusation being made against John and Jesus for the purpose of trying to discredit them. Jesus said that they lacked "wisdom."
6. **Matthew 11:20-24**—All peoples have opportunities to repent, but where repentance is not forthcoming, then a severe but just punishment is certain (Heb. 10:29). As certain as eternal punishment is for those who reject God, the degree of the punishment will coincide with the degree to which one responded to God's opportunities (cf. Luke 12:47-48). God is the righteous Judge (Gen. 18:25; 2 Tim. 4:8)!
7. **Matthew 11:27**—Christ revealed the Father to us, for the Father and the Son are one (John 14:8-11; 10:30).
8. **Matthew 11:28-30**—The rest that Christians enjoy in this life is truly a peace of soul that surpasses all understanding (Phil. 4:6-7).
9. **Matthew 12:3-4**—Jesus was not condoning what David did, but His point was that the Pharisees did not condemn David for his actions, but they were condemning the disciples for something that God did not condemn (but only their traditions did).

(continued on next page)

Mark Your Bible

10. **Matthew 12:8**—There is no justification in this passage for setting aside God's law for any reason. Jesus was more qualified than these Pharisees to assess the law and its proper application.

11. **Matthew 12:24-32**—They blasphemed the Holy Spirit when they claimed of Jesus, "He has an unclean spirit" (Mark 3:30). Rather than casting out demons by the power of the devil (which was nonsensical and would be a counter-productive idea), Jesus was casting out demons by the only power that could—God. (See Mark 3.)

12. **Matthew 12:40**—While many believe the story of Jonah in the great fish to be fictitious, Jesus taught that it was historically factual.

13. **Matthew 12:40**—Jews counted any part of a day as a whole day (Matt. 16:21; 27:63-64; cf. Gen. 7:12, 17; 1 Kgs. 12:5, 12).

14. **Matthew 12:41**—The Ninevites repented "at" the preaching of Jonah (which is the Greek word *eis*). Some suggest this is a usage of the term that points backward, meaning "because of." But scholars note that the preposition *eis* always points forward, as it does here. This verse means that the Ninevites "repented into [the life required by] the preaching of Jonah."

15. **Matthew 13:11**—The word "mysteries" simply means truths that had not been revealed previously, but they were at that time being revealed.

16. **Matthew 13:12-13**—Parables served a sifting-like purpose—identifying those who were genuinely interested in learning God's truths and those who were not. If someone does not want to understand, they will not (13:14-15; cf. Matt. 5:6; John 7:17; 2 Thess. 2:10).

17. **Matthew 13:23**—The good soil represents the heart that is "honest and good" (Luke 8:15), who "hears the word and understands it" (Matt. 13:23), "accepts it" (Mark 4:20), "keeps it" (Luke 8:15) and "bears fruit and produces" more followers of Christ (Matt. 13:23). This should be our goal!

18. **Matthew 13:41-42**—Some have tried to teach that this parable teaches against the practice of church discipline. If the "field" is the

Mark Your Bible

"world" (13:38), as Jesus specifies, then the focus is not on two different seeds in the church/kingdom but in the world. Even if this parable is about the church (13:24, 41), Jesus is the one who taught (Matt. 18:15-18) and led the apostles to teach (1 Cor. 5:1-13; 2 Thess. 3:6-15; Rom. 16:17; Tit. 3:10-11) for the church to practice withdrawing of fellowship. A parable is not to be used against clear Bible teaching.

19. **Matthew 13:46**—Representing the kingdom/church, there is only "one" pearl of great price. Circle the word "one."
20. **Matthew 13:55-56**—Mary was not a perpetual virgin, as she had other children after Jesus (cf. Matt. 1:25; Luke 2:7).
21. **Matthew 14:4**—"Had said" is in the Greek imperfect tense, denoting that John kept on saying this over and over.
22. **Matthew 14:5**—Herodias wanted to kill John also (Mark 6:19).
23. **Matthew 14:14**—"Moved with compassion" is from the Greek word *splagchnizomai,* which means to "be moved as to one's bowels or inwards (Greek *splanchnon*)." This was a deep pity and yearning with tender compassion
24. **Matthew 14:22, 27, 31**—Underline and connect the three uses of the word "immediately."
25. **Matthew 14:25**—Some have tried to find a natural explanation for this, but there is none. This is a miracle. John tells us that they were 3-4 miles out (John 6:19), "in the middle of the sea" (Matt. 14:24).
26. **Matthew 14:33**—Jesus is worthy of worship, for He is God.
27. **Matthew 15:3**—To elevate human law is to violate Divine law.
28. **Matthew 15:8-9**—Teaching false doctrine and practicing human traditions makes one's worship null and void. Underline this verse.
29. **Matthew 15:13**—By the word "plant," Jesus was referring to every human doctrine, tradition or practice that man initiated but was not authorized by God. God will not tolerate them but will punish.

(continued on next page)

Mark Your Bible

30. **Matthew 15:22-25**—There are three imperfect tense verbs used in these verses, which denote ongoing activity in a past tense. The woman "kept on crying out" to Jesus (v. 22). The disciples "kept on urging" Jesus to send her away (v. 23). The woman "kept on worshiping Jesus" (v. 25).
31. **Matthew 15:26-27**—Jesus was not being harsh or insulting toward the woman. Compare Mark 7:27, where He says, "Let the children be filled first." Jesus was "sent" to the "Jews" (i.e., "the children") "first," by which He was implying that there was something for the Gentiles coming, and He was giving the woman an argumentative handle to grab and use. And she did. The woman simply asked for a "crumb" of that from Jesus now. (The word for "dog" was a diminutive form of the word, indicating a tame pet, a little puppy, who had to wait until after the meal to get crumbs. Jesus was not calling the woman a dog; He was referring to the common practice of that day and opening the door for her to plead her case.)
32. **Matthew 15:37**—These large baskets were like a hamper, large enough to hold a man (Acts 9:25).

Day of Reflection

Take time today to reflect on the five chapters that you read this week. You may choose to read all five chapters again, in one sitting, or certain parts of them. Take time today to answer at least one of these questions below. You may or may not write anything down—you can choose to write or simply reflect.

1. What personal application do I need to make from the chapters I have read this week?

2. How can these five chapters help draw me closer to Jesus?

3. What words, phrases or verses in these chapters do I want to go back and study more in depth?

4. What questions do I have about what I have read this week on which I need to do some further Biblical research?

Week 4

January 22-28

January 22	Read Matthew 16
January 23	Read Matthew 17
January 24	Read Matthew 18
January 25	Read Matthew 19
January 26	Read Matthew 20
January 27	Mark Your Bible
January 28	Day of Reflection

Prayer for this week:

"Heavenly Father,
please help me to understand what I am reading."

January 22 Week 4, Day 1

Matthew 16

Helpful Notes:

1. **Son of Man** = This expression was used only by Christ for Himself (over 80 times), to identify Himself as the promised Messiah (Dan. 7:13); the term emphasizes His human nature and His union with mankind (used of His atoning death in Mark 10:45 and of His role in executing judgment in John 5:27), and it also denotes His Divine authority, which no one else possessed; "Son of Man" is used interchangeably with "Son of God" (Matt. 16:13-19).
2. **Church** = The word is from the Greek *ekklesia,* meaning "called out"; it is the prophesied (2 Sam. 7:12-13; Isa. 2:2-4; Dan. 2:44) kingdom of God (Matt. 16:18-19), that was part of the eternal plan of God (Eph. 3:10-11) and is comprised of God's saved (Acts 2:47); it is the "one body" of Christ (Eph. 4:4), that was established in Acts 2 and will be taken by Christ into heaven (1 Cor. 15:24; Heb. 12:23); denominations are not the church established in the N.T.
3. **Soul** = The word "soul" is used in various ways in the Bible, including to speak of life (Gen. 2:7) or of individual persons (Ezek. 18:20; 1 Pet. 3:20); most often it is used of the eternal, immortal essence of man, that is made in the image of God and will separate from the body at death and dwell eternally in heaven or hell; in this sense, it is often used synonymously with one's "spirit."

1. In warning about the doctrine of the Pharisees and Sadducees, what word did Jesus use? Why do you think He used that word?

2. What did Jesus call Peter when he focused on earthly desires rather than God's desires?

3. What three things did Jesus say a person must do if he "desires to come after" Him?

Verse for Meditation and Prayer: **Matthew 16:18**

"And I also say to you that you are Peter, and on this rock
I will build My church, and the gates of Hades
shall not prevail against it."

Matthew 17

Helpful Notes:

1. **Transfiguration** = The Greek verb for "transfigured" is *metamorphoo,* and it means "to change into another form or appearance"; there was significant and noticeable change when Jesus was transfigured: "the appearance of His face was altered" (Luke 9:29), "His face shone like the sun" (Matt. 17:2), "His clothes became shining, exceedingly white, like snow" (Mark 9:3); there was nothing natural about these changes or merely a bright light shining on Him.
2. **Elijah** = The prophet Elijah appeared with Jesus on the mountain of transfiguration; the prophecies of Malachi regarding the coming of Elijah were fulfilled in John the Baptist (Matt. 17:13; 11:14; Mal. 3:1; 4:5-6); Elijah was a great prophet of the O.T., who "went up by a whirlwind into heaven" (2 Kgs. 2:11).
3. **Moses** = Moses was the great lawgiver of the Old Testament, the penmen of the first five books of the Bible, the one who led the children of Israel out of Egyptian bondage, the one who received the law from God for the Jews while at Mount Sinai, and the one who prophesied of the "Prophet" who would come "like" Moses (Deut. 18:15-18); there was not another human prophet like Moses (Deut. 34:10); after he died, the Lord buried him (Deut. 34:5-6).

1. After identifying Jesus (not Moses or Elijah) as His beloved Son, what did the voice from heaven command the disciples to do?

2. Why did Jesus say that the disciples were unable to cast the demon out of the boy?

3. Although God's Son was technically exempt from paying the tax on the temple (i.e., His Father's house), what did Jesus do?

Verse for Meditation and Prayer: **Matthew 17:5**

"While he was still speaking, behold, a bright cloud overshadowed them; and suddenly a voice came out of the cloud, saying, 'This is My beloved Son, in whom I am well pleased. Hear Him!'"

January 24

Week 4, Day 3

Matthew 18

Helpful Notes:

1. **Talent** = The talent was the largest weight used by the Jews, and it weighed about 75 pounds; when considering currency, it was worth about $1,000; the first servant in this parable owed his master roughly $10 million; however, his day's wage was only 17 cents, so it would take about 200,000 years to pay; our debt to God is incalculable and unpayable.
2. **Denarius** = This was the most common Roman coin during the first century (usually made of silver); it was the daily wage for the common Palestinian worker (20:2), worth about 17 cents; thus, in this parable, the servant was forgiven by his master of a debt around $10 million, but he would not forgive his fellow servant of a debt around $17.
3. **Forgive** = The Greek word *aphiemi* means "to send away, to let go, set free"; as we want God to have "compassion" and "patience" with us and to "forgive" us, we must also do for others (Matt. 6:14-15); in following the example of our Lord, we must show mercy toward all who repent and seek our forgiveness (Jas. 2:13; Luke 17:3); forgiveness starts with the heart (Matt. 18:35).

1. Why do you think Jesus was (and is) so very protective of children, giving such stern warnings in this text?

2. If a fellow Christian sins against you, what process did Jesus teach to follow, in order to rectify the situation?

3. How often did Jesus teach that we should be ready to forgive a brother who sins against us?

Verse for Meditation and Prayer: **Matthew 18:3**

"Assuredly, I say to you, unless you are converted and become as little children, you will by no means enter the kingdom of heaven."

Matthew 19

Helpful Notes:

1. **Divorce** = The Greek word *apoluo* means "to set free, release; let go, send away," and is often used of setting someone free; in the context of marriage, the word means to "put away" (as it is best translated), which involves a mental, intentional act, then a legal act; it was never part of God's will from the beginning because He "hates divorce" (Mal. 2:16); He permits it now for only one cause.
2. **Fornication** = The Greek word *porneia* means "every kind of unlawful sexual intercourse," which is every kind not between a husband and his lawful (in God's eyes) wife; it includes sex between unmarried people (1 Cor. 7:2), between individuals who may be married but not to each other (Matt. 19:9), homosexuality (Jude 7), incest, pedophilia, bestiality, etc.; this is Jesus' one exception.
3. **Adultery** = The Greek word *moicheia* is a specific type of fornication, involving "unlawful intercourse with the spouse of another"; this is a sexual act where at least one party is married to someone else; this sin can be committed even if a court-approved divorce has taken place, if God views a previous marriage as still binding; adultery is not the wedding or vows that take place but the sexual union of persons who are not husband and wife in God's eyes.

1. What two genders did God create, and was it ever God's design for two of the same gender to marry each other?

2. What illustration does Jesus use to show how hard it is for those who trust in riches to enter the kingdom of God?

3. Although a person's decision to follow Christ may cost him relationships with his family, what new family does he "receive a hundredfold" when he is baptized?

Verse for Meditation and Prayer: **Matthew 19:26**

"But Jesus looked at them and said to them,
'With men this is impossible, but with God all things are possible.'"

January 26 Week 4, Day 5

Matthew 20

Helpful Notes:

1. **Laborers for His vineyard** = In Jesus' parable, the vineyard represents the church/kingdom, into which different people would come at different times; the word "laborers" emphasizes that there is real labor expected by the Lord and available to do inside His church; while the parable has often been used to talk about end-of-life conversions, Jesus' primary application was to Jews (who would come in the kingdom first) and the Gentiles (who came in later), but they were all "equal" (v. 12) in God's sight.
2. **Ransom** = The Greek word *lutron* literally means "a means by which to loose someone," and it was used of the "price of release" paid to release a slave from bondage; Jesus paid the price (with His own His blood, Acts 20:28; 1 Cor. 6:19) to redeem/ransom man out of the bondage of sin (John 8:34; Rom. 6:6-7).
3. **Son of David** = The Jews knew that the Messiah was to be a descendent of David, and their hopes were fixed on that Davidic king coming to establish His kingdom (2 Sam. 7:12-16); among the Jews, the name "Son of David" was a commonly recognized identification of the expected Messiah; it is a Messianic title to them.

1. Jesus said that if a person desires "to be first among" others, what must he become?

2. While some in authority "lord it over" those subject to them, what kind of leaders did Jesus tell the apostles to be?

3. What were the blind men asking Jesus to "have on" them? And "Jesus had" what for them in the last verse?

Verse for Meditation and Prayer: **Matthew 20:28**

"...Just as the Son of Man did not come to be served, but to serve, and to give His life a ransom for many."

Mark Your Bible

1. **Matthew 16:3**—"The signs of the times" were the obvious evidences that the Messiah had arrived, as authenticated by His miracles.
2. **Matthew 16:11-12**—Underline and draw a line from the word "leaven" (v. 11) to the word "doctrine" (v. 12).
3. **Matthew 16:18**—Jesus would build HIS church on the "rock" (*petra,* bedrock) of the truth of His deity (16:16), and not on Peter (*petros,* a stone) (see 1 Cor. 3:11). Those are two different words with two different meanings. Peter is no different from any of the other apostles (cf. Eph. 2:20). Jesus' church was built upon Jesus!
4. **Matthew 16:18**—The forces of Hades and death would not prevent the coming of His church or the continued existence of His church.
5. **Matthew 16:18-19**—It is important to see that Jesus uses the terms "church" and "kingdom" interchangeably in these verses. Circle those words and connect them with a line. In simple terms, the word "church" reflects the Christian's relationship with the world (i.e., "called out") and the word "kingdom" reflects the Christian's relationship with Christ (i.e., He is the king with all authority).
6. **Matthew 16:19**—The Greek perfect tense emphasizes that what Peter would bind and loose on earth had already been bound or loosed in heaven. The binding and loosing was already done by God and was not being initiated by any man. Note in your Bible that this same statement was made to ALL of the apostles in 18:18. So it was not limited to Peter alone.
7. **Matthew 16:28**—Jesus would come in the establishing of His church in Acts 2. Compare this with Mark 9:1.
8. **Matthew 17:1**—Peter, James and John appear to be Jesus' closest friends, for they were taken alone with the Lord several times (Matt. 17:1; Mark 5:37; 14:33).
9. **Matthew 17:5**—Jesus has all authority; we must hear and follow Him (not the O.T. prophets). The word "hear" is a present imperative, emphasizing to get busy hearing Him now and then keep on hearing Him. Hearing implies heeding.

(continued on next page)

Mark Your Bible

10. **Matthew 17:11-13**—It is critical to see that Jesus identified John the Baptist as the fulfillment of the prophecies made about the coming Elijah. There is not another Elijah. Jesus said it was John.
11. **Matthew 17:20**—The disciples had just encountered a "mountain" that tested the strength of their faith. Jesus rebuked their "unbelief" in not being able to "move" the mountain (in this case, the demon). Jesus was not talking about physical mountains but about the many obstacles that lay before His apostles in preaching the gospel.
12. **Matthew 17:24-26**—Jesus had taught that the temple was "My Father's house" (John 2:16). Thus, as the Son, He was exempt from paying the tax to His Father's house. Lest He offend, He paid it anyway.
13. **Matthew 18:3**—The words of Jesus help to establish the truth that a child does not enter this world having inherited sin (Ezek. 18:20).
14. **Matthew 18:3**—One must truly become humble and teachable (like a child) in order to enter the kingdom now and in eternity.
15. **Matthew 18:6**—Millstones were so large that they had to be turned at the mill by a beast of burden, particularly a donkey or mule.
16. **Matthew 18:8-9**—By using hyperbole, Jesus emphasized that we must remove any and all potential stumbling blocks that could lead us to hell.
17. **Matthew 18:15**—Underline "you and him alone." This is critical. When there is a problem between two persons, the problem should first and only be addressed between those two persons and no others. It should not be discussed with others. (Note also Luke 17:3-5.)
18. **Matthew 18:17**—A brother who is lost in sin and resistant to efforts to restore him is to be regarded as an outsider, excluded from fellowship with the church. Jesus teaches withdraw of fellowship, which is detailed again later (1 Cor. 5:1-13; 2 Thess. 3:6-15).
19. **Matthew 18:18**—The Greek perfect tense emphasizes that what the apostles would bind and loose on earth had already been bound or loosed by God in heaven.

Mark Your Bible

20. **Matthew 18:20**—The context of this verse is brethren trying to solve a dispute. Verses must be kept in their context.
21. **Matthew 18:21**—The Jewish rabbis taught that forgiving someone three times was sufficient. So, Peter was being extra generous here. But Jesus said that there was to be no limit to our forgiveness.
22. **Matthew 19:4-5**—God's plan regarding marriage (and divorce) goes all the way back to the beginning. That plan is still binding today.
23. **Matthew 19:4**—God only created two genders; therefore, only two genders exist. Every person is born biologically a male or a female, and that does not and cannot be changed.
24. **Matthew 19:7-8**—In the O.T., God only "permitted" divorce due to "hardness of hearts"; He did not command it out of desire or a permanent change to His will. That was Jesus' point and the reason Jesus took His answer all the way back to "the beginning" (v. 4).
25. **Matthew 19:8**—"It was not so" is in the Greek perfect tense, which denotes, "It was not God's will then and that has never changed."
26. **Matthew 19:9**—The two words "except for" are critical. (1) "Except" means "if and only if"; there is no consideration apart from this (see the same word in John 3:5). The Greek word for "except" in Matthew 5:32 means "apart from, saving for," emphasizing the one and only exception. (2) The preposition "for" is "the marker of basis for an action," denoting the cause for the action. Fornication is the only basis/cause for divorce and it must actually be the known basis/cause in order to remarry without committing adultery.
27. **Matthew 19:24**—Some have wrongly thought that Jesus was referencing some gate in Jerusalem. He was actually illustrating the tremendous difficulty love for money creates in one's life. The physician Luke used the word for a surgeon's needle in Luke 18:25.
28. **Matthew 19:28**—When Jesus ascended (Dan. 7:13-14; Luke 24:46), He sat on His throne (Acts 2:30-33) to reign (1 Cor. 15:25), and the apostles were given authority to bind and loose His will, which He Himself had authorized (18:18).

(continued on next page)

Mark Your Bible

29. **Matthew 20:12**—It matters not when one enters the church—all are "equal" inside and on the day of judgment. Circle "equal."
30. **Matthew 20:15**—Whatever is "lawful" to God is what is "right" in the eyes of God (v. 4). Draw a line connecting those two words.
31. **Matthew 20:18-19**—Jesus knew exactly what was going to happen to Him, and He still did it. This is the first time the word "crucify" appears in the N.T. It was not merely that Jesus was going to die, but the manner of His death was specified.
32. **Matthew 20:22**—There was a "cup" of suffering that awaited Jesus (Luke 22:42), and He was willing and ready to "drink" it (John 18:10-11). In Acts 12, this same James was killed, thus drinking of the same cup of suffering that Jesus Himself drank.
33. **Matthew 20:30**—There is no contradiction between this verse and Mark 10:46, as some allege. Mark's account does not say that there was only one man sitting and begging. If it had, that would be a contradiction. Instead, Mark simply focuses on one of the two. It is supplementary information, not contradictory.

January 28 Week 4, Day 7

Day of Reflection

Take time today to reflect on the five chapters that you read this week. You may choose to read all five chapters again, in one sitting, or certain parts of them. Take time today to answer at least one of these questions below. You may or may not write anything down—you can choose to write or simply reflect.

1. What personal application do I need to make from the chapters I have read this week?

2. How can these five chapters help draw me closer to Jesus?

3. What words, phrases or verses in these chapters do I want to go back and study more in depth?

4. What questions do I have about what I have read this week on which I need to do some further Biblical research?

Week 5

January 29-February 4

January 29	Read Matthew 21
January 30	Read Matthew 22
January 31	Read Matthew 23
February 1	Read Matthew 24
February 2	Read Matthew 25
February 3	Mark Your Bible
February 4	Day of Reflection

Prayer for this week:

"Heavenly Father,
thank You for making Your Word understandable!"

January 29 Week 5, Day 1

Matthew 21

Helpful Notes:

1. **Hosanna** = This word is a transliteration of a Hebrew (or possibly Aramaic) word, and it means ,"Save, we pray"; it was originally a Hebrew prayer addressed to God, but it later became an acclamation of joyous praise to God.
2. **Vinedresser** = The word is also translated "husbandmen," "vine-growers" and "tenants"; it identifies those who were "keepers of the vineyard" (i.e., tenant farmers) for another, who were responsible for planting, pruning and cultivating the vines, so that they would produce a rich harvest for the owner; in the parable, the vinedressers represent the Jewish leaders (21:45).
3. **Stone** = It was prophesied in Psalm 118:22 that Jesus would be like a stone rejected by the "builders" (i.e., Jewish leaders); this verse from Psalm 118 is quoted at least five times in the N.T., and it has obvious reference to Jesus, who in His death, became the Chief Cornerstone of His church (Eph. 2:20; 1 Pet. 2:6-7), which is the "nation bearing the fruits" (1 Pet. 2:9); Jesus' promise to build His church (Matt. 16:18) would not be thwarted.

1. In fulfillment of prophecy, on what great beast did King Jesus ride into Jerusalem?

2. In what city (outside Jerusalem) did Jesus lodge during this last week of His life?

3. After hearing the Parables of the Two Sons and the Wicked Vinedressers, what did the chief priests and Pharisees perceive?

Verse for Meditation and Prayer: **Matthew 21:22**

"And whatever things you ask in prayer, believing, you will receive."

January 30 Week 5, Day 2

Matthew 22

Helpful Notes:

1. **Herodians** = This appears to be a political (not religious) group, who were partisans of (and therefore, serving the interests of) the dynasty of Herod the Great, and specifically Herod Antipas at this time; not much is known about them or what persons composed the group; they aligned themselves on at least two occasions with the Pharisees in opposition to Christ.
2. **Caesar** = Title given to and taken by each Roman Emperor after Julius Caesar; the title was used by Jesus both figuratively (of any earthly ruler/government) and specifically (referring to Tiberius, who ruled as Caesar during Jesus' ministry [Luke 3:1]); when Paul "appealed to Caesar" in Acts 25, Nero was the Roman Emperor at that time; the term came to symbolize the Roman state in general.
3. **Chosen** = Those "chosen" by God are those who are "in Christ" (Eph. 1:3-4); this is not an unconditional or arbitrary election/choosing, for "all" who obey the Lord are accepted by Him (Acts 10:35); His "chosen" are those who "choose" to follow Him by keeping His commands.

1. How is the church/kingdom like a wedding of a King's son? Is the church married?

2. What did Jesus say are the two greatest commands?

3. As a summation of our responsibilities to both God and man, what did Jesus say "hangs" on the two greatest commands?

Verse for Meditation and Prayer: **Matthew 22:37**

"Jesus said to him, 'You shall love the Lord your God with all your heart, with all your soul, and with all your mind.'"

January 31

Week 5, Day 3

Matthew 23

Helpful Notes:

1. **Woe** = This is an interjection of displeasure and denunciation; the word is used 31 times total by Jesus in the gospel accounts, and Jesus used it eight times in Matthew 23 to draw attention to and warn about the dangerous and destructive ways of the largest Jewish sect—the Pharisees and their special class of scribes.
2. **Abel to Zechariah** = God's people were persecuted from the beginning of Old Testament history (with Abel) to the end of Old Testament history (with Zechariah the priest in 2 Chronicles 24:20) by their own countrymen, and the price for that "blood shed" would be paid by "this generation," when Jerusalem and the temple were destroyed in A.D. 70 (23:36, 38; 24:1-34); "this generation" is a key phrase in these chapters.
3. **Rabbi, Father, Teacher** = Like today, the religious leaders of that day preferred special titles; Jesus plainly said not to give special titles to any man, but only to God; the best title today is that of a humble "servant"; Peter referred to the great apostle to the Gentiles as "our beloved brother Paul" (2 Pet. 3:15); truly, "holy and reverend is His name" (Psa. 111:9) and not any man's.

1. Jesus gives the precise definition of hypocrisy in the last words of verse 3. What is it?

2. Jesus gives a summation and motivation of the Pharisees' works at the beginning of verse 5. What is it?

3. While the Pharisees had been focused on making sure to tithe even the smallest things to God, what had they left undone?

Verse for Meditation and Prayer: **Matthew 23:12**

"And whoever exalts himself will be humbled, and he who humbles himself will be exalted."

Matthew 24

Helpful Notes: ** See also the notes and markings for Mark 13 and Luke 21.*

1. **Temple** = The temple complex was about 25-30 acres in size and could hold well over 100,000 people; it consisted of various courts, porticos, buildings and the sanctuary itself; it was the center of the Jewish religion, where the Jews gathered, sacrificed, worshiped, learned and mingled; to destroy it would be to destroy Judaism itself; the old covenant died with Jesus on the cross (Col. 2:14) and the Jewish system was visually destroyed in A.D. 70.
2. **The end** = In context, "the end" of which Jesus spoke was "the end of the age" (the word in verse 3 is not "world" but the Greek *aion,* meaning "age"); Biblically, the term was used of the "end" of the Jewish dispensation/age (see Heb. 9:26; 1 Cor. 10:11); Jesus said the temple would be destroyed, which would mark "the end of the age" of Judaism; when one reads Matthew 24:1-34 in context, it is quite apparent that it is not about the end of the world.
3. **All these things** = This expression (in 23:36 and six times in chapter 24) has reference to "all these things" of the temple and all the signs of the impending destruction of which Jesus was warning His friends; verse 34 is the absolute key—"all these things" would "take place" during the lifetime of "this generation" to whom Jesus spoke; there is nothing of the "all these things" in verses 1-34 that would take place after "this generation" in Jesus' day.

1. As a general rule, when "lawlessness abounds," what happens to the love some may have for the Lord and His ways?
2. When individuals claim to predict the day on which Jesus will return, what can we know for certain (see v. 36)?
3. When the Master returns, who will be considered "a faithful and wise servant" (according to verse 46)?

Verse for Meditation and Prayer: **Matthew 24:44**

"Therefore you also be ready, for the Son of Man is coming at an hour you do not expect."

February 2 Week 5, Day 5

Matthew 25

Helpful Notes:

1. **Angel** = The Greek term *angelos* means "messenger" and is sometimes translated that way; the term was used of both "angels" sent by God or by Satan (Matt. 25:41); usually it denotes a heavenly order of spirit beings (created by God), who "minister" to God's people at His direction (Heb. 1:14); how they operate is not known, nor is there any sensual perception of their activity.
2. **Eternal life** = More than merely existing forever, the righteous (who have obeyed God's will) will "enter the joy" (25:23) of everlasting fellowship with God, Christ and the redeemed of all ages, to worship, serve and commune forever and ever; what a gracious, joyful gift from God!
3. **Eternal punishment** = More than merely existing forever, the unrighteous (who have not obeyed God's will) will be "cast" into "everlasting fire," where there will be "weeping and gnashing of teeth" (25:30, 41), along with the devil, his angels and the "wicked" of all ages, to be separated from God and tormented forever and ever; it will last as long as heaven lasts; the consciousness of its inhabitants is emphasized by the word "punishment."

1. What does Jesus say is the main point of the Parable of the Ten Virgins?

2. What does the Parable of the Talents teach us about the danger of being inactive as a Christian (although we may not be doing really bad things)?

3. In our efforts to serve others, who in particular does Jesus tell us to be mindful of, so that our service is truly unto Him?

Verse for Meditation and Prayer: **Matthew 25:23**

"Well done, good and faithful servant; you have been faithful over a few things, I will make you ruler over many things. Enter into the joy of your lord."

Mark Your Bible

1. **Matthew 21:2-5**—Jesus' disciples were told that they would find two donkeys, one was a colt or foal (a young donkey which had never been ridden). The King would ride on a young donkey, fulfilling Zechariah 9:9.
2. **Matthew 21:12**—Jesus did this at the beginning of His ministry (John 2:13-22), and He is now doing it again at the end of His ministry. The people did not learn the lesson the first time.
3. **Matthew 21:13**—God's temple was designed as a place of prayer and focusing on God "for all nations" (Isa. 56:7; Mark 11:17). They made it a "den of thieves" (Jer. 7:11) either by their financial transactions or by stealing the attention away from God where it belonged.
4. **Matthew 21:21**—See note for Matthew 17:20.
5. **Matthew 21:25**—This is the question we should ask about every doctrine and practice of various religious groups: "Is it from heaven or from men?"
6. **Matthew 21:28-29**—This is a good illustration to show someone what repentance is—it is a change of mind that leads to a change of action.
7. **Matthew 21:43**—The "nation" is the church (1 Pet. 2:9), the new, spiritual Israel of God (Gal. 6:16).
8. **Matthew 22:7**—After the Jews rejected God's invitation into His kingdom, He sent "His armies" (i.e., the Roman army) to destroy Jerusalem in A.D. 70.
9. **Matthew 22:8-10**—When the Jews rejected the gospel, the call then went to the Gentiles, among whom there was great success.
10. **Matthew 22:11-13**—The man without a wedding garment is one who does not make the personal, necessary preparations by putting on Christ (Gal. 3:26-27) and keeping on Christ in faithful living (Rom. 13:14). He was professing identification with Christ, but he was not "in Christ" or "of Christ," for he had refused the true garment of Christ. (This is similar to Matthew 7:21-23).

(continued on next page)

Mark Your Bible

11. **Matthew 22:17-21**—Jesus teaches the responsibility to submit to government and pay taxes. Rendering ourselves to God requires rendering taxes to the proper authorities (Rom. 13:6-7).
12. **Matthew 22:21**—Man bears the image of God and is responsible to submit, to obey and to use himself for his God.
13. **Matthew 22:31**—The Bible was written by inspiration "to you by God." Make it personal. Underline "to you."
14. **Matthew 22:32**—"I am" and "the living" are present tense verbs. Jesus was teaching that the patriarchs were/are still alive and their bodies will be resurrected.
15. **Matthew 22:40**—In the eyes of God, law and love are inseparable.
16. **Matthew 22:43-45**—Psalm 110:1 attests to both the humanity (as David's offspring) and the deity (as David's Lord) of Jesus Christ (John 1:1, 14).
17. **Matthew 23:3**—Underline "they say, and do not do." That is a simple, yet precise definition of hypocrisy (which Jesus condemns in this chapter).
18. **Matthew 23:5**—Underline "all their works they do to be seen by men." This is a summary of the life and motivation of the Pharisees (cf. 6:1, 5, 16).
19. **Matthew 23:25-28**—There is a danger even today of God's people being more concerned about their outward actions and appearances than their inward attitudes and motivations.
20. **Matthew 23:36**—Underline "all these things" and "this generation." Those expressions are key in the context of Matthew 24.
21. **Matthew 23:37**—God gave man free will. As much as God wants to save man, man can choose whatever path he wants.
22. **Matthew 23:38**—"Your house" is the temple that would be destroyed in A.D. 70. This is leading into Jesus' discussion of that in chapter 24.

Mark Your Bible

23. **Matthew 24:3-4**—The "you" is Peter, Andrew, James and John (Mark 13:3). You may want to circle "you" throughout this chapter.
24. **Matthew 24:14**—Paul wrote in about the year 62 A.D. that the gospel had been "preached to every creature under heaven" (Col. 1:6, 23). So it did happen before Jerusalem was destroyed in A.D. 70.
25. **Matthew 24:20**—This has nothing to do with Christians keeping the Sabbath. The gates of Jerusalem were closed on the Sabbath (Neh. 13:19).
26. **Matthew 24:29**—This imagery is used in the O.T. for the fall of a nation: Babylon (Isa. 13:6-22), Idumea (Isa. 34:4-5), Egypt (Ezek. 32:7-8). The Jews would have understood this language was not literal, but it was figuratively describing the fall of Jerusalem.
27. **Matthew 24:30**—The fulfillment of the prophecies of the destruction of Jerusalem will be a "sign" that the Son of Man has ascended and is reigning in heaven (cf. Acts 2:30-33).
28. **Matthew 24:31**—The word "angels" can mean "messengers," representing His teachers taking the gospel to save the world. When the preachers of the gospel went forth to preach the gospel on Pentecost and thereafter, it was like the trumpet of the year of Jubilee (Lev. 25) that announced the salvation of God, as the church (i.e., the elect, Eph. 1:4) was established and the saved flowed into it.
29. **Matthew 24:34**—Underline or highlight this whole verse. Everything before this verse had to be fulfilled in their lifetime.
30. **Matthew 24:35**—See 2 Peter 3:10-13 and 1 Peter 1:23-25.
31. **Matthew 24:36**—Circle the word "But." Jesus is transitioning to a singular "day," whereas before this verse it was "days" plural. Before verse 34 focuses on the "days" of the destruction of Jerusalem. Verse 36 starts a discussion of the final "day" at the end of time.
32. **Matthew 24:40-41**—This is not the so-called "rapture." Jesus is simply illustrating the sudden and unexpected nature of His coming, which will result in a sudden and unexpected separation of people.

(continued on next page)

Mark Your Bible

33. **Matthew 24:43**—Jesus taught that the timing of His coming would be like a "thief" coming—no way to predict, no way to set a date (1 Thess. 5:2; 2 Pet. 3:10).
34. **Matthew 25:10**—Underline the word "ready." Those who go "in" to heaven are those who have made the necessary preparations.
35. **Matthew 25:12**—This is similar to Matthew 7:22-23.
36. **Matthew 25:13**—It is impossible to predict when Jesus will return.
37. **Matthew 25:15**—A talent was a measurement of weight and used as a sum of money—in this case, about $1,000 each. The talents represent responsibilities in the parable.
38. **Matthew 25:15**—God gives responsibilities "each according to his ability" (underline that phrase), and God expects us to serve and give "according to our ability" (2 Cor. 8:3).
39. **Matthew 25:21, 23, 26**—Underline "good and faithful servant" and then connect to "wicked and lazy servant."
40. **Matthew 25:31-32**—Judgment will take place at the moment of Christ's return, not 1,000 years later. Circle the words "When" and "then," and connect with a line.
41. **Matthew 25:45**—Sins of omission are just as sinful as sins of commission (cf. Jas. 4:17).
42. **Matthew 25:46**—Hell will be conscious punishment for just as long as heaven is conscious joy.

February 4 Week 5, Day 7

Day of Reflection

Take time today to reflect on the five chapters that you read this week. You may choose to read all five chapters again, in one sitting, or certain parts of them. Take time today to answer at least one of these questions below. You may or may not write anything down—you can choose to write or simply reflect.

1. What personal application do I need to make from the chapters I have read this week?

2. How can these five chapters help draw me closer to Jesus?

3. What words, phrases or verses in these chapters do I want to go back and study more in depth?

4. What questions do I have about what I have read this week on which I need to do some further Biblical research?

Week 6

February 5-11

February 5	Read Matthew 26
February 6	Read Matthew 27
February 7	Read Matthew 28
February 8	Read Mark 1
February 9	Read Mark 2
February 10	Mark Your Bible
February 11	Day of Reflection

Prayer for this week:

"Heavenly Father,
thank You for sending Jesus!"

February 5 Week 6, Day 1

Matthew 26

Helpful Notes:

1. **Passover** = The oldest and most important of all the Jewish feasts, commemorating God's deliverance of the Jews from Egyptian bondage (specifically a deliverance from death through the sacrifice of a lamb, typifying Christ's death and deliverance); all Jewish males were to assemble in Jerusalem; the Feast of Unleavened Bread continued for seven days after Passover (and they were considered the same event , with the terms being used interchangeably [Luke 22:1; Mark 14:1]), in which all leaven was removed from their homes.
2. **Legion** = A major division of the Roman army consisting usually of 6,000 soldiers; a legion was divided into ten cohorts, and a cohort was further divided into six centuries; Jesus' use of "twelve legions" emphasizes that God could have sent more than 72,000 angels (symbolic number) to deliver Him, if He so chose.
3. **Council/Sanhedrin** = "Council" is from the Greek word "Sanhedrin"; the Sanhedrin was the highest Jewish court, having judicial and legislative power over Judea; it was composed of 70 or 71 Jewish men, namely chief priests (former high priests), scribes and elders (tribal and family heads).

1. Who made the choice for Judas to betray Jesus? Was it his choice or was it forced upon him?

2. What did Jesus pray three times?

3. When Jesus was arrested, what does it say that "all the disciples" did?

Verse for Meditation and Prayer: **Matthew 26:28**

"For this is My blood of the new covenant,
which is shed for many for the remission of sins."

February 6 Week 6, Day 2

Matthew 27

Helpful Notes:

1. **Pontius Pilate** = He was appointed by Tiberius Caesar as the Roman procurator/governor of Judea, Samaria and Idumea (26-36 A.D.); he was hated by the Jews for his many offenses against them and their religion, but he was used by the Jews to sentence Christ to crucifixion, though he found no fault in Him.
2. **Time/Hour (Jewish)** = The Jews divided time between sunrise and sunset into twelve hours; the beginning hour = 6:00 a.m.; the third hour = 9:00 a.m.; the sixth hour = 12:00 p.m.; the ninth hour = 3:00 p.m.; the twelve hour = 6:00 p.m.
3. **Veil of the temple** = The veil separated the holy place from the most holy place in the temple; it was reported to be 60 feet tall, 20 feet wide and hand-width thick; only an act of God could tear such from top to bottom; the miracle symbolized the end of the Mosaic/Levitical system and the start of the Christian system, which gives all Christians direct access to God all the time (while only the high priest could enter into the presence of God behind the veil under the old system, and that was only once a year).

1. What was purchased with the money of betrayal that Judas returned?

2. What did Pilate's own wife warn him about?

3. What did Joseph of Arimathea do for and give to Jesus that no one else appears to have been willing or able to do or give?

Verse for Meditation and Prayer: **Matthew 27:54**

"So when the centurion and those with him, who were guarding Jesus, saw the earthquake and the things that had happened, they feared greatly, saying, 'Truly this was the Son of God!'"

Matthew 28

Helpful Notes:

1. **First day of the week** = Rather than the Sabbath of the old covenant, the first day took on great significance in the N.T.: it was the day Jesus was raised from the dead, the day that He met with His disciples after His resurrection (John 20:19-29), the day the church was established in Acts 2, the day on which the N.T. church assembled (1 Cor. 16:1-2) to worship and partake of the Lord's Supper (Acts 20:7); that day must have significance to us today.
2. **Chief Priests and Jewish Elders** = These were the leaders among the Jews: "Chief Priests" (a.k.a. "rulers") held high positions in Judaism, likely being the heads of the 24 courses of priests and perhaps former high priests; the "elders" held high positions in the community as tribal and family heads, likely serving as representatives of the people, community leaders and/or judges; together they composed much of the Sanhedrin.
3. **All authority** = Christ possesses absolute authority and power; no man stands in the place of Christ or possesses any of His authority; Christ alone has the power to make and exact law, and His authority is inherent in His Word (Matt. 7:28-29; 17:5; Acts 3:22-23; John 12:48); we must submit to His authority and obey Him.

1. Who rolled the stone away from the tomb opening, despite Pilate and the Jews making it "secure"?

2. What lie were the tomb guards paid money to tell?

3. While we carry out Jesus' Great Commission, where did He say that He would be?

Verse for Meditation and Prayer: **Matthew 28:19**

"Go therefore and make disciples of all the nations, baptizing them in the name of the Father and of the Son and of the Holy Spirit."

Mark 1

Helpful Notes: ** See Brief Introduction to Mark on page 632.*

1. **Baptize** = The English word "baptize" is merely a transliteration of the Greek word *baptizo,* which means "to dip, immerse, submerge"; the example of Jesus' baptism shows it is immersion, by using the words "into" the Jordan and coming "out of" the water (1:9-10); the baptism of the Ethiopian in Acts 8:38-39 also shows going "down into" and coming "up out of the water"; Bible baptism is always a burial (Col. 2:12) in water; it is never sprinkling.
2. **Immediately** = This is a key word in Mark; the Greek word *eutheos* is found 40 times in the book, with 9 in the first chapter; Mark emphasizes Jesus was a man of action and energy, which would have appealed to Mark's Roman audience; Jesus was always busy in ministering, healing, teaching and guiding.
3. **Unclean spirit** = The terms "unclean spirit," "evil spirit" and "demon" are used interchangeably of evil beings permitted unusual activity on the earth during Christ's ministry, perhaps to show His Divine power over them; demons know and "believe" who Jesus is (Jas. 2:19), but He did not want or need their testimony or any association with them.

1. What did the angels do for Jesus that they also do for us (Heb. 1:14)?

2. What can we learn about prayer from the example of Jesus in verse 35?

3. Having been "moved with compassion," what did Jesus physically and personally do toward the leper?

Verse for Meditation and Prayer: **Mark 1:22**

"And they were astonished at His teaching,
for He taught them as one having authority,
and not as the scribes."

Mark 2

Helpful Notes:

1. **Paralytic** = The KJV says, "one sick with palsy," which is a less familiar term; this was a neurological disease, common in the N.T., which involved loss of control of muscles due to disease or nerve damage; the severity varied from person to person.
2. **Levi** = This was another name for Matthew, the son of Alphaeus, who became one of Jesus' twelve apostles; Matthew always refers to himself as "Matthew"; Mark and Luke introduce him as "Levi" and then call him "Matthew" in listing the twelve apostles; some think he was the brother of James the son of Alphaeus.
3. **Sabbath** = The word designated the seventh day; the Hebrew word meant "cessation," which ties the word to its purpose (intended as a day of rest and worship for the Jews); there is no evidence that anyone before the Jews in Exodus observed the day as a holy day (Deut. 5:1-15; Ezek. 20:12; Neh. 9:13-14); the Pharisees created many traditions regarding the Sabbath that were not aligned with God's Word; Christians do not observe the Sabbath today, as it was taken out of the way as a "holy day," along with the rest of the old covenant (Col. 2:14-17; Rom. 7:1-7).

1. Although they remained in unbelief, who did the scribes realize was the only one who could forgive sin?

2. When the paralytic was healed and took up his bed, what did the people's amazement lead them to do?

3. The Pharisees believed they were "well" and "righteous," but what was Jesus (the Physician) saying they were?

Verse for Meditation and Prayer: **Mark 2:12**

"Immediately he arose, took up the bed, and went out in the presence of them all, so that all were amazed and glorified God, saying, 'We never saw anything like this!'"

Mark Your Bible

1. **Matthew 26:7**—This is Mary, the sister of Martha (John 12:1-3), and not the "sinful woman" in Luke 7:36-39.
2. **Matthew 26:14-16**—While he gave into Satan's temptations (Luke 22:3; John 13:27), Judas was acting of his own free will. He could have resisted the devil (Jas. 4:7; 1 Pet. 5:9), but he chose to give in.
3. **Matthew 26:15**—Thirty pieces of silver was the common price for a slave (Ex. 21:32). Its value today would be about $15.
4. **Matthew 26:26, 28**—The fact that Jesus was still in His body and still had His blood shows that He was not speaking literally but metaphorically. The elements are not, nor do they become, the actual body and blood of the Lord. Scripture does not support that.
5. **Matthew 26:27**—Underline the word "all." All disciples are to drink of the cup and not just the so-called "clergy."
6. **Matthew 26:28**—Jesus' blood would authorize the execution of His new covenant, thus removing the old covenant (Heb. 8:8-13; 9:15-17).
7. **Matthew 26:28**—"For the remission of sins" is prospective, looking to the purpose of Jesus shedding His blood—this same grammatical structure and meaning is used in Acts 2:38.
8. **Matthew 26:29**—In our weekly communion, Christ communes with us.
9. **Matthew 26:44**—This event is described in Hebrews 5:7-8.
10. **Matthew 26:64**—A simple meaning is likely here: the day is coming when Jesus will be the Judge (sitting at God's right hand) and they would be on trial. "Coming on the clouds of heaven" was used often in the O.T. of judgment upon fallen nations. (See Luke 21:27 note.)
11. **Matthew 27:5**—The word for "temple" indicates the inner sanctuary of the temple itself, consisting of the holy place and most holy place (fulfilling Zechariah 11:12-13).
12. **Matthew 27:11**—Jesus was the King, in fulfillment of Scripture (2 Sam. 7:12-13; Zech. 9:9; Isa. 9:6-7), but not in a political sense.

(continued on next page)

Mark Your Bible

13. **Matthew 27:14**—"Answered him not a word" is fulfillment of Isaiah 53:7. It does not mean total silence, for Jesus did speak limited words. It means that He made no strong defense for Himself, arguing for His release.

14. **Matthew 27:45-46**—Matthew ties the darkness to the Father forsaking the Son on the cross. The Lord laid on Him the sins of the world for Him to bear, and sin separates man from the God of light (Isa. 59:1-2; Hab. 1:13; 1 John 1:5). Jesus did not become a sinner, but He "bore our sins in His own body on the tree" (1 Pet. 2:24).

15. **Matthew 27:50**—This shows the difference between one's body and his spirit. "The body without the spirit is dead" (Jas. 2:26). Jesus truly died.

16. **Matthew 27:61**—It is sometimes claimed that the women came to the wrong tomb on Sunday morning, but "they observed the tomb" (Luke 23:55) and kept on "sitting opposite the tomb." They knew precisely in which tomb the body of Jesus was laid.

17. **Matthew 27:64-66**—Note the word "secure" (3 times), along with the governor's seal and the Roman guard. Usually they would use four squads of four soldiers each (cf. Acts 12:4), with 16 guards present and sleeping in shifts. Pilate and the Jews did all they could to keep the tomb shut and Jesus' body inside. Only God could open it!

18. **Matthew 28:1**—Underline "first day of the week," and note that every record of His resurrection specified this day (Mark 16:1-2, 9; Luke 24:1; John 20:1).

19. **Matthew 28:6**—The word "lay" is in the Greek imperfect tense, which emphasizes that He was laying continually for some time in the past, but that activity is no longer occurring. The "laying" has ended.

20. **Matthew 28:19**—"Baptizing" is a present participle, which points back to the leading verb "make disciples," and denotes the manner in which an action was performed, emphasizing action at the same time as the main verb. Disciples are made by baptizing people. One is not a disciple (i.e., a Christian, Acts 11:26) before baptism.

Mark Your Bible

21. **Matthew 28:19**—"In the name of" is better translated "into the name of" (as in the ASV). It is a prepositional phrase emphasizing a change in relationship from outside to inside. One is baptized "into" a new relationship with the Godhead. We then belong to God.

22. **Mark 1:4**—John's baptism required repentance, as does the baptism of the Great Commission (Acts 2:38).

23. **Mark 1:4**—The purpose of John's baptism was "for the remission of sins"—the same purpose of Christ's "one baptism" today (Acts 2:38; Eph. 4:5; Mark 16:16).

24. **Mark 1:9**—Jesus traveled at least 70 miles for the express purpose of being baptized.

25. **Mark 1:9**—The Greek word for "in" is the word *eis,* which means to be baptized "into" the Jordan. Baptism is immersion, not sprinkling.

26. **Mark 1:15**—Jesus came at exactly the time God had planned (Gal. 4:4). The prophecy of the kingdom was being fulfilled in the days of the Romans kings, just as Daniel prophesied (Dan. 2:44-45).

27. **Mark 1:22, 27**—The Jews recognized Jesus' "authority" in His teaching (v. 22) and in His power/miracles (v. 27). There was no one like Him!

28. **Mark 1:27**—The word "new" (*kainos*) is not "new in time" (as having never existed), but "new in quality" (as having a different and fresh nature).

29. **Mark 2:5**—True faith is something that is seen in one's conduct (Jas. 2:18).

30. **Mark 2:8**—Jesus knows the thoughts of man (John 2:24-25).

31. **Mark 2:21-22**—The new dispensation was not intended as a patch for the old or to be placed within the old. The new dispensation, with its laws and principles, would replace the old.

February 11 Week 6, Day 7

Day of Reflection

Take time today to reflect on the five chapters that you read this week. You may choose to read all five chapters again, in one sitting, or certain parts of them. Take time today to answer at least one of these questions below. You may or may not write anything down—you can choose to write or simply reflect.

1. What personal application do I need to make from the chapters I have read this week?

2. How can these five chapters help draw me closer to Jesus?

3. What words, phrases or verses in these chapters do I want to go back and study more in depth?

4. What questions do I have about what I have read this week on which I need to do some further Biblical research?

Week 7

February 12-18

February 12	Read Mark 3
February 13	Read Mark 4
February 14	Read Mark 5
February 15	Read Mark 6
February 16	Read Mark 7
February 17	Mark Your Bible
February 18	Day of Reflection

Prayer for this week:

"Heavenly Father,
help me to write Your Word on my heart
as I study it."

Mark 3

Helpful Notes:

1. **Beyond the Jordan** = The location is mentioned several times in the gospel accounts, and it usually refers to the land on the east side of the Jordan River, known as Perea (south of Decapolis).
2. **Boanerges** = This was the surname given by Jesus to the sons of Zebedee (James and John), when they were chosen as apostles; the name means "Sons of Thunder," which may refer to their fiery zeal and dispositions (Mark 9:38; Luke 9:51-56).
3. **Blasphemy of the Holy Spirit** = "Blasphemy" means "to speak a word against" (Matt. 12:32); blasphemy of the Holy Spirit is something they could commit when they said about Jesus, "He has an unclean spirit" (Mark 3:30); the sin of blasphemy of the Holy Spirit appears to have been unique to that setting and Jesus dealt with the matter immediately; the N.T. teaches that no man will be forgiven of any sin for which he does not repent and confess to God, but "all" sin/unrighteousness is forgiven by God when properly "confessed" (1 John 1:9), including blasphemy (1 Tim. 1:13).

1. Why did Jesus look around at the Pharisees "with anger"?

2. What are the three purposes that Mark gives for Jesus appointing His twelve apostles?

3. What excuse did Jesus' family try to make for Him in verse 21?

Verse for Meditation and Prayer: **Mark 3:25**

"And if a house is divided against itself, that house cannot stand."

Mark 4

Helpful Notes:

1. **Ears to hear** = While all men have ears and can hear (even the deaf can "hear"/read signs), not all ears want to hear or are tuned in to hear; the point that Jesus is making is that if a man does not want to hear and understand the Bible, then that man will not understand it; but the one who has ears that want to hear has the ability to understand and act accordingly, if he so chooses.
2. **Apostasy** = The seed on the stony ground represents hearts that hear, receive with gladness and endure (for a time), which indicates persons who respond favorably to the gospel and are saved; however, when hard times come for being a Christian, they "fall away" (NASB); Jesus taught that once someone is saved, he can fall away and be lost.
3. **Choke** = The things of this life can choke the Word out of someone's life, making the Word unfruitful; the Greek word means choking by "crowding around" and "being pressed upon"; some things in life may not be sinful in themselves, but they can crowd out the Word from our lives.

1. When a great multitude gathered to Jesus in verse 1, from what unique place did He preach to the people?

2. A person's "lamp" is his influence upon others. Where does Jesus say that good influence is needed?

3. Where was Jesus during the great windstorm, when waves were beating "into" the boat? What allowed Him to do that?

Verse for Meditation and Prayer: **Mark 4:20**

"But these are the ones sown on good ground,
those who hear the word, accept it, and bear fruit:
some thirtyfold, some sixty, and some a hundred."

Mark 5

Helpful Notes:

1. **Legion** = As noted in the notes on Matthew 26, this term represented a large division of the Roman army, consisting of 6,000 soldiers; in this case, the name signified that it was not just one demon possessing the man but "many"; when they were cast out, they entered 2,000 swine.
2. **Decapolis** = This was the territory on the east side of the Jordan River; this land was given to the tribe of Manasseh, but was conquered by Alexander the Great and redistributed; it originally consisted of 10 cities (thus, the name), and eventually grew to 18; they were permitted their own coinage, courts and army.
3. **Tell no one** = Jesus often told His disciples and those He healed to "tell no one"; that may seem strange and counter-productive, at first, but He likely did it (1) for the safety and security of the ones healed, and (2) to suppress excitement and prevent too large of crowds and frenzied followers, that would hinder His efforts, purpose and timing; today, we are told to tell everyone!

1. When the people of the city came out to see the man once possessed by many demons, what did they see?

2. What did Jesus tell the man, formerly possessed of many demons, to do instead of staying with Him?

3. Who were the only apostles Jesus permitted to enter Jairus' house and witness the miracle?

Verse for Meditation and Prayer: **Mark 5:19**

"Go home to your friends, and tell them what great things the Lord has done for you, and how He has had compassion on you."

Mark 6

Helpful Notes:

1. **Carpenter** = Jesus is called a carpenter, as was His earthly father, Joseph (Matt. 13:55); it was the father's duty to teach his son a trade; this is the work Jesus did until He was 30 years old; Jesus was a strong, tough man, and He knew the value of hard work.
2. **Herodias** = She was the daughter of Aristobulus, one of the sons of Herod the Great; she had been married to one of her uncles (Philip, son of Mariamne), but she divorced him to marry another uncle named Antipas; her brother was Herod Agrippa I, who killed the apostle James (Acts 12).
3. **Compassion** = The Greek word means to "have pity, feel sympathy"; the root word of this Greek term is the word for one's bowels, entrails or inward parts; literally, Jesus was moved deeply, down in His most inward, visceral emotions for the shepherdless people; true compassion is not merely a feeling that is possessed but a motivation that leads one to act on someone's behalf.

1. Why is it that a hard place for one to be respected is in his hometown and among his own relatives?

2. What kind of man did Herod know John the Baptist to be?

3. When Jesus was moved with compassion for the people, before He gave them food to eat for their bodies, what did He do in verse 34?

Verse for Meditation and Prayer: **Mark 6:50**

"But immediately He talked with them and said to them, 'Be of good cheer! It is I; do not be afraid.'"

Mark 7

Helpful Notes:

1. **Corban** = Some hypocritical Jews thought they found a way around keeping the law to honor and care for parents; if they designated certain monies and valuables as "Corban," they could claim that what they had was "given to God" (the meaning of Corban) and they had nothing left for their parents; they violated a law of God through their human tradition.
2. **All foods clean** = While certain foods under the O.T. system were forbidden to eat (Lev. 11; Deut. 14), Jesus "declared all foods clean" (7:19, NASB); this was also taught to/by Peter (Acts 10:11-18) and Paul (1 Tim. 4:1-5); this is not justification for drinking alcohol, for that is forbidden (Eph. 5:18; 1 Pet. 4:1-3; 2:11; Gal. 5:19-21) and the context is Jewish law.
3. **Syro-Phoenician** = The city of Tyre (where the woman lived) was in the region of Phoenicia (which was in the larger Roman province of Syria), thus a Syro-Phoenician; she was a Greek (Gentile) of great faith; Matthew identifies her as a "Canaanite" (Matt. 15:22).

1. In what ways can manmade traditions (although good and beneficial at times) be dangerous and destructive?

2. What unusual thing did Jesus do in healing the deaf and mute man?

3. The more Jesus commanded the people to "tell no one," the more they did what?

Verse for Meditation and Prayer: **Mark 7:37**

"And they were astonished beyond measure, saying, 'He has done all things well. He makes both the deaf to hear and the mute to speak.'"

Mark Your Bible

1. **Mark 3:1**—The withered hand suffered from some kind of muscle atrophy, which caused the hand to shrivel and be of little to no use.
2. **Mark 3:19**—Every time Judas is named in the gospel accounts, he is always identified as the one who betrayed Jesus.
3. **Mark 3:21**—Translations vary in the identity of these people. The Greek term means, "those by His side," and likely is a reference to His family.
4. **Mark 3:27**—While Satan is "a strong man," Jesus is stronger and rid many persons from having the devil and demons "housing" themselves within them (cf. 1 John 4:4).
5. **Mark 3:30**—Underline this whole verse. This is how they committed the blasphemy of the Holy Spirit, something that appears unique to that situation.
6. **Mark 4:11**—"Mystery" does not mean "mysterious" or requiring "clues" to unravel; it simply means the wisdom, counsel and will of God which had been hidden and were awaiting revelation from God.
7. **Mark 4:13-20**—The different soils represent the different hearts/ attitudes toward God's Word.
8. **Mark 4:27**—As man does not fully understand the intricacies of the growth and development of a seed and plant, man does not fully understand exactly how the seed of God's Word grows and develops in the heart of man; but the evidence of such is visibly apparent (in the growth from a physical seed and from the Word of God).
9. **Mark 4:37**—The word "filling" is in the present tense, denoting a continual activity of water filling the boat.
10. **Mark 4:38**—"Perishing" is the same Greek word for "destroy" in Matthew 10:28. The disciples were not being annihilated in the storm. It was their well-being that was being lost and ruined.

(continued on next page)

Mark Your Bible

11. **Mark 5:7**—The demons knew who Jesus was and where He was going (by the power of God) to return them.
12. **Mark 5:15**—This is clear evidence of the power of God at work.
13. **Mark 5:24**—"Thronged" meant "to press together" or to "press on all sides," to the point of not being able to move.
14. **Mark 5:29, 34**—The Greek word for "affliction" (*mastix*) was a word used for "a whip or scourging" (Acts 22:24; Heb. 11:36). It is used metaphorically here to denote how severe her suffering was.
15. **Mark 5:36**—"Believe" is in the present tense, emphasizing to "keep on believing." Don't quit. Don't give up. Don't lose faith.
16. **Mark 6:3**—They noted every form of identification they had for Jesus to prove He was just a man, lest they should believe in Him.
17. **Mark 6:6**—God gives man free will and does not choose who has faith and who does not. Yet, disbelief (especially in the face of so much evidence to believe) still disappoints and amazes Him.
18. **Mark 6:18**—The words "had said" are in the Greek imperfect tense, emphasizing that he warned the king repeatedly.
19. **Mark 6:19**—In the Greek imperfect tense, Herodias had a sustained, incessant desire to kill John the Baptist.
20. **Mark 6:48**—It was the middle of the night, and the disciples were in the middle of the Sea of Galilee (3-4 miles out, according to John 6:19), and it was during a horrible storm, but Jesus still "saw" them. He sees you whatever you're going through.
21. **Mark 6:52**—Even for the apostles, it took a while for everything to sink in. They were not willfully hardened; they were slow to perceive and reason through all the amazing evidence being displayed for them that day.
22. **Mark 7:2, 5**—The Pharisees concern about "unwashed hands" was not due to germs from dirt or grime, but from contamination of a Gentile—that is what they guarded themselves against the most.

Mark Your Bible

23. **Mark 7:3**—The words "in a special way" and "holding the tradition" emphasize that the Pharisees had created their own laws, and they were more concerned about their laws than the laws of God.

24. **Mark 7:8, 9, 13**—Underline the words "you" and "your" in these verses; that is where the Pharisees and scribes placed their focus.

25. **Mark 7:8, 9, 13**—Underline the words "laying aside," "reject" and "made of no effect" and connect them with a line—that is what holding to human traditions does to the commandments of God.

26. **Mark 7:21**—Man is not sinful because of birth or genetics. Man is sinful because of what his own heart leads him to think, say and do.

27. **Mark 7:27**—By saying the word "first," Jesus may have intentionally been opening a door for the woman to walk through in her request.

February 18 Week 7, Day 7

Day of Reflection

Take time today to reflect on the five chapters that you read this week. You may choose to read all five chapters again, in one sitting, or certain parts of them. Take time today to answer at least one of these questions below. You may or may not write anything down—you can choose to write or simply reflect.

1. What personal application do I need to make from the chapters I have read this week?

2. How can these five chapters help draw me closer to Jesus?

3. What words, phrases or verses in these chapters do I want to go back and study more in depth?

4. What questions do I have about what I have read this week on which I need to do some further Biblical research?

Week 8

February 19-25

February 19	Read Mark 8
February 20	Read Mark 9
February 21	Read Mark 10
February 22	Read Mark 11
February 23	Read Mark 12
February 24	Mark Your Bible
February 25	Day of Reflection

Prayer for this week:

"Heavenly Father,
help me to love studying Your Word."

Mark 8

Helpful Notes:

1. **Leaven** = This is a fermenting agent that causes dough to rise; at least two characteristics of leaven are emphasized by Jesus: (1) it works in a quiet, subtle and almost unnoticeable way; (2) it was a corrupting influence that spread until the whole was affected; the doctrines and evil influence of the Pharisees, Sadducees (Matt. 16:6) and Herodians (Mark 8:15) was subtle and wholly corrupting; thus, "Beware!"
2. **Caesarea Philippi** = This was a city at the extreme northern boundary of Palestine, in the hill country of the southern slopes of Mount Hermon; it was renamed by Philip the tetrarch (son of Herod the Great and Cleopatra of Jerusalem), in honor of Tiberius Caesar; the transfiguration may have occurred here.
3. **The Christ** = "Christ" is not merely a name attached to "Jesus" but is the N.T. equivalent title of the O.T. "Messiah" (John 1:41); Jesus of Nazareth is the Christ, having fulfilled all O.T. prophecies of the coming Messiah; the word "Christ" means "the anointed one," which was the role Jesus fulfilled perfectly and completely as prophet, priest and king.

1. Why does Jesus refer to Peter as "Satan"?

2. For whose sake and for what's sake is losing one's life truly worth it?

3. If one is ashamed of Jesus in this life, what did Jesus say would be His response?

Verse for Meditation and Prayer: **Mark 8:31**

"And He began to teach them that the Son of Man must suffer many things, and be rejected by the elders and chief priests and scribes, and be killed, and after three days rise again."

Mark 9

Helpful Notes:

1. **Kingdom of God** = The word "kingdom" signifies a type of government, which is ruled by a King (which would be Jesus); the kingdom was prophesied in the O.T. (2 Sam. 7:12-16; Isa. 2:2-3; Dan. 2:44); Jesus predicted it was "at hand" (Matt. 4:17) and identified it as His church (Matt. 16:18-19); His kingdom/church was established with power (Mark 9:1) in Acts 2 and Christians are part of it today (Col. 1:13; Rev. 1:9); in the end, Christ will come and deliver those in His kingdom/church to the Father (1 Cor. 15:24).
2. **Miracle** = A miracle is a supernatural act of God on this earth to establish His supreme, Divine authority; genuine miracles could only be performed by someone given that power by God (Satan could not do miracles); miracles would (and did) cease when the N.T. was completed (1 Cor. 13:8-13).
3. **Greatest** = The disciples were human, and therefore subject to human desires and pursuits, including pride and power; man wants to be "greatest" and "first," but followers of Christ will gladly choose to be like Him—"last of all and servant of all"; humility is a choice (Phil. 2:3-8).

1. Who appears to have been Jesus' closest friends, for He took them with Him alone several times (Mark 5:37; 9:2; 14:33)?

2. What were the apostles of Jesus still questioning within themselves and not understanding (9:10, 31-32)?

3. In what vivid way did Jesus describe the suffering and anguish in hell (three times)?

Verse for Meditation and Prayer: **Mark 9:1**

"Assuredly, I say to you that
there are some standing here who will not taste death
till they see the kingdom of God present with power."

February 21 Week 8, Day 3

Mark 10

Helpful Notes:

1. **From the beginning** = Jesus taught that God's design for marriage at the beginning was the design intended for mankind for all time and nothing was to change; thus, when Jesus was asked about divorce, He took the matter all the way back to God's original plan in Genesis 2; Jesus also taught that humanity was at the beginning and did not come about millions of years later.
2. **Receive a hundredfold** = To be a disciple of Christ involves sacrifice, and often that sacrifice is of relationships and possessions; Jesus promised that those who make those sacrifices to follow Him will receive it back in overflowing abundance "now" (with a huge church family and all spiritual blessings in Christ) and in "eternal life."
3. **Baptism of suffering** = "The cup" and "the baptism" in this passage are parallel; "the cup" is the suffering Jesus would endure on the cross (14:36), therefore, the baptism of which Jesus spoke was fulfilled on the cross, when He was immersed, submerged and overwhelmed with suffering; His disciples would also be immersed in suffering for Him.

1. When God has joined a man and woman together in marriage, what does He not want them to do?

2. Why did the rich young ruler go away sorrowful from Jesus?

3. What specifics did Jesus know about how He was going to be treated in His final hours (verses 33-34)?

Verse for Meditation and Prayer: **Mark 10:45**

"For even the Son of Man did not come to be served, but to serve, and to give His life a ransom for many."

February 22 Week 8, Day 4

Mark 11

Helpful Notes:

1. **Moneychangers** = Many enterprising Jews had set up business inside the temple complex, in order to accommodate Jews coming from great distance to offer various animals as sacrifice; there were those who exchanged currency and those who sold the animals; Jesus would not tolerate a sacred place being desecrated by materialism.
2. **Cursed** = Jesus did not use profanity or sin in "cursing" the fig tree; He simply doomed the tree so that "no one eat fruit from it ever again" (11:14); having leaves was a promise of fruit, but it had none; this was symbolic of the future doom of the Jewish nation for not bearing fruit as they should.
3. **From heaven or from men** = The question that Jesus asked regarding the baptism of John is the perfect question to ask about any religious doctrine or religious practice of a religious group today; the origin of the various doctrines and groups that exist today (and by what authority they exist) must be determined; anything short of having heaven's authority based upon the clear teaching of Scripture must be rejected.

1. Not only were the people saying, "Blessed" is the King coming into Jerusalem, but they also said "Blessed" is what else?

2. For what reason does Mark say that the scribes and chief priests "feared" Jesus?

3. Jesus' words in verse 22 represent the condition of heart that children (of all ages) need to develop. What are those words?

Verse for Meditation and Prayer: **Mark 11:25**

"And whenever you stand praying, if you have anything against anyone, forgive him, that your Father in heaven may also forgive you your trespasses."

Mark 12

Helpful Notes:

1. **Said by the Holy Spirit** = Jesus affirms the verbal inspiration of the Bible by noting that what "David himself said" was "by the Holy Spirit"; David would also say, "The Spirit of the Lord spoke by me, and His word was on my tongue" (2 Sam. 23:2); the Holy Spirit was responsible for the revelation of God's Word and guiding the writers of the Bible—no part of Scripture was the result of man's own ingenuity (2 Tim. 3:16; 2 Pet. 1:20-21; 1 Cor. 2:10-13).
2. **Treasury** = This area of the temple complex was also called "the court of women"; this area (large enough for Jesus to teach crowds, John 8:20) is where the Jews deposited their offerings (for the expenses of the temple services) into 13 containers that looked like inverted trumpets.
3. **Mite** = This was the smallest Jewish coin, known as a lepton, which was worth about 1/8 of a cent; her two mites (making a quadrans/kodrantes or farthing) was worth about 1/64 of a denarius (a day's wage for a laborer); she truly was "poor," as this was her "whole livelihood," but she "put in more than all those" who gave "out of their abundance."

1. On this day, just days before the crucifixion, what four groups came one after another to test Jesus (verses 13, 18, 28)?

2. What did Jesus say the Sadducees did "not know," which caused them to be "mistaken/wrong" in their conclusions?

3. Who did Jesus say wrote the book of Exodus?

Verse for Meditation and Prayer: **Mark 12:44**

"For they all put in out of their abundance,
but she out of her poverty put in all that she had,
her whole livelihood."

February 24 Week 8, Day 6

Mark Your Bible

1. **Mark 8:10**—This village was on the west shore of the Sea of Galilee, likely near or the same as Magdala/Magadan in the parallel passage (Matt. 15:39).
2. **Mark 8:12**—The Greek for "sighed deeply" indicates that Jesus literally "groaned aloud upwardly" from the depths of His being for these antagonists—He loved them.
3. **Mark 8:24-25**—It is inappropriate to question the power or wisdom of Jesus. He was always in perfect control of His power, and, no doubt, He was purposeful in this healing process. The actions here were likely designed to have an impact on the man.
4. **Mark 8:32**—The imperfect tense emphasizes that Jesus kept speaking openly and repeatedly about His impending death and resurrection.
5. **Mark 8:38**—"Adulterous" is used symbolically (as used by O.T. prophets) of their unfaithfulness to their God, to whom they were married (Ex. 34:15; Jer. 3:14, 20).
6. **Mark 9:1**—Underline this KEY verse! The kingdom/church would come with "power" in their lifetime. The "power" would come from "on high" (Luke 24:49), "when the Holy Spirit" would "come upon" the apostles (Acts 1:8). In Acts 2, all of this was fulfilled.
7. **Mark 9:38**—It is not enough to claim to do something in Jesus' name (Matt. 7:22-23). It must be evident that one's teaching is conforming to the will of God (Matt. 7:21; Acts 17:11; 1 Pet. 4:11; 1 Cor. 1:10).
8. **Mark 9:39-40**—This does not justify denominationalism, as some so attempt. This man was doing miracles only if he was teaching Jesus' truth. The two always went together. He was preaching Divine truth.
9. **Mark 10:2**—The imperfect tense emphasizes that they "kept asking" Jesus—pestering Him.

(continued on next page)

Mark Your Bible

10. **Mark 10:12**—Christ's law regarding marriage and divorce applies equally to male and female.
11. **Mark 10:24**—Jesus' emphasis is not merely on those who have riches but on those who "trust in riches." (See 1 Timothy 6:10.)
12. **Mark 10:42**—Jesus uses the word "over" three times to describe those who like to rule and be in charge. Some followers of Christ will be in positions of authority, but they must not "lord it over" others (1 Pet. 5:3).
13. **Mark 10:46**—It is not a contradiction that Matthew mentions two men (20:30) and Mark and Luke (18:35) mention one. The information is merely supplementary, since Mark and Luke did not say "only one man."
14. **Mark 11:13**—The fig tree was presenting itself as if it had fruit, to draw people to it, but it was barren. This represented the Jewish leaders and their empty, fruitless teachings and promise.
15. **Mark 11:16**—To maintain the sacredness of the temple, Jesus prohibited the people from carrying any vessel, container or sack that could be construed as making the holy place appear to be some common market.
16. **Mark 11:17**—Note carefully that God intended His temple to be for all nations, including Gentiles (2 Chron. 6:32).
17. **Mark 11:23**—Jesus was not talking about physical mountains but about the many obstacles that lay before His apostles in preaching the gospel.
18. **Mark 11:25**—Underline the "any" in "anything" and "anyone." If we want our prayers to be heard and if we want to be forgiven ourselves, we must "forgive" <u>any</u>one for <u>any</u>thing.
19. **Mark 12:14**—Jesus always spoke the truth and was not concerned about pleasing man, seeking his favor or changing His message to fit the people's wishes or the moment.

Mark Your Bible

20. **Mark 12:26**—The only part of the O.T. that the Sadducees accepted was the Pentateuch, so Jesus appealed to "their" Scriptures.
21. **Mark 12:26**—The Bible had not yet been divided into chapters and verses, so it was easiest to quote the Bible by the subject of the passage.
22. **Mark 12:27**—God is not the God of nothing. He is the God of something. He is "the God of the living," which means the Patriarchs were still alive.
23. **Mark 12:34**—This scribe/Pharisee (who usually emphasized the external only) recognized that obedience is nothing without the heart. Those two components (heart and obedience) are essential to enter the kingdom.

Day of Reflection

Take time today to reflect on the five chapters that you read this week. You may choose to read all five chapters again, in one sitting, or certain parts of them. Take time today to answer at least one of these questions below. You may or may not write anything down—you can choose to write or simply reflect.

1. What personal application do I need to make from the chapters I have read this week?

2. How can these five chapters help draw me closer to Jesus?

3. What words, phrases or verses in these chapters do I want to go back and study more in depth?

4. What questions do I have about what I have read this week on which I need to do some further Biblical research?

Week 9

February 26-March 4

February 26	Read Mark 13
February 27	Read Mark 14
February 28	Read Mark 15
March 1	Read Mark 16
March 2	Read Luke 1
March 3	Mark Your Bible
March 4	Day of Reflection

Prayer for this week:

*"Heavenly Father,
You are an amazing God and have
blessed me tremendously!"*

February 26 Week 9, Day 1

Mark 13

Helpful Notes: ** See also the notes and markings for Matthew 24 and Luke 21.*

1. **Tribulation** = The word means "a pressure, affliction, oppression" that is brought on from outside; Jesus called this "great tribulation" the worst that ever occurred; this took place in the destruction of Jerusalem because: (1) Jesus said it happened in that "generation" (13:30); (2) the Jews, as a nation, were more blessed than any people and, therefore, more subject to punishment for willfully rejecting and defying their God and their blessed position as His people; (3) the historian Josephus described the utter horror of Rome's vicious devastation of Jerusalem and its people; Jesus was not talking about a tribulation at the end of time.
2. **This generation** = Jesus said that "all these things" (i.e., the signs of the destruction of Jerusalem) would "take place" in "this generation"; "generation" is all people living at a given time, who are contemporaries with one another; Jesus used that word for those living in His day (Matt. 11:16; 12:41-42, 45; 23:36); thus, none of those signs have application to anything today.
3. **That day** = In verse 32, Jesus contrasts what He had been talking about regarding Jerusalem's destruction in "those days" (with various "signs" preceding) with "that day" in the future when the Son of Man would come unexpectedly (with no signs preceding it) and the world would pass away; "that [final] day" (singular) is much different than "those [A.D. 70] days" (plural).

1. Amazingly, what would some family members do to each other when persecution arose?

2. While we know that all material things are transitory in nature, what reassuring reality do we know about God's Word?

3. Since we "do not know when the time is" that Jesus will return, what two things does He tell us to do?

Verse for Meditation and Prayer: **Mark 13:31**

"Heaven and earth will pass away,
but My words will by no means pass away."

February 27

Week 9, Day 2

Mark 14

Helpful Notes:

1. **Gethsemane** = This was a garden off the Mount of Olives, across the Kidron Valley from Jerusalem (John 18:1), where Jesus was "accustomed" to go (Luke 22:39); the name means "olive press" or "oil press," which seems fitting for what Jesus endured there.
2. **Abba** = This term of endearment is always tied with "Father" in the N.T. and always in the context of prayer; this was the word that Jewish children (from infancy) used in addressing their father, which emphasizes complete trust and loving familiarity.
3. **This cup** = Jesus prayed three times, "Take this cup away from Me"; what exactly Jesus meant has been a point of disagreement; Mark says that Jesus prayed that "the hour might pass from Him" (14:35), and then He prayed in the next verse to "Take this cup away from Me" (14:36); thus, the cup which was causing Jesus so much trouble, distress and agony was every bit of the "hour" (used figuratively) of suffering (mental, physical and spiritual) that He would endure over the next several hours; Jesus was Divine and human, and He suffered tremendously for us.

1. In a simple note of praise, how did Jesus honor the woman anointing Him in the first part of verse 8?

2. As if Jesus was a violent criminal, what did the mob bring with them to arrest Jesus?

3. What signal (of a common greeting in that day) did Judas give to identify Jesus?

Verse for Meditation and Prayer: **Mark 14:38**

"Watch and pray, lest you enter into temptation. The spirit indeed is willing, but the flesh is weak."

Mark 15

Helpful Notes:

1. **Crucifixion** = Used extensively by the Persians, the Romans seemed to perfect every torturous aspect of crucifixion; the upright part of the cross (the stipes) was usually already secured in the ground, and the victim carried the crossbar (the patibulum), which weighed about 110 pounds; nails were driven through the hands (probably wrists) and feet; victims would die of blood loss and/or build up of CO_2 due to the inability to exhale while the body was suspended on nails; this was the most vicious and humiliating execution reserved for the worst criminals and most worthless slaves.
2. **Golgotha** = This was an Aramaic term meaning "Place of the Skull"; the place was "near" (John 19:20) but "outside" (Heb. 13:12) the city; this public execution site was close enough for city residents and passers by to gawk at and chide the victims.
3. **Preparation Day** = This was "the day before the Sabbath," which would be Friday; this was the weekly day on which they made ready for the Sabbath (the day on which no work was permitted); the Bible identifies Friday (the sixth day of the week) as the day of Christ's crucifixion.

1. For what reason did Pilate know that the chief priests "had handed [Jesus] over" to him to crucify Him?

2. Who got involved in blaspheming, mocking and reviling Jesus while He was on the cross?

3. While most of the disciples had fled, who was still there watching the crucifixion from afar?

Verse for Meditation and Prayer: **Mark 15:34**

"And at the ninth hour Jesus cried out with a loud voice, saying, 'Eloi, Eloi, lama sabachthani?' which is translated, 'My God, My God, why have You forsaken Me?'"

Mark 16

<u>Helpful Notes:</u>

1. **Saved** = The word means "to rescue, deliver or preserve one from danger, suffering or death"; in this context, it is being saved or preserved from eternal judgment and death in hell; Jesus came to save mankind from their sins (Matt. 1:21), and our obedience to the gospel (which includes baptism) is how we can be saved from our sins and their eternal consequences in hell; it is essential to use Bible words (like "saved") in the way that the Bible uses them, incorporating all that the Bible has to say on the subject.
2. **Condemned** = The Greek word means "to give judgment against, to pronounce a sentence after determination of guilt"; when one is found guilty of sin and has not been saved from those sins by obeying God's plan, he is sentenced to eternal hell.
3. **Confirming the Word** = The purpose of miracles was to "confirm" (i.e., to establish as valid, authenticate, guarantee as reliable) the message that was being preached (Heb. 2:2-4); the N.T. was still being written and could not be personally verified, which was the purpose of God providing the ability to do miracles; once the written N.T. was completed, the signs would cease (1 Cor. 13:8-13).

1. What detail about the stone does Mark give, which would have made it difficult for the woman to remove?

2. What did Jesus do to the apostles when they did not believe the reports of His resurrection?

3. After giving His disciples the Great Commission, where did Jesus go?

Verse for Meditation and Prayer: **<u>Mark 16:15</u>**

"And He said to them, 'Go into all the world and preach the gospel to every creature.'"

Luke 1

Helpful Notes: ** See Brief Introduction to Luke on page 633.*

1. **Division of the priests** = David divided the priests into 24 divisions (1 Chron. 24:1-19); the divisions rotated service at the temple, each serving for one week, two separate times a year; one priest was chosen each day (by lot) to preside over the two times of prayer—a once-in-a-lifetime opportunity; Zacharias was of the 8th division of Abijah.
2. **Throne of David** = The Lord promised David that, from his seed, He would "establish the throne of his kingdom forever" (2 Sam. 7:12-16); the Jews had been waiting for the Messiah to fulfill this prophecy; this new "forever, no end" (Isa. 2:2-4; 9:6; Dan. 2:44) kingdom (the "house of David/Jacob/Israel") was the now, soon-to-be-established spiritual Israel (Gal. 6:16; 1 Pet. 2:9), which is the church (Matt. 16:18-19).
3. **Judea** = This is the southern part of Palestine, with Galilee in the north and Samaria between the two; much of Judea was "hill country" (1:63) and "wilderness" (Matt. 3:1); in Judea, and especially near the Jordan River, is where John the Baptist did most of his preaching; the city of Jerusalem was in Judea.

1. In his great service to the Lord, what would John the Baptist not drink?

2. What was the name of the angel who appeared to Zacharias and Mary (and also appeared to the prophet Daniel)?

3. After hearing the plans that the Lord had for her, how did Mary respond (v. 38)? What did she call herself?

Verse for Meditation and Prayer: **Luke 1:68**

"Blessed is the Lord God of Israel,
For He has visited and redeemed His people."

Mark Your Bible

1. **Mark 13:28-29**—When His disciples would "see" these signs take place, they would "know" that the destruction of Jerusalem was near.
2. **Mark 13:30**—This verse gives context to every verse before it. Underline it.
3. **Mark 13:32**—Even when He was on the earth, "the Son" did not know the day or hour when He would return the second time.
4. **Mark 13:32**—Circle the word "But," denoting a change of subject to the final return of Christ—the timing of which one cannot "know." Draw a line connecting the words "know" in verses 28-29 and the words "no one knows" and "not know" in verses 32-33, to note the contrast. The disciples in Jesus' day could "know" when the city of Jerusalem was going to be destroyed based upon seeing the signs. No disciple today can "know" when Jesus will return, for there will be no signs preceding it.
5. **Mark 14:23**—Jesus told them to "all" drink and "they all drank." There is no Scriptural support for only clergy to drink.
6. **Mark 14:24**—"Shed" or "poured out" emphasizes that His death would be one of violence (Isa. 53:12; Zech. 12:10).
7. **Mark 14:25**—"That day in the kingdom of God" pointed to the establishment of the church in Acts 2 and Jesus communing with His people every Sunday.
8. **Mark 14:30**—The rooster would usually crow several times in the night, but especially at midnight and at 3:00 a.m. The other gospel writers mention the last one (3:00 a.m.), while Mark mentions both.
9. **Mark 14:71**—Peter called a curse "down on himself" (the emphasis of the Greek), in desperation and irritation, to bind himself (in their eyes) under a curse that he had never known Jesus.
10. **Mark 15:16-20**—Jesus was tortured by Roman soldiers (not Jewish), who feigned respect (giving royal robe of purple and a crown) and feigned worship (bowing down before Him). How despicable!

(continued on next page)

Mark Your Bible

11. **Mark 15:20**—His own garments were necessary to fulfill Scripture (Matt. 27:35; Psa. 22:18).
12. **Mark 15:21**—It is possible that Mark's readers knew these individuals; perhaps they had been converted to Christ (Rom. 16:13).
13. **Mark 15:23**—"Gave" is in the imperfect tense, indicating they kept trying to give it to Him repeatedly.
14. **Mark 15:23**—This concoction was designed to deaden the pain and perhaps prolong the torture; Christ refused, choosing rather to suffer the full agony.
15. **Mark 15:43**—Not all of the Sanhedrin voted to put Jesus to death.
16. **Mark 15:44-45**—This is absolute confirmation that Jesus really died and did not merely go unconscious. The Roman centurion knew death.
17. **Mark 16:7**—The last time Peter saw Jesus before His death is when he denied Him three times and then locked eyes with Him (Luke 22:61). Underline "and Peter."
18. **Mark 16:9**—The Bible explicitly tells us exactly when Jesus was raised.
19. **Mark 16:11, 13, 14**—Three times (underline them) the text says the disciples still "did not believe." No wonder the first thing Jesus says one must do to be saved is to "believe."
20. **Mark 16:15**—Salvation is universally available to "all/every," just as it was prophesied (Isa. 2:2-4).
21. **Mark 16:16**—The coordinating conjunction "and" joins two items of equal grammatical importance. Both elements (believe and baptized) are equally necessary to obtain the result of being saved.
22. **Mark 16:17**—The Greek word for "new" is not a chronological newness (of something that never existed before) but a qualitative newness (of a fresh language to them to speak to others who knew it).

Mark Your Bible

23. **Mark 16:18**—In fulfillment of this promise, Paul was bitten by a deadly viper and suffered no harm (see Acts 28:3-6).
24. **Luke 1:3**— The title "most excellent" may indicate that Theophilus was a government official (Acts 26:25), perhaps in Rome (Phil. 1:12-13).
25. **Luke 1:3**—The name Theophilus means "lover (or loved) of God."
26. **Luke 1:4**—The truths and doctrines of Christ can be known with "certainty."
27. **Luke 1:10**—The hour of incense was the hour of prayer (either at 9:00 a.m. or 3:00 p.m.).
28. **Luke 1:32-33**—This prophecy is fulfilled in Acts 2:30-33, with Christ reigning in heaven (not the earth) over His kingdom.
29. **Luke 1:41, 44**—Circle the word "baby" and note the same word is used in 2:12, 16 (circle it there). God (and Dr. Luke) used the same word for a "baby" in the womb and a "baby" out of the womb. The practice of "abortion" is the practice of murdering a living baby.
30. **Luke 1:78**—The Dayspring or Sunshine was an O.T. depiction of the coming Messiah (Isa. 9:2; 60:1-3; Mal. 4:2).

Day of Reflection

Take time today to reflect on the five chapters that you read this week. You may choose to read all five chapters again, in one sitting, or certain parts of them. Take time today to answer at least one of these questions below. You may or may not write anything down—you can choose to write or simply reflect.

1. What personal application do I need to make from the chapters I have read this week?

2. How can these five chapters help draw me closer to Jesus?

3. What words, phrases or verses in these chapters do I want to go back and study more in depth?

4. What questions do I have about what I have read this week on which I need to do some further Biblical research?

Week 10

March 5-11

March 5	Read Luke 2
March 6	Read Luke 3
March 7	Read Luke 4
March 8	Read Luke 5
March 9	Read Luke 6
March 10	Mark Your Bible
March 11	Day of Reflection

Prayer for this week:

"Heavenly Father,
I love You! Please help me
to deepen that love every day!"

March 5

Week 10, Day 1

Luke 2

Helpful Notes:

1. **Obey the law of the land** = Before He was born, Jesus' parents were diligent to obey civil law, including traveling some 90 miles from Nazareth to Bethlehem, in order to register to pay taxes (while Mary "was with child"); God's people must obey the law of the land (Rom. 13:1-7; 1 Pet. 2:13-17).
2. **Obey the law of the Lord** = Jesus learned to be obedient to the law of Moses/the law of the Lord from infancy—His parents had Him circumcised on the 8th day (Lev. 12:3), they went to the temple to make an offering (Lev. 12:4-8), and they went to Jerusalem every year for Passover (Ex. 23:15-17).
3. **Nazareth and Bethlehem** = Jesus' parents lived in Nazareth (Luke 1:26) and that is where He would be raised (Matt. 2:23); but prophecy specified He would be born in Bethlehem of Judah (Mic. 5:2; Matt. 2:6); to fulfill this prophecy, God's providence worked to have a decree from the Roman emperor himself that "all" peoples were to be registered in their hometowns, and Joseph's hometown was Bethlehem (Luke 2:1-5).

1. In the song of the angels, what did they say that the birth of Jesus had brought on earth for those well-pleasing to God?

2. Simeon had received a revelation from God that Jesus would be "a light for revelation" to what people?

3. In what four key areas did Jesus continue to grow from age 12 to age 30?

Verse for Meditation and Prayer: **Luke 2:49**

"And He said to them, 'Why did you seek Me?
Did you not know that I must be about My Father's business?'"

Luke 3

Helpful Notes:

1. **Philip the tetrarch** = When Herod the Great died, his territory was divided among three of his sons: Archelaus took Judea, Samaria and Idumea; Antipas took Galilee and Perea; Philip took Trachonitis and Iturea (in NE Galilee); this Philip (son of Cleopatra) is different than the Philip (son of Mariamne) who was married to Herodias.
2. **Baptism of fire** = The baptism of the Holy Spirit is distinct from the baptism with fire, but both would be administered by the Lord; the word "baptize" means an "immersion" in fire, and this is the same "unquenchable fire" (3:17) in which the chaff would "burn"; baptism of fire is for those who are cast into the "furnace of fire" (Matt. 13:42, 50) in hell; no one should desire the baptism of fire.
3. **Genealogy** = Matthew traces Jesus' ancestry through Joseph back to Abraham, to prove His pure Jewish heritage; Luke traces Jesus' ancestry through Mary back to Adam, to emphasize His human descent for the Greek reader; the Jewish Talmud says Mary was the daughter of Heli (but Luke does not record women in his genealogy for the Greeks).

1. Why were people being baptized by John? Was it because they already had the remission of sins?

2. What sorts of changes did John tell specific people to make, lest the ax cut them down?

3. What did the great John the Baptist say about his worthiness before Jesus?

Verse for Meditation and Prayer: **Luke 3:17**

"His winnowing fan is in His hand, and He will thoroughly clean out His threshing floor, and gather the wheat into His barn; but the chaff He will burn with unquenchable fire."

Luke 4

Helpful Notes:

1. **Synagogue** = The Greek term means "a place of assembly, a gathering place"; they are believed to have their origin during the Babylonian exile, when Jews could not go to Jerusalem; their primary purpose was for instruction in the law, only later to become a place of worship for some Jews, instead of going to Jerusalem; historians indicate that regular meetings occurred on Monday, Thursday and the Sabbath; a synagogue was to be set up in any community with ten Jewish men.
2. **Book** = The word is from the Greek word *biblion,* from which we derive the word "Bible"; the word denoted a written document and usually referred to a scroll; the O.T. was divided out onto multiple scrolls, which were usually stored at the synagogue or temple for public readings.
3. **Anointed** = Jesus was "the anointed one," which is the meaning of the Hebrew term "Messiah" and the Greek term "Christ"; Jesus fulfilled all prophesied roles of those who were anointed—prophet (1 Kgs. 19:16; Acts 3:22-23), priest (Ex. 28:41; Heb. 3:1) and king (1 Sam. 9:16; Luke 1:32-33).

1. What did Jesus make a priority to do every Sabbath?

2. What miraculously happened to Naaman, of which Jesus testifies as an actual event and a real miracle?

3. What did Jesus say was the purpose for which He had been sent?

Verse for Meditation and Prayer: **Luke 4:8**

"Get behind Me, Satan! For it is written,
'You shall worship the LORD your God,
and Him only you shall serve.'"

Luke 5

Helpful Notes:

1. **Catch men** = Various metaphors are used for evangelism (like planting seeds); Jesus taught that the church is "like a dragnet" (Matt. 13:47); the responsibility of Christians is to cast the net far and wide, allowing the gospel to do the "catching" and the Lord to do the "increasing" (1 Cor. 3:6); the victories of Pentecost and beyond were foreshadowed here.
2. **Jesus prayed** = Jesus often got away on His own to spend time in prayer (Matt. 14:23; Mark 1:35; Luke 5:16); He prayed before meals (John 6:11), before important decisions (Luke 6:12-13), for others (John 17:6-26), when facing and immersed in trials (Matt. 26:36-46; 27:46), etc.; if Jesus devoted so much time to prayer, what does that teach Christians today?
3. **Bridegroom** = The N.T. depicts Jesus as the bridegroom (Matt. 25:1-13; Luke 5:34-35), or the husband (2 Cor. 11:2), to whom the church is married (Rom. 7:4); the church is the bride of Christ (Eph. 5:23-27; Rev. 22:17); the N.T. uses this figurative language to help us to understand the close relationship that Jesus longs to have with His church, and to provide a vivid illustration to husbands and wives of what their relationship should look like.

1. Even though Simon argued back with the Lord at first, why did he finally let down the net?

2. When it finally clicked with Peter that he was in the presence of deity at the miraculous catch of fish, how did he respond?

3. What relationship did Peter and Andrew have with James and John before Jesus called them as His disciples?

Verse for Meditation and Prayer: **Luke 5:8**

"When Simon Peter saw it, he fell down at Jesus' knees, saying, 'Depart from me, for I am a sinful man, O Lord!'"

Luke 6

Helpful Notes:

1. **Apostles** = The Greek word means "one sent forth"; the term is usually applied to the men chosen by Jesus for His special work—the original twelve (Luke 6:13), Matthias (Acts 1:21-26) and then Paul (1 Cor. 15:8-9); there are no apostles today, for they would be unqualified to serve in such a role, having not been with Jesus during His ministry or witnessed His resurrection (Acts 1:21-22).
2. **Heal** = Jesus had the ability to heal people of diseases (Matt. 11:5), and the healing was 100% effective and immediate ("perfect soundness," Acts 3:16); Jesus gave this healing ability to His apostles (Acts 3:6-11), who could pass it on to other Christians by laying hands on them (Acts 8:14-19; 1 Cor. 12:7-11); healing, like all miracles, ceased in the first century (1 Cor. 13:8-13).
3. **Reward** = While "reward" can mean "wages, pay, remuneration," there is no sense in which one earns the rewarded blessings of God in this life or the next; the reward to a Christian is always based on the grace of God and extended only to those who meet His conditions (Eph. 2:1-10; Tit. 2:11-14).

1. Before making the important decision of choosing His twelve apostles, what did Jesus do all night?

2. When we take a stand for Christ, what did Jesus say we should expect in verse 22?

3. What did Jesus tell us to do toward those who are unthankful?

Verse for Meditation and Prayer: **Luke 6:31**

"And just as you want men to do to you, you also do to them likewise."

Mark Your Bible

1. **Luke 2:1**—Augustus was the Roman Caesar at Christ's birth and Tiberius was Caesar during His ministry (Luke 3:1).
2. **Luke 2:8**—Shepherds would not have had their flocks in the fields at night during the winter. Jesus was not born in December.
3. **Luke 2:11**—Note three designations for Jesus: Savior, Christ and Lord. Mark these words.
4. **Luke 2:22, 24**—"The law of Moses" is "the law of the Lord." (Draw a line connecting these two phrases.) The argument that "the law of Moses" was abrogated in the cross but "the law of the Lord" (supposedly containing the Sabbath remembrance) was not done away at the cross is absolutely false.
5. **Luke 2:24**—Jesus' parents were poor. Instead of being able to offer a lamb, they offered the less-expensive substitute. Poverty is not dishonorable.
6. **Luke 2:41**—"Went" is the Greek imperfect tense, indicating this was a regular habit of Jesus' parents.
7. **Luke 2:48-49**—12-year-old Jesus drew a distinction between His earthly "father" (v. 48) and His heavenly "Father" (v. 49).
8. **Luke 3:6**—The prophet specified (Isa. 40:5) that salvation would not just come to the Jews but to "all flesh," including the Gentiles.
9. **Luke 3:8**—Repentance is a change of mind. It must then lead to a change of action, bearing fruits of repentance; otherwise, it is not true repentance.
10. **Luke 3:17**—The unquenchable fire is hell (same as the fire in verses 9 and 16).
11. **Luke 3:23**—Underline the age of Jesus when He began His ministry.
12. **Luke 4:13**—Even with Jesus, the devil leaves for a while and then comes back at "an opportune time."

(continued on next page)

Mark Your Bible

13. **Luke 4:16**—Jesus made it His custom and priority to gather in the synagogue every Sabbath.
14. **Luke 4:19**—"The year of the Lord" was a reference to the year of Jubilee (Lev. 25:10), when slaves were set free, which is what Christ came to do for those in bondage to sin.
15. **Luke 4:25-27**—Gentiles were the ones who received Divine favor in the past, and if Jesus' "own" were to reject Him now, the Gentiles would receive Divine favor again.
16. **Luke 4:30**—This was a miracle (see Luke 24:31; John 8:59; 10:39; 20:19, 26).
17. **Luke 5:1**—Another name for the Sea of Galilee. Gennesaret was a small plain on the northwest side of the Sea.
18. **Luke 5:23**—The power of God can heal one of physical infirmity and spiritual infirmity with the same ease.
19. **Luke 5:39**—Some Jews would prefer to stay with "the old" covenant and consider it "better" than "the new" covenant.
20. **Luke 6:16**—Judas the son of James is another name for "Lebbaeus, whose surname was Thaddaeus" (Matt. 10:3).
21. **Luke 6:20**—This is the "poor in spirit" (Matt. 5:3)—those who are humble.
22. **Luke 6:21**—This is those who "weep" or "mourn" over sin and its effects (Matt. 5:4; Jas. 4:9).
23. **Luke 6:27**—This is *agape* love, which is not based upon or motivated by emotion, but is a conscious choice to seek and work what is in the best interest of the other person, even when such calls for self-sacrifice.
24. **Luke 6:46**—This is very similar to Matthew 7:21, another passage that emphasizes obedience is required beyond mere verbal calling.

March 11 Week 10, Day 7

Day of Reflection

Take time today to reflect on the five chapters that you read this week. You may choose to read all five chapters again, in one sitting, or certain parts of them. Take time today to answer at least one of these questions below. You may or may not write anything down—you can choose to write or simply reflect.

1. What personal application do I need to make from the chapters I have read this week?

2. How can these five chapters help draw me closer to Jesus?

3. What words, phrases or verses in these chapters do I want to go back and study more in depth?

4. What questions do I have about what I have read this week on which I need to do some further Biblical research?

Week 11

March 12-18

March 12	Read Luke 7
March 13	Read Luke 8
March 14	Read Luke 9
March 15	Read Luke 10
March 16	Read Luke 11
March 17	Mark Your Bible
March 18	Day of Reflection

Prayer for this week:

"Heavenly Father,
help me to draw closer to Jesus as I am reading."

March 12 Week 11, Day 1

Luke 7

Helpful Notes:

1. **Such great faith** = Jesus commented on the "great faith" of two persons in His ministry, and they were both Gentiles (Matt. 8:10; 15:28); the centurion's "great faith" is described for us to emulate: (1) Believes Jesus can solve problems we cannot, so go to Him; (2) Recognizes unworthiness in the presence of Christ; (3) Surrenders to the supreme authority of Jesus.
2. **Rejecting baptism** = Note carefully that those who "rejected the will of God for themselves" were those who had "not been baptized" by John the Baptizer; when men reject God's plain truth about baptism today, they are, therefore, rejecting the will of God for themselves; a stronger statement could not be made to emphasize the God-given essentiality of baptism.
3. **Like children** = In their non-sensical objection of Jesus, the Jewish leaders were acting like children and making childish accusations against John and Jesus (verse 32); the problem was not with John and Jesus, as the Jews demanded, but it was with the "evil generation," who lacked "wisdom" to recognize the true nature of Jesus.

1. When the people of Nain saw Jesus raise the boy from the dead, what did they realize?

2. What does the fact that Jesus "answered" Simon after Simon "spoke to himself" reveal about Jesus?

3. Having been forgiven of many sins ourselves, what should be our response of love toward Jesus?

Verse for Meditation and Prayer: **Luke 7:16**

"Then fear came upon all, and they glorified God, saying,
'A great prophet has risen up among us';
and, 'God has visited His people.'"

March 13 Week 11, Day 2

Luke 8

Helpful Notes:

1. **The good news of the kingdom of God** = The word for "gospel" means "good news"; the good news throughout the N.T. is about Jesus' death, burial and resurrection (1 Cor. 15:1-4); but note that Jesus includes His kingdom/church in the good news/glad tidings; one cannot have Jesus without His kingdom/church, for the good news of one necessitates the good news of the other.
2. **Mary Magdalene** = She was from the city of Magdala, on the west side of the Sea of Galilee; Jesus cast seven demons out of her (8:2), but there is zero evidence that she was a promiscuous, social derelict or harlot; nor is there any evidence of any kind of sexual relations between her and Jesus; she was among other women who ministered to Jesus, and she was the first disciple to see the resurrected Savior (Mark 16:9).
3. **Abyss** = This simply means a bottomless pit, and it is a reference to the abode of the demons (Rom. 10:7; Rev. 9:1-2; 11:7; 17:8; 20:1, 3); they had been permitted temporary escape, so that Jesus could prove His power over them, but they would be going back.

1. What did the physician Luke reveal about the sick woman's physicians?

2. What evidence was there that the sick woman had faith in Jesus?

3. How does the sick woman's faith compare with the apostles' faith in the boat during the storm?

Verse for Meditation and Prayer: **Luke 8:14**

"Now the ones that fell among thorns are those who, when they have heard, go out and are choked with cares, riches, and pleasures of life, and bring no fruit to maturity."

Luke 9

Helpful Notes:

1. **Preach the kingdom** = Five times in this chapter alone (along with dozens throughout the gospel accounts), Jesus and His disciples went around preaching about the kingdom; balanced preaching today must regularly focus on the kingdom/church; preaching about the King necessitates His kingdom (cf. Acts 1:3; 8:12; 19:8; 20:25; 28:23, 31).
2. **Hear Him** = While the word "hear" can denote merely the faculty of "hearing" sounds or words, the meaning is greater here; as used in this text, it means, "to give careful attention to, listen to, heed, obey"; those who will not do that will be "utterly destroyed" (Acts 3:22-23); it is important that we define and use terms in the way that the Bible uses them.
3. **First** = The Lord places a great emphasis on that which is first in our lives, and He demands that nothing should take priority over our Savior and serving Him (Matt. 6:33; Col. 1:18); some things in this life may not be intrinsically wrong, but they become so when they push Christ out of first place.

1. What did Jesus know full well "must" happen to Him in Jerusalem, although His disciples didn't grasp it?

2. How often did Jesus say His followers must take up their cross?

3. What did Jesus say about the person who enters into His service (i.e., puts his hand to the plow) but then "looks back" with regret?

Verse for Meditation and Prayer: **Luke 9:23**

"Then He said to them all,
'If anyone desires to come after Me, let him deny himself,
and take up his cross daily, and follow Me.'"

March 15 Week 11, Day 4

Luke 10

Helpful Notes:

1. **Near to you** = Twice in this chapter, Jesus said, "the kingdom of God has come near to you" (10:9, 11); Jesus and His disciples had been preaching "the kingdom of God is at hand" (Matt. 3:2; 4:17; 10:7; Mark 1:15) and "has come upon you" (Matt. 12:28); the kingdom was not thousands of years in the future, but it was right upon them (see "at hand" in Mark 14:42); the kingdom is His church, which was established in Acts 2, according to His eternal plan.
2. **Satan fall like lightning** = This has nothing to do with Satan's original fall; Jesus said that "He was seeing" (Greek imperfect tense indicating continuous activity) Satan fall, as the apostles were casting out demons, which was a precursor to future defeats and his ultimate overthrow; he was not falling from heaven, but his destruction and fall was "like" lightning falling from heaven.
3. **Neighbor** = Followers of God are to love their neighbor as themselves; a neighbor is "the one who is near or close by, fellow human beings"; this includes everyone we know and encounter, and we are responsible to help anyone who needs our help.

1. When someone rejects a messenger of Jesus and the message he/she is preaching, who did Jesus say they ultimately reject?

2. Why is it so significant that the "good-deed-doer," who showed mercy, was a Samaritan?

3. How did Jesus respond to Martha's complaint about her sister, Mary?

Verse for Meditation and Prayer: **Luke 10:20**

"Rejoice because your names are written in heaven."

March 16 Week 11, Day 5

Luke 11

Helpful Notes:

1. **Pray** = Jesus taught that prayer should be directed to the Father (not to Him or any saints), for the Father's will to be done, and that one should pray persistently, repeatedly and fervently; our Father will hear every prayer and respond to every prayer according to His will (1 John 5:14-15); prayer is a tremendous (and yet underused) blessing and tool of every Christian.
2. **Lead me not into temptation** = God does not tempt us (Jas. 1:13); but He can permit us to be led into temptation, while at the very same time providing the open way of escape from it (1 Cor. 10:13; 2 Pet. 2:9), which leaves the choice in our hands; when we pray this, we must strive to fulfill it by keeping ourselves away from temptation.
3. **The finger of God** = Anthropomorphism is often used in describing attributes or activities of God, in order to depict God in a way that would be understood in human terms; God Himself does not have physical, human features; Jesus casting out demons by "the finger of God" demonstrates the immense and immeasurable power of the one true and living God (Ex. 8:19; 31:18; Psa. 8:3).

1. How many should I forgive (11:4), if I want God to forgive me?

2. When a woman said, "Blessed is the womb who bore You," who did Jesus say is truly "blessed"?

3. While the Pharisees wanted the outside (of the cup) to look clean, what did Jesus say their inward part was full of?

Verse for Meditation and Prayer: **Luke 11:9**

"So I say to you, ask, and it will be given to you; seek, and you will find; knock, and it will be opened to you."

Mark Your Bible

1. **Luke 7:14**—The "open coffin" or "bier" was an open stretcher, open bed or flat wooden frame on which the dead were placed for public viewing in the home and then carried to the grave.
2. **Luke 7:38**—The verbs "wiped, kissed, anointed" are in the Greek imperfect tense, indicating continual and repeated action. (This is not Mary, the sister of Martha, who washed Jesus' feet in John 12.)
3. **Luke 7:48**—"Forgiven" is in the perfect tense, indicating she had already been forgiven prior to this time. She came now to express her "much love" for all the sins which Jesus forgave. Her love was the result of her forgiveness, not the cause.
4. **Luke 8:14**—It is not possible to mature as a Christian when the cares, riches and pleasures of life are permitted access to our hearts. In fact, they will choke God's Word out of our lives.
5. **Luke 8:15**—Growth and service as a Christian requires hard work and endurance, which is built on God's Word.
6. **Luke 8:50**—Fear and faith cannot coexist.
7. **Luke 8:55**—When her "spirit returned" to her body, she came to life. Thus, death occurs when the spirit leaves the body (Jas. 2:26).
8. **Luke 9:9**—Herod was exceedingly glad to see Jesus in Luke 23:8, for "he hoped to see some miracle done by Him," as if Jesus was performing.
9. **Luke 9:23**—Salvation and discipleship is universally available to "all" who will obey.
10. **Luke 9:23**—Underline the word "daily."
11. **Luke 9:24-26**—Each of these verses begins with "for," giving a reason for denying self and following Christ.
12. **Luke 9:31**—Luke is the only one to tell us what they were talking about. "Decease" comes from the Greek word *exodus,* indicating His departure from among the living, which must involve great suffering (9:22).

(continued on next page)

Mark Your Bible

13. **Luke 9:43**—"Majesty" means "splendor, magnificence, impressiveness." They were in awe of God and His might.
14. **Luke 9:59**—"Follow me" means "to accompany, imitate, obey, be a disciple."
15. **Luke 10:7**—Paul quotes this verse in 1 Timothy 5:18 and refers to it as "Scripture."
16. **Luke 10:16**—When Israel rejected Samuel's leadership and counsel, God said that they were rejecting Him (1 Sam. 8:7).
17. **Luke 10:19**—This is symbolic of the powers of evil (cf. John 12:31; Eph. 6:12).
18. **Luke 10:20**—Nothing compares with the joy of being in heaven, and they were "registered" there already (Heb. 12:23; Rev. 3:5; 20:12).
19. **Luke 10:28, 37**—"Do" is in the present tense, denoting continuous and ongoing activity. The question he asked (v. 25) had "do" (in the Greek aorist tense) as a one-time, over-and-done activity.
20. **Luke 11:13**—Compared to the perfect Father in heaven, we are "evil" and sinful; the parental care in us is magnified infinitely in our heavenly Father.
21. **Luke 11:13**—This is parallel with Matthew 7:11, in which Jesus said that God would "give good things to those who ask." Those good things came from the Holy Spirit operating providentially in the lives of His people to answer their prayers.
22. **Luke 11:24-26**—We cannot be neutral toward evil. It will progressively take over our lives if we leave it room.
23. **Luke 11:50**—Man has been around "from the foundation of the world" (contrary to the false doctrine of evolution).
24. **Luke 11:50-51**—The blood of His people that was shed would be avenged/required of this generation when Jerusalem was destroyed in A.D. 70.

Day of Reflection

Take time today to reflect on the five chapters that you read this week. You may choose to read all five chapters again, in one sitting, or certain parts of them. Take time today to answer at least one of these questions below. You may or may not write anything down—you can choose to write or simply reflect.

1. What personal application do I need to make from the chapters I have read this week?

2. How can these five chapters help draw me closer to Jesus?

3. What words, phrases or verses in these chapters do I want to go back and study more in depth?

4. What questions do I have about what I have read this week on which I need to do some further Biblical research?

Week 12

March 19-25

March 19	Read Luke 12
March 20	Read Luke 13
March 21	Read Luke 14
March 22	Read Luke 15
March 23	Read Luke 16
March 24	Mark Your Bible
March 25	Day of Reflection

Prayer for this week:

"Heavenly Father,
I need You!
Please be with me as I study Your Word!"

Luke 12

<u>Helpful Notes:</u>

1. **Fear God** = True, healthy fear of God is not a slavish fear or a dreadful terror; "the fear of the Lord is the beginning of wisdom" (Prov. 9:10); it is an awe, respect and reverence for who He is, what He has done and what He can/will do; true fear takes note of God's providential care of little things and applies that to His care for me (see Acts 5).
2. **Coming when not expected** = Many have and will try to set the date of Christ's return, believing that there are/will be signs preceding it; however, Jesus repeatedly says it will be at the hour that is not expected, like a thief; therefore, we must always remain ready and vigilant, so that the Lord finds us serving and ready to go.
3. **Confess** = The Greek word *homologeo* literally means, "to say the same thing"; Jesus said (and proved) that He is the Son of God, and I must be willing to say that same thing (in order to be saved, Rom. 10:9-10) and to continue to live by that confession, holding fast to it (Heb. 4:14; 10:23; 1 Tim. 6:12).

1. If "one's life" is not about the things he possesses, of what then does "one's life" truly "consist"?

2. Instead of having an "anxious mind," especially about things we "are not able to do," on what did Jesus say to focus?

3. When we lay up treasures in heaven, how did Jesus describe that "money bag" where we carry those eternal treasures?

Verse for Meditation and Prayer: **<u>Luke 12:34</u>**

"For where your treasure is, there your heart will be also."

March 20 Week 12, Day 2

Luke 13

Helpful Notes:

1. **Worst sinners** = It was thought that one's sinfulness could be measured by the misfortunes that he suffered; Jesus taught that such is not the case; suffering takes place in life as a result of humanity's sin, in general; bad things are not necessarily tied to one's personal sins (Ecc. 9:11); to avoid eternal punishment for one's sins, he must repent now.
2. **Glorified God** = While some were rejecting Christ, we have read several times in Luke of those who heard Him and witnessed His miraculous power and "glorified God"; the word means "to magnify, extol, praise, ascribing honor to Him for His glory; to adore, worship"; these hearts were open, receptive and excited by Jesus—are ours?
3. **Strive** = Look at the Greek word—*agonizomai;* one must "agonize" to be saved and to enter the narrow gate of heaven; originally the word meant to contend for the prize in the games; we must push ourselves, make all sacrifices necessary, fight and exert every effort to "enter" heaven, which will be worth it all (1 Cor. 9:24-27; 1 Tim. 6:12; 2 Tim. 4:7; Phil. 2:12-13; 2 Pet. 1:5-11).

1. What do you think is the significance of Jesus saying back-to-back, "unless you repent you will all likewise perish"?

2. Once the door to heaven is shut, what does Jesus say about those on the outside?

3. Why do you think Jesus called Herod Antipas a "fox"?

Verse for Meditation and Prayer: **Luke 13:24**

"Strive to enter through the narrow gate, for many, I say to you, will seek to enter and will not be able."

Luke 14

Helpful Notes:

1. **Dropsy** = This is caused by too much fluid in the tissues, which could be the result of heart failure, cancer or liver or kidney disease; this is the only time mentioned in the New Testament.
2. **Hate** = Jesus teaches to "honor father and mother" (Matt. 15:4), so He does not contradict that here; the parallel in Matthew 10:37 defines "hate" in this passage to mean "to love less"; Christ will not accept second place to anyone; we must love Him supremely more than anyone else (see also Gen. 29:29-31).
3. **Count the cost** = In living the Christian life as it is intended to be lived, there are challenges, sacrifices and requirements that must be taken into consideration and only entered into with strong conviction and total commitment; it is more than "worth it" for those who devote themselves entirely to it.

1. In His line of argumentation (from less to greater), Jesus argued that if man would do good toward an animal, why would he not do good (at least equally) to man. How can that apply to us today?

2. What is the practical meaning for us to "sit down in the lowest place"?

3. To whom in particular should we seek to do good according to Jesus' explanation in verse 14?

Verse for Meditation and Prayer: **Luke 14:23**

"Then the master said to the servant,
'Go out into the highways and hedges,
and compel them to come in, that my house may be filled.'"

March 22 Week 12, Day 4

Luke 15

Helpful Notes:

1. **Lost** = The Greek *apollumi* is used for "perishing" (Luke 13:3) and being "destroyed" (Matt. 10:28), so there is a desperation involved in it and a connection to these terms; here it means to be separated from a normal connection and where one should be; it is a spiritual destitution, spiritual ruin and loss of spiritual well-being; when our sins lead us away from God (where we should be), we are "lost" (19:10), and we can remain "lost" (i.e., "perish") for eternity if we do not repent.
2. **One sinner** = Jesus emphasized the exceeding value of one soul and the length to which we should go to find and return them; we must "go after" and "search carefully" to find one, so that we can "rejoice" together; each soul is wanted, loved and treasured by the Lord and should be by us.
3. **Prodigal** = The Greek word means a "wasteful, dissolute spendthrift, lacking restraint"; the word is often associated (as here) with immorality, debauchery, lasciviousness (v. 30); the son was as far into the far country as he could go.

1. How does God (and the entirety of heaven) respond when one sinner repents?

2. What finally caused the prodigal son to "come to himself"?

3. What does "the far country" represent in a life of sin?

Verse for Meditation and Prayer: **Luke 15:10**

"Likewise, I say to you, there is joy in the presence of the angels of God over one sinner who repents."

March 23 Week 12, Day 5

Luke 16

Helpful Notes:

1. **Steward** = One who manages his master's property; the property does not belong to him, but he is responsible for maintaining it, using it properly and increasing it for the master's good; we are stewards of all that God has given to us and we must be faithful (1 Cor. 4:2; Matt. 25:14-30).
2. **God knows our hearts** = "Man looks at the outward appearance" (1 Sam. 16:7) and wants to be "highly esteemed among men" (Luke 16:15); but God looks at the heart, for He knows "what is in man" (John 2:24-25); our concern should not be what man thinks of us (Gal. 1:10) but being right "in the sight of God"; Jesus knows hearts (Matt. 12:25), therefore, He is God!
3. **Abraham's bosom** = At the death of a body, the soul is taken to the realm of the departed spirits called "Hades"; the unrighteous enter "torments," and the righteous enter into "Abraham's bosom" or "Paradise" (Luke 23:43); resting in one's "bosom" was a place of honor and blessedness (John 13:23; 1:18); what a stark contrast with "torments."

1. For what reasons does Jesus state one cannot serve two masters? How does this apply to us?

2. With the rich man and Lazarus, how did their life before death determine their life after death?

3. What does reading about life after death motivate us to do?

Verse for Meditation and Prayer: **Luke 16:13**

"No servant can serve two masters; for either he will hate the one and love the other, or else he will be loyal to the one and despise the other. You cannot serve God and mammon."

Mark Your Bible

1. **Luke 12:6**—This coin was an assarion, worth about 1/16 of a denarius (so about one penny). One sparrow was worth about 4/10 of a penny. Since God takes care of birds of such little value, Jesus' point is that He will take more care of you.
2. **Luke 12:12**—This promise was specifically to first-century disciples and not to us. We have the Bible (complete from the Holy Spirit) to teach us what to teach today.
3. **Luke 12:17-19**—The rich fool said "I" (6 times) and "my" (5 times). Riches can cause us to be very "I"-centered.
4. **Luke 12:47-48**—Everyone who does "not know God" and everyone who does "not obey the gospel" will be punished (2 Thess. 1:8). While Jesus spoke of possible degrees of punishment, it is the punishment of hell for each one nonetheless.
5. **Luke 13:1**—Pilate was a corrupt and cruel governor. When some Jews from Galilee came to offer sacrifices in Jerusalem, he killed them while they were slaying their animals. (Galilee was under Herod Antipas' rule at that time.)
6. **Luke 13:6-9**—The Jewish nation was fruitless in their response to God's blessings, and they would be cut down.
7. **Luke 13:17**—When one speaks only the truth and is able to reason soundly and effectively, those who do not do so will be "put to shame."
8. **Luke 13:27**—"Iniquity" literally is "unrightness"; it is simply doing what is wrong in the eyes of God.
9. **Luke 13:34**—As much as God wants to save everyone, the words "not willing" emphasize man's free will to do as he chooses (but to suffer consequences thereof).
10. **Luke 14:18-20**—These seem like flimsy excuses because they are. Any excuse offered to reject the invitation of Christ (no matter how valid it may seem) is flimsy.

(continued on next page)

Mark Your Bible

11. **Luke 14:21**—Underline the word "angry," and note that this is the response of the Master (God) to excuses offered in rejecting His preparations and invitation.
12. **Luke 14:23**—This was the Gentiles.
13. **Luke 14:26, 27, 33**—Underline the three times Jesus says, "cannot be my disciple," and consider the reason for each carefully.
14. **Luke 14:34-35**—As salt with no flavor is useless, so is a Christian with no true dedication to "forsake all" and sacrificially follow Christ.
15. **Luke 15:1-2**—This is the context of the three parables. The sinners "kept drawing near to Jesus" (imperfect tense denotes continuous action), and the Pharisees "kept complaining" about it (imperfect).
16. **Luke 15:4-7**—Throughout the chapter, underline each use of words like "lost," "find," "found," "joy" and "rejoicing."
17. **Luke 15:15**—For a Jew, anything to do with swine would have been the lowest of the lows.
18. **Luke 15:17**—He had been as far from self (and as far from home) as he could get; now sound reasoning was returning.
19. **Luke 15:17-19**—This is a picture of repentance.
20. **Luke 15:20**—This is what our heavenly Father does with every sinner (every one of us), who repents and returns to Him.
21. **Luke 15:25-28**—The elder brother and his attitude is really the focus of this parable (see verses 1-2).
22. **Luke 16:8**—Jesus called the man, "unjust/unrighteous." Jesus did not condone the man's dishonesty.
23. **Luke 16:8**—The world is often better at advancing their material efforts than Christians are at advancing their spiritual efforts.

Mark Your Bible

24. **Luke 16:9**—Have the foresight to use the things of this world now (which have been given to us by God) to help prepare you and welcome you into the eternal, heavenly home (Matt. 6:19-20).
25. **Luke 16:9**—This implies that there will be recognition in heaven.
26. **Luke 16:23**—"Being" is in the present tense, denoting continued conscious existence after death. Nothing in this passage supports the false doctrine of "soul-sleeping" after death.
27. **Luke 16:26**—"Fixed" is in the perfect tense, which emphasizes that it was fixed in the past and it remains permanently fixed today.
28. **Luke 16:26**—After death, one's destiny cannot be altered.
29. **Luke 16:31**—God's Word is the only means by which one can learn truth and be saved.

Day of Reflection

Take time today to reflect on the five chapters that you read this week. You may choose to read all five chapters again, in one sitting, or certain parts of them. Take time today to answer at least one of these questions below. You may or may not write anything down—you can choose to write or simply reflect.

1. What personal application do I need to make from the chapters I have read this week?

2. How can these five chapters help draw me closer to Jesus?

3. What words, phrases or verses in these chapters do I want to go back and study more in depth?

4. What questions do I have about what I have read this week on which I need to do some further Biblical research?

Week 13

March 26-April 1

March 26	Read Luke 17
March 27	Read Luke 18
March 28	Read Luke 19
March 29	Read Luke 20
March 30	Read Luke 21
March 31	Mark Your Bible
April 1	Day of Reflection

Prayer for this week:

"Heavenly Father,
You have been so good to me!
Thank You for all You do!"

March 26 Week 13, Day 1

Luke 17

Helpful Notes:

1. **Unprofitable servants** = To "increase our faith" (17:5), we need to remember in Whom our faith is founded—it's in our Master who is the holy and awesome God, who permits us into His service; it ought to be our greatest and most humbling joy to serve our God—so much so that when we have done all we can do for Him, we still humbly view ourselves as (not deserving, but) unprofitable servants, just doing as we should for our Lord.
2. **Must suffer** = Jesus repeatedly told His disciples that He "must suffer many things"; the word "must" indicates a "necessity of happening"; all the "many things" that Jesus "suffered" on our behalf were NOT optional—every single one of those heinous things was a "must."
3. **His day** = In the last half of the chapter, Jesus emphasizes the need for constant preparation for His return; the word "days" is found five times of the "days" leading up to an end, but then the word "day" is found five times to isolate the final day; "that day" will be "His day" and we must be ready.

1. What did the disciples ask the Lord to do, which ought to be our aim as well?

2. What lesson does it teach us that only one leper returned to thank Jesus?

3. What woman does Jesus say to remember, as one who was centered on earthly things more than heavenly instruction?

Verse for Meditation and Prayer: **Luke 17:24**

"For as the lightning that flashes out of one part under heaven shines to the other part under heaven, so also the Son of Man will be in His day."

Luke 18

Helpful Notes:

1. **Pray always** = God gives His children an open line of communication to talk to Him at any time, all the time; thus, Christians are urged to pray to God continually (Col. 4:2; 1 Thess. 5:17), and He has promised to hear and answer us (1 John 5:14-15; 3:22; Jas. 5:16), especially in times of persecution, so that we do "not lose heart."
2. **Fasting** = Abstaining from food and drink was done for spiritual reasons, to focus cravings on God and His Word; the O.T. only commanded one fast on the Day of Atonement (Lev. 16:31), although the Jews fasted at other times; there are spiritual benefits to fasting for Christians, but it is not commanded; it is voluntary and should not be flaunted (Matt. 6:16-18) or thought to make one superior to others (Luke 18:9-14).
3. **Tithe** = The word means "tenth"; under Mosaic law, Jews were required to tithe (Lev. 27:30-33), and actually gave well over 10% in all their offerings; in the N.T. , Christians are not commanded to "tithe"; rather, Christians are to give proportionally (1 Cor. 16:2), generously (Rom. 12:8), purposefully (2 Cor. 9:7) and cheerfully (2 Cor. 9:7).

1. What key principles are taught in these parables on prayer?

2. What did Jesus mean by receiving the kingdom as a little child?

3. What specific things did Jesus know were going to happen to Him when they got to Jerusalem?

Verse for Meditation and Prayer: **Luke 18:31**

"Then He took the twelve aside and said to them, 'Behold, we are going up to Jerusalem, and all things that are written by the prophets concerning the Son of Man will be accomplished.'"

Luke 19

Helpful Notes:

1. **Jericho** = It was strategically located between Jerusalem and the Jordan River, so it was frequently passed through by all Jews, particularly those traveling to and from Galilee, who crossed to the east side of the Jordan to avoid Samaria; it was about 800 feet below sea level, while Jerusalem was 2,500 feet above sea level.
2. **Reign over** = Jesus is the nobleman who received His kingdom when He ascended into heaven (Dan. 7:13-14), but many reject His reign as King and reject His kingdom; Jesus is "the King" (19:38; cf. 1 Tim. 1:17), who reigns now over His kingdom (1 Cor. 15:24-25); to reject Him or His kingdom is to become His enemy.
3. **Wept over Jerusalem** = The word for "wept" indicates "bursting into tears, with sobbing, wailing and loud expressions of grief and anguish"; this was not just a single tear rolling down Jesus' cheek; the sinful condition of the people, their unrepentant hearts and knowing the destruction that awaited them broke Jesus' heart.

1. Zacchaeus wanted to see Jesus, and when he met him, how did he receive Him?

2. What did Jesus say would cry out if the people should keep silent?

3. Why were the Jewish leaders unable to do anything against Jesus at this time?

Verse for Meditation and Prayer: **Luke 19:10**

"For the Son of Man has come
to seek and to save that which was lost."

March 29 Week 13, Day 4

Luke 20

Helpful Notes:

1. **Render to God** = Man bears the image of God, for we are made in His image (Gen. 1:26-27; Acts 17:28-29; Jas. 3:8-9); therefore, those things that belong to God (i.e., His people) should be "given back to" God for His service.
2. **The dead are raised** = The Sadducees did not believe in the resurrection of the dead, and they tried to trick Jesus; instead, He taught emphatically and unanswerably that the dead are still "living" now and will be raised to die no more; this ought to both encourage us and motivate us.
3. **Rejected** = The Son of God came to earth, and those who should have welcomed Him with joy and respect, instead cast Him out and killed Him; premillennialists assert that the Jews' rejection (especially of the kingdom) was unexpected; however, the rejection was prophesied in Psalm 118:22 and Isaiah 53; and the result of the rejection leading to the establishment of His kingdom/church was also prophesied (2 Sam. 7:12-16; Isa. 2:2-4; Dan. 2:44); this was all part of God's plan (Psa. 118:23).

1. What were the spies sent by the Pharisees trying to do?

2. How was both the humanity and the deity of Jesus proven in verses 42-44?

3. What behavior of the scribes did Jesus warn about?

Verse for Meditation and Prayer: **Luke 20:25**

"And He said to them, 'Render therefore to Caesar the things that are Caesar's, and to God the things that are God's.'"

Luke 21

Helpful Notes: ** See also the notes and markings for Matthew 24 and Mark 13.*

1. **Sign** = This word is found three times in this chapter of a "sign of things to come," as an indication that an event is going to take place; note that the word "sign" appears only in the context of the destruction of Jerusalem and never in the context of the final coming of Jesus in the judgment—there are no signs for that day, as it will come "unexpectedly."
2. **Jerusalem surrounded by armies** = This identifies specifically the event Jesus was discussing (i.e., the destruction of Jerusalem in A.D. 70) and explains that "the abomination of desolation" (Dan. 9:24-27; Matt. 24:15) was the Roman armies besieging the city.
3. **Coming of the Son of Man** = The Bible speaks of at least five "comings" of Jesus Christ: (1) His first coming in the flesh (2 John 7), (2) possibly a rendezvous with His apostles (Matt. 10:23), (3) His coming in the establishment of His kingdom on Pentecost (Matt. 16:28; Acts 2:30-33), (4) His coming in judgment against Jerusalem (Matt. 24:27-30), (5) His coming at the end of time to judge mankind (Matt. 24:36-44); numbers 3 and 4 were not visible but He came nonetheless.

1. How had Jesus' disciples been describing the temple to Him, which is the background and lead-in to this whole context?

2. What did Jesus tell His disciples to "take heed" to avoid doing lest "that Day come on you unexpectedly"?

3. How did Jesus spend His daytime hours during His last week?

Verse for Meditation and Prayer: **Luke 21:32**

"Assuredly, I say to you, this generation will by no means pass away till all things take place."

Mark Your Bible

1. **Luke 17:1-4**—Sin is a huge deal! Causing someone to sin is appalling! Forgiving someone who has sinned is essential!
2. **Luke 17:2**—This was a huge stone used at the mill to grind grain, and the large ones were so heavy that they had to be turned by a mule or donkey.
3. **Luke 17:14**—They were cleansed when they obeyed what they were told to do without questioning it.
4. **Luke 17:15-16**—"Glorifying" and "giving" are in the present tense, indicating a continuous activity and not a quick "one and done."
5. **Luke 17:16**—This likely implies the other nine were Jews and not Samaritans.
6. **Luke 17:19**—Jesus identified their obedience as "faith."
7. **Luke 17:31**—While the terminology is similar to Matthew 24, it is not the same event. There is no warning to flee to the mountains (Matt. 24:16). It is emphasizing the need for constant preparedness for His return.
8. **Luke 17:34**—The word "men" is not in the original.
9. **Luke 17:34-36**—The sudden and unexpected nature of His coming will result in a sudden and unexpected separation of people.
10. **Luke 18:3**—"Came" is in the imperfect tense, emphasizing constant coming, without letting up.
11. **Luke 18:7**—God protects His "elect," who are those who are "in Christ" (Eph. 1:4) through obedience to His will (Rom. 6:3-4).
12. **Luke 18:11**—"Prayed" is in the imperfect tense, emphasizing a long prayer going on and on.
13. **Luke 18:11**—"With himself" denotes an arrogant and self-serving purpose.

(continued on next page)

Mark Your Bible

14. **Luke 18:13**—Beating the breast was a sign of anguish at the awareness of one's sinfulness and unworthiness (23:48; Nah. 2:7).
15. **Luke 18:22**—"One thing" can keep you out of the kingdom.
16. **Luke 18:31**—Not "some" or "most" things, but "all things."
17. **Luke 19:9**—The Jews rejected him as a son of Abraham because he was a tax collector. Jesus affirmed his heritage.
18. **Luke 19:10**—Jesus' purpose must be my/our purpose.
19. **Luke 19:13**—A mina was worth about 100 days' wages (or 3 months).
20. **Luke 19:26**—Final rewards and punishments will be in proportion to one's ability and opportunity.
21. **Luke 19:28**—There was significant elevation change ("up") from Jericho to Jerusalem.
22. **Luke 19:43-44**—Rome would besiege and completely destroy Jerusalem in A.D. 70.
23. **Luke 19:44**—"The time of your visitation" was the visit of God's grace, when Jesus came to save them from destruction.
24. **Luke 19:47**—He was teaching there daily, just as He would later remind them (22:53).
25. **Luke 20:17**—The Greek indicates that He looked directly and intently at them with a piercing glance.
26. **Luke 20:17-18**—The Jews rejected Christ (the stone) and the nation was ground into powder by the Romans in A.D. 70.
27. **Luke 20:35-36**—Those raised from the dead will be "like angels," in that they will not marry and they will not die.
28. **Luke 20:35-38**—Jesus came right at the Sadducees. They didn't believe in the resurrection of the dead, angels or spirits, and Jesus affirmed emphatically all three in this short answer.

Mark Your Bible

29. **Luke 20:42**—Modern scholars disagree on who wrote Psalm 110, but Jesus clearly says it was David.
30. **Luke 21:22**—Because the Jews had thoroughly and incessantly rejected God and His will for their lives, the destruction of Jerusalem was a just act of God's vengeance.
31. **Luke 21:23**—Underline "this people," for this emphasizes that everything of which Jesus was speaking pertained to the Jews in Jerusalem.
32. **Luke 21:27**—The O.T. describes the Lord coming on clouds in the fall of nations (Psa. 97:2-3; 104:3; Isa. 19:1). See Matthew 24:30 note.
33. **Luke 21:32**—Underline this verse. It is key.
34. **Luke 21:33**—"The word of God...lives and abides forever" (1 Pet. 1:23-25). It will never fail!
35. **Luke 21:34**—Jesus warns of not being ready for His coming by using two different terms with regard to alcohol consumption. Alcohol is dangerous to the Christian (Prov. 20:1).

April 1 Week 13, Day 7

Day of Reflection

Take time today to reflect on the five chapters that you read this week. You may choose to read all five chapters again, in one sitting, or certain parts of them. Take time today to answer at least one of these questions below. You may or may not write anything down—you can choose to write or simply reflect.

1. What personal application do I need to make from the chapters I have read this week?

2. How can these five chapters help draw me closer to Jesus?

3. What words, phrases or verses in these chapters do I want to go back and study more in depth?

4. What questions do I have about what I have read this week on which I need to do some further Biblical research?

Week 14

April 2-8

April 2	Read Luke 22
April 3	Read Luke 23
April 4	Read Luke 24
April 5	Read John 1
April 6	Read John 2
April 7	Mark Your Bible
April 8	Day of Reflection

Prayer for this week:

"Heavenly Father,
I love Your Word!"

April 2 Week 14, Day 1

Luke 22

Helpful Notes:

1. **Blood** = In a physical sense, "the life of the flesh is in the blood" (Lev. 17:11); God took this and gave it a much more significant, eternal application; under the old covenant, the blood of animals was used to atone for man's sins (Ex. 30:10; Heb. 9:22), but it could not take away sins (Heb. 10:4); the blood of Jesus, the lamb of God (John 1:29), was "shed for the remission of sins" (Matt. 26:28), redeeming us from our sins (Eph. 1:7), when we are baptized "into Christ," even "into His death" (Rom. 6:3-4); Christians remember this every Sunday in the Lord's Supper (1 Cor. 11:25-26).
2. **Twelve thrones judging twelve tribes** = The apostles were given authority to teach and bind what had already been bound by Christ in heaven (Matt. 18:18); their teachings (in spoken and written word) would be authoritative over the spiritual Israel of God, which is the church (Gal. 6:16; 3:29).
3. **Not My will, but Yours** = Jesus humbled Himself and yielded to the will of God for His life; may we pray the same (Matt. 6:10) and live the same (Jas. 4:15).

1. What disciples did Jesus send to prepare the Passover meal?

2. Who did Jesus give as the ultimate example of someone who was great and yet "serves"?

3. What did Jesus do after Peter denied Him the third time? What does that indicate about the proximity of the two men?

Verse for Meditation and Prayer: **Luke 22:44**

"And being in agony, He prayed more earnestly. Then His sweat became like great drops of blood falling down to the ground."

Luke 23

Helpful Notes:

1. **The King of the Jews** = Jesus was not a king in the political sense, as some supposed, which would rival Caesar or other government leaders; Jesus was "King of the Jews," as He was the anointed Messiah and fulfillment of the Davidic promise, having come to establish His kingdom/church (2 Sam. 7:12-16; Luke 1:32-33).
2. **No fault** = The Bible says that three times Pilate told the Jews that he found "no fault" in Jesus (23:4, 14, 22); he questioned Jesus but knew there was "nothing deserving of death"; however, in his spineless efforts to please to the mob, he sentenced Jesus (an admittedly innocent man) to crucifixion.
3. **The thief on the cross** = Much has been made about the thief being saved by Jesus but not being baptized; the thief has been used to deny the essentiality of baptism for salvation; however, (1) he could have been baptized (Mark 1:5) and fallen back into sin; (2) the thief did not live under the new covenant that requires baptism (Heb. 9:15-17; Mark 16:15-16); (3) Jesus had the power to forgive anyone He wanted while on earth (Matt. 9:6; Mark 2:5; Luke 7:48; 19:9); regardless of what he did or did not do, man today is commanded to be baptized in order to be saved (Mark 16:16; Acts 2:38; 1 Pet. 3:21).

1. While Herod Antipas was "exceedingly glad" to see Jesus, how did he and his soldiers treat Jesus?

2. Who was also crucified with Jesus, indicating for whom this form of execution was reserved?

3. What was Jesus' attitude toward those who crucified Him?

Verse for Meditation and Prayer: **Luke 23:46**

"And when Jesus had cried out with a loud voice, He said, 'Father, "into Your hands I commit My spirit."' Having said this, He breathed His last."

Luke 24

Helpful Notes:

1. **All things must be fulfilled** = The O.T. contained 332 prophecies about the coming Messiah; for Jesus of Nazareth to be the Christ, He "MUST" fulfill "ALL" of them, and He did; Jesus helped them to see that His death and resurrection were part of the "all things" to be fulfilled (see 24:27); the O.T. was written primarily, Jesus affirmed, "concerning Me."
2. **All nations** = While the Jews considered themselves the elite people in relationship with God, the O.T. had made clear that "all nations" were part of God's eternal plan of redemption (Gen. 22:18; Joel 2:28-32) and His kingdom (Isa. 2:2-4; Dan. 7:14); thus, Jesus commissioned His people to "go into all the world and preach the gospel to every creature" (Mark 16:15); all nations/people can be saved (Acts 10:34-35).
3. **Power** = Jesus' use of the word "power" had great significance; He said that the kingdom would come "with power" (Mark 9:1); He told His disciples to stay in Jerusalem to be "endued with power from on high" (Luke 24:49); He told the apostles that they would "receive power" when the Holy Spirit came upon them (Acts 1:8); the Lord's church was established with "power" in Acts 2, just as He promised.

1. Who were the first disciples to witness the empty tomb?

2. When the women told the disciples of the empty tomb, what was their response to the news?

3. What did Jesus tell the disciples to do to know He was alive?

Verse for Meditation and Prayer: **Luke 24:44**

"These are the words which I spoke to you while I was still with you, that all things must be fulfilled which were written in the Law of Moses and the Prophets and the Psalms concerning Me."

April 5 Week 14, Day 4

John 1

Helpful Notes: * *See Brief Introduction to John on page 634.*

1. **The Word** = Jesus being called "the Word" (Greek *logos*) is a term representing communication—Jesus is the full and complete revelation of deity to the world (He "declared" the Father, 1:18); Jesus is eternal and He is Divine (He is the "I AM" and always has been, John 8:58; Phil. 2:6); He is not a created being, rather "all things were made through Him" (1:3); He "became flesh" (1:14) to reveal "the glory" of God and to give His "grace and truth."
2. **The only begotten** = Jesus truly is the only one of God (i.e., unique in kind), coming to this earth in the perfect combination of Divine (Jesus is God!) and human (taking on flesh, in order that He might reveal Himself to His creation and offer salvation to them); Jesus truly possesses the same nature as the Father (as only He does), for they are the one God.
3. **The Lamb of God** = The Passover Lamb was the O.T. type of Jesus coming as the ultimate Lamb, given by the Father, to suffer in our place, to bear the guilt and penalty of our sins, in order to cancel the punishment deserved for our sins (1 Pet. 1:19; Rev. 5:12; 7:14; Isa. 53:6-11; Ex. 12).

1. John wrote that Jesus "came to His own," but what did His creation do?

2. What did John say that Jesus is "full of"? (Those two things go together and are both equally essential.)

3. When Andrew found Jesus, what the first thing that he did?

Verse for Meditation and Prayer: **John 1:1**

"In the beginning was the Word, and the Word was with God, and the Word was God."

April 6 Week 14, Day 5

John 2

Helpful Notes:

1. **Wine** = The word does not necessarily mean an intoxicating drink; the Greek word *oinos* is a generic term that simply means "liquid from a grape"; it can mean fresh grape juice (Isa. 16:10; 65:8; Prov. 3:10; Joel 2:24; Rev. 19:15) or fermented beverage (Eph. 5:18; 1 Tim. 3:8); it is shameful and erroneous to believe or teach that the Son of God made 120-180 gallons of intoxicating beverage (Prov. 20:1; 23:29-35; Hab. 2:15; 1 Cor. 5:11; Gal. 5:21; Eph. 5:18).
2. **My hour** = Several times, Jesus stated that "His hour" had not yet come (2:4; 7:6, 8, 30; 8:20), but then He would say "His hour" had come (12:23, 27; 13:1; 16:32; 17:1); this supreme "hour" or "sign" as God's Son would be demonstrated in His passion and crucifixion.
3. **Destroy this temple** = John tells us that Jesus was "speaking of the temple of His body," but the Jews would intentionally use this against Jesus in His trial and in their mockery (Matt. 26:61; 27:40); His resurrection was the ultimate sign!

1. Jesus' mother gave great advice for any occasion. What did she tell the servants to do at the wedding feast?

2. John records seven specific miracles of Jesus to prove that He is God's Son (20:30-31). What was the first miracle?

3. When did Jesus' disciples make the connection and understand what He meant about raising the temple in three days?

Verse for Meditation and Prayer: **John 2:19**

"Jesus answered and said to them,
'Destroy this temple, and in three days I will raise it up.'"

Mark Your Bible

1. **Luke 22:7**—Jesus and His disciples ate the Passover on Thursday evening after sunset, which would be the Jewish Friday.
2. **Luke 22:17**—They were eating the Passover meal, which also included a cup. Jesus took the Passover cup first, BEFORE He instituted the Lord's Supper. The Passover typified Christ's death *before* it occurred; the Lord's Supper is emblematic of Christ's death *after* it occurred. The cup of the Lord's Supper comes after the bread (1 Cor. 11:23-26).
3. **Luke 22:19**—Underline "do this in remembrance of Me." That is our purpose when we partake. That is our mindset every Sunday.
4. **Luke 22:31-32**—The "you" in verse 31 is plural; Satan was after all of them. The "you" in verse 32 in singular; Peter, in particular, was facing a great failure and would need to return to Jesus personally.
5. **Luke 22:32**—Peter would not "strengthen" the church alone as its supposed "head." Timothy and Paul also strengthened (same Greek word) the church (Rom. 1:11; 1 Thess. 3:2; 2 Pet. 1:12).
6. **Luke 22:44**—Hematidrosis is real medical phenomenon that can occur during moments of extreme physical or emotional distress.
7. **Luke 22:62**—"Godly sorrow produces repentance" (2 Cor. 7:9-10).
8. **Luke 23:1**—The Jews had no legal authority to execute anyone, so they had to bring their argument to the Roman governor.
9. **Luke 23:7**—This is Herod Antipas (cf. 9:7-9). (See notes on him.)
10. **Luke 23:23**—The words "insistent" and "prevailed" are in the imperfect tense, denoting their incessant shouting, creating a tumult.
11. **Luke 23:26**—John states that Jesus was "bearing His cross" (John 19:17), but the weight of the cross on His battered and weakened body must have been too much for him to bear.
12. **Luke 23:33**—The word "Calvary" is not in the Greek. The word here is *kranion*, which meant "skull" (see Matt. 27:33).

(continued on next page)

Mark Your Bible

13. **Luke 24:21** – They mistakenly thought that the Messiah was going to free Israel from the Roman yoke and set up His own earthly rule. Little did they realize from what He really did "redeem" them.

14. **Luke 24:21** – Sunday (24:1, 13) was the third day. Jesus was crucified on Friday. The Jews considered any part of a day to be a full day (see "today, tomorrow and the third day" in Luke 13:32).

15. **Luke 24:39** – God is spirit (John 4:24), but He is not a physical being with "flesh and bones." But Jesus was a real, human, physical being.

16. **Luke 24:47** – The apostles fulfilled this only a few days later on Pentecost. Cross reference Acts 2:38.

17. **Luke 24:49** – "The Promise of the Father" was the outpouring of the Spirit on all flesh (Jews and Gentiles), fulfilled in Acts 2 and Acts 10.

18. **John 1:1** – The word "was" in this verse is the imperfect tense, emphasizing Jesus always "was" in existence and always "was" God.

19. **John 1:3** – There is "nothing" (including Jesus Himself) that was made that Jesus didn't make! Jesus is NOT a created being!

20. **John 1:12** – Those who "believe" are not saved by faith alone, but they obtain the privilege to move forward and become saved.

21. **John 1:14** – "Dwelt among" means "to tabernacle or to pitch a tent," emphasizing the temporary nature of His earthly pilgrimage.

22. **John 1:51** – Jesus is the fulfillment of Jacob's dream of a "ladder" (Gen. 28:12), who descended from heaven and died on the cross to give access for man to ascend into heaven.

23. **John 2:6** – These waterpots were there for the sole purpose of fulfilling their strict tradition of handwashing.

24. **John 2:7** – The waterpots were filled "to the brim," so that nothing could be added to them to appear like a miracle had been done.

25. **John 2:13** – John records three Passovers in the ministry of Jesus (2:13; 6:4; 11:55), and maybe a fourth in 5:1.

26. **John 2:24-25** – Jesus possessed supernatural knowledge of man.

Day of Reflection

Take time today to reflect on the five chapters that you read this week. You may choose to read all five chapters again, in one sitting, or certain parts of them. Take time today to answer at least one of these questions below. You may or may not write anything down—you can choose to write or simply reflect.

1. What personal application do I need to make from the chapters I have read this week?

2. How can these five chapters help draw me closer to Jesus?

3. What words, phrases or verses in these chapters do I want to go back and study more in depth?

4. What questions do I have about what I have read this week on which I need to do some further Biblical research?

Week 15

April 9-15

April 9	Read John 3
April 10	Read John 4
April 11	Read John 5
April 12	Read John 6
April 13	Read John 7
April 14	Mark Your Bible
April 15	Day of Reflection

Prayer for this week:

*"Heavenly Father,
Your Word has changed me and made me
a better person! Thank You!"*

April 9 Week 15, Day 1

John 3

Helpful Notes:

1. **Born again; New birth** = Being "born again" is essential to "enter the kingdom of God" (to be saved and to be in His church); Jesus said, "You must be born again"; there is ONE birth with TWO elements: (1) "water" refers to baptism (coming out of the water), (2) "Spirit" refers to the message of the Spirit in the gospel, which produces faith; note parallel statements (1 Cor. 12:13; Eph. 5:26; Tit. 3:5), which identify water with baptism, the Spirit with the Word, and the kingdom with the body and salvation. Baptism is essential!
2. **Believe** = The N.T. uses the word "believe" to speak about an active, working, obedient faith (not just a mental assent or acceptance of information); the Greek *pistis* is defined as a (1) conviction which (2) trusts and (3) obeys; John himself equates belief with obedience in the last verse (3:36).
3. **Darkness** = This is a frequent metaphor in the N.T. for sin, evil, wickedness and error; many choose (and it is a choice) to live in it, in order to hide from the light (of Christ and His gospel), which they know is antithetical to their way of life.

1. How did Nicodemus know that Jesus had come from God?

2. Is baptism (being born again) necessary to be saved and to receive God's eternal blessings?

3. Why do people living in darkness "hate the light"?

Verse for Meditation and Prayer: **John 3:17**

"For God did not send His Son into the world to condemn the world, but that the world through Him might be saved."

April 10 Week 15, Day 2

John 4

Helpful Notes:

1. **Samaritans** = It is commonly believed that the Samaritans were a mixed race of the Jews remaining in the northern kingdom of Israel and the Assyrians who settled in the land; thus, because they were "half-breeds," there was great animosity between the Jews and the Samaritans (4:9), and the Jews usually went around Samaria to avoid any possible interaction; still Jesus intentionally went through the land, and speaking with a Samaritan woman was even more abnormal and against their modern culture (4:27).
2. **True worship** = By identifying "true worshipers," Jesus implied there are false worshipers; God is seeking true worshipers and true worship; true worship is directed toward the right object (God), from the right attitude (in spirit), and by the right standard (in truth); all worship must be authorized by Christ (Col. 3:17), or it is not acceptable to God.
3. **White unto harvest** = There are souls ready to hear the gospel all around; the Samaritans "came to" Jesus—the imperfect tense emphasizing a steady stream; "more believed," then "many more" (4:30, 39-41); in Acts 8, "multitudes" of Samaritans heeded the gospel being preached (8:5-13).

1. What ordinary substance did Jesus turn into a spiritual lesson for the woman at the well?

2. What did Jesus say was His "food"?

3. When was the nobleman's son healed?

Verse for Meditation and Prayer: **John 4:35**

"Do you not say, 'There are still four months and then comes the harvest'? Behold, I say to you, lift up your eyes and look at the fields, for they are already white for harvest!"

John 5

Helpful Notes:

1. **Equal with the Father** = By calling God, "My Father" (which He does 36 times in the book of John), Jesus was "making Himself equal with God"; He was claiming a unity with, an identification with and an operation with the Father that declared He and the Father to be of the same nature and on the same level; Jesus said, "I and My Father are one" (10:30)—one in purpose and essence (see Col. 2:9).
2. **Dead raised in the same hour** = Jesus said in John 5:28-29 that in the same "hour" (not 1,000 years apart), "all" of the dead (good and bad) would hear His voice and be raised, and they would be separated unto eternal "life" and eternal "condemnation" at His return.
3. **Witnesses to the deity of Christ** = The O.T. required that a matter be established by two or three witnesses (Deut. 17:6; 19:15), so Jesus provided more; the witnesses to prove the Divine nature of Jesus are: Jesus (5:31), the Father (5:32, 37-38), John (5:33-35), the works/miracles of Jesus (5:36-37), the Scriptures (5:38-47).

1. What could be a "worse thing" to suffer (than a 38-year infirmity) if the man did not stop sinning?
2. To whom has "all judgment" been committed?
3. While the Jews did search the Scriptures, what obvious teaching did they miss (verse 39)?

Verse for Meditation and Prayer: **John 5:24**

"Most assuredly, I say to you, he who hears My word and believes in Him who sent Me has everlasting life, and shall not come into judgment, but has passed from death into life."

April 12 — Week 15, Day 4

John 6

Helpful Notes:

1. **Believing is a work** = When Jesus emphasized the need to "labor" (work, v. 27), the Jews asked how to "work" the works of God (v. 28); Jesus said, "This is the work of God, that you believe" (v. 29); while many attempts have been made to teach that salvation is by faith and not by works, Jesus said that believing in Him is a work; believing involves yielding to Him (continuously), "coming" to Him (continuously, v. 35) and obeying Him (continuously).
2. **The bread of life** = Jesus came down from heaven to give life; whoever "eats" of Christ will "live forever"; this is not literal, nor is it a reference to the Lord's Supper; eating His flesh and drinking His blood involved ingesting (i.e., receiving and accepting) the life and mission of Christ, His sacrifice for our sins, His teaching and the requirements of personal sacrifice and obedience thereto; truly "keeping His commandments" (1 John 3:24) is "hard/difficult" for some.
3. **Words of eternal life** = Through Christ alone and through His teachings alone can one obtain eternal life; His words are the means by which one is "drawn to" Christ (v. 44), and they will sift the true faith from the artificial (v. 60-66).

1. What prompted Jesus to depart to the mountain alone?

2. What did Peter say that the apostles had come "to believe and know"?

3. What did Jesus say Judas was (at the end of the chapter)?

Verse for Meditation and Prayer: **John 6:68**

"But Simon Peter answered Him, 'Lord, to whom shall we go? You have the words of eternal life.'"

April 13 Week 15, Day 5

John 7

Helpful Notes:

1. **Feast of Tabernacles** = This is also called the Feast of Booths or Ingathering (Lev. 23:33-43); it began five days after the Day of Atonement and lasted seven days; it celebrated the end of the harvest season and remembered God's care for His people while they wandered in the wilderness and lived in booths; during the festival, they would usually construct tents/booths/huts out of tree branches and stay in them.
2. **Judge with righteous judgment** = Some allege that it is never right to judge another (misquoting Matthew 7:1); however, Jesus commands judging here, as long as the judgment is in harmony with the principles of God's Word and not man's.
3. **No man ever spoke like this man** = How true were these words! Jesus spoke with authority (Matt. 7:28-29); He spoke the words of God (John 3:34; 12:49-50); He spoke heavenly things (John 3:12-13), which He had seen with His Father (John 8:38); He spoke the words of eternal life (John 6:63, 68).

1. Why did Jesus not want to walk in Judea?

2. What do we learn about the relationship between Jesus and His brothers?

3. Why did the world hate Jesus, according to what He said to His brothers?

Verse for Meditation and Prayer: **John 7:24**

"Do not judge according to appearance,
but judge with righteous judgment."

Mark Your Bible

1. **John 3:1**—Not all Pharisees or members of the Sanhedrin were against Jesus. A few believed openly (7:50-52; 19:38-39).
2. **John 3:2**—There was an obvious connection between the supernatural signs that Jesus was doing and the power behind them—God.
3. **John 3:8**—This is the only place (out of 386 uses) where the Greek *pneuma* is translated "wind." It should be translated "Spirit" (as it is every other time, including five other times in this chapter). The word "blows" can be translated "breathes," so the verse is about how the Spirit works through His God-breathed Word, which creates faith and leads to baptism (Mark 16:15-16).
4. **John 3:14-15**—As the serpent which was lifted up provided life to the dying, so the Son who was lifted up on the cross provides life to the dying in sin.
5. **John 3:15-16**—"Believes" is in the present tense, emphasizing an ongoing, persistent faith.
6. **John 3:15-18**—The emphasis is not simply "believing in Him," but it is that the one who believes can "have eternal life in Him." The emphasis is on being "in Christ" to be blessed (cf. Eph. 1:3-11).
7. **John 3:16**—"Loved" is *agape* love—the unselfish, unconditional, noblest love that seeks what is best for others. That does not mean that salvation is unconditional; it means that God loves everyone and wants the best for everyone, which is salvation in Christ.
8. **John 3:23**—This affirms emphatically that baptism is immersion.
9. **John 3:34**—The power that Christ had by the Spirit was limitless and unmeasured. This implies the Spirit was given "by measure" to others (including apostles and those on whom they laid hands).
10. **John 4:4**—No Jews ever "needed to go through Samaria," but Jesus did, so that He could find and teach lost souls.

(continued on next page)

Mark Your Bible

11. **John 4:6**—It is unclear if John followed Jewish time (which would be noon in this verse) or Roman time (which could be 6:00 a.m. or 6:00 p.m. in this verse).
12. **John 4:10**—"Living water" bestows life from the Lord—abundant life now in Christ, forgiven of all sins, and then eternal life in heaven. Those with living water (i.e., Christ) will "never thirst again."
13. **John 4:11**—The well has measured from 100 to 125 feet deep.
14. **John 4:24**—At least one modern religion claims that the Father has flesh and bones like man. Jesus specifically says that "God is spirit," and later said that "a spirit does not have flesh and bones" (Luke 24:39; cf. Isa. 31:3; Hos. 11:9; Matt. 16:17).
15. **John 4:46**—Capernaum is at least 16 miles away from Cana. Jesus healed the man's son from long distance.
16. **John 4:46**—A "nobleman" was an officer of the king (a royal official); he may have served Herod Antipas, who was over Galilee.
17. **John 5:9**—"Walked" is in the imperfect tense, indicating constant activity.
18. **John 5:10**—It was "not lawful" according to their traditions; the law of Moses did not forbid carrying his pallet.
19. **John 5:16**—The words "persecuted" and "sought to kill" are in the imperfect tense, indicating constant, ongoing activity.
20. **John 5:20**—God both *agapao* "loves" the Son (3:35) and *phileo* "loves" (warm, tender affection for) the Son (5:20).
21. **John 5:22**—Jesus will judge all mankind (12:48; Acts 17:31).
22. **John 5:27**—Jesus will not only judge as "the Son of God" (having Divine authority) but as "the Son of Man" (having unique understanding and sympathy for living the human life, Heb. 2:17; 4:15).
23. **John 5:46**—By rejecting Jesus, they were rejecting their Moses.

Mark Your Bible

24. **John 6:23**—Part of what was remembered about Jesus feeding the 5,000 was that He "had given thanks" (6:11). Do we give thanks?
25. **John 6:35, 37**—The words "comes" and "believes" are in the present tense, indicating continuous and sustained endeavor.
26. **John 6:39, 40, 44, 54**—Four times in this chapter Jesus speaks of "the last day." There will not be multiple days or years. Just one last day.
27. **John 6:44**—God "draws" people through His Word, but the "drawn" come and abide (present tense) of their own free will.
28. **John 7:5**—During Jesus' lifetime, His own "brothers did not believe in Him." But after His resurrection, that all changed (1 Cor. 15:7; Acts 1:14). Jesus' resurrection changes people and creates faith.
29. **John 7:8**—The contextual emphasis is that it was not His time to go up to the city publicly or demonstrably, as His brothers suggested, but to go up "in secret" (without attention).
30. **John 7:15**—Jesus had not attended a rabbinical school, so they marveled at His skill in the written law and their traditions.
31. **John 7:17**—If someone has a strong determination to find and know the truth, they will find it (Jer. 29:13; Matt. 5:6).
32. **John 7:21**—This is probably a reference to healing the man in chapter 5.
33. **John 7:39**—This is probably a reference to the gift of the Holy Spirit that was promised to all who were baptized into Christ (Acts 2:38; 5:32).

April 15 Week 15, Day 7

Day of Reflection

Take time today to reflect on the five chapters that you read this week. You may choose to read all five chapters again, in one sitting, or certain parts of them. Take time today to answer at least one of these questions below. You may or may not write anything down—you can choose to write or simply reflect.

1. What personal application do I need to make from the chapters I have read this week?

2. How can these five chapters help draw me closer to Jesus?

3. What words, phrases or verses in these chapters do I want to go back and study more in depth?

4. What questions do I have about what I have read this week on which I need to do some further Biblical research?

Week 16

April 16-22

April 16	Read John 8
April 17	Read John 9
April 18	Read John 10
April 19	Read John 11
April 20	Read John 12
April 21	Mark Your Bible
April 22	Day of Reflection

Prayer for this week:

"Heavenly Father,
You are awesome and deserve my very best!"

John 8

Helpful Notes:

1. **Light of the world** = Mankind was living in darkness (sin, evil, error); Jesus not only brought the light (representing truth), but He is the light (of truth) Himself; coming into the world of darkness, Jesus desperately wanted all to see the way to salvation and to His Father, so He showed how to walk in the light and to let it shine for others to see.
2. **The truth shall make you free** = There is an objective body of moral and religious information that can be known and kept (v. 51); that truth (as given by the Light of the world) must be known and kept, for only that truth can set free from bondage to sin, the world, the devil and death, for sin is enslaving.
3. **Before Abraham was, I AM** = Abraham came to be at a particular point in time (the emphasis of the verb "was"); before that point in time, Jesus said, "I AM"; the verb is in the present tense, emphasizing continuous existence—"I always have been"; the expression also identifies Jesus as Jehovah, who is the "I AM" (Ex. 3:14); Jesus was claiming the nature of eternal deity, and we must "believe" He is "I AM" (v. 24).

1. In relationship to His Father, what did Jesus say that He was always doing?

2. The Jews said they had "never been in bondage to anyone." Can you think of any time they were slaves or in captivity?

3. What insults did the Jews throw at Jesus in verse 48?

Verse for Meditation and Prayer: **John 8:32**

"And you shall know the truth,
and the truth shall make you free."

April 17 Week 16, Day 2

John 9

Helpful Notes:

1. **We must work the works of God** = We "must" (this is not optional); we must "work" (present tense indicates continual action); "the works of God" (not the works of the devil or the works that please men); "while it is day" (while there is time and opportunity, as life is fleeting); "night is coming" (there must be a real sense of urgency, realizing the end is coming); this was not just true of Jesus, but of us also!
2. **God does not hear sinners** = This verse is used and misused to prove a point; note that an uninspired, formerly-blind man is stating what was commonly believed; "The Lord is far from the wicked" and is not obligated to hear or answer their prayers (Prov. 15:29; 28:9; Psa. 34:14-15; 66:18); an alien sinner is certainly not saved by saying a prayer (Matt. 7:21; Acts 9:9-11; 22:16); however, God does hear every word from every person's mouth (Matt. 12:36-37), and He can choose to hear a sinner seeking truth (Matt. 5:6; John 7:17), without saving him/her by that prayer.
3. **For judgment Jesus came** = In some cases, He said that He didn't come to judge (12:47; 3:17), but the context must be considered; here "judgment" involves separation, and for that purpose Jesus did come (7:43; 9:16; 10:19; Luke 12:51-53).

1. Why were this man's parents resistant to cooperate?

2. While this man didn't know a full explanation for what had happened to him, what "one thing" did he say that he knew?

3. The man deduced if Jesus were "not from God," then what?

Verse for Meditation and Prayer: **John 9:4**

"I must work the works of Him who sent Me while it is day; the night is coming when no one can work."

John 10

Helpful Notes:

1. **The door of the sheep and the good shepherd** = Using metaphors, Jesus said that He was both (speaking of them interchangeably); as "the door," Jesus is the one and only entrance into His sheepfold (14:6; Acts 4:12), and all others are thieves and robbers; as "the shepherd," Jesus lovingly cares for His followers/sheep, knows them personally and lays down His life for them (15:13; Matt. 20:28); the sheep recognize His voice from all the others and will only follow Him.
2. **One flock and one shepherd** = Jesus is the one shepherd; there are as many flocks (one) as there are shepherds (one); Jesus is the one head (Eph. 5:23) of His one church (Eph. 4:4; 1:22-23); His one church is made up of Jews (the first flock) and Gentiles (the "other sheep") in one body (Eph. 2:11-22; Gal. 3:28).
3. **Feast of Dedication** = This feast was not one commanded by God but was started by the Jews during the intertestamental period, when they recaptured, cleansed and rededicated the temple (December of 165 B.C.), after Antiochus IV Epiphanes defiled it; the feast (a.k.a. Feast of Lights) was celebrated for eight days in December and is now called Hanukkah.

1. What sheep does a shepherd call by name?

2. What sort of life does Jesus offer to His sheep in this life?

3. To what ultimate end was Jesus going to go for His sheep?

Verse for Meditation and Prayer: **John 10:27**

"My sheep hear My voice, and I know them, and they follow Me."

April 19 Week 16, Day 4

John 11

Helpful Notes:

1. **The sleep of death** = Jesus spoke of death as "sleeping" (Matt. 9:24; John 11:11-14); it was figurative of the position of the body, in a position of rest (even in the grave, Dan. 12:2); however, Jesus only spoke of the body as sleeping and NEVER the soul (Luke 16:19-31; cf. Rev. 6:9-11); the dead are conscious in spirit in the Hadean realm, for only the body has died (Jas. 2:26).
2. **The resurrection and the life** = Only Jesus ("I am," and no other) had the power residing in Him to raise the dead and to give life again, even eternal life; though faithful followers (continuous "believers" who "keep His Word," 8:51) would die physically, they "shall live" eternally and "never die" spiritually (saved from the second death in hell).
3. **Jesus wept** = When Jesus saw His friends "weeping," He "groaned in the spirit" (conveys anger and indignation, perhaps with death itself and Satan), "was troubled" (to the point of shuddering or shaking), and He "wept" (burst into tears). Jesus experienced real human emotions (Heb. 4:15).

1. According to verses 4, 15 and 42, why did Jesus delay His trip to Bethany and allow Lazarus to die?

2. While we usually characterize him as a "doubter," how did Thomas exhibit bold faith?

3. What did Martha and Mary both say to Jesus, exhibiting a true faith in Him (although limited)?

Verse for Meditation and Prayer: **John 11:25**

"Jesus said to her, 'I am the resurrection and the life. He who believes in Me, though he may die, he shall live.'"

April 20 Week 16, Day 5

John 12

Helpful Notes:

1. **The hour has come** = After stating many times that His hour had not yet come, now it has (12:23, 27; 13:1; 16:32; 17:1); He was in His final week and the time of His suffering and death was drawing near; while He was "troubled" (12:27), He was fulfilling the "purpose" for which He came, and He would be "glorified" and His Father honored as a result.
2. **The ruler of this world will be cast out** = The decisive event (Gen. 3:15) had arrived, when Satan's dominion (as ruler of this world) would begin coming to an end, when the power over death was ripped from Satan's control by the death and the resurrection of Christ (Heb. 2:14-15); this was the moment of "judgment" (Greek *krisis)*, when the rightful ruler would be determined.
3. **The Word of Christ will judge man** = In the "last day," the standard of final judgment will not be man's traditions but the all-authoritative Word of Christ; the very thing that man was rejecting is the very thing that will judge him (2 Cor. 5:10); we must adhere to His Word, without modification.

1. Why did Judas complain about Mary's generous act?

2. When did Jesus' disciples understand the significance of His triumphal entry?

3. For what reason did the believing rulers not confess Jesus?

Verse for Meditation and Prayer: **John 12:48**

"He who rejects Me, and does not receive My words, has that which judges him – the word that I have spoken will judge him in the last day."

Mark Your Bible

1. **John 8:11**—Jesus was not condoning adultery. He condemned the sin (Matt. 5:32). Jesus was not pressing for stoning her to death.
2. **John 8:15**—Jesus did not judge anyone on the basis of the flesh.
3. **John 8:28**—"Lift up" was a reference to His crucifixion (12:32-33).
4. **John 8:30-31**—Underline "believed" in these verses. Jesus told those who "believed" in Him that they were not of God (v. 42) but were "of the devil" (v. 44). Faith alone will not and does not save.
5. **John 8:31**—To be His disciples, we must steadfastly follow Christ and abide by His teachings. Salvation requires faithfulness.
6. **John 8:34**—The word "commits" is present tense, denoting a habitual way of life (not just one sin). Sin is enslaving, if we let it.
7. **John 8:44**—The devil murdered Adam and Eve (and every human since) by bringing death upon them. That was "the beginning" of sin.
8. **John 8:51**—Not only must one believe His Word, but "anyone" (universal) who "keeps" (obeys) His Word will have eternal life.
9. **John 9:2**—It was a common misunderstanding that misfortunes were tied to sins (cf. Job 4:3-4). While our sins (and the sins of others) can bring misfortunes, the latter is not a measure of the former (Ecc. 9:11).
10. **John 9:7**—Jesus could have healed without the clay. This was, no doubt, a test of the man's faith, to see if he would obey.
11. **John 9:15**—The word "again" is found 5 times in this chapter. The Pharisees were determined "again" and "again" to find some explanation for this great miracle other than the truth—Jesus is God!
12. **John 9:16**—John uses the word "division" three times (7:43; 9:16; 10:19) to describe the impact of the truth of Jesus among the Jews.

(continued on next page)

Mark Your Bible

13. **John 9:38**—This man's growing faith in Jesus went from talking about "a man called Jesus" (9:11), to "a prophet" (9:17), to "from God" (9:33), to "Lord, I believe" (9:38).
14. **John 10:10**—The "thief" is reference to any religious leader who teaches salvation through any one or way other than Jesus Christ.
15. **John 10:10**—The word "have" (twice), in the present tense, emphasizes bountiful blessings overflowing in the life of a Christian now.
16. **John 10:16**—The "other sheep" is reference to the Gentiles (Eph. 2:11-22; 3:1-12), not manmade denominations that would arise later.
17. **John 10:27-28**—No one is able to snatch Jesus' sheep from His hand because they "hear" Him and "follow" Him (which are both present tense verbs, denoting ongoing behavior). If/When someone (of their own will) chooses to stop hearing and following, they can be snatched. This does not teach "once saved, always saved."
18. **John 10:30, 33**—Draw a line from "I and My Father are one" to "You make Yourself God." Jesus possessed the Divine nature.
19. **John 10:35**—Scripture truly cannot be broken, set aside, undone or annulled at will. It truly "endures forever" (1 Pet. 1:23-25).
20. **John 11:1**—Bethany was two miles from Jerusalem (11:18), on the eastern slopes of the Mount of Olives; it was the hometown of Jesus' friends: Mary, Martha and Lazarus.
21. **John 11:2**—Mary anointed the Lord in John 12 (cf. Matt. 26:7), but she was not the "sinful woman" who anointed Him in Luke 7:36-37.
22. **John 11:3, 5, 36**—Jesus loved *(phileo)* Lazarus, Mary and Martha (11:3, 36) and He loved *(agapao)* them (11:5). *Phileo* is the warm, tender, brotherly affection for a friend; *agapao* wants the best for them.
23. **John 11:4**—His death would not be permanent; the ultimate end was life.

Mark Your Bible

24. **John 11:19**—The Jewish custom was seven days of public mourning after the death and thirty days of private mourning.
25. **John 11:24**—Martha knew the dead would be raised, and it would happen "at the last day" (not after 1,000 years millennium).
26. **John 11:48**—The real issue is revealed. They are concerned about their political power and their position of authority.
27. **John 11:49-51**—Unbeknownst to Caiaphas, God guided His words.
28. **John 11:52**—Jesus would die for the Jews ("the nation) and for the Gentiles ("scattered abroad"), and gather them into "one" church.
29. **John 12:3**—Mary is not the "sinful woman" of Luke 7:36-37.
30. **John 12:20**—The "Greeks" were Jewish proselytes (Acts 2:10), who had been circumcised in the process of conversion to Judaism.
31. **John 12:27**—This was the third time the Father spoke from heaven (Matt. 3:17; 17:5); each time it was to benefit the people; the voice "thundered" (perfect tense indicating the effect was still present).
32. **John 12:32**—Jesus knew exactly how He would die (it was part of the plan, 3:14; 8:28); while man and Satan may have thought they were victorious, the gospel of the cross would draw people to salvation.
33. **John 12:39-40**—These people had hardened their hearts so much that they made themselves immune (by their own will) to deity.

April 22 Week 16, Day 7

Day of Reflection

Take time today to reflect on the five chapters that you read this week. You may choose to read all five chapters again, in one sitting, or certain parts of them. Take time today to answer at least one of these questions below. You may or may not write anything down—you can choose to write or simply reflect.

1. What personal application do I need to make from the chapters I have read this week?

2. How can these five chapters help draw me closer to Jesus?

3. What words, phrases or verses in these chapters do I want to go back and study more in depth?

4. What questions do I have about what I have read this week on which I need to do some further Biblical research?

Week 17

April 23-29

April 23	Read John 13
April 24	Read John 14
April 25	Read John 15
April 26	Read John 16
April 27	Read John 17
April 28	Mark Your Bible
April 29	Day of Reflection

Prayer for this week:

*"Heavenly Father,
give me peace and comfort as I study Your Word."*

John 13

Helpful Notes:

1. **The devil and Judas** = The devil cannot make anyone do anything against their own will; temptation involves one's own "desires," when he is "enticed" to sin (Jas. 1:13-15); Judas had a love for money (12:6; Matt. 26:15), and he willingly allowed the devil into his heart; the devil worked gradually (Luke 22:3; John 13:27), but only because Judas permitted it.
2. **Wash disciples' feet** = The disciples had been arguing in the upper room about who would be "the greatest" (Luke 22:24); Jesus gave them "an example" of true humility and service, by assuming the role of a servant and washing dirty feet; He was not intending this to be a church ritual but a lesson in the value of service, the key to "greatness" in God's eyes.
3. **Love one another** = Jesus gave His disciples a "new commandment"; loving one's neighbor was part of the old covenant (Lev. 19:18), but this was a "new" commandment based upon a "new" standard—Jesus; the motivation, extent and expression of Jesus' love is our standard for loving our brethren; and this would be the badge of true discipleship.

1. If you were washing the apostles' feet, what would you have thought about washing Peter's feet and Judas' feet?

2. How did Jesus identity the one who would betray Him?

3. What time of day was it when Judas left the room? When is it often easier to do a dark deed, which you know to be wrong?

Verse for Meditation and Prayer: **John 13:34**

"A new commandment I give to you, that you love one another; as I have loved you, that you also love one another."

John 14

Helpful Notes:

1. **Prepare a place** = Jesus told His disciples that He was going "to the Father" (13:1; 14:12, 28; 16:10, 16, 28); His Father was in "heaven" (Matt. 5:16, 45, 48; 6:1, 9; 7:11, 21); therefore, Jesus was going away from earth to heaven to prepare a place; He distinguished between heaven and earth (Matt. 5:18; 6:10, 19-20; 28:18); the "place" prepared and reserved (1 Pet. 1:3-5) is not on earth but "in heaven," where the Father is.
2. **The way, the truth, the life** = Note the definite article "the" before each term (it indicates there is one and only one); Jesus is the "one way" to heaven (Heb. 10:20); Jesus is the "one truth" that will set free (John 8:32); Jesus is the "one life" who provides eternal life (John 10:28); there is no other way to the Father, to salvation from sin or to eternity in heaven than through Jesus (Acts 4:12; Heb. 7:25).
3. **The Holy Spirit** = The Spirit is a Divine entity/person of the Godhead (separate from the Father and Son), who was responsible for guiding the penmen of the Bible to write the very words of God (2 Pet. 1:20-21; 1 Cor. 2:11-13); when Jesus ascended into heaven, He sent the Holy Spirit as a Comforter/Helper to directly guide the apostles.

1. How did Jesus describe heaven?

2. Twice in this chapter, Jesus said, "Let not your heart be troubled." How can a follower of God make that a reality?

3. What proof is there that Jesus loved the Father?

Verse for Meditation and Prayer: **John 14:6**

"Jesus said to him, 'I am the way, the truth, and the life. No one comes to the Father except through Me.'"

April 25 Week 17, Day 3

John 15

Helpful Notes:

1. **The vine and the branches** = Faithful Christians are each a branch "in" Christ; we must abide in Christ, abide in His Word, ensure His words abide in us and be productive in leading others to Christ; otherwise, we will be cut off and cast into the fire; the image is of living, continual growth.
2. **Friends** = Three times Jesus refers to His faithful followers as His "friends"; we receive His love and friendship if we keep His commandments, including His command to love one another as He has loved us (15:12); doing "whatever" He commands should make our "joy...full" (15:11).
3. **The Helper/Comforter** = When Jesus ascended into heaven, "another Helper" would be sent (noting Jesus as the first); the Holy Spirit was the "Helper/Comforter" (Greek *parakletos*), which literally means "called to one's side"; for the apostles (underline the word "you"), He would "teach you all things," "remind you of all things," "testify of Jesus," and "guide you into all truth" (14:26; 15:26; 16:13); this direct operation was promised only to the apostles, not to us.

1. What sort of fruit are faithful Christians to bear? (You can include the "fruit of the Spirit," but think beyond that.)
2. What connection does Jesus make between us abiding in Him and His words abiding in us?
3. For what reason did Jesus say the world hates His people?

Verse for Meditation and Prayer: **John 15:13**

"Greater love has no one than this,
than to lay down one's life for his friends."

John 16

Helpful Notes:

1. **Convict of sin** = Jesus said the Holy Spirit would come to the apostles and "convict the world of sin"; that is not a direct operation of the Spirit upon the heart of man, for (1) the whole thrust of John 14-16 is Jesus telling His apostles that the Holy Spirit would teach, remind and guide them in what to say—the words would convict, and (2) the first time the Spirit convicted of sin on Pentecost was done through the words preached (2:37); the Spirit still convicts of sin today, but only through His "sword"—His Word (Eph. 6:17).
2. **Guide you into all truth** = Underline "you" and "all truth"; when the Holy Spirit was done revealing God's truth to the apostles, they would have written "all" the truth; the Bible is "complete" (2 Tim. 3:16-17), supplying "all things" that we need (2 Pet. 1:3), for "all" God's truth has been "once for all delivered" (Jude 3); there are no modern revelations.
3. **Ask the Father in Jesus' name** = Jesus instructed that prayer is to be directed to the Father (cf. Matt. 6:9), and we are to "ask in His name" (i.e., in harmony with the will and authority of Christ); Jesus gave these conditions for prayer.

1. Into how much truth would the Spirit guide the apostles?

2. While all of His disciples would desert Him, how was it that Jesus would still not be alone?

3. Bringing reassuring peace and cheer are the last five words of the chapter. What are they?

Verse for Meditation and Prayer: **John 16:33**

*"These things I have spoken to you, that in Me you may have peace.
In the world you will have tribulation; but be of good cheer,
I have overcome the world."*

John 17

Helpful Notes:

1. **In the world, not of the world** = Jesus had been "in the world," but He was getting ready to go back to His Father; His disciples would remain "in the world," to carry out His mission; however, just as Jesus had not been "of the world," He prayed that they might not be "of the world"; in other words, although we live here, we must not love, approve of or participate in the evils "of this world" (1 John 2:15; Jas. 4:4).
2. **Sanctify by Your truth** = To be "sanctified" is to "be set apart by God *for* holy purposes, *from* the world and sin *to* His faithful service"; sanctification is not accomplished by a direct operation of the Holy Spirit, where man is passive; it is God's Word and obedience to God's Word (Eph. 5:26; 1 Cor. 6:11) that makes one holy and keeps him from living worldly.
3. **That they all may be one** = Jesus prays that all believers may be united as "one"—one in faith, doctrine, practice, purpose, love; the model of unity is the Father and Son (who do not differ in their doctrine, purpose, love, etc.); oneness is only possible through full submission to Christ's authority; denominationalism is foreign to this Divine precept and actually produces more disbelief as a result (just as Jesus said such division would).

1. What did Jesus say that He had finished?

2. When God's people are "one," what can result (verse 23)?

3. Ultimately, what did Jesus want for His people (verse 24)?

Verse for Meditation and Prayer: **John 17:21**

"...that they all may be one, as You, Father, are in Me,
and I in You; that they also may be one in Us,
that the world may believe that You sent Me."

Mark Your Bible

1. **John 13:17**—God's blessings are always conditional. True happiness is found in serving others and obeying our Lord.
2. **John 13:20**—The chain of authority is emphasized: the Father→the Son→the apostles. To reject the apostles was to reject the Godhead.
3. **John 13:21**—Speaking of His betrayal deeply "troubled" Jesus, to the point of shuddering and shaking (same word in 11:33; 12:27).
4. **John 13:23**—The Holy Spirit inspired the author of this book (John, the apostle) to identify himself as "the disciple whom Jesus loved."
5. **John 13:31**—"Now" (with the betrayal imminent) the final events are set in motion for Jesus' death, burial and resurrection.
6. **John 13:30-36**—Lord's Supper was instituted between verses 30-36.
7. **John 14:3**—Jesus promised (guaranteed) that He would return.
8. **John 14:9**—Jesus is not the Father. He is "the express image" of God on this earth (Heb. 1:3; Col. 1:15); therefore, His "words" and His "works" (14:10) were from the Father and united with the Father.
9. **John 14:12**—The works of the followers of Christ are greater in "extent," going to "every creature under heaven" in "the uttermost parts of the earth" with the gospel.
10. **John 14:15**—Love is the greatest motivator for obedience, not fear.
11. **John 14:16**—The Spirit would abide with the apostles throughout their work and His teaching would abide forever (1 Pet. 1:22-25).
12. **John 14:22**—Judas was also known as Thaddaeus (Mark 3:18).
13. **John 14:27**—Jesus' peace is not a worldly, absence-of-conflict peace, but an inner peace that dismisses anxiety and fear, and it surpasses all understanding (Phil. 4:6-7).
14. **John 15:5**—Underline "without Me you can do nothing."
15. **John 15:7, 10, 14**—Circle the word "if" in these verses. God's promises are more than we deserve, but they are also conditional.

(continued on next page)

Mark Your Bible

16. **John 15:6**—The Bible does not teach "once saved, always saved."
17. **John 15:13**—"For" means "in the place of." Jesus substituted His precious life on our behalf. Self-sacrificing love is the highest love.
18. **John 15:18-19, 23**—"Hates" is in the present tense, indicating ongoing, ceaseless hatred for who you are and Whose you are.
19. **John 15:22**—The Jews could not have rejected Christ if He had not come, but He did come, and they have no excuse for rejecting Him.
20. **John 16:1-33**—You may choose to circle the word "you" in this chapter, as a reminder that Jesus was speaking to the apostles.
21. **John 16:2**—This certainly fits Saul of Tarsus (Acts 9:1-5; 23:1).
22. **John 16:13**—Jesus said that He did not speak on His own authority (12:49), and neither does the Spirit. The Godhead was united in their message; they all spoke the same truth and did not deviate.
23. **John 16:20-22**—The crucifixion of Jesus would have very different effects (on His followers and on the world), but then His resurrection would completely reverse those emotions.
24. **John 16:23**—Jesus used the expression "that day" three times in these chapters (14:20; 16:23, 26). They each probably refer to the day of Pentecost, when the Spirit would be poured out on the apostles.
25. **John 16:27**—The Father "loves" *(phileo)* you with a tender, warm, caring affection. He also "loves" *(agapao)* you with an unconditional desire for your very best.
26. **John 16:32**—Just as He predicted, "they all forsook Him and fled" (Mark 14:50).
27. **John 16:33**—Jesus' peace is only for those who are "in" Him.
28. **John 17:11, 25**—Note that in His prayer, Jesus calls God "Father" (3 times) but also "Holy Father" and "Righteous Father."
29. **John 17:4-5**—Jesus was glorified and began His reign over His kingdom when He ascended into heaven (Dan. 7:13-14).

Mark Your Bible

30. **John 17:5**—Jesus shared an eternal glory with the Father, but He emptied Himself of some portion of that glory (but NOT His deity) to come to earth and save mankind (Phil. 2:5-11). What a thought!
31. **John 17:6, 8**—God is manifested to others through the Word.
32. **John 17:8**—Note the connection between faith and knowledge. Faith is not some blind leap in the dark. It is based upon evidence.
33. **John 17:12**—Judas was "lost" of his own free will. All the apostles were taught, guarded and warned. Judas, who was once saved, chose to sin, and as "the perishing one," he is deserving of hell.
34. **John 17:21-23**—Disunity leads to disbelief. Lack of unity leads to lack of conversions.

Day of Reflection

Take time today to reflect on the five chapters that you read this week. You may choose to read all five chapters again, in one sitting, or certain parts of them. Take time today to answer at least one of these questions below. You may or may not write anything down—you can choose to write or simply reflect.

1. What personal application do I need to make from the chapters I have read this week?

2. How can these five chapters help draw me closer to Jesus?

3. What words, phrases or verses in these chapters do I want to go back and study more in depth?

4. What questions do I have about what I have read this week on which I need to do some further Biblical research?

Week 18

April 30-May 6

April 30	Read John 18
May 1	Read John 19
May 2	Read John 20
May 3	Read John 21
May 4	Read Acts 1
May 5	Mark Your Bible
May 6	Day of Reflection

Prayer for this week:

"Heavenly Father,
You are beautiful beyond description!
May I live with that thought every day!"

April 30 Week 18, Day 1

John 18

Helpful Notes:

1. **Annas and Caiaphas** = The Romans took charge of appointing the high priests for the Jews—none of them were qualified by Mosaic law; Annas had been high priest but was deposed by Rome; his son-in-law, Caiaphas, was the official high priest at this time, but Annas continued to have power and influence in the people's eyes; so they went to Annas first.
2. **Praetorium** = This was the headquarters or provincial residence of the governor Pilate, while he was in Jerusalem (the Roman governor usually resided in Caesarea); in this context, it is the judgment hall; its location is uncertain—either Herod the Great's palace in the west side of the city or the Antonia tower connected to the outer court of the temple.
3. **My kingdom is not of this world** = While the Jews anticipated an earthly kingdom like David's, Jesus declared that His kingdom was spiritual in nature (not political), and therefore would not pose a threat of violence against the Jews; Jesus' kingdom is His church, and He resides as its head in heaven (Matt. 16:18-19; Eph. 1:22-23; 5:23).

1. When Judas came to betray Jesus, who did he bring and what were they carrying?

2. When Jesus first told the troops, "I am He," what did they do?

3. For what purpose did Jesus tell Pilate that He had come into the world?

Verse for Meditation and Prayer: **John 18:36**

"My kingdom is not of this world. If My kingdom were of this world, My servants would fight, so that I should not be delivered to the Jews; but now My kingdom is not from here."

John 19

Helpful Notes:

1. **Scourging** = The Roman soldiers gathered the whole garrison around Jesus and stripped Him (Matt. 27:27-28); His hands were tied above His head, and He was beaten with a flagrum that usually had three thongs with pieces of metal and bone tied into them; while the Jews limited to 40 blows (Deut. 25:3), the Romans had no such limit; the body would be literally torn to shreds on front and back; victims often did not survive the scourging.
2. **Times on the cross** = John used Roman time, which his audience would recognize; Pilate sentenced Jesus to crucifixion at the sixth hour—6:00 a.m. (19:14); Jesus was nailed to the cross at 9:00 a.m. (Mark 15:25); darkness came over the land at noon for three hours (Mark 15:33); Jesus died at 3:00 p.m. (Mark 15:34-37), after six hours on the cross.
3. **It is finished** = His death was the culmination of many things; "finished" was His life, His mission, His suffering, His shame, His separation, His redemptive plan; the perfect passive tense emphasizes abiding results.

1. "According to the law," why did the Jews say that Jesus "ought to die"?

2. What ruler did the Jews use as their trump card to finally get Pilate to concede to their demands?

3. What two unexpected disciples came to bury Jesus' body?

Verse for Meditation and Prayer: **John 19:5**

"Then Jesus came out, wearing the crown of thorns and the purple robe. And Pilate said to them, 'Behold the Man!'"

John 20

Helpful Notes:

1. **Jesus breathed on the apostles** = Simply, this was a symbolic and prophetic act of reassurance to the apostles that the Holy Spirit would come upon them in Jerusalem (Luke 24:49; Acts 1:8), when they began to fulfill being sent out by Jesus (Mark 16:15-16) and they preached the gospel so that people could be forgiven of sins (Luke 24:47; Acts 2:38).
2. **Written that you may believe** = The purpose of the inspired writings (especially the writings about the "signs" Jesus did, proving His deity) was to produce faith (cf. Rom. 10:17), and reading the written truths was to be just as credible as seeing the visual acts themselves; we are "blessed" (20:29) to have and to be able to read the full revelation of God!
3. **The Son of God** = "Son of" does not mean a descendant or an inferior; Scripture sometimes uses "son of" to depict the nature of a person (Mark 3:17; John 17:12); the expression "Son of God" is understood as Jesus being "God" (10:33; cf. 1:1), "one" with the "Father" (10:30), "equal with God" (5:18), and worthy of the same "honor" as the Father (5:23).

1. What did John note about the handkerchief or face cloth?

2. What did Thomas want to do, in order to believe?

3. What did Thomas call Jesus when he realized He had been raised?

Verse for Meditation and Prayer: **John 20:31**

"But these are written that you may believe
that Jesus is the Christ, the Son of God, and that believing
you may have life in His name."

John 21

Helpful Notes:

1. **Sea of Tiberias** = This is another name for the Sea of Galilee, which is often what the Gentiles called it; Tiberias was a town on the western shore of the Sea of Galilee; it was built by Herod Antipas and named after the reigning emperor Tiberius.
2. **Do you love me?** = Jesus used two different words for "love" in His restorative conversation with Peter; the first two times He used the word *agapao,* which is the highest form of love—an unconditional, unselfish, self-sacrificing devotion to the greatest needs of the one loved; Peter answered, "I *phileo* You," which was a warm, tender affection of dear friends; in the third question, Jesus asked "Do you *phileo* Me?" to get Peter to reflect on the depth of his love and to truly mean it.
3. **Feed My lambs** = Jesus used two different verbs: "feed" meaning "to provide food, nourish," and then "tend" meaning "to shepherd, protect"; Jesus used two different metaphors: "lambs" for "young ones" and "sheep" for "more mature ones"; Jesus was restoring Peter and reaffirming his usefulness to Christ and his meaningful work in the kingdom.

1. From 100 yards away, how did Jesus know where they could catch so many fish (when they had caught nothing)?

2. What two words did Jesus tell Peter in verses 19 and 22?

3. In the last two verses, what two things did John say about the things He had written?

Verse for Meditation and Prayer: **John 21:25**

"And there are also many other things that Jesus did, which if they were written one by one, I suppose that even the world itself could not contain the books that would be written. Amen."

Acts 1

Helpful Notes: ** See Brief Introduction to Acts on page 635.*

1. **Proof** = The Greek word means "that which causes something to be known in a convincing and decisive manner; demonstrative proof"; it was not merely hearsay that Jesus was raised from the dead, there were "many" pieces of solid, confirmed evidence that Jesus was truly alive after His death; it was not a matter of opinion or blind faith.
2. **Kingdom** = John the Baptist and Jesus came promising "the kingdom" to be near (Matt. 3:2; 4:17), and now (in Acts 1:5), it was "not many days" away; the kingdom of God is the church (Matt. 16:18-19), which was purchased by the blood of Christ (Acts 20:28) and established in Acts 2; Christians in the first century had been "conveyed into the kingdom" (Col. 1:13; cf. Rev. 1:9); the kingdom is not still to be established—it is a present reality.
3. **Baptism of the Holy Spirit** = The immersion/overwhelming of the Holy Spirit was administered by Jesus Himself (John 1:33) only twice in the N.T.—with the apostles (Jews) in Acts 2 and the Gentiles in Acts 10; it is not the "one baptism" (Eph. 4:5) to be taught and practiced today.

1. How long was Jesus with His disciples between His resurrection and His ascension?

2. Who was gathered with the apostles in the upper room, who had not believed in Jesus before His resurrection?

3. Who took Judas' place as an apostle?

Verse for Meditation and Prayer: **Acts 1:3**

"...to whom He also presented Himself alive after His suffering by many infallible proofs, being seen by them during forty days and speaking of the things pertaining to the kingdom of God."

Mark Your Bible

1. **John 18:3**—All of this to arrest Jesus! To arrest deity!
2. **John 18:6**—They expected resistance but received cooperation. They may have been filled with awe, being startled in His presence.
3. **John 18:11**—Jesus had known "the cup" of suffering was coming (Mark 10:38; 14:36), and He willingly drank of it.
4. **John 18:12**—They treated Jesus like a criminal, yet He went willingly.
5. **John 18:28**—These hypocritical frauds would not violate their traditions, but they had no problem murdering an innocent man.
6. **John 18:31**—The Romans took capital punishment away from the Jews, so the Jews had to bring death cases to Roman officials.
7. **John 18:31-32**—Jewish capital punishment was done by stoning; however, in O.T. prophecy (Psa. 22:16) and Jesus' own words (Matt. 20:19; John 12:32), the Lord was to die by crucifixion. So the Jews took this case to the Romans, unwittingly fulfilling God's plan.
8. **John 19:2-3**—This was a full mockery of Jesus as "King," giving Him a crown, a royal robe and bowing to salute Him. Shameful!
9. **John 19:11**—Pilate's authority/power (truly that of all nations and leaders) is granted by the sovereign God (Dan. 2:21; 4:17, 25, 32).
10. **John 19:11**—"Greater sin" because they had the Scriptures and greater knowledge of God's plan for the Messiah.
11. **John 19:23**—To inflict even greater humiliation, Jesus was most likely completely naked on the cross. They took all His garments.
12. **John 19:24**—Psalm 22 is a detailed (and moving) prophecy of Jesus' final moments, written 1,000 years before it ever happened.
13. **John 19:26**—It appears Joseph was already dead, and may have been for some time. And Jesus' brothers were not even believers.
14. **John 19:33**—Underline "He was already dead." The Roman soldiers knew what death looked like; they were experts in it.

(continued on next page)

Mark Your Bible

15. **John 19:33**—Just like the Passover lamb, Jesus ("the Lamb of God," 1:29) had no bones broken (Ex. 12:46; Num. 9:12).
16. **John 19:34**—The spear did not kill Jesus. "He gave up His spirit" (19:30) and was "already dead" (19:33). But the blood and water certainly confirmed that He was dead.
17. **John 20:1**—The word "saw" is used 7 times in this chapter and the word "see" (in some form) is used 5 times. Our faith in the resurrection is based upon established EYE-witness testimony.
18. **John 20:7**—The cloths were still there and "folded." There was no haste in leaving the tomb; the body was not stolen. If Jesus just "woke up," did He just leave the tomb naked? He was raised!
19. **John 20:15**—The term "Woman" was one of tender respect.
20. **John 20:16**—"Rabboni" meant "great teacher."
21. **John 20:17**—Jesus had a unique relationship with the Father that no one else did, so He did not use the term "our Father."
22. **John 20:19, 26**—Jesus met with His disciples twice, and it was on the first day of the week both times. That is significant.
23. **John 20:23**—Only God can forgive sin (Mark 2:7). When the gospel is preached, it makes forgiveness available to accept or reject.
24. **John 20:27**—Jesus literally said, "Stop disbelieving, start believing."
25. **John 20:31**—Saving faith is always an obedient faith (3:36).
26. **John 21:6**—Obedience brings abundant blessings.
27. **John 21:7**—Peter wanted to be appropriately attired when he saw Jesus, even if it made the swimming more difficult.
28. **John 21:14**—Read Matthew 28, Luke 24 and 1 Corinthians 15:4-9 for all of the post-resurrection appearances of Jesus.
29. **John 21:15-17**—There is NO reason to conclude that Jesus was placing Peter over all of His flock/church. The N.T. does not teach that.

Mark Your Bible

30. **John 21:18-19**—Historians state that Peter was crucified and even, at his request, crucified upside down.
31. **John 21:15-19**—Peter had denied Jesus three times, now he reaffirms his love for Jesus three times. Jesus has a place for him still.
32. **Acts 1:4**—The Promise of the Father was the outpouring of the Spirit on all flesh (Jews and Gentiles), fulfilled in Acts 2 (2:1-4, 33) and Acts 10 (10:44-46+11:15-17).
33. **Acts 1:8**—Underline the word "power" (it is a key term). Jesus promised that His kingdom would come with "power" within His generation (Mark 9:1), and then told His apostles that they would be endued with "power" from on high while in Jerusalem (Luke 24:49). All of this was fulfilled in Acts 2.
34. **Acts 1:8**—This verse provides an outline of the book: (1) Spreading the gospel in Jerusalem [chap. 1-7], (2) Spreading the gospel in Judea and Samaria [chap. 8-12], (3) Spreading the gospel in the uttermost parts of the earth [chap. 13-28].
35. **Acts 1:11**—Jesus will return in like manner as He ascended—literally and visibly (Rev. 1:7), personally (1 Thess. 4:16) and in the clouds (1 Thess. 4:17). It will not be in secret.
36. **Acts 1:14**—Underline "His brothers." Before Jesus' resurrection, they did not believe in Him (John 7:5). The resurrection changed these men (1 Cor. 15:7).
37. **Acts 1:16**—David wrote Psalm 41:9, but Peter affirms that "the Holy Spirit spoke...by the mouth of David." The words of David were inspired of God (2 Sam. 23:2; 2 Pet. 1:20-21).
38. **Acts 1:21-22**—Two qualifications were given for one to be an apostle: (1) Must have been among Jesus' disciples from the beginning (i.e., the baptism of John) to the end (i.e., the ascension of Jesus) of Jesus' ministry; (2) Must have been a witness of the resurrection of Christ. Thus, it is impossible for anyone to be an apostle today.
39. **Acts 1:26**—Underline "apostles." This is the antecedent of the pronoun "they" in the next verse (2:1).

May 6 Week 18, Day 7

Day of Reflection

Take time today to reflect on the five chapters that you read this week. You may choose to read all five chapters again, in one sitting, or certain parts of them. Take time today to answer at least one of these questions below. You may or may not write anything down—you can choose to write or simply reflect.

1. What personal application do I need to make from the chapters I have read this week?

2. How can these five chapters help draw me closer to Jesus?

3. What words, phrases or verses in these chapters do I want to go back and study more in depth?

4. What questions do I have about what I have read this week on which I need to do some further Biblical research?

Week 19

May 7-13

May 7	Read Acts 2
May 8	Read Acts 3
May 9	Read Acts 4
May 10	Read Acts 5
May 11	Read Acts 6
May 12	Mark Your Bible
May 13	Day of Reflection

Prayer for this week:

"Heavenly Father,
help me to not be ashamed that I'm a Christian
but to be bold and happy!"

Acts 2

Helpful Notes:

1. **Pentecost** = This was one of the three annual Jewish feasts which required all Jewish males to be present in Jerusalem; the Greek word means "fiftieth," thus denoting that the day of Pentecost was 50 days after Passover, as detailed in Leviticus 23:15-22; therefore, the day of Pentecost was always on a Sunday; the first day of the week has had great significance to Christians from the very beginning; the Sabbath is no longer a holy day (Col. 2:14-17).
2. **Tongues** = Speaking in tongues was a miraculous gift of the Holy Spirit (1 Cor. 12:7-11), by which one was able to speak in a language that he had not studied; the gift of tongues ceased upon the completion of the N.T. in the first century (1 Cor. 13:8-13); that which was spoken was not unintelligible sounds, but it was a real, known, existing language of the day (see the word "tongues" and "language" used interchangeably in Acts 2:4, 6, 8, 11), which could be understood and interpreted (1 Cor. 12:10; 14:13, 27-28).
3. **Last days** = This Biblical expression refers to the final dispensation of time (i.e., the Christian age), when the church was established (Isa. 2:2-4); Peter said, "this is what was spoken by the prophet Joel" (Acts 2:16; Joel 2:28-32); even Christians in the first century were living in "the last days" (2 Tim. 3:1-5).

1. In fulfillment of prophecy, who was dwelling in Jerusalem on the day of Pentecost?

2. How many people were baptized for the forgiveness of their sins?

3. When one is saved by God's plan of salvation, where does God add Him? Could one be saved but not in His church?

Verse for Meditation and Prayer: **Acts 2:38**

"Then Peter said to them, 'Repent, and let every one of you be baptized in the name of Jesus Christ for the remission of sins; and you shall receive the gift of the Holy Spirit.'"

Acts 3

Helpful Notes:

1. **Hour of prayer** = The Jews practiced a morning sacrifice and an evening sacrifice, which was accompanied by public prayer; the evening sacrifice and hour of prayer was the ninth hour (3:00 p.m.); the apostles were going there (not for Jewish worship) because many would be gathered and it would be the ideal opportunity to teach the gospel to a large crowd.
2. **Name** = While the word "name" can be used to stand for the person himself, it is often used (especially in the case of Jesus) to emphasize and identify authority; the miracle was done "in the name of Jesus Christ" (3:6), their preaching was done "in the name of Jesus" (4:17-18), and Bible baptism is done "in the name of Jesus Christ" (2:38); all of these stress the authority of Christ as the basis for all that is done (cf. Col. 3:17).
3. **Prophet** = The word "prophet" generally means "one who speaks forth for another"; while Moses was a prophet himself, he prophesied (in Deut. 18:15-18) of the ultimate Prophet who would come and must be heard in all things; this Prophet is Jesus Himself (Acts 3:22-23), who came speaking the words of God (Heb. 1:1; John 12:48-50); He must be heard and obeyed.

1. For a man who had never walked a day in his life, what was the lame man doing (and continuously so) after he was healed?

2. By what interesting name did Peter call Jesus in verses 13 and 26?

3. What will happen to those who will not hear Jesus?

Verse for Meditation and Prayer: **Acts 3:22**

"For Moses truly said to the fathers, 'The LORD your God will raise up for you a Prophet like me from your brethren. Him you shall hear in all things, whatever He says to you.'"

Acts 4

Helpful Notes:

1. **Captain of the temple** = These men were in charge of the guard posts around the temple courtyard and the Levites who manned those 24 posts; the "captain of the temple" was basically the "chief of police" among the Jewish leaders; the size of the temple compound (25-30 acres) and the size of the crowds that could gather there (at least 100,000) required the presence of law and order.
2. **Common** = The common and committed devotion to Christ of early Christians brought a true sense of selflessness and belonging; they did not practice communism, socialism or exact any laws to be obeyed in giving donations; rather, those who were able (that's key) voluntarily (that's key) helped each other based upon "need" (that's key) (Acts 4:32-35).
3. **Barnabas** = His given name was Joses/Joseph, but the apostles gave him a new name suited to his character, which meant "Son of Encouragement"; he was a "good man" (11:24), who reconciled Saul with the apostles, encouraged the church in Antioch to walk faithfully with the Lord, and traveled with Paul on his first missionary journey.

1. What did the enemies of Peter and John realize about them in verse 13?

2. When Peter and John were severely threatened and commanded to not speak at all in the name of Jesus, what was their response?

3. For what two things did the apostles pray in verse 29?

Verse for Meditation and Prayer: **Acts 4:20**

"For we cannot but speak the things which we have seen and heard."

Acts 5

Helpful Notes:

1. **Fear** = Fear can involve terror or dread (as in Rev. 18:10, 15) or cowardice or timidity (as in 2 Tim. 1:7, John 14:27), or it can involve awe, respect and reverence (a holy fear for the majesty and holiness of God, His Word and His will); all fear can motivate, but reverential fear is a healthy fear that motivates man to respect God's authority, obey His commands, turn from evil and pursue holiness.
2. **Gamaliel** = He was a highly respected teacher/Rabbi among the Jews in Jerusalem (perhaps the most respected of his day), who gave counsel to the council/Sanhedrin during the trial of the apostles; Saul of Tarsus was "brought up at his feet" (22:3), and Saul may have been aware of this event (perhaps even present for it).
3. **Beaten** = The Greek word originally meant "to skin, flay," and was used of the whipping inflicted on the front and back of a naked body; from the Jews, this would have been 39 lashes (Deut. 25:3; 2 Cor. 11:24); those who received this brutal scourging sometimes did not survive.

1. To whom was God giving the Holy Spirit (according to verse 32)?

2. According to Gamaliel's counsel, if the plan and work of the apostles was "of God," what could the Sanhedrin do about it?

3. After being beaten and commanded not to speak in the name of Christ, how did the apostles respond and what did they do?

Verse for Meditation and Prayer: **Acts 5:29**

"But Peter and the other apostles answered and said: 'We ought to obey God rather than men.'"

Acts 6

Helpful Notes:

1. **Hellenists** = The Hellenists (or Grecian Jews) were Jews who were born outside of Palestine, educated in the Greek culture and spoke Greek (rather than Aramaic, which most Palestinian-born Jews spoke); Grecian Jews would sometimes return to Jerusalem in their later years; Jews native to Palestine often looked down on Grecian Jews.
2. **Priests** = The priests served at the temple in Jerusalem, with an estimated 18,000 living in Jerusalem; religious leaders are often the most resistant to changing their beliefs; so when "a great many priests" (at least in the hundreds, if not more) are converted, it evidences a major shift taking place in Jerusalem.
3. **The faith** = The definite article "the" identifies this not as a personal belief but as an objective body of truth (Jude 3); "the faith" is "the gospel" (Gal. 1:11+23); the gospel involves facts to be believed, commands to be obeyed and promises to be received; obedience is required to "the faith" to be saved, and there is only "one faith" (Eph. 4:5).

1. Rather than merely adding, what was the number of the disciples doing in verse 1?

2. What did the apostles say that they needed to be able to continue doing themselves?

3. What were those who heard Stephen preaching not able to do?

Verse for Meditation and Prayer: **Acts 6:7**

"Then the word of God spread, and the number of the disciples multiplied greatly in Jerusalem, and a great many of the priests were obedient to the faith."

Mark Your Bible

1. **Acts 2:1**—The "they" who were "all" baptized with the Holy Spirit in Acts 2 were the "apostles" (1:26). Draw a line from the pronoun "they" in 2:1 to its antecedent, "apostles," in 1:26.
2. **Acts 2:16-17**—Draw a line from "this is what" to "last days." These events were happening in "the last days."
3. **Acts 2:17**—"All flesh" is representative of Jews and Gentiles. Joel's prophecy of Holy Spirit baptism on "all flesh" was fulfilled in Acts 2 (with the Jews) and Acts 10 (with the Gentiles).
4. **Acts 2:21, 38**—These two verses complement each other. Being "saved" (v. 21) is equivalent to "remission of sins" (v. 38). "Calling on the name of the Lord" takes place after one believes (Rom. 10:13-14), but it is not merely a verbal call (Matt. 7:21). Thus, the "calling" takes place in the acts of repentance and baptism (see Acts 22:16).
5. **Acts 2:27, 31**—See "Helpful Notes" on "Hades" in Matthew 11.
6. **Acts 2:27-31**—At death, souls/spirits go to Hades and bodies go to the grave (Jas. 2:26; Ecc. 12:7; Luke 16:19-31). But, Jesus' spirit did not remain in Hades, for it came forth and gave life back to His body in the tomb.
7. **Acts 2:34**—Christ is reigning right now in heaven, having received His kingdom when He ascended into heaven (Dan. 7:13-14).
8. **Acts 2:37**—The "hearing" of the gospel led them to "believe" (Rom. 10:17). Their hearts were pierced with faith in the resurrected Lord and sorrow for their sinful deeds.
9. **Acts 2:38**—The word "for" is from the Greek preposition *eis*, which always (without exception) looks forward ("in order to obtain") and never looks backward (to mean "because of"). The very same grammatical structure is found in Matthew 26:28—"For this is My blood... which is shed for many for the remission of sins." Jesus did not shed His blood "because of" sins already being forgiven, but He shed His blood "in order that" sins might be forgiven. The same meaning is here in Acts 2:38. Baptism is essential for salvation.

(continued on next page)

Mark Your Bible

10. **Acts 2:42**—"The breaking of bread" (with the definite article "the") is a figure of speech for the Lord's Supper. It differs from a common meal, where the definite article is not used (as in v. 46). Also, by use of synecdoche, the bread is representing a part for the whole, and it includes the partaking of the cup (Matt. 26:27).
11. **Acts 2:47**—One does not "join" the church; God "adds" the saved to His church.
12. **Acts 3:2**—The man was 40 years old (4:22).
13. **Acts 3:7**—Underline the word "immediately."
14. **Acts 3:2, 10**—The "Beautiful Gate" is likely the gate on the east side of the Court of Women (also called "the treasury" in John 8:20)—the ideal place to beg for money as people entered.
15. **Acts 3:11**—Solomon's "porch" was along the eastern side of the Court of the Gentiles; it was a covered area about 45 feet wide with rows of columns 38 feet tall. This was a common place for gatherings; the church met here in its early days (5:12).
16. **Acts 3:16**—It was the "faith" of the apostles (not the lame man) in the "authority" of Christ that brought about the healing.
17. **Acts 3:18, 21**—Note the singular "mouth" from which the "prophets" (plural) spoke—they all spoke the same truth from God.
18. **Acts 3:19**—This verse parallels 2:38. "Be converted" or "turn again" is what happens in baptism. "The times of refreshing" parallels "the gift of the Holy Spirit."
19. **Acts 3:21**—"The times of restoration" is the "these days" (v. 24), in which God was seeking to restore fallen man back to Himself through the preaching of the gospel.
20. **Acts 4:4**—Underline the number "five thousand."
21. **Acts 4:7, 10**—To do something in the "name" of Jesus means to do it by His "power" or by His "authority." Underline and connect these words in these two verses.

Mark Your Bible

22. **Acts 4:12**—This is a powerful injunction against any doctrine or religion that does not conform to the authority of Christ. There is no salvation other than through Christ, through His authority and through obeying His commands.
23. **Acts 4:13**—The boldness exhibited itself in unrestrained speech. They were bold in their preaching and would not back down.
24. **Acts 4:17, 18, 20, 29, 31**—Circle the words "speak" and "spoke" in these verses and draw lines connecting them. That is what the Lord sent them to do and they would not stop.
25. **Acts 4:27**—Pilate and Herod were enemies but became friends in opposing Jesus (Luke 23:12).
26. **Acts 5:1-2**—This was all voluntary. There was no obligation to sell possessions or give any proceeds from a sale.
27. **Acts 5:1-4**—Their lie was bringing part of the proceeds and representing it as all the proceeds (5:8).
28. **Acts 5:3**—Satan did not make him lie. Ananias and Sapphira planned it together (5:9).
29. **Acts 5:3**—The Holy Spirit is a person (who can be lied to). The Holy Spirit is "God" (5:4).
30. **Acts 5:3**—Lying is a horrible sin (Prov. 6:16-19), and it will cost you your soul (Rev. 21:8, 27; 22:15).
31. **Acts 5:12, 20, 21, 25**—This is where they were arrested in the first place in chapter 3. Now, they were to go back again (to the same place) and keep preaching.
32. **Acts 5:14**—"Added" is in the imperfect tense, indicating a steady and persistent growth of the church (cf. Isa. 2:2-4).
33. **Acts 5:15**—This is not mentioned as hyperbole. With God, this was very much possible (Luke 8:44; Acts 19:12).
34. **Acts 5:28**—They had already asked for that in Matthew 27:25.

(continued on next page)

Mark Your Bible

35. **Acts 5:41**—Peter (one of these men) later wrote about how to properly handle suffering for the name of Christ (1 Pet. 4:16).

36. **Acts 5:42**—The verbs "teaching" and "preaching" are in the Greek present tense, denoting continuous action. They did not stop!

37. **Acts 6:2, 4, 7**—To help identify "the faith" (in v. 7), connect it to "the word" in verses 2, 4 and 7.

38. **Acts 6:3**—The congregation was involved in identifying men who met the Divine qualifications.

39. **Acts 6:3**—The delegation of responsibility put these men "under" the authority of the apostles' guidance but "over" the work assigned to them. While these men are not called "deacons," it is a good representation of deacons in a congregation being "under" the eldership but "over" their assigned duty.

40. **Acts 6:5**—All of the names of those who were selected to help the Grecian widows were Greek names. The complaint of neglect was brought by the Hellenists, and the instruction was to search "among" them to find qualified men. So the problem was going to be solved by getting Hellenists involved in helping the Hellenists.

41. **Acts 6:7**—There is a direct correlation between the Word of God spreading and the number of the disciples growing. Both verbs are in the imperfect tense, indicating ongoing activity of both.

42. **Acts 6:7**—The "chief priests" were some of the first earwitnesses to the resurrection of Jesus (Matt. 28:11). Perhaps that helped to prepare their hearts to obey the gospel when they heard it preached.

43. **Acts 6:8**—Stephen is the first person mentioned as doing miracles in the book of Acts other than the apostles.

Day of Reflection

Take time today to reflect on the five chapters that you read this week. You may choose to read all five chapters again, in one sitting, or certain parts of them. Take time today to answer at least one of these questions below. You may or may not write anything down—you can choose to write or simply reflect.

1. What personal application do I need to make from the chapters I have read this week?

2. How can these five chapters help draw me closer to Jesus?

3. What words, phrases or verses in these chapters do I want to go back and study more in depth?

4. What questions do I have about what I have read this week on which I need to do some further Biblical research?

Week 20

May 14-20

May 14	Read Acts 7
May 15	Read Acts 8
May 16	Read Acts 9
May 17	Read Acts 10
May 18	Read Acts 11
May 19	Mark Your Bible
May 20	Day of Reflection

Prayer for this week:

"Heavenly Father,
help me to have the strength of faith
that early Christians had!"

Acts 7

Helpful Notes:

1. **God does not dwell in temples made with hands** = Stephen spent the first 48 verses of the sermon proving that God's presence and God's providential care are not restricted to Palestine or the temple (which is what his hearers were concerned about, see 6:11-14); God had been active in the lives of His people in Mesopotamia, Haran, Egypt, Midian, etc.
2. **The Angel of the Lord** = Stephen recounts that "the Angel of the Lord appeared" to Moses "in a flame of fire from the midst of a bush" (7:30; Ex. 3:2); in the next two chapters of the book of Exodus, the Angel is called "God" (23 times), "LORD" (23 times) and "I AM" (3:14); "the Angel of the Lord" is referred to more than 60 times in the O.T., and the evidence points conclusively to the Angel of the Lord being deity—pre-incarnate appearances and interactions of the Christ to man.
3. **Cut to the heart** = The gospel sparks different reactions: in Acts 2:37, hearers were "cut to the heart" (they believed) when they heard about the Christ; in Acts 7:54, hearers were "cut to the heart" (literally, "sawn asunder" in their hearts with rage); some "ears" want to "hear" and others do not.

1. What did the Jews do after making the golden calf?

2. The hearers' "fathers" killed the prophets who foretold of the coming Christ. What had Stephen's hearers done to Christ?

3. What was Jesus doing when Stephen saw Him?

Verse for Meditation and Prayer: **Acts 7:51**

"You stiffnecked and uncircumcised in heart and ears!
You always resist the Holy Spirit; as your fathers did, so do you."

Acts 8

Helpful Notes:

1. **Persecution** = The first persecution against the Christians came from the Jews, who had persecuted God's prophets and killed God's Son; they had threatened, imprisoned and beaten the Christians; now they had killed one; the persecutors would stop at nothing, but the persecuted would not stop either—the scattering resulted in wider preaching.
2. **Receive miraculous gifts of the Holy Spirit** = The apostles dispatched two of their number, Peter and John, to Samaria, in order that the new Christians "might receive the Holy Spirit" (v. 15); when the apostles "laid hands on them...they received the Holy Spirit" (v. 17); the only means of imparting the miraculous gift (and powers) of the Spirit was through the apostles' hands, which shows the limited duration of the miraculous gifts.
3. **Second law of pardon** = God has a law of pardon for non-Christians (i.e., His plan of salvation), and a law of pardon for Christians who sin (which proves Christians are not "always saved," but can be lost); a Christian who has sinned must "Repent and pray" to "be forgiven" (v. 22).

1. What had Jesus said several years earlier about the harvest of souls in Samaria (John 4:35)?

2. When Simon saw the genuine miracles done by Philip, what did he realize about his sorcery?

3. What did the eunuch do *after* his baptism, but not *before*?

Verse for Meditation and Prayer: **Acts 8:4**

"Therefore those who were scattered went everywhere preaching the word."

Acts 9

Helpful Notes:

1. **Saul of Tarsus** = Saul (Hebrew name) was later known as Paul (Greek name); Saul was born in Tarsus (on the NE corner of the Mediterranean Sea), as a Roman citizen (Acts 22:28) and learned the trade of tentmaking (18:3); he had a strong Jewish heritage, was of pure Jewish blood, a Pharisee, who studied under the famous Rabbi Gamaliel (Phil. 3:4-6; Acts 22:3; 23:6; 26:4-5); he actively opposed Christianity and led persecution against it (7:58-8:3; 9:1-2; 26:10-11); the fact that he was converted shows the power of the gospel.
2. **The Way** = This term is used six times in Acts (9:2; 19:9, 23; 22:4, 14; 24:22) as a designation of the unique Christian faith and the exclusive nature of Christ's followers (there was something very identifiable about them); each time the term is used it is found in the context of hostility toward the gospel and Christians; there is only one way (Matt. 7:13-14), through Christ (John 14:6; Acts 4:12) to heaven.
3. **Saul's salvation** = Contrary to common belief, Saul was not saved on the road to Damascus; Jesus told him to enter the city to be told what he "must do"; he fasted and prayed for three days, but he still had his "sins" when Ananias arrived (22:16); Saul was saved when he did what all others did in the book of Acts—he arose and was baptized to wash away his sins.

1. To whom did the Lord say that He had chosen Saul to bear His name?

2. How soon was Saul baptized after Ananias came and preached to him?

3. What man of encouragement took it upon himself to defend Saul to the apostles?

Verse for Meditation and Prayer: **Acts 9:20**

"Immediately he preached the Christ in the synagogues, that He is the Son of God."

Mark Your Bible

1. **Acts 7:6**—Israel would be slaves in Egypt for roughly 400 years (perhaps rounding off the number, like in Genesis 15:13).
2. **Acts 7:33**—The ground was "holy" because the Lord was there.
3. **Acts 7:35-39**—The Jews had rejected Moses in his day, just as the Jews in Stephen's day had rejected their Deliverer, whom Moses prophesied was coming to redeem His people.
4. **Acts 7:42**—When people reject God, He "gives them up" and allows them to engage fully in their rebellious evil (Rom. 1:24-28).
5. **Acts 7:43**—Moloch (or Molech) was an Ammonite god whose worshipers offered children as sacrifices.
6. **Acts 7:51-52**—Circle the word "you." This is the first time that Stephen directs his words openly and bluntly at his listeners.
7. **Acts 7:51**—"Stiff-necked" denoted ones who were stubborn and unyielding, like farm animals refusing a yoke. "Uncircumcised in heart" denounced them as acting like pagans and heathens.
8. **Acts 7:56**—Even in heaven, Jesus was still seen as "the Son of Man," denoting His incarnation and human nature.
9. **Acts 7:58**—The Greek for "young man" indicates 24-40 years old.
10. **Acts 7:59**—The imperfect tense indicates they were ceaselessly "stoning" him, and the present tense indicates that Stephen kept on "calling" on the Lord in prayer. They kept on and he kept on.
11. **Acts 7:59-60**—At death, the "spirit" leaves the body and continues to live, and the body goes to "sleep" at the separation of the spirit.
12. **Acts 8:3**—The verb "made havoc" is in the imperfect tense, emphasizing ongoing, continual ravaging of the Christians.
13. **Acts 8:4, 12, 25, 35, 40**—The Greek word for "preached" in these verses is *euangelizo,* which means "to bring good news, glad tidings." You can see the English "evangelize," which is our responsibility to announce the good news of Jesus Christ and His salvation.

(continued on next page)

Mark Your Bible

14. **Acts 8:4, 5, 12, 25, 35**—Mark and connect what they were preaching (all parallel to each other and essentials for N.T. preaching): "the word," "Christ," "the kingdom of God," "the name of Jesus Christ," "the word of the Lord," "the gospel" and "Jesus."
15. **Acts 8:5**—This Philip is one of the seven in Acts 6, not the apostle.
16. **Acts 8:10-13**—Preaching the gospel and Christ involves commands to be obeyed—they "heeded...believed...were baptized."
17. **Acts 8:12-13**—The people "believed and were baptized" to be saved, just as Jesus taught (Mark 16:16).
18. **Acts 8:26**—God's providence was at work to send Philip from the very populated Samaria to teach one man in a desolate place about 50 miles away. Philip had to leave at least one day or more before the Ethiopian left Jerusalem, in order to meet at the right place.
19. **Acts 8:27**—The Ethiopian eunuch was a dedicated proselyte to Judaism, who had traveled 200 miles to worship.
20. **Acts 8:34**—Jesus said that Isaiah 53 was about Him (Luke 22:37).
21. **Acts 8:35**—Preaching "Jesus" includes the essentiality of baptism.
22. **Acts 8:38-39**—Baptism is an "immersion"—going down, coming up.
23. **Acts 8:39**—The "rejoicing" took place after the baptism, not before.
24. **Acts 9:2**—Saul was receiving authoritative arrest warrants from the Jewish council to "bind all who call" on Christ (v. 14, 21).
25. **Acts 9:2**—It was 140 miles from Jerusalem to Damascus and would take a week to travel. Saul was determined to exterminate Christians everywhere.
26. **Acts 9:3-6**—In order to be an apostle, one of the qualifications was to see the resurrected Lord (1:22). This was one purpose for this event (1 Cor. 9:1; 15:8).
27. **Acts 9:4**—In persecuting the church and its saints (v. 13), Saul was persecuting Christ Himself. Christ and the church are inseparably connected.

Mark Your Bible

28. **Acts 9:6**—Underline "must do." Whatever Saul would be told in the city was a "must." Baptism is not optional but a must (22:16)!
29. **Acts 9:18**—There is no essential connection between the scales falling from his eyes and salvation. They were scales, not sins.
30. **Acts 9:20**—The Greek imperfect tense emphasizes that Saul was "continually preaching" Christ "is" (present tense) the Son of God.
31. **Acts 9:22**—The Greek word for "proving" literally means "to bring together." He was bringing together (1) the O.T. prophecies with (2) the facts about Jesus to draw a logical, irrefutable conclusion.
32. **Acts 9:23**—The "many days" are likely when he went to Arabia (Gal. 1:17).
33. **Acts 9:26**—It had been three years since Saul was there persecuting the Christians (Gal. 1:18), but his reputation remained.
34. **Acts 9:28**—He was in Jerusalem for 15 days (Gal. 1:18).
35. **Acts 9:30**—Saul was in Tarsus for about 6 years until Acts 11:25.
36. **Acts 9:31**—The word "multiplied" is in the Greek imperfect tense, which indicates that the church "kept on multiplying" repeatedly.
37. **Acts 9:35**—Many "turned to the Lord," which is an indication of their conversion. Acts 11:21 shows that "turning to the Lord" takes place after believing, and Acts 26:20 shows it takes place after repentance. So, what does their "turning to the Lord" involve? Comparing Acts 2:38 and 3:19 shows they did not fully turn to the Lord until, after believing and repenting, they were baptized.
38. **Acts 9:39**—Her body was still there but she was no longer "with them." She was absent from the body but present with the Lord (2 Cor. 5:1-8). There is a difference between a person and his/her body.
39. **Acts 9:42**—The "believing on the Lord" involves the same thing as the "turning to the Lord" (v. 35) and being "baptized" (v. 18), which is all the fullness of God's plan of salvation.

(continued on next page)

Mark Your Bible

40. **Acts 10:1**—Caesarea was 30 miles north of Joppa, 70 miles NW of Jerusalem and was the Roman headquarters in Palestine.
41. **Acts 10:6**—Underline "He will tell you what you must do." This is the same thing that Jesus told Saul in Acts 9:6. Those who are lost must be "told" God's Word in order to learn, obey and be saved.
42. **Acts 10:15**—Under Christ's new covenant, (1) all animals are clean (Mark 7:19; 1 Tim. 4:3-4), (2) the law of Moses was void (Col. 2:14; Eph. 2:13-15), (3) the Gentiles (and all nations) are to be brought into God's fold (Eph. 3:6), and (4) all are one in Christ (Gal. 3:28).
43. **Acts 10:25-26**—Peter did not accept any worship. Peter was not the first Pope and no man should be bowed before in worship today.
44. **Acts 10:28**—While Peter was doing that which was "unlawful" according to Jewish custom, he was doing what God had told him to do.
45. **Acts 10:30**—Cornelius was not saved by praying to God (cf. v. 4).
46. **Acts 10:34-43**—The gospel is for all! Underline the words "every," "all," "people" and "whoever."
47. **Acts 10:35**—Cornelius had already "feared" God (10:2, 22), but he had not yet obeyed God's commands (righteousness). Thus, he was not yet "accepted" (i.e., saved), though he was a very devout man. To "work righteousness" is to obey God (Matt. 3:15; Rom. 6:16).
48. **Acts 10:43, 48**—"Believes" is in the present tense and stands as a summary term of all that is necessary in order to receive "remission of sins." God is no respecter of persons. The Jews were commanded to "repent and be baptized in the name of the Lord" to be saved (2:38) and so were the Gentiles (10:48; 11:18). God's plan is the same for all—believe (10:43), repent (11:18) and be baptized (10:48).
49. **Acts 10:44**—Draw a line from "still speaking these things" to "began to speak" in 11:15. The Holy Spirit fell on them before Peter told them about Jesus and His salvation. They were not saved yet.

Mark Your Bible

50. **Acts 10:45-46**—This was the purpose of the Gentiles being baptized with the Holy Spirit.

51. **Acts 10:47**—Water baptism is distinct from Holy Spirit baptism. Today, there is only "one baptism" (Eph. 4:5)—water baptism.

52. **Acts 11:9-18**—Peter defended his actions to the Jews by saying it was God's will and not his. Underline "God," "Spirit," "Holy Spirit," "Lord," "He" and "angel" in these verses. The key is verse 17.

53. **Acts 11:14**—Underline this whole verse. This is key. They were not saved until they heard and responded to the "words" from God.

54. **Acts 11:15-17**—Holy Spirit baptism occurred only twice (Acts 2 and 10). Peter's memory had to go back to Pentecost for a parallel to what he was seeing and he remembered the promise of Jesus about baptizing with the Holy Spirit. These verses connect Acts 2 and 10. Draw a line from "at the beginning" (11:15) to "same gift" (11:17) to "also" (10:45) to "just as we" (10:47)—this fulfilled Joel 2:28.

55. **Acts 11:18**—What God granted them was the opportunity (viewed as a gift) to repent and get their lives right with God. It is used as a synecdoche of all the steps needed for salvation as "believes" is in 10:43. The "sum" of God's Word is truth (Psa. 119:160), not "some."

56. **Acts 11:19-20**—Antioch of Syria was the third largest city in Roman Empire (behind Rome and Alexandria) with about 500,000 people.

57. **Acts 11:21**—"Turned to the Lord" takes place in baptism (3:19).

58. **Acts 11:23**—There would be no purpose in continually urging (the tense of the verb) the Christians to keep on continuing (the tense of the verb) with the Lord if they could not fall away and be lost.

59. **Acts 11:25**—Tarsus was about 120 miles to the west of Antioch. Paul had been there for about 6-8 years, preaching "the faith" (Gal. 1:23).

60. **Acts 11:30**—This is the first time "elders" of the church are mentioned in Scripture.

Day of Reflection

Take time today to reflect on the five chapters that you read this week. You may choose to read all five chapters again, in one sitting, or certain parts of them. Take time today to answer at least one of these questions below. You may or may not write anything down—you can choose to write or simply reflect.

1. What personal application do I need to make from the chapters I have read this week?

2. How can these five chapters help draw me closer to Jesus?

3. What words, phrases or verses in these chapters do I want to go back and study more in depth?

4. What questions do I have about what I have read this week on which I need to do some further Biblical research?

Week 21

May 21-27

May 21	Read Acts 12
May 22	Read Acts 13
May 23	Read Acts 14
May 24	Read Acts 15
May 25	Read Acts 16
May 26	Mark Your Bible
May 27	Day of Reflection

Prayer for this week:

"Heavenly Father,
please help me to trust You more
and lean on my own understanding less."

Acts 12

Helpful Notes:

1. **Herod Agrippa I** = This Herod is the grandson of Herod the Great (who tried to murder baby Jesus), the nephew of Herod Antipas (who beheaded John the Baptist) and the father of Herod Agrippa II (who was "almost persuaded" by Paul); he was made king over Judea and Samaria by Claudius Caesar in A.D. 41.
2. **Confidence in prayer** = The church was in "constant prayer" for Peter when he was imprisoned by Herod; they were "gathered together praying" (present tense emphasizes constancy); but when Peter (for whom they were praying) came to the house, they did not believe and were "astonished"; we must have "confidence toward God" in our prayers that He "hears us" and that "we have the petitions" we ask of Him (1 John 5:14-15; 3:21-22; Jas. 1:6-8).
3. **James** = There are two men named James in this chapter; the first, who was killed by Herod, was the son of Zebedee and brother of the apostle John; the second was the brother of Jesus (Matt. 13:55), who did not believe in Jesus until after His resurrection (John 7:5; Acts 1:14), when Jesus appeared to him (1 Cor. 15:7); he was becoming an influential leader in the Jerusalem church (15:13; 21:18; Gal. 2:9); he wrote the book of James in the New Testament.

1. Why did Herod seize Peter after he murdered James?

2. What did Peter not realize when the angel was freeing him from prison?

3. What reason does the Bible give that Herod was struck dead?

Verse for Meditation and Prayer: **Acts 12:23**

"Then immediately an angel of the Lord struck him, because he did not give glory to God."

Acts 13

Helpful Notes:

1. **Laid hands** = The expression "laid hands on them" is used in various ways in the N.T. and the context will determine the meaning; only the apostles could impart a miraculous gift to another through their hands (Acts 8:14-18; 19:6; 2 Tim. 1:6); others, like elders (1 Tim. 4:14) and Christian brethren, laid hands (perhaps in a ceremony) as a sign of confidence and commissioning to work.
2. **Word of this salvation** = The word "word" is found nine times in this chapter; the phrases "the word of God" and "the word of the Lord" refer to the objective message of truth that was preached and written; here God's Word is "the word of this salvation," emphasizing that salvation is tied to an objective standard that can be understood alike, taught alike and obeyed alike.
3. **Appointed to eternal life** = Some attempt to teach predestination in verse 48, but that ignores the context and grammar; in verse 46, the Jews had "rejected for (i.e., thrust away from) themselves" (middle voice) the gospel and "determined" themselves to be "unworthy of eternal life" (they made the choice); verse 48 is contrasting the Gentiles with the Jews; the Gentiles had "believed" (i.e., fully obeyed) the gospel, having "determined" themselves (middle voice) to have been offered "eternal life" from God (they made the choice); both made choices that affected their eternity.

1. What did Paul do to Elymas as a punitive miracle for constantly opposing the truth?
2. To whom did Paul turn when the Jews continued rejecting the Word?
3. What did Paul and Barnabas do when expelled from the city?

Verse for Meditation and Prayer: **Acts 13:38**

"Therefore let it be known to you, brethren, that through this Man is preached to you the forgiveness of sins."

May 23

Week 21, Day 3

Acts 14

Helpful Notes:

1. **God's general providence** = Providence involves God's active preservation and care over His creation; Paul told the idolaters that they needed to "turn" to "the living God," who not only "made all things," but He sustains all things; His providential care (the rain, the seasons, the food and gladness) is a perpetual "witness" of His Divine power and loving care.
2. **Enter the kingdom** = One enters the present phase of "the kingdom" (i.e., the church) when one is baptized into Christ, being "born again" (John 3:3-5; 1 Cor. 12:13); the word "kingdom" is also used in some passages to describe "the eternal kingdom" in "heaven" (2 Pet. 1:11; 2 Tim. 4:18), into which one "must through many tribulations enter"; one must be in the kingdom now in order to be delivered into the heavenly kingdom (1 Cor. 15:24).
3. **Elders in every church** = God's design for His church is that each congregation should have qualified men (1 Tim. 3:1-7; Tit. 1:5-9) from "among" the congregation (Acts 20:28; 1 Pet. 5:2) overseeing the work and shepherding the members; every N.T. passage emphasizes that congregations have a plurality of men serving as elders, never just one man (i.e., elder/pastor); it is likely that these early elders had spiritual gifts imparted to them (Eph. 4:8, 11).

1. What did Paul and Barnabas do when the people of Lystra started calling them "gods"?

2. What had God done to "not leave Himself without witness"?

3. What did Paul and Barnabas do on their way back to Antioch of Syria (v. 22)?

Verse for Meditation and Prayer: **Acts 14:17**

"Nevertheless He did not leave Himself without witness,
in that He did good, gave us rain from heaven and fruitful seasons,
filling our hearts with food and gladness."

May 24 Week 21, Day 4

Acts 15

Helpful Notes:

1. **Dissension and dispute** = Some people are so uncomfortable with disagreements that they suggest we should just "go along to get along"; however, false teaching must never be tolerated (Tit. 1:9-11), and Christians must contend for God's truth (Jude 3); there was an "uproar from strife that led to discord" (i.e., "dissension") and vigorous "debate"; such must happen when error is espoused, for compromise is not an option, even for an hour (Gal. 2:5).
2. **Judaizers** = While the Bible does not give this group a particular name, this is the designation commonly given to those Christians who were of a strong Jewish background and were troubling the church by demanding adherence to both the law of Moses and the gospel, teaching that circumcision was a condition of salvation (15:1, 6); Paul fought against these false teachers regularly, in life and letter, emphasizing there is "not another" gospel (Gal. 1:6-9).
3. **Saved in the same manner** = God's plan of salvation is universally available (Tit. 2:11; Mark 16:15) and its conditions are universally applicable (Acts 10:34-35); the Gentiles were saved by the same gospel as the Jews, and the same requirements were made of both groups—believers in Christ were commanded to "repent" (Acts 2:38; 11:18) and be "baptized (2:38; 10:48); God "made no distinction" (15:9), and He does not make any distinction today either!

1. What response was prompted by hearing of the conversion of the Gentiles?

2. What did Barnabas and Paul report that God had done among the Gentiles?

3. Who did Paul choose as his new travel companion?

Verse for Meditation and Prayer: **Acts 15:18**

"Known to God from eternity are all His works."

Acts 16

Helpful Notes:

1. **Timothy** = Timothy was from Lystra and had a good reputation; he was raised by a Jewish mother who became a Christian but his father was a Greek (and not a Christian, and perhaps deceased); he learned the Scriptures early (2 Tim. 1:5; 3:15) and was probably converted by Paul (1 Tim. 1:2) on Paul's first missionary journey (Acts 14:6; 2 Tim. 3:11); although their age difference was maybe 30 years, Paul and Timothy became close friends (Phil. 2:19-22).
2. **The Lord opened her heart** = Some contend that the Lord took the initiative through a direct operation of the Holy Spirit to open her heart without her awareness or direction, but such is false; the order of events is (1) Paul "spoke" (imperfect, ongoing message), then (2) Lydia "heard" (imperfect, kept listening with interest), then (3) her heart was "opened" to "the things spoken by Paul"; it was the Word of God that opened her heart. (See Mark Your Bible)
3. **Believe, having believed** = "Believe" in verse 31 is an aorist imperative marking urgency and point of action; he was not being taught "faith only"—as a pagan, he needed to hear about and believe on the Lord (16:32; Rom. 10:17); but Biblical belief is a comprehensive term for full obedience (14:1-2; John 3:36); "believed" in verse 34 is perfect tense, denoting abiding belief, which summarizes and encompasses the entire conversion process, including baptism; baptism and belief are inseparable in salvation (Mark 16:16).

1. From what region did Paul receive a vision to preach the gospel?

2. What city in that region was the foremost city where Paul worked?

3. What were Paul and Silas doing while in prison?

Verse for Meditation and Prayer: **Acts 16:9**

"And a vision appeared to Paul in the night.
A man of Macedonia stood and pleaded with him, saying,
'Come over to Macedonia and help us.'"

Mark Your Bible

1. **Acts 12:2**—This fulfilled Jesus' prophecy to James that he would "drink the cup" of suffering that Jesus drank (Mark 10:39).
2. **Acts 12:4**—Peter was guarded by four squads of four soldiers each, who alternated shifts every three hours during the night. This would have been the same arrangement at Jesus' tomb (Matt. 27:65-66).
3. **Acts 12:4**—The last word is "Passover," not "Easter" as in the KJV.
4. **Acts 12:6**—The fact that Peter was sleeping on the night before his execution shows his faith and confidence in His Lord.
5. **Acts 12:19**—It was standard procedure to execute guards who lost their charge, which sheds light on the Philippian jailer who was getting ready to kill himself in Acts 16:27. It also shows the vileness that surrounded the execution of Jesus, seeing that His guards were not executed.
6. **Acts 12:19**—Caesarea was the headquarters of the Roman government in Palestine.
7. **Acts 12:22**—The phrase "kept shouting" is a Greek imperfect tense, emphasizing a continuing and ongoing chant. Herod had plenty of time to stop them, correct them and refuse their praise.
8. **Acts 12:24**—Circle the word "But." The verbs "grew" and "multiplied" are both imperfect tense, emphasizing continual, steady progress. It seemed that the more the disciples were persecuted, the faster and wider the church grew.
9. **Acts 12:25**—John Mark was a cousin of Barnabas (Col. 4:10).
10. **Acts 13:1**—Manaen was the foster brother of Herod Antipas, who executed John the Baptist. The gospel is powerful and impartial. The church had welcomed him into the fellowship.
11. **Acts 13:2**—The Holy Spirit is a person of the Godhead (not a mystical force). He "said" and called Himself, "Me." Only a person does that (cf. John 14:26; Acts 10:19-20; 15:28; 16:6).

(continued on next page)

Mark Your Bible

12. **Acts 13:3**—Note these facts about Paul's First Missionary Journey: recorded in 13:1-14:28, covering 47-49 A.D. (approx.). Travel companions included Barnabas and John Mark.

13. **Acts 13:8**—The word "withstood" means to "set oneself against," even in a face-to-face confrontation, and the imperfect tense indicates that Elymas kept on opposing Barnabas and Saul repeatedly.

14. **Acts 13:8**—There is "one" objective body of truth called "the faith."

15. **Acts 13:9-10**—The expression "son of the devil" means that Elymas took on the character or nature of the devil.

16. **Acts 13:12**—The word "believed" summarizes his full obedience to the gospel (cf. 16:34; 4:32; 5:14). The proconsul became a Christian.

17. **Acts 13:13**—The reason for John Mark's departure is not stated. He returned to Jerusalem, his hometown and where his mother lived (12:12). Whatever the reason was did not please Paul (15:37-39).

18. **Acts 13:16, 26**—"You who fear God" refers to the Gentiles (cf. 10:2).

19. **Acts 13:22, 36**—Draw a line from the prophecy that David "will do all My will" to fulfillment that "he had served...by the will of God."

20. **Acts 13:33**—This Messianic prophecy embraces Jesus' incarnation (Heb. 1:5), resurrection (Acts 13:22) and priesthood (Heb. 5:5).

21. **Acts 13:34**—The resurrection of Jesus was permanent (never to die again), and due to His resurrection the "blessings of David," promised through Isaiah (55:3), are now available. This has nothing to do with a future 1,000–year reign of Christ. Paul said it was fulfilled in the Christian age upon the resurrection of Christ.

22. **Acts 13:43**—These had obviously been converted, as they are now urged to "continue in the grace of God." One cannot continue in something in which he has not entered. If they needed to continue, then grace is not irresistible, as some claim. One saved can be lost.

23. **Acts 13:47**—It was prophesied that the gospel would be taken to the Gentiles (Isa. 49:6). What Isaiah wrote was from "the Lord."

Mark Your Bible

24. **Acts 14:1-2**—The inspired author contrasts those who "believed" (v. 1) with those who were "disobedient" (v. 2, ASV). In the book of Acts, to "believe" was to "obey" (cf. John 3:36; Heb. 3:18-19).
25. **Acts 14:3**—The Biblical purpose of miracles was to "confirm," "bear witness" to the validity of the message (Mark 16:17-20; Heb. 2:3-4).
26. **Acts 14:4**—"Apostles" is used in its generic sense, meaning "ones sent," not in its specific sense. Barnabas was not an authorized apostle like Paul, but he was a messenger sent (Phil. 2:25; Gal. 1:19).
27. **Acts 14:12**—There was a temple of Zeus outside the city of Lystra and a statue of Hermes that was dedicated to Zeus.
28. **Acts 14:19**—Likely Timothy was there (16:1; 2 Tim. 3:11).
29. **Acts 14:21**—Disciples are made, according to Jesus, by teaching and baptizing them (Matt. 28:19-20). A disciple is a Christian (11:26).
30. **Acts 14:22**—Christians need to be strengthened and encouraged. The fact that they are urged to "continue" emphasizes that one can choose to not continue and that there would be consequences.
31. **Acts 14:22**—While some discount the importance of doctrine, Christians are urged to continue in "the faith"—the pure gospel system (Gal. 1:11+23), of which there is only "one" (Eph. 4:5).
32. **Acts 14:28**—There are two possible dates for the writing of the book of Galatians (an early and a late date). If the early date is correct, it was likely written during this "long" stay in Antioch.
33. **Acts 15:2**—Paul was an apostle and his authority (from God) should have been sufficient. This shows that Paul was still not viewed on an equal level with the other apostles, and it also shows Paul's humility to go, when he knew he was an equal (2 Cor. 11:5).
34. **Acts 15:3**—The word "conversion" is from the Greek *epistrepho,* which literally means "to turn about, to turn towards." The Gentiles were "changing their way of thinking" from error to truth.

(continued on next page)

Mark Your Bible

35. **Acts 15:4**—The events in this chapter seem to parallel Paul's recounting in Galatians 2:1-10.

36. **Acts 15:4**—In this discussion about the relationship of the law of Moses to Christianity, everyone who spoke focused their attention squarely on "God," as the authority and as the one deserving the credit. Circle "God" in verses 4, 7, 8, 10, 12, 14, 18, 19 and circle "prophets" in verse 15 (who spoke for God) and "Lord" in verse 17.

37. **Acts 15:9**—"Faith" at the end of this verse is "the faith" (the definite article is in the Greek). Salvation is by "the faith" (i.e., the gospel system, Gal. 1:23, Jude 3) and not the law of Moses. Peter later wrote souls are "purified" by "obeying the truth" (1 Pet. 1:22).

38. **Acts 15:10**—Demanding the keeping of the law of Moses was a "yoke" because (1) the law must be kept perfectly (Gal. 3:10) and (2) keeping one part obligated them to the whole law (Gal. 5:3).

39. **Acts 15:13**—This James is the brother of Jesus, introduced in Acts 12 as a leader in the Jerusalem church (12:17; cf. Gal. 1:19; 2:9).

40. **Acts 15:15-18**—Inspiration applies the prophecy from Amos 9:11-15 to the inclusion of the Gentiles in the church in the first century. This was part of God's plan "from eternity," and it has nothing to do with a supposed "national Israel" in a so-called "millennium."

41. **Acts 15:20**—Animals that were not properly bled were referred to as "strangled" (cf. Lev. 17:13-14).

42. **Acts 15:20, 21, 28**—These regulations are "necessary things" and were to be binding long-term. Their principles are even found in the law of Moses, although that is no longer binding as law.

43. **Acts 15:24**—The Greek word for "unsettling" (*anaskeuazo*) meant "to tear down, dismantle, cause inward distress." In the military, it meant to plunder a town, pack it up and carry it off.

44. **Acts 15:36**—Note these facts about Paul's Second Missionary Journey: recorded in 15:36-18:22, covering 50-52 A.D. (approx.). Travel companions included Silas, Timothy and Luke.

Mark Your Bible

45. **Acts 15:36**—It is not enough just to baptize people. Every effort must be made to help them mature in the faith and remain steadfast.

46. **Acts 15:37-38**—The verbs "was determined" and "insisted" are both in the imperfect tense, indicating a constant, unyielding action. Neither man was giving up his position.

47. **Acts 15:37-39**—While Paul did not want to work with John Mark at this point, later Paul said that Mark "is useful to me for ministry" (2 Tim. 4:11).

48. **Acts 16:1**—Paul was stoned and left for dead in this city (14:19-21).

49. **Acts 16:3**—Paul circumcised Timothy as a matter of expediency and not a matter of salvation. They did not want to unnecessarily offend the Jews while working among them (cf. 1 Cor. 9:20).

50. **Acts 16:3**—This is likely when Paul laid hands on Timothy to impart a miraculous gift (2 Tim. 1:6), if he had not on the first journey. In leaving his home congregation, this must have been when the elders laid their hands on Timothy in prayerful confidence and commissioning him for the work (1 Tim. 4:14; cf. Acts 13:3).

51. **Acts 16:5**—Both verbs ("strengthened" and "increased") are in the imperfect tense, denoting ongoing, sustained progress.

52. **Acts 16:10**—The pronoun now changes from "they" to "we." This is when Luke joins the mission team for a time. Circle "we."

53. **Acts 16:12**—The gospel (and Paul's mission team) reaches Europe.

54. **Acts 16:13**—This may indicate the city did not have a synagogue, which required a minimum of ten Jewish men in a city.

55. **Acts 16:14**—"To heed" (present tense) means that she was obedient to the things that she heard (8:6, 12). In obeying, she was baptized.

(continued on next page)

Mark Your Bible

56. **Acts 16:15**—There is no Scriptural basis for using this verse to justify infant baptism. No infants are mentioned. "Household" is from the Greek *oikos,* which often meant or included "property," like servants (which is most likely its use here). Whoever was baptized was mature enough to believe in Christ and to repent of sins. If "household" includes infants being baptized in this verse, then "household" must include infants believing in 18:8 and fearing God in 10:2.

57. **Acts 16:17-18**—Demons always spoke the truth about Christ (Mark 1:24; 3:11), but demons were not the witnesses Christ wanted.

58. **Acts 16:22-23**—The Jews limited their beatings to 40 stripes (but they stopped at 39, 2 Cor. 11:24), but the Romans had no limits. This is one of the three times that Paul referenced (2 Cor. 11:25).

59. **Acts 16:27**—Roman law required the death of one whose prisoners escaped (12:19). Taking his own life was thought to be more noble.

60. **Acts 16:33**—He was baptized "the same hour of the night" and "immediately." If baptism is not essential for salvation, why not wait?

61. **Act 16:34**—The "rejoicing" took place after the baptism, not before.

62. **Acts 16:40**—Circle the two uses of "they" in the last part of the verse. "They" saw the brethren and "they" departed indicates that Luke stayed in Philippi. (There was a famous medical school there. Perhaps that was the reason that he stayed, and also to work with the church in Philippi.) Also of interest is that "they encouraged them," meaning instead of the church encouraging the missionaries who had been beaten, the beaten missionaries encouraged the new converts.

Day of Reflection

Take time today to reflect on the five chapters that you read this week. You may choose to read all five chapters again, in one sitting, or certain parts of them. Take time today to answer at least one of these questions below. You may or may not write anything down—you can choose to write or simply reflect.

1. What personal application do I need to make from the chapters I have read this week?

2. How can these five chapters help draw me closer to Jesus?

3. What words, phrases or verses in these chapters do I want to go back and study more in depth?

4. What questions do I have about what I have read this week on which I need to do some further Biblical research?

Week 22

May 28-June 3

May 28	Read Acts 17
May 29	Read Acts 18
May 30	Read Acts 19
May 31	Read Acts 20
June 1	Read Acts 21
June 2	Mark Your Bible
June 3	Day of Reflection

Prayer for this week:

"Heavenly Father,
help me to see souls around me every day
who need the gospel."

May 28 Week 22, Day 1

Acts 17

Helpful Notes:

1. **Reasoned** = The Greek word literally means "to speak through or thoroughly"; it involved "bringing together different reasons," which would often result in "disputes"; by using reasoning, Paul would (1) "explain," literally "open up completely," taking the O.T. prophecies about the Messiah; then (2) "demonstrate," literally "place beside or set before" the historical facts about Jesus of Nazareth; finally (3) draw the only reasonable conclusion that "Jesus is the Christ," the promised Messiah of the O.T.; this is the effective way to use the Bible to teach the Bible.
2. **To the Unknown God** = The word for "unknown" is *agnostos,* combining the negative *a* ("without" or "not") and *gnosis* ("knowledge"); in verse 24, the Greek definite article precedes "God" to emphasize that Paul is going to preach to them about "the God," not merely "one of the gods," as they were inclined to worship many; the one true God can and must be known.
3. **Made from one** = All "nations" (Greek *ethnos*) have been "made" (not evolved, but the result of a creative act) "from" (Greek word *ek* is literally, "out of") "one"; the word "blood" or "man" is not in the original; the word "one" is masculine denoting that all persons have their origin in "one male" (i.e., Adam); there are not multiple races of people—there is only one race, that is, the human race!

1. Why would Paul make it his custom to go to a Jewish synagogue?

2. What made the Bereans "more fair-minded" than others?

3. Who has been appointed as our Judge and what assurance is there?

Verse for Meditation and Prayer: **Acts 17:30**

"Truly, these times of ignorance God overlooked, but now commands all men everywhere to repent."

Acts 18

Helpful Notes:

1. **Believed and baptized** = The term "believed" at the beginning of verse 8 is a summary term that includes everything necessary for one to become a Christian, including baptism (16:33-34); this is evidenced by the fact that Crispus (who "believed") was personally baptized by Paul (1 Cor. 1:14); this verse does not teach salvation by "faith alone," as evidenced by the further explanation at the end of the verse—those who "believed" were "baptized" in order to be "saved" (Mark 16:16).
2. **Providence in judgment** = Paul was put on trial before the proconsul/governor Gallio for preaching the gospel, but the governor was not interested in bringing church issues into the civil court (perhaps "words and names" meant talking about things like "Jesus" and "Messiah," which didn't belong in a civil court); it has been suggested that the governor's decision on this day was God's providential way of opening the door for the gospel and the advancement of the kingdom throughout the Roman empire.
3. **Correction** = One may "instruct" others "in the way of the Lord" but still be in error and need correction; Apollos (1) was sincere and fervent but he was wrong; (2) was taught incorrectly and needed to be corrected; (3) was right about so much but wrong about baptism and was, therefore, not truly teaching "the way of God"; (4) learned the "one baptism" of N.T. Christianity.

1. Why did Paul shake his garments?

2. How long did Paul stay teaching in Corinth?

3. On what topic did Apollos need to be corrected?

Verse for Meditation and Prayer: **Acts 18:8**

"Then Crispus, the ruler of the synagogue, believed on the Lord with all his household. And many of the Corinthians, hearing, believed and were baptized.

Acts 19

Helpful Notes:

1. **The one baptism** = Twelve men were baptized with John's baptism years after John's baptism was no longer a valid baptism, as they were taught to "believe on [Christ Jesus] who would come after," but Christ had already come; when they learned that their baptism was not the "one baptism" (Eph. 4:5) that Christ gave, they were "baptized in the name of the Lord Jesus"; being baptized is not sufficient (and is not acceptable to God) if it is not the one baptism of the N.T.; one must be taught and obey properly.
2. **Miracles** = Key truths are learned about miracles in verses 11-15: (1) miracles were done "by" (Greek *dia*) the hands of those with such abilities, as the preposition emphasizes the person was merely the channel through which it was worked; (2) God was the one who "worked" the miracles; (3) the power was not in the miracle worker but in God; (4) only those given the power by God could actually do miracles, others could only "feign" such power; (5) genuine Bible miracles are not done today, only "feigning" efforts.
3. **Confess** = The Greek word here (*exomologeo*) is the common word for confess with the added prefix *ex* ("out"), meaning, "to confess forth, openly, freely; make a public admission of wrong-doing/sin"; the confession of wrong was made as widely as the offense was known; when a sin is realized, it must be admitted and abandoned.

1. Why were 12 men baptized when they had already been baptized?

2. How much were the magic books that were burned worth?

3. What did the Ephesian mob keep chanting?

Verse for Meditation and Prayer: **Acts 19:10**

"And this continued for two years, so that all who dwelt in Asia heard the word of the Lord Jesus, both Jews and Greeks."

Acts 20

Helpful Notes:

1. **To break bread** = The first day of the week had great significance to N.T. Christians (see note for 20:7); Scripture uses "the breaking of the bread" (Acts 2:42) as a figure of speech for the Lord's Supper; the prepositional phrase "to break bread" is an infinitive of purpose, denoting the reason and authority for the church to assemble every week; only in the first-day-of-the-week assembly is the Lord's Supper to be observed, and it is to be done every Sunday; the Lord's Supper cannot be separated from the Lord's Day, and vice versa.
2. **The whole counsel of God** = God's truth must not be compromised, added to, taken from or modified in any way (Rev. 22:18-19; Gal. 1:6-9); the entirety of God's plan for saving man must be taught, without "keeping back anything" (v. 20) or being selective based upon personal likes and dislikes (or based upon likes or dislikes of the listeners); Paul taught the same thing every place that he went (1 Cor. 4:17; 7:17; 14:33; 16:1).
3. **False teachers and teachings** = False teachers are "savage wolves" (vicious enemies of the truth, Matt. 7:15); some may "come in" from without and some may "rise up" "from among" the church (and even from the leadership), but none of them (the persons or their doctrines) can be tolerated one iota because there are souls at stake; this warning matters because Christians can fall away and be lost.

1. For what purpose did the church come together every Sunday?

2. Although "chains and tribulations" awaited Paul, what did he say about that?

3. What is one major reason that elders must watch over the flock?

Verse for Meditation and Prayer: **Acts 20:28**

"Therefore take heed to yourselves and to all the flock, among which the Holy Spirit has made you overseers, to shepherd the church of God which He purchased with His own blood."

June 1

Week 22, Day 5

Acts 21

Helpful Notes:

1. **Daughters who prophesied** = It was prophesied that both "sons and daughters shall prophesy" (2:17-18), which likely indicates that these ladies had the miraculous, spiritual gift of prophecy (1 Cor. 12:10); they, no doubt, found opportunities to speak and exercise this gift in full harmony with the specified role of women in the church (1 Cor. 14:34; 1 Tim. 2:12; Tit. 2:3-5; Acts 18:26); there is no indication that they taught over a man in an assembly.
2. **Ready to die** = Although Paul knew that "chains and tribulations" (20:23; 21:4, 11) awaited him in Jerusalem, "none" of those things moved him and he did not "count [his] life dear" to himself (20:24), for he was "ready," if necessary, "to die" for Christ (21:13) and to go to Christ, which is "far better" (Phil. 1:21-23); Paul places a premium on eternal life over physical life (Rev. 2:10; 2 Tim. 4:6-8).
3. **Purification** = The event of Paul and the purification is difficult, so consider this: Paul had circumcised Timothy as a matter of expediency, but not as a matter of salvation; Paul had written clearly of the abolition of the law (2 Cor. 3; Rom. 7; Gal. 5), so he was not practicing a Jewish custom for religious purposes; Paul could have "purified" himself strictly in conformity to the nationalistic Jewish practice (as a matter of expediency to relieve tension and accomplish a greater good), and not as a redemptive sacrifice in place of Christ's sacrifice to obtain personal forgiveness; the Divine system of Judaism took a while to fully phase out until A.D. 70.

1. What was Paul ready to do for the Lord?

2. Who carried Paul up the stairs to avoid the mob?

3. What two languages could Paul speak?

Verse for Meditation and Prayer: **Acts 21:13**

"Then Paul answered, 'What do you mean by weeping and breaking my heart? For I am ready not only to be bound, but also to die at Jerusalem for the name of the Lord Jesus.'"

Mark Your Bible

1. **Acts 17:4**—The Greek word for "persuaded" is *peitho* and means "to convince, to believe, to obey as a result of persuasion through the influence of reason." These people were converted.
2. **Acts 17:6**—The word used for "world" here was often used specifically for the Roman empire (cf. Luke 2:1).
3. **Acts 17:6**—The Greek for "turned the world upside down" means "to upset the stability of a person or group; disturb, trouble, upset." The gospel, when properly taught, must stir hearts.
4. **Acts 17:11**—"Readiness of mind" is from the Greek *prothumia,* which literally means "a forward mind," expressing an exceptional interest and eagerness to learn the truth.
5. **Acts 17:11**—The word for "search" is *anakrino* and it denotes one who "engages in a careful study of a question" and "examines it thoroughly." It is in the present tense, emphasizing an ongoing activity on their part. They wanted to know the truth and were determined to make sure that what they were being taught "was so."
6. **Acts 17:16**—The word for "provoked" means to "become irritated, angry" and is in the imperfect tense, denoting a constant agitation as he was constantly "beholding" (present tense) all the idols.
7. **Acts 17:16**—It is estimated in that day that there were 30,000 public idols in Athens (not counting the ones in private homes) and about 10,000 residents. They were truly "given over to idols" (3-to-1).
8. **Acts 17:18**—Epicureans were pagan deists (polytheistic evolutionists), who saw the pursuit of pleasure as life's ultimate goal.
9. **Acts 17:18**—Stoics were materialistic pantheists, who believed god is all and all is god, and fate ruled the world.
10. **Acts 17:19**—Areopagus has often been identified as "Mars Hill" in Athens, but it is the name of the highest Athenian legislative body.
11. **Acts 17:24**—The Greek for "world" is *kosmos,* which carries the meaning of "a harmonious arrangement or order." The universe

(continued on next page)

Mark Your Bible

and everything in it (by definition of the word) has been arranged or ordered with precision and did not happen by chance.

12. **Acts 17:25**—The Law of Biogenesis states that "life comes only from life." Therefore, if there is life on earth, it had to come from life.
13. **Acts 17:26**—All human beings are equal in the eyes of God (Acts 10:34) and especially "in Christ" (Gal. 3:28).
14. **Acts 17:27**—God has revealed Himself in a general way through nature (Rom. 1:20; Psa. 19:1) and in a direct way through Scripture (1 Cor. 2:10-13).
15. **Acts 17:30**—God exercised patience with man while Divine revelation was being completed, but with Christ and the fullness of revelation complete, the universal requirement is for all to repent.
16. **Acts 17:34**—"Believed" in this book is always an obedient belief, which includes all compliance with all elements of the gospel, including baptism (Acts 16:33-34).
17. **Acts 18:2**—Jews (and Jewish Christians) were expelled from Rome because of an ongoing and sharp conflict between Jews and Christians over the preaching of Christ.
18. **Acts 18:5**—This would have been the time that Paul wrote First Thessalonians (around 51 A.D.). This is the first of the epistles of Paul that we have in our New Testament.
19. **Acts 18:5**—The "Spirit" is better translated "word." The imperfect tense and middle voice emphasizes that Paul was continually constraining and restricting himself to the Word and preaching it.
20. **Acts 18:6**—Paul's major emphasis shifted from this point forward to the Gentiles, but that does not mean he avoided all teaching to the Jews (Rom. 11:13; 1 Tim. 2:7; 2 Tim. 1:11). Crispus was a Jew.
21. **Acts 18:8**—Some claim that the recording that a "household" was baptized in 16:15, 33-34 is evidence that infants were baptized. If so, then the recording that a "household" believed in this verse must be evidence that infants "believed on the Lord" also (see 10:2 also).

Mark Your Bible

22. **Acts 18:9**—"Do not be afraid" is a present imperative which literally means, "Stop being afraid" (cf. 1 Cor. 2:3; 2 Tim. 1:7).
23. **Acts 18:10**—This promise is fulfilled in verse 16. Draw a line.
24. **Acts 18:11**—While Paul was in Corinth for 18 months, he wrote First Thessalonians (around the time that Silas and Timothy returned from Macedonia in 18:5; cf. 1 Thess. 3:6) and wrote Second Thessalonians a few months later during the 18 months of 18:11.
25. **Acts 18:12**—The *bema* "judgment seat" was a raised platform about 7.5 feet high, where citizens appeared before the officials and where speakers would make their orations.
26. **Acts 18:17**—Sosthenes may have eventually become a Christian (see 1 Cor. 1:1).
27. **Acts 18:18**—The facts of the "vow" are not known. It is possible that it was a personal matter with Paul or that he was seeking to accommodate a Jewish custom for the furtherance of the gospel (cf. 1 Cor. 9:20). There is nothing intrinsically sinful about taking a vow and there is no condemnation of the vow in this text. It is irresponsible to state or assume more than the text states.
28. **Acts 18:21**—Underline "God willing" and note James 4:15.
29. **Acts 18:22-23**—The Second Missionary Journey ends in verse 22, and the Third Missionary Journey begins in verse 23.
30. **Acts 18:23**—Note these facts about Paul's Third Missionary Journey: recorded in 18:23-21:17, covering 53-57 A.D. (approx.). Travel companions included Titus, Luke, Timothy, Erastus (and others).
31. **Acts 18:26**—Both Aquila and Priscilla ("they") were involved in the teaching of Apollos. A woman may teach a man, as long as it does not violate 1 Timothy 2:8-14, putting her in a position of exercising authority "over" the man.
32. **Acts 19:1**—These men were "students" (the meaning of "disciples"), but they were not Christians, saved from their sins.

(continued on next page)

Mark Your Bible

33. **Acts 19:2**—"Believed" is a summary term to denote all that one does in proper obedience to the will of God to be saved.

34. **Acts 19:3-5**—There were several things right about John's baptism: it was an immersion in water (based upon a penitent heart) for the remission of sins (Mark 1:4), and it required a level of faith, but the faith was in the One who *would* come, rather than in the One who *had* come. Although baptism is a right thing to do, it can be ineffective (thus, not actually Bible baptism) if it is not done properly, with the proper understanding and for the proper reason.

35. **Acts 19:5**—"In the name of" in this verse indicates a change of relationship that takes place in baptism. One "becomes the possession of and bears the name of" Christ upon baptism (cf. Matt. 28:19).

36. **Acts 19:6**—These men were given miraculous, spiritual gifts through the apostle's hands (8:14-18), speaking in real languages they did not know and speaking forth for the Lord.

37. **Acts 19:8**—The kingdom of God was/is a present reality (not in a future millennium), entered by the new birth (Matt. 16:18-19; Col. 1:13; John 3:3-5).

38. **Acts 19:9, 23**—See "Helpful Notes" on Acts 9 for "the Way."

39. **Acts 19:9**—Little is known of the school of Tyrannus. This may have been some kind of lecture hall that was used by various teachers.

40. **Acts 19:10**—This could have been the time when congregations were established in Colossae and Laodicea in the region of Asia.

41. **Acts 19:10**—During Paul's total of three years in Ephesus (cf. 20:31) is likely when he wrote our First Corinthians (circa 55 A.D.).

42. **Acts 19:15**—The demon distinguished between Jesus and Paul by using two different verbs: "I *ginosko* Jesus" (know and acknowledge His authority through experience); "I *epistamai* Paul" (am acquainted with). Jesus is greater than Paul.

43. **Acts 19:19**—Repentance is more than feeling sorry; it requires taking action to get away from that sin and rectify one's soul with

Mark Your Bible

God. Sometimes that is costly. These Christians did not merely step away from that which was causing them to sin or give it away to someone else. They destroyed it. Sin (and its devices) is serious!

44. **Acts 19:24**—The temple of Diana (Artemis) was one of the seven wonders of the ancient world. Artemis was a goddess of fertility and many came to "worship" in this temple.

45. **Acts 19:29, 32**—Draw a line from "confusion" in verse 29 to "confused" in verse 32. Sometimes people (even today) go along with what they have heard without investigating for themselves.

46. **Acts 20:1**—While in Macedonia, this is probably when Paul wrote our Second Corinthians (circa 56 A.D.).

47. **Acts 20:2-3**—While in Corinth, this is probably when Paul wrote Romans (circa 56-57 A.D.) and perhaps Galatians (see 14:28).

48. **Acts 20:5-6**—Circle the words "us" and "we." Luke has rejoined the traveling group, probably at Philippi where he was left in 16:40.

49. **Acts 20:6**—Paul was in a hurry to get to Jerusalem (v. 16). Why stay in Troas for seven days? Likely it was to meet with the saints on the Lord's Day (v. 7).

50. **Acts 20:7**—The "first day of the week" is (1) when Christ was raised from the dead (Mark 16:1-2), (2) when the disciples were meeting together from the beginning (John 20:19, 26), (3) when the church was established (Acts 2:1), (4) when the congregation in Troas was meeting (20:7), (5) when the Christians contributed to the church every week (1 Cor. 16:1-2), (6) called "the Lord's Day" (Rev. 1:10). God has sanctified this day for N.T. Christians.

51. **Acts 20:7**—Luke was using Roman time, not Jewish time. They met on Sunday evening, not Saturday evening.

52. **Acts 20:11**—This was a regular meal, not the Lord's Supper (see Acts 2:46): only Paul was eating (singular verbs); the Greek verb for "eat" was used for ordinary meals, not communion; this was eaten on Monday, which was not the meal for which they "came together" on "the first" (not second) day of the week.

(continued on next page)

Mark Your Bible

53. **Acts 20:16**—Paul was going to Jerusalem to find large crowds to whom to preach the gospel of Jesus Christ, who was the fulfillment of the old law. He was not going there to observe a feast of the old law.

54. **Acts 20:17, 28**—Paul was talking to "elders," when he called them "overseers" and told them that their task was to "shepherd" the church. These three terms are from three distinct Greek words describing the same men. (See "Helpful Notes" for 1 Peter 5.) The Greek word for "shepherd" is the same word for "pastor." A pastor is an elder, and the elders are the pastors. The local minister of the church is not identified as "pastor" in the N.T.

55. **Acts 20:26**—Paul may be using terminology from Ezekiel 33:1-6 to describe himself like a watchman, who has proclaimed the gospel and is not responsible for those who rejected it.

56. **Acts 20:28**—The "church" is "the kingdom" (v. 25) and a "flock" (v. 28), which was currently in existence (Acts 2:47; Col. 1:13) and must be loved, protected and preached.

57. **Acts 20:28**—Elders are "made overseers" by "the Holy Spirit" for they must meet the qualifications given by the Holy Spirit (1 Tim. 3:1-7; Tit. 1:5-9). Also, these specific elders were appointed by the apostle Paul and endowed with spiritual gifts (14:23; 19:6).

58. **Acts 20:28**—The blood of Christ "purchased the church." This same blood saves those who obey Him (Matt. 26:28; Rom. 5:8; Eph. 1:7; Rev. 1:5). The two concepts are not separated in Scripture. Those who are "saved" by the blood of Jesus are "added to the church" that was purchased by the blood of Jesus (Acts 2:38-47). One must be in His church to be saved, and only the saved are in His church.

59. **Acts 20:28**—Jesus is God! Jesus shed His blood, and "God… purchased the church." Therefore, Jesus is God (Tit. 2:13; Heb. 1:8).

60. **Acts 20:35**—The Greek word for "support" is *antilambano,* which literally means "to take up facing," denoting the concept of picking up and helping someone carry a heavy load. The present tense shows this is to be an ongoing, regular part of the Christian life.

Mark Your Bible

61. **Acts 20:35**—The Greek word for "blessed" is *makarios,* which means "happy." The word "give" is in the present tense, denoting habitual activity. (The word "receive" is also in the present tense.) One is "happiest" in giving because it is then that he most resembles His Savior (John 3:16; 1 John 3:16; Eph. 5:2).
62. **Acts 21:4-5**—Those who share a "like precious faith" (2 Pet. 1:1) can form strong bonds over a period of years (as Paul did with the Ephesian elders, cf. 20:36-38), or in just a week (21:5).
63. **Acts 21:8**—Philip was last mentioned, after baptizing the Ethiopian, as having gone to Caesarea (8:40). An evangelist is "one who announces good news" (cf. Eph. 4:11; 2 Tim. 4:5) and is tied to the Greek word for "gospel" (*euaggelion*).
64. **Acts 21:9**—The term "virgins" does not necessitate a young age, and it may indicate they had devoted themselves to full-time service of the Lord, without choosing to marry (cf. 1 Cor. 7:34).
65. **Acts 21:10**—This is likely the same Agabus who prophesied of the famine in 11:27-28.
66. **Acts 21:12**—This is the third time that it is stated that dangers awaited Paul in Jerusalem (20:23; 21:4). And even though they continually and repeatedly begged Paul (the force of the imperfect tense) not to go with incessant loud crying (present tense of Greek word *klaio*), Paul would not be dissuaded.
67. **Acts 21:14**—Put it in the Lord's hands and leave it (cf. Luke 22:42).
68. **Acts 21:19-20**—Two imperfect tense verbs are used, emphasizing continuous activity. Paul "kept on telling" what God had done and those who heard it "kept on glorifying" the Lord.
69. **Acts 21:20**—The word "believed" is a summary term for their full obedience to the gospel.
70. **Acts 21:26**—While these verses are difficult, it is improper to accuse Paul of compromise or sin, and it would be improper to use this to justify participation in unauthorized worship.

(continued on next page)

Mark Your Bible

71. **Acts 21:28-29**—Verse 29 shows the inconsistency of their argument in verse 28. Paul had not violated any Jewish laws. In fact, even if Trophimus had been to the temple (for which there was no evidence), Gentiles were permitted in the larger court area around the temple, which was called "The Court of the Gentiles."

72. **Acts 21:27, 30, 31, 34, 35**—Connect the words "stirred up," "disturbed," "uproar," "tumult," "violence." These were Paul's own Jewish countrymen exhibiting such hatred and violence toward him because of his association with the Gentiles.

73. **Acts 21:31**—The "commander," as he is called several times in these chapters, is later identified as Claudius Lysias (23:26; cf. 24:7, 22). He was the Roman commander of the garrison stationed at the temple.

74. **Acts 21:37, 40**—Paul could speak both Greek (which was Koine Greek, the common language of that day) and Hebrew (his own native tongue as a Jew). This helped him, no doubt, in his efforts to teach the gospel to both Jews and Gentiles.

Day of Reflection

Take time today to reflect on the five chapters that you read this week. You may choose to read all five chapters again, in one sitting, or certain parts of them. Take time today to answer at least one of these questions below. You may or may not write anything down—you can choose to write or simply reflect.

1. What personal application do I need to make from the chapters I have read this week?

2. How can these five chapters help draw me closer to Jesus?

3. What words, phrases or verses in these chapters do I want to go back and study more in depth?

4. What questions do I have about what I have read this week on which I need to do some further Biblical research?

Week 23

June 4-10

June 4	Read Acts 22
June 5	Read Acts 23
June 6	Read Acts 24
June 7	Read Acts 25
June 8	Read Acts 26
June 9	Mark Your Bible
June 10	Day of Reflection

Prayer for this week:

"Heavenly Father,
help me to endure all the world throws at me
and to serve You faithfully."

Acts 22

Helpful Notes:

1. **Be baptized** = In Greek, this is an aorist middle imperative, which denotes immediate and urgent action must be taken; the middle voice denotes action taken toward oneself, literally meaning here, "get yourself baptized"; so Saul was commanded to make the arrangements to have himself baptized right away—it was "a decisive and immediate action"; the purpose and personal nature of the urgency is found in the words, "and wash away your sins."
2. **Calling on the name** = "Calling" is not merely a verbal plea expressed in a prayer (that is not Biblical); the word "calling " here is an aorist participle; this adverbial participle points back to the leading verbs of the sentence ("be baptized" and "wash away") to denote the means or manner in which it is carried out; an aorist participle denotes action taking place simultaneously as the main verb; so it is at the moment one is baptized to have his sins washed away that one is then "calling" on the Lord to do as He promised and take away one's sins (compare 2:21 and 2:38; see 1 Peter 3:21).
3. **Roman citizenship** = This made a non-Roman (like a Jew) equal in judicial rights to the natives of Rome; it was granted for special services that had been rendered to the empire or the emperor, or it could be purchased; Roman citizens had exemption from shameful punishments (like scourging or crucifixion) and it gave the right to appeal to Caesar in certain situations.

1. Under which famous Jewish Rabbi was Saul trained?

2. What time was it when the bright light shone from heaven?

3. Where was Saul when Stephen was stoned?

Verse for Meditation and Prayer: **Acts 22:16**

"And now why are you waiting? Arise and be baptized, and wash away your sins, calling on the name of the Lord."

Acts 23

Helpful Notes:

1. **Good conscience** = The conscience is one's inner sense of right and wrong, which guides in making choices; Paul had lived his life consistent with the knowledge that he had and believed that he was right in the eyes of God for persecuting Christians, but one's feelings are not always a safe guide (cf. Prov. 14:12); Saul had been wrong in his actions (1 Tim. 1:12-15), although he thought he was right, which shows a conscience must be properly trained by the truth of God's Word to make one right with God.
2. **Ananias** = Ananias was high priest in A.D. 47-59, and he was very corrupt, as Paul knew; the Greek word used for "know" in verse 5 (*oida*) and its use in the imperfect Greek tense indicates that Paul's answer was, "I have not and I do not now acknowledge or regard this man as 'God's high priest'"; Paul was not admitting wrong or even ignorance, but he was stating that Ananias was not a legitimate high priest in God's eyes.
3. **Felix** = His name at birth was Antonius Claudius, and he had been a slave; he was freed by Claudius and eventually became governor of Judea (A.D. 52-60)—the same position Pilate had; he was married to Drusilla (24:24), whom he had seduced from her husband; Drusilla was the sister of Agrippa II (25:13); Felix was a wicked, cruel governor and often sought bribes (24:26).

1. For what reason did Paul say that he was being judged?

2. Where did Jesus promise Paul that he would "bear witness"?

3. Who learned of the conspiracy and saved Paul's life?

Verse for Meditation and Prayer: **Acts 23:11**

"But the following night the Lord stood by him and said,
'Be of good cheer, Paul; for as you have testified for Me in Jerusalem,
so you must also bear witness at Rome.'"

Acts 24

Helpful Notes:

1. **Sect** = The Greek word for "sect" is *hairesis* (from which we get the word "heresy"), and the word involves a "choosing," as if the Christians had chosen distinctive tenets or doctrines to which to hold, in order to make them peculiar from others (cf. 24:5, 14; 28:22); the Pharisees and Sadducees were "sects" of the Jews (5:17; 15:5), but Christianity is NOT a sect; Christianity and the teaching of Christ is the only Way of access to God (9:2); the religion of Jesus Christ is exclusive and must never be compromised or tarnished.
2. **Resurrection of the just and unjust** = Both the O.T. (ex: Job 19:25-26; Heb. 11:19; Dan. 12:2) and the N.T. (1 Cor. 15) attest to the resurrection of the dead; Jesus and Paul (thus, all of Scripture) affirm that there will be only one resurrection, in which both the good and the evil (the just and the unjust) will be raised in the same hour (John 5:28-29); this is a literal resurrection of all the dead.
3. **Drusilla** = She came from a violent family, who had shed much blood against Christ and His cause; she was the great-granddaughter of Herod the Great (who tried to murder infant Jesus), the great niece of Herod Antipas (who beheaded John the Baptist), the daughter of Herod Agrippa I (who killed the apostle James), and the sister of Herod Agrippa II and Bernice (25:13); Felix seduced her from Aziz, the king of Emesa, when she was 16.

1. Again, for what reason did Paul say he was being judged?

2. What did Paul preach to Felix and Drusilla about?

3. How did Felix respond to Paul when he was afraid?

Verse for Meditation and Prayer: **Acts 24:25**

"Now as he reasoned about righteousness, self-control, and the judgment to come, Felix was afraid and answered, 'Go away for now; when I have a convenient time I will call for you.'"

Acts 25

Helpful Notes:

1. **Festus** = Festus succeeded Felix as governor of Judea; he is presented in history as a better, more efficient and more agreeable governor than Felix; still, he was more interested in pleasing the Jews than he was in true justice, and he appeared cowardly when Paul was before him, asking permission of the prisoner to make certain decisions regarding where he was to be tried.
2. **Appeal to Caesar** = As a Roman citizen, Paul had the right to appeal his case directly to Caesar's judgment seat, and he felt that he had no choice (28:19); for the sake of the gospel he made this appeal, that it might continue to be spread; Paul had longed to go to Rome (Rom. 1:10) and the Lord promised that he would (Acts 23:11), but Paul may not have envisioned such as a prisoner; the Caesar at this time was Nero (A.D. 54-68).
3. **Herod Agrippa II** = He was the great-grandson of Herod the Great, the great nephew of Herod Antipas (who beheaded John the Baptist), the son Herod Agrippa I (who killed the apostle James), the brother of Drusilla (24:24) and Bernice (25:13, 23; 26:30); he was king over much of Palestine and would be the last Jewish king, as his reign ended in A.D. 70, when Jerusalem was destroyed; he and Bernice were in an incestuous relationship.

1. What favor did the Jewish leaders ask of Festus?

2. Why did Paul appeal to Caesar?

3. With what did Festus say that he wanted Agrippa's help?

Verse for Meditation and Prayer: **Acts 25:10**

"So Paul said, 'I stand at Caesar's judgment seat, where I ought to be judged. To the Jews I have done no wrong, as you very well know.'"

Acts 26

Helpful Notes:

1. **The hope of the promise** = Paul preached that Jesus was the fulfillment of "the hope of Israel" (28:20), which was based upon "the promise made by God" (26:6); Jesus was the promised Messiah of the O.T., and man's "hope" lies in Christ's greatest accomplishment of being raised from the dead; we have "hope" (absolute assurance) in "the resurrection from the dead" (23:6; 24:15; 26:6-7) because Christ was raised from the dead; Paul was willing to give his life for the preaching of this vital and guaranteed truth.
2. **Kick against the goads** = A goad was a sharp stick used for prodding cattle, particularly during plowing to keep them moving straight; Jesus uses the term to indicate that Saul must have been struggling with his conscience while persecuting Christians and his heart was being poked by the gospel to realize he was wrong; but Saul kept "kicking against" that sharp stick, which was hard.
3. **Repent and turn to God** = God distinguishes the act of repentance from the act of turning to God; repentance is a turn in mind, and what follows is baptism (2:38); baptism is the point at which one fully turns to the Lord (see 11:21); Acts 2:38 and 3:19 are parallel teachings that both command repentance in order that sins may be forgiven or blotted out, and the other parallel command in those verses is "be baptized" (2:38) and "turn again" (3:19).

1. What work did Jesus have for Saul upon his conversion (verse 18)?

2. How did Paul respond to Festus' claim that he was "mad"?

3. What did Paul say that he knew about Agrippa?

Verse for Meditation and Prayer: **Acts 26:25**

"But he said, 'I am not mad, most noble Festus, but speak the words of truth and reason.'"

Mark Your Bible

1. **Acts 22:1**—For the word "defense," see Philippians 1 and 1 Peter 3.
2. **Acts 22:2-5**—Paul was trying to identify himself with his audience, in order to get them to listen to what he was going to say.
3. **Acts 22:4**—Acts has placed a great emphasis on "the Way" of Christ and Christianity being singular, exclusive and identifiable (9:2; 19:9, 23; 24:14, 22). This must have been an identifying designation given to Christians and Christianity.
4. **Acts 22:6-16**—See Acts 9, where this event happened, for additional notes. The fact that Paul's conversion is recorded three times in the book of Acts indicates how significant this was in proving the resurrection of Christ and validating the Christian movement.
5. **Acts 22:13**—The fact that Ananias called Saul, "brother," does not prove that he was already a Christian. Both men were Jews, and this was a common way of addressing each other in a nationalistic sense. Peter addressed the crowd in Acts 2 as "brethren" (2:29), but they had not repented of sins yet and were not saved (2:38). It was common among Jews, just as it is now among Christians.
6. **Acts 22:15**—The "all men" included "the Gentiles" (22:21). Draw a line connecting those words.
7. **Acts 22:16**—After three days of praying and fasting (9:9-11), Saul still had his sins. It was not until he was baptized that his sins were washed away and he was saved in the eyes of God.
8. **Acts 22:17**—This visit to Jerusalem is mentioned in 9:26, and it took place about 3 years after his conversion (Gal. 1:18).
9. **Acts 22:19-20**—Paul was trying to prove to these Jews that his conversion was genuine and based on solid, incontrovertible evidence that Jesus of Nazareth had really been raised from the dead—Paul had seen Him and heard Him.
10. **Acts 22:28**—Paul's Roman citizenship had been passed down from his parents (more authentic than buying it). Roman citizens may have carried their birth certificate as proof.

(continued on next page)

Mark Your Bible

11. **Acts 23:3**—"Whitewashed wall" was a way of calling him a hypocrite (cf. Matt. 23:27).
12. **Acts 23:3**—It was Jewish law that a man's case must be heard first before he was beaten (Deut. 25:1-2).
13. **Acts 23:6**—The resurrection of Jesus Christ and man's future resurrection was the focus of first-century preaching and persecution.
14. **Acts 23:8**—See "Helpful Notes" on Matthew 3 for more on the Sadducees. They believed that the soul dies with the body, while the Pharisees believed wholeheartedly in the immortality of the soul.
15. **Acts 23:9**—Saying, "We find no evil in this man," was limited to this matter of the resurrection and not their overall evaluation.
16. **Acts 23:10**—This fulfilled the prophecy of Agabus in 21:11.
17. **Acts 23:11**—The Lord standing with Paul is seen at other times of distress (cf. 2 Tim. 4:16-17).
18. **Acts 23:11**—The Lord uses a present imperative to urge Paul to "keep up his courage continually." Don't lose heart. The word "must" is used by Jesus (see 9:6) as a Divine imperative.
19. **Acts 23:23-24**—Caesarea is where the Roman governor had his residence. The "third hour of the night" would have been 9:00 p.m. Caesarea was about 60 miles to the west of Jerusalem. They traveled about 35 miles the first night (23:31) and then 25 miles the next (23:32-33). Paul's Roman citizenship had to be respected.
20. **Acts 23:29**—Paul was preaching about Jesus Christ, which was not against Roman law. Roman magistrates continually found that Paul had done nothing, according to Roman law, "deserving of death."
21. **Acts 23:35**—Herod the Great had built a royal palace in Caesarea on a massive scale. Paul was kept imprisoned there.
22. **Acts 24:1**—Tertullus was there as an "attorney" to prosecute the case.
23. **Acts 24:5**—"Nazarenes" is a term used derogatorily by the enemies of Christ and is not an authoritative title for God's people.

Mark Your Bible

24. **Acts 24:5**—The Greek word for "plague" means "a pestilence, any deadly, infectious malady." Additionally, he was charged with instigating "dissension" or "insurrections," which was a serious matter among the Romans (cf. Mark 15:7).
25. **Acts 24:6**—This was a lie (see 21:28-29).
26. **Acts 24:10**—The Greek word for "answer" is *apologeomai,* which is a verbal defense against charges. Paul used this same word several times while on trials (24:10; 25:8; 26:1, 2, 24), along with the noun form, *apologia* (22:1; 25:16). The English word "apologetics" is from this Greek term.
27. **Acts 24:11**—Start calculating in 21:17, and Paul says there has not been sufficient time to create the kind of uproar of which he was being accused. He had been a prisoner more than half of that time.
28. **Acts 24:14**—Paul believed the O.T. He preached the O.T. He did so, in connection with the gospel, to prove that Jesus Christ was raised from the dead and is the Son of God. The O.T. (i.e., "the Law and the Prophets") and the gospel are not contradictory or "antagonistic" to one another. They go hand-in-hand (26:22-23).
29. **Acts 24:14-16**—Circle and connect the three uses of "God" in these verses. Paul worshiped "God," had hope in "God" and strove to live pleasing to "God."
30. **Acts 24:21**—It was a religious issue for which Paul had been charged.
31. **Acts 24:24**—The word "in" in the expression "in Christ" is the Greek word *eis.* It could denote faith "toward" Christ or faith that leads "into" Christ—essentially the same result.
32. **Acts 24:25**—The Greek word for "afraid" (*emphobos*) means to be terrified, with great mental agitation. Hearing about the judgment sobered and frightened this governor.
33. **Acts 24:26**—The present tense "sent" and imperfect tense "conversed" indicate regular meetings between these men.
34. **Acts 24:27**—Felix knew that Paul was innocent. If he was an honest man, he would have released him.

(continued on next page)

Mark Your Bible

35. **Acts 25:2**—Even after two years, the Jewish leaders in Jerusalem were still focused on Paul, who had been in prison in Caesarea. The leaders incessantly begged (imperfect tense) Festus to do them a favor and help them to kill Paul.

36. **Acts 25:8**—Paul defends himself against three major indictments: he had not sinned against (1) the law, for it was part of God's eternal plan of redemption; (2) the temple, for he had not desecrated it by taking a Gentile into it; (3) Rome, for he was not stirring up riots or disturbing Roman peace. He was innocent of all three charges.

37. **Acts 25:9**—Draw a line from Festus wanting to do the Jews "a favor" to 24:27, where Felix was wanting to do the Jews a "favor." In such a setting, justice for Paul was not possible.

38. **Acts 25:19**—This was not a legal matter but a religious matter, and it should have been dismissed and Paul found not guilty. Festus believed that Jesus was still "dead," but Paul "kept on, repeatedly affirming" (imperfect tense) that Jesus "is" (present tense, continually and ongoing) "alive." This was the foundation of Christianity.

39. **Acts 25:21, 25**—The KJV and NKJV have "Augustus" in these verses. The Greek word *sebastos* means "august one, revered one." This became the title used for each Roman emperor and is better translated "emperor." Caesar Augustus died in A.D. 14.

40. **Acts 25:21**—The Greek word for "decision" is *diagnosis.*

41. **Acts 25:24-25**—Repeatedly, the Roman judges before whom Paul appeared concluded the same thing: Paul had done "nothing deserving of death" (cf. 23:29; 25:8, 11; 26:31). It did not matter how loudly and how incessantly (present tense) his enemies kept crying out that "he was not fit to live any longer."

42. **Acts 25:26**—"My lord" is a reference to Nero, who claimed to not only be the emperor but "lord," as well. Starting with Caligula, the emperors embraced and demanded Divine titles.

43. **Acts 26:8**—The present tense "raises" emphasizes that God has the ability to raise the dead because He already has, in raising Jesus

Mark Your Bible

from the dead. Draw lines from this to "hope" (three times in verses 6-7), "this" in verse 7, and "rise from the dead" in verse 23.

44. **Acts 26:9**—Underline "I myself thought I must do." What we feel in our hearts is not a safe guide for how to please God (23:1; Prov. 14:12; 2 Kgs. 5:11). Circle Paul's seven uses of the first person pronoun "I" in verses 9-11. God's truth must trump our feelings.
45. **Acts 26:10, 12**—Connect "authority" in verses 10 and 12. Paul received authority (cf. 9:2) from "the chief priests" (i.e., the Sanhedrin), having been "commissioned" with full powers of the highest Jewish court to arrest, imprison and persecute Christians.
46. **Acts 26:16, 22**—Draw a line from "witness" in verse 16 to "witnessing" in verse 22. Paul was fulfilling his Christ-given task.
47. **Acts 26:17**—"Deliver" is not a promise of freedom from hardships (cf. 2 Cor. 11:23-28), but a promise of Christ's presence and strength to endure (23:11; 27:23), even if such meant death (2 Tim. 4:8, 18).
48. **Acts 26:18**—"Faith" in Acts (and the N.T.) is always an obedient faith (6:7; 16:34). God ties "forgiveness of sins" (through obedience) with "sanctified" (through obedience) (cf. Eph. 5:25-27).
49. **Acts 26:22**—See note on 24:14.
50. **Acts 26:23**—Jesus was "the first to rise from the dead," who was raised permanently, never to die again. That He was "the first" emphasizes that others would follow in such manner (1 Cor. 15:20, 23).
51. **Acts 26:25**—God's truth is conveyed through "words" (1 Cor. 2:13), not feelings or hunches. And God's words can be understood, proven and reasoned through (2 Tim. 2:15).
52. **Acts 26:26**—Christianity is founded upon real, historical events, which are knowable, checkable, and therefore, believable.
53. **Acts 26:28**—The name "Christian" is only found three times in the New Testament—Acts 11:26; 26:28; 1 Peter 4:16.

June 10 Week 23, Day 7

Day of Reflection

Take time today to reflect on the five chapters that you read this week. You may choose to read all five chapters again, in one sitting, or certain parts of them. Take time today to answer at least one of these questions below. You may or may not write anything down—you can choose to write or simply reflect.

1. What personal application do I need to make from the chapters I have read this week?

2. How can these five chapters help draw me closer to Jesus?

3. What words, phrases or verses in these chapters do I want to go back and study more in depth?

4. What questions do I have about what I have read this week on which I need to do some further Biblical research?

Week 24

June 11-17

June 11	Read Acts 27
June 12	Read Acts 28
June 13	Read Romans 1
June 14	Read Romans 2
June 15	Read Romans 3
June 16	Mark Your Bible
June 17	Day of Reflection

Prayer for this week:

"Heavenly Father,
You are better to me than I deserve!"

Acts 27

Helpful Notes:

1. **"God" in the storm** = Even when in a dangerous storm and seemingly without hope, Paul had an unwavering faith in God; in verses 23-25, he made three "I" statements regarding his relationship with his God: (1) "I belong to God"—He bought me and owns me, even now (1 Cor. 6:19-10); (2) "I serve God"—present tense, indicating continuous serving, even in the storm; (3) "I believe God"—present tense verb, emphasizing Paul's persistent trust and confidence in God's power, plans and promises.
2. **Conditional salvation** = God promised that the men would be saved (27:22, 24, 34; cf. 27:44), but their free gift of salvation was conditioned upon their adherence to His conditions ("stay in the ship"); the words "unless" and "cannot" are used by Jesus in John 3:3-5, emphasizing that one's free gift of eternal salvation (i.e., entering the kingdom) is conditioned upon one's baptism; God's promises are free gifts that He gives us, but His gifts come with conditions that must be met in order to obtain (cf. Josh. 6:1-5).
3. **Gave thanks** = In the midst of a horrible, life-threatening storm, Paul "gave thanks to God" for the food, and he did this "in the presence of them all"; giving thanks for our food should be a regular practice of every Christian (1 Tim. 4:4-5); it was a regular practice of Jesus Himself (Luke 9:16; 24:30).

1. What appointment did the angel remind Paul that he had?

2. For how long had they gone without eating?

3. Why did the centurion stop the soldiers from killing the prisoners?

Verse for Meditation and Prayer: **Acts 27:25**

"Therefore take heart, men,
for I believe God that it will be just as it was told me."

Acts 28

Helpful Notes:

1. **Poisonous viper** = The Greek word for "viper" (*echidna*) indicated a poisonous snake; Paul "suffered no harm" (stated twice in verses 5-6); this miracle is precisely what Jesus had promised to His first-century disciples (Mark 16:18; Luke 10:19); such miraculous capabilities ceased in the first century (1 Cor. 13:8-13; Eph. 4:8-13), but they were designed then to confirm the Word that was preached and to lead to faith.
2. **Rome** = Rome was the largest city of the ancient world at that time, with the city's circumference over 13 miles and an estimated population (in A.D. 14) of over 4 million; the city was built on seven hills on the east bank of the Tiber River; while it was the literary and artistic center of the world, and while "all roads led to Rome," it was a center of worldliness and ungodliness.
3. **Kingdom of God** = The theme of Paul's preaching was Jesus Christ (the Lord and King) and His kingdom; the kingdom of God was prophesied in the O.T. (2 Sam. 7:12-16; Isa. 2:2-4; 9:6-7; Dan. 2:44) and was established by Christ in the N.T. on the day of Pentecost (Mark 9:1; Luke 24:49; Acts 1:8; 2:1-47); the kingdom of God is the church of Christ (Matt. 16:18-19), and Christians are part of it today (Col. 1:13; Rev. 1:9), having been baptized into it (John 3:3-5; 1 Cor. 12:13); in the end, Christ will deliver the kingdom (with all of its citizens) to the Father in heaven (1 Cor. 15:24).

1. What did the Maltans think Paul was when no harm came to him?

2. What did the Jews tell Paul about the church (which they called "this sect")?

3. What did Luke record that Paul did for two years in Rome?

Verse for Meditation and Prayer: **Acts 28:23**

"...to whom he explained and solemnly testified of the kingdom of God, persuading them concerning Jesus from both the Law of Moses and the Prophets, from morning till evening."

Romans 1

Helpful Notes: * *See Brief Introduction to Romans on page 636.*

1. **Declared to be the Son of God with power** = The resurrection of Jesus Christ is the pivotal proof of His deity, accompanied by "many infallible proofs" (Acts 1:3); its certainty brought about full conversion and complete conviction of millions, including His disciples and even His brothers.
2. **Obedience of faith** = The design of the gospel is to "bring about the obedience of faith"; the N.T. nowhere teaches justification by "faith alone," for Biblical faith is not merely a mental assent; the book of Romans places great emphasis on faith, and it defines that faith which justifies as an obedient faith (1:5; 6:16-18; 16:26; cf. 1:8; 2:8; 5:19; 10:16; 16:19).
3. **His invisible attributes are clearly seen** = The exquisite and intricate design in the universe demands a designer; the design, according to Scripture, is evidence of God's eternal power and Divine nature; the "material effect" that is "seen" is proof that they were "made" (created) by an "adequate cause," which was greater than and existed before the universe; those lost in disbelief are "without excuse."

1. For what reason did Paul give thanks for their faith?

2. While Paul really wanted to visit the church in Rome, how did he eventually make it to Rome (Acts 27:1)?

3. Read the list of sins in 1:29-31. Which ones really stand out to you?

Verse for Meditation and Prayer: **Romans 1:16**

"For I am not ashamed of the gospel of Christ, for it is the power of God to salvation for everyone who believes, for the Jew first and also for the Greek."

Romans 2

Helpful Notes:

1. **Practice what you preach** = The Jews thought themselves superior to the Gentiles, so they condemned the Gentiles for their sins (such as found in chapter 1); however, the Jews were themselves "practicing the same things"; they were arrogant, condescending and hypocritical, and they would be judged for that (as much as the Gentiles for their sins).
2. **The goodness of God leads to repentance** = Mankind (and especially the Jews) has been a constant witness and recipient of the goodness of God, particularly evidenced in His "forbearance and longsuffering," as He patiently waits for His people to obey Him; such goodness ought to drive conscientious people to repent of their sins and turn to God.
3. **Render to each according to his deeds** = Each person will be judged "according to truth" based upon his individual response to the will of God (positive or negative); eternal life awaits those who continually do the will of God; eternal condemnation awaits those who do not obey the truth; and when it comes to judgment, there is no partiality with God.

1. What is there about the goodness of God toward us today that ought to drive us to repentance?

2. By what standard will the secrets of men be judged?

3. Why was the name of God being blasphemed among the Gentiles? Who was causing that to happen?

Verse for Meditation and Prayer: **Romans 2:4**

"Or do you despise the riches of His goodness, forbearance, and longsuffering, not knowing that the goodness of God leads you to repentance?"

Romans 3

Helpful Notes:

1. **Sin** = The Greek *harmartia* means "missing the mark"; a sin is a transgression of God's law—whether an act of commission (1 John 3:4) or omission (Jas. 4:17); sin is a universal problem (Rom. 3:9-12, 23), as it is a choice (not inherited, Ezek. 18:20) that accountable persons make that transgresses the law of God; sin separates man from God (Isa. 59:1-2).
2. **Justification** = Since all men sin and suffer the consequences, God designed a way for the sinner to be acquitted and declared righteous before God and free from guilt; this is not the result of man's meritorious works (Eph. 2:8-9) or by "faith alone" (Jas. 2:14-26); it is extended by the gracious sacrifice of Christ to those who respond with obedient faith.
3. **Propitiation** = Our sin brings condemnation (Rom. 6:23), which must be satisfied, because God is holy (Hab. 1:13; Isa. 6:3) and justice is demanded (Heb. 10:28-31); Christ came and offered Himself as a sinless sacrifice in our behalf (1 Pet. 1:19-20; 2 Cor. 5:21), and His blood is the "mercy seat" (O.T. term for propitiation), the necessary price that had to be paid to satisfy the wrath of God toward sin and account us as righteous in His sight.

1. What was committed to the Jews, which should have proven to them their place of privilege in the eyes of God?

2. What knowledge did the law bring?

3. While verse 23 is sobering, how does verse 24 overcome it?

Verse for Meditation and Prayer: **Romans 3:23**

"For all have sinned and fall short of the glory of God."

Mark Your Bible

1. **Acts 27:1**—Circle the word "we." Luke joined the mission team again. Luke has been called a master historian. The details that he gives in the book of Acts are precise and accurate—regarding persons, places, historical events, etc. Also, his account in this chapter has been scrutinized and found again to be completely accurate in geography and nautical navigation and practices of the time.
2. **Acts 27:2**—Aristarchus traveled with Paul on his third journey (20:4), was dragged into the theater during the Ephesian mob (19:29) and was a "fellow prisoner" with Paul in Rome (Col. 4:10; Phile. 24).
3. **Acts 27:6**—This was a large ship, able to fit 276 people (27:37).
4. **Acts 27:9**—"The fast" mentioned here was associated with the Day of Atonement, which occurred in early October.
5. **Acts 27:9, 11**—Two imperfect tense verbs are used. Paul "kept on advising" repeatedly, but the centurion "kept on being more persuaded" by the helmsman and owner of the ship.
6. **Acts 27:20**—Without the sun and stars, they were not able to verify their location. They did not know where they were in the Mediterranean Sea.
7. **Acts 27:23**—The Lord often "stood" with Paul, either in person or through an angel (18:9; 23:11; 26:17; 27:23; 2 Tim. 4:17).
8. **Acts 27:24**—The present imperative, "Do not be afraid," is a prohibition to stop doing what you are doing. Like everyone on the ship, Paul was afraid, and God told Him to "Stop being afraid."
9. **Acts 27:29**—The word "prayed" or "wished" is in the Greek imperfect tense, denoting that they kept on praying all night.
10. **Acts 27:42**—If the prisoners escaped, the soldiers would be killed (cf. 12:18-19; 16:27-28), so they planned to kill the prisoners instead.
11. **Acts 27:44**—God kept His promise (27:22, 24, 34). See "Helpful Notes."

(continued on next page)

Mark Your Bible

12. **Acts 28:4**—The word "justice" is probably best understand as the personification of a false goddess named "Justice."
13. **Acts 28:14**—The word "toward" is one of the 1,767 times that the Greek preposition *eis* is found in the Greek New Testament. The word always points forward, never backward. It is the Greek preposition in Acts 2:38, "*for* the remission of sins." If it means "because of" in Acts 2:38, then it must mean "because of" in 28:14.
14. **Acts 28:15**—When Paul saw the brethren from Rome, he "thanked God" for answering his prayers (Rom. 1:10; 15:30-32).
15. **Acts 28:16**—Paul was shown great respect by officials who interacted with him (which must be indicative of the respect he showed to them). Rather than being kept with the general criminal population in prison, he was permitted to live in his own hired dwelling (28:30), large enough to accommodate crowds (28:23), with a soldier guarding him regularly.
16. **Acts 28:17**—Addressing the Jews as "brethren" reflected a nationalistic ancestry (2:29; 22:5) and not a Christian relationship. There were an estimated 20,000 Jews in Rome at that time.
17. **Acts 28:20**—See "Helpful Notes" for Acts 26.
18. **Acts 28:22**—See "Helpful Notes" for Acts 24.
19. **Acts 28:23**—Paul's custom was to go to the synagogue in a city and reason with them from the Scriptures. There were an estimated 13 synagogues in Rome, but as a prisoner, Paul could not go. Instead, he invited the synagogue (i.e., the Jews) to come to him.
20. **Acts 28:23**—The central theme of the Old Testament (the Scriptures of his Jewish listeners) was Jesus Christ.
21. **Acts 28:24**—"Persuaded" indicates that some were converted and became Christians (17:4; 18:4), while some did not obey.
22. **Acts 28:25**—The Holy Spirit "spoke through" the prophets, moving the men to write the very words of God (2 Pet. 1:20-21; 2 Tim. 3:16).

Mark Your Bible

23. **Acts 28:28**—The Jews did not want to hear the word "Gentiles," but the "salvation" offered and conditioned by God was sent to both the Jews and the Gentiles. That is what the book of Acts is about.
24. **Acts 28:30**—During Paul's two-year imprisonment: (1) he enjoyed freedom to preach the gospel to all who came to him; (2) he wrote Ephesians, Philippians, Colossians and Philemon (often called "The Prison Epistles"); (3) he met and converted Onesimus; (4) many brethren came and visited him; (5) he preached to Roman guards and Caesar's household. These facts (and others) are learned about his two-year imprisonment from reading the Prison Epistles.
25. **Acts 28:30**—The fact that Luke records that Paul "dwelt two whole years" as a prisoner in Rome implies that he was released after two years. After he was released, he wrote First Timothy, Titus and Second Timothy (in that order), from which we learn that he traveled quite a bit in further endeavors to preach the gospel. Historical records indicate that after 2-3 years of freedom Paul was imprisoned in Rome again and penned Second Timothy from there. It is believed that Paul was beheaded during Nero's persecution of Christians (around A.D. 68).
26. **Romans 1:15**—The gospel makes one a "debtor," having a memory of one's past, knowing the vile consequences of sin, which demanded the sacrifice of Christ on our behalf. We are debtors to tell all.
27. **Romans 1:16**—What is there to be ashamed of? It is from God, it is made possible by Jesus Christ, it offers salvation and eternal life!
28. **Romans 1:16**—The salvation of God is available to "everyone," including both Jews and Greeks. There is no such Bible doctrine as "unconditional election" or "limited atonement."
29. **Romans 1:17**—The "righteousness of God" involves God's plan to account man as "righteous" in His eyes through the sacrifice of Jesus Christ, which requires man's obedient faith (6:16-18).
30. **Romans 1:18**—God's wrath is not like human tempers. It is a just and measured judgment against sin and not an emotional outburst.

(continued on next page)

Mark Your Bible

31. **Romans 1:18**—Generally speaking, "ungodliness" is wrong done toward God and "unrighteousness" is wrong done toward man.
32. **Romans 1:20**—Humanity has existed since the beginning of creation (cf. Mark 10:6) and did not come around billions of years later.
33. **Romans 1:23, 25, 26**—Underline the three times that it says mankind "changed" or "exchanged" something that belonged to God.
34. **Romans 1:24, 26, 28**—When man willfully rebelled against God and entrenched himself in sin, God "gave them up" to the life they wanted to live and permitted them to suffer the consequences.
35. **Romans 1:26-28**—Homosexuality is "vile" (rejecting God), "against nature" (not born that way), "shameful" and "error."
36. **Romans 1:32**—Those who "give approval/consent" to the "practice" of unrighteous acts are as guilty of sin as those who commit them.
37. **Romans 2:6-10**—Underline words that emphasize the need for obedience, including "deeds," "works," "doing," "obey," "does," etc. "Faith only" will not save. True faith acts and obeys God's will.
38. **Romans 2:11**—God makes no exceptions—He will be obeyed or He will punish, without partiality (Eph. 6:9; Col. 3:25; 1 Pet. 1:17).
39. **Romans 2:13-15**—This is a parentheses in the flow of thought. It is not that the Gentiles were "a law to themselves" (i.e., they made up their own law), but their God-given conscience (which instinctively knows some things are right and some are wrong) caused them to obey the law of God better than those who knew it. The Gentiles were obviously under a law of some kind (4:15; 1 John 3:4).
40. **Romans 2:28-29**—The Jews prided themselves on the name "Jew" (2:17), but God says that a "true Jew" (cf. Gal. 6:16) was not made so by circumcision of the flesh but of the heart, removing stubbornness and sinful desires and seeking the praise of God and not men.
41. **Romans 3:4**—Regardless of what man does, God's unchanging character remains unaltered (2 Tim. 2:13).

Mark Your Bible

42. **Romans 3:18**—The universal and horrible nature of man's sin is the result of having no fear/reverence for God, or regard for fellow man.
43. **Romans 3:21-22**—The "righteousness of God" is His plan to account sinful people as righteous in His sight, and it is available to all.
44. **Romans 3:22-23**—Draw a line from the "all" who can be made righteous by God (v. 22) to the "all" who sin and need it (v. 23).
45. **Romans 3:25**—The Greek definite article "the" is found before "faith," to identify the objective faith of God's gospel saving system.
46. **Romans 3:26**—The sacrifice of Christ for sin was God's way of redeeming man without compromising His righteousness or condoning man's unrighteousness.
47. **Romans 3:27**—The "law of faith" is God's gospel plan of salvation that requires man's obedient faith to be justified by the grace of God.

Day of Reflection

Take time today to reflect on the five chapters that you read this week. You may choose to read all five chapters again, in one sitting, or certain parts of them. Take time today to answer at least one of these questions below. You may or may not write anything down—you can choose to write or simply reflect.

1. What personal application do I need to make from the chapters I have read this week?

2. How can these five chapters help draw me closer to Jesus?

3. What words, phrases or verses in these chapters do I want to go back and study more in depth?

4. What questions do I have about what I have read this week on which I need to do some further Biblical research?

Week 25

June 18-24

June 18	Read Romans 4
June 19	Read Romans 5
June 20	Read Romans 6
June 21	Read Romans 7
June 22	Read Romans 8
June 23	Mark Your Bible
June 24	Day of Reflection

Prayer for this week:

"Heavenly Father,
help me to be eager to study Your Word."

June 18 Week 25, Day 1

Romans 4

Helpful Notes:

1. **Works of merit** = It is essential when reading Bible words to keep them in context—not all "works" in the N.T. are the same; in this context, the "works" have to do with keeping the law perfectly, which would give reason to "boast" before God and even put God in "debt" to the perfect works; it is not possible to keep the law perfectly, thus we need God! (This does not nullify the essentiality of works of faith.)
2. **Accounted to him for righteousness** = Some think it was only Abraham's belief in God (like an alien sinner coming to believe in God) that made him righteous; but the verse quoted is Genesis 15:6, which was about 11 years after Genesis 12; Abraham was not justified before he obeyed; his faith was accounted to him for righteousness *when* he obeyed.
3. **Father of us all** = God told Abraham that through his seed "all" nations would be blessed (Gen. 22:18); Abraham is not the "father of us all" through the old law but through Christ (his Seed, Gal. 3:16); when we have an obedient faith like Abraham, then we are "Abraham's seed" (Gal. 3:26-29).

1. Who did David say is "Blessed"?

2. The word "promise" is found five times in this chapter. What "promise" did God make about Abraham's "seed"?

3. For whose sake did Paul say these things were written about Abraham?

Verse for Meditation and Prayer: **Romans 4:7**

"Blessed are those whose lawless deeds are forgiven,
And whose sins are covered."

Romans 5

Helpful Notes:

1. **Rejoice in tribulation** = Suffering is not considered a rejoicing opportunity, but it has the strong potential for positive, spiritual results in our lives; it can lead to endurance, then proven character before God, then hope that does not disappoint; we can be renewed every day through it, knowing that it is working an eternal reward (8:18; 2 Cor. 4:16-18).
2. **God demonstrates His love** = True, Biblical, *agape* love is not merely an emotion of the heart, but it is active and working for the good of its recipients; God's love sent Jesus to die for those who were "weak...ungodly...sinners...enemies"; no greater love has ever existed or been demonstrated than the love of our perfect God.
3. **Reconciled** = The terms "saved" and "reconciled" are used interchangeably in this text; reconciliation is a change that takes place when estranged parties are brought back together; our own sins have estranged us from God (Eph. 2:12; 4:18), but Jesus' blood reconciles us back into beautiful fellowship with God when we are baptized (Eph. 2:16; 5:26) and we cease to be enemies (2 Cor. 5:18).

1. When we are justified by an obedient faith, what blessings flow as a result?

2. What do we learn about sin in this chapter that ought to cause us to hate it and flee from it?

3. Where man's sin abounds, what is God's grace doing?

Verse for Meditation and Prayer: **Romans 5:8**

"But God demonstrates His own love toward us, in that while we were still sinners, Christ died for us."

Romans 6

Helpful Notes:

1. **Into Christ** = Being "in Christ" is absolutely critical in order to be right with God (Eph. 1:3-11) and to go to heaven; "eternal life" is only found "in Christ Jesus" (Rom. 6:23), and Scripture only gives one path "into Christ" and that is through baptism (6:3; Gal. 3:27); no other path exists.
2. **That form of doctrine** = The Greek word for "form" means "pattern"; there is a "pattern" that must be "obeyed," in order to be "set free from sin," and Paul gives that pattern in verses 2-4—as Christ died, one must die to his old ways in repentance; as Christ was buried, one must be buried in baptism; as Christ was raised, one must be raised to walk a new life, apart from sin; the "form" centers around baptism, and one is "united" with Christ in this pattern of baptism.
3. **Wages of sin is death** = When one violates the law of God (i.e., sins, 1 John 3:4), he dies (Gen. 2:17), suffering a spiritual death (Rom. 6:23; Jas. 1:15), which is separation from God (Isa. 59:1-2); unlike salvation, this is something that we earn and are hence paid our wages in full.

1. When we are baptized, what happens to the old man of sin?

2. What does it mean to be "alive to God"?

3. What does it mean to be a "slave of righteousness for holiness"?

Verse for Meditation and Prayer: **Romans 6:23**

"For the wages of sin is death, but the gift of God is eternal life in Christ Jesus our Lord."

June 21 Week 25, Day 4

Romans 7

Helpful Notes:

1. **Marriage is for life** = Paul is actually using marriage as an illustration here, but a Divine truth is taught about it; God designed marriage to be "bound" "as long as" the husband or wife "lives"; to marry another, while married in God's eyes, makes one "an adulteress"; the only exception provided by Jesus was fornication committed by one's spouse.
2. **Dead to the law** = When a spouse dies, the living spouse is no longer "bound" to that dead spouse; the point is the Jews were "released from," "free from," "dead to" (i.e., separated, Jas. 2:26) and "delivered from the law" of Moses; when Christ died on the cross, the old law died as a law, as well (Col. 2:14; Eph. 2:13-16); no one is "bound" to it any longer.
3. **The law included the Ten Commandments** = Some seventh-day religions today argue that the Ten Commandments (esp. the Sabbath) are still binding today; Paul used the phrase "the law" seven times in verses 1-7, teaching it was "dead," and then specified that included in that "dead" law was the Ten Commandments which said, "You shall not covet."

1. How long is the wife bound to her husband (and vice versa)?

2. To whom are Christians married?

3. While Christians struggle not to sin, is it ok to give in to sin? When we do sin, whose responsibility is it?

Verse for Meditation and Prayer: **Romans 7:4**

"Therefore, my brethren, you also have become dead to the law through the body of Christ, that you may be married to another – to Him who was raised from the dead, that we should bear fruit to God."

June 22

Week 25, Day 5

Romans 8

Helpful Notes:

1. **No condemnation in Christ** = Those who are "in Christ" know that they are saved and have eternal life, and they are not condemned for their sins; those "in Christ" have been "baptized into Christ" (6:3) and continually (present tense) "walk according to" the teachings of the Holy Spirit found in the New Testament.
2. **The Spirit of God dwells in Christians** = When one is "baptized into Christ," he becomes a child of God (Gal. 3:26-27) and receives "the gift of the Holy Spirit," for the Spirit of God "dwells in" "children of God"; as the "child" of God continues to be "led by" and "live according to" the teachings of the Holy Spirit (i.e., obeys God's Word), God continues to "dwell" in him; the present tense verbs, "live" and "led by," emphasize this promise of God is conditional.
3. **The providence of God** = There is the general providence of God for all of His creation (Matt. 5:45), and there is the special providence of God for His children; God's special providence is active for His people, who love Him, obey Him (John 14:15) and continue to accept and live after His "purpose"; His providence takes care of us now (according to His will) and will see to our ultimate "good" in heaven.

1. As children of God, with whom are we joint heirs?

2. Along with Jesus, who also makes intercession for us in our prayers?

3. Having given His Son for us, what is there God won't give?

Verse for Meditation and Prayer: **Romans 8:28**

"And we know that all things work together for good to those who love God, to those who are the called according to His purpose."

Mark Your Bible

1. **Romans 4:5**—Paul defined faith/belief at the beginning of the book. Whenever you read the word "faith" or "believe" in this letter, if it is a saving faith, then it is a trusting and obeying faith (every time).
2. **Romans 4:10**—The Gentiles can be righteous without circumcision, just as Abraham was righteous before God without circumcision.
3. **Romans 4:12**—Note that "faith" has "steps" (plural) in which man must "walk." Abraham's faith was obedient (Heb. 11:8-10).
4. **Romans 4:13**—Abraham lived 400 years before the law of Moses was given, so he was not justified by the old law (neither are we).
5. **Romans 4:16-22**—God made promises to Abraham that may have seemed impossible, but Abraham trusted every promise and obeyed, knowing God was "able to perform." Trust and obey!
6. **Romans 5:1**—Nowhere does the Bible ever teach justification by "faith alone." Biblical faith (acceptable to God) is an obedient faith.
7. **Romans 5:5**—The Holy Spirit is given to indwell in every Christian upon baptism (Acts 2:38; Gal. 4:6). This is not miraculous or illuminating. He only operates on us through His Word (Eph. 6:17).
8. **Romans 5:12**—The guilt of sin is not inherited from Adam (guilt is tied to one's own personal sins and not someone else's, Ezek. 18:20). But the penalty of sin (i.e., physical death because of sin, Gen. 2:16-17; 1 Cor. 15:22) is now the lot of all mankind (Heb. 9:27).
9. **Romans 5:13**—This proves there was a law before the law of Moses (cf. 4:15; 1 John 3:4). Man has never lived when not under law.
10. **Romans 5:13-17**—These verses are a parentheses to explain the magnitude of man's sin and then how much greater the gift of God.
11. **Romans 5:9, 10, 15, 17, 20**—Underline "much more." Sin is heinous, but the gift of God "much more" (than enough) covers our sin.
12. **Romans 5:13-19**—Adam is a "type" of Christ (5:14). Note the many contrasts between Adam and our glorious Savior in these verses.

(continued on next page)

Mark Your Bible

13. **Romans 5:19**—A person is made a "sinner" or "righteous" by his own personal choice. Nothing is chosen for him apart from his will.
14. **Romans 5:20**—The law was given to see the enormity of sin (and its consequences) and man's hopeless condition without God's grace.
15. **Romans 6:2**—To "die to sin" is to die to the love and practice of sin, making a decision to stop living in it. This takes place in repentance.
16. **Romans 6:3**—The baptism in this text is water baptism, not Spirit baptism. They ("we/us") were all baptized with the same baptism (Acts 9:18; 22:16). A word should be taken in its literal, most obvious sense, unless the context demands otherwise.
17. **Romans 6:3**—Baptized "into His death" brings us into the saving, cleansing and freeing benefits of His blood (Rev. 1:5; Acts 22:16).
18. **Romans 6:4**—Bible baptism is a burial—being "buried" in water and "raised" up (see also Col. 2:12; Matt. 3:16; Acts 8:38-39).
19. **Romans 6:6, 7, 18, 22**—Baptism is the moment in which one who was a "slave of sin" is "freed from sin" and "the body of sin."
20. **Romans 6:11**—"Alive" is in the present tense, emphasizing continuous, ongoing action.
21. **Romans 6:12**—Sin can be controlled and must not be permitted to control our lives. Obeying sin (6:16) is a choice, not forced.
22. **Romans 6:14**—We are under a law (3:27; Gal. 6:2; Jas. 1:25), but it is not a law that demands perfect obedience. When we sin (by violating His law, which we are under), the grace of God forgives us.
23. **Romans 6:23**—While "death" from sin is earned, eternal life is a "gift" not earned. But God's gifts are conditional (Josh. 6:1-5; Heb. 11:30). We must "work" for what God "gives" us (John 6:27-29).
24. **Romans 7:4**—The word "that" sets forth two purposes for the death of Christ freeing man from the law—(1) to be married to (i.e., belong to) Christ, (2) to bear fruit (i.e., spiritual offspring) to God.

Mark Your Bible

25. **Romans 7:8-9**—One learns what sin is through the law. As a child, Paul had no sin (had not violated the law), but when he became of age, sin came alive when he violated God's commandment.
26. **Romans 7:7-13**—Sin is personified to show that it is not the law that is sinful, but sin is the agent that leads us to disobey God's law. The law convicts and condemns sin, but the sinner is responsible for sin.
27. **Romans 7:12**—Here is the answer to the question in verse 7.
28. **Romans 7:14-23**—The present tense verbs in this section indicate this was a present struggle in which Paul was dealing with sin.
29. **Romans 7:25**—The first statement in this verse shows Paul's direction in this whole section—only "through Jesus Christ" is one delivered from the old law, from sin and from death.
30. **Romans 8:2**—"The law of the Spirit of life" is the gospel conveyed by the Holy Spirit ("the law of Christ" [Gal. 6:2] to which we are amenable); "the law of sin and death" is the law of Moses.
31. **Romans 8:3**—Jesus came in human flesh that was able to be tempted to sin, but He never sinned (Heb. 4:15; 2:14, 17; 1 Pet. 2:22).
32. **Romans 8:7-8**—Being "in the flesh" here means being devoted to fulfilling the desires of the flesh. So, for a Christian, being "in the Spirit" denotes one who is devoted to fulfilling the desires of God.
33. **Romans 8:19-22**—Creation is personified as longing to fulfill its purpose when earthly affairs are ended and the sons of God receive their future glory in heaven. Creation is often personified in Scripture (Psa. 96:12; 98:8; Isa. 35:1; 55:12), particularly when aiding God in fulfilling His purpose (Psa. 114). This has nothing to do with a restored earth at the end of time as the eternal heaven for the saints.
34. **Romans 8:17-30**—This whole section is to encourage Christians suffering for Christ. When we are suffering, our "spirit" doesn't like it and groans (8:23), and so also (in sympathy) the creation doesn't like it and groans (8:20-22), and the Holy Spirit doesn't like it and groans on our behalf (8:26).

(continued on next page)

Mark Your Bible

35. **Romans 8:29**—In His eternal purpose, God "foreknew" and "predestined" a group of people, not specific individuals. That group is the church (Eph. 1:4-7; 3:9-11), for they are the ones who are the "called out" (1 Pet. 2:9), having obeyed the gospel (2 Thess. 2:14). Calvinism is not taught in this verse.
36. **Romans 8:35-39**—No external force can separate us from Christ's love, but an individual Christian can choose to reject that love, fall away and be lost (Jas. 5:19-20; 2 Pet. 2:20-22; Gal. 5:4).
37. **Romans 8:39**—The saving love of God is only found "in Christ."

Day of Reflection

Take time today to reflect on the five chapters that you read this week. You may choose to read all five chapters again, in one sitting, or certain parts of them. Take time today to answer at least one of these questions below. You may or may not write anything down—you can choose to write or simply reflect.

1. What personal application do I need to make from the chapters I have read this week?

2. How can these five chapters help draw me closer to Jesus?

3. What words, phrases or verses in these chapters do I want to go back and study more in depth?

4. What questions do I have about what I have read this week on which I need to do some further Biblical research?

Week 26

June 25-July 1

June 25	Read Romans 9
June 26	Read Romans 10
June 27	Read Romans 11
June 28	Read Romans 12
June 29	Read Romans 13
June 30	Mark Your Bible
July 1	Day of Reflection

Prayer for this week:

*"Heavenly Father,
help me to not just be a hearer of the Word
but a doer of it!"*

June 25 Week 26, Day 1

Romans 9

Helpful Notes:

1. **Spiritual Israel** = God's redemptive plan went beyond just physical Israel; a spiritual Israel would come forth from His physical Israel nation; the Jews (physical Israel) brought forth the Christ, but they rejected Him; God's "spiritual Israel" is comprised of "the children of God" today (i.e., the church, New Testament Christians), who are "the children of promise" (cf. "twelve tribes" [Acts 26:7], "Abraham's seed" [Gal. 3:29], "the Israel of God" [Gal. 6:16]).
2. **Hardens** = God does not arbitrarily harden a heart; rather, this is a Hebrew idiom which represents God actively doing something which He merely permitted (see 2 Thess. 2:11-12); Pharaoh had already hardened his heart himself (Ex. 7:14; 8:15; 9:34) against God's miraculous demonstrations; God was simply giving him over to his heart's desires (cf. Rom. 1:24, 26, 28) and providentially using him to accomplish His will of delivering His people.
3. **Stumbling stone** = Rather than humble themselves before God, as their rock of refuge, they rejected Christ because He did not fulfill their nationalistic, militaristic expectations; trusting in themselves, they stumbled over God's real plan.

1. What do we learn about the heart of Paul in verses 1-3?

2. According to verse 5, what does Paul tell us about Jesus?

3. How do we compare to our God (verse 20)?

Verse for Meditation and Prayer: **Romans 9:20**

"But indeed, O man, who are you to reply against God?
Will the thing formed say to him who formed it,
'Why have you made me like this?'"

Romans 10

Helpful Notes:

1. **Establish own righteousness** = There is a stark difference between God's plan for righteousness (i.e., making man right with God) and man's plan for righteousness; when man rejects God's plan, he usually seeks to create his "own righteousness" (i.e., his own way of pleasing God) by enacting his own laws and traditions; such will never please God!
2. **The end of the law** = Paul says that "Christ is the end of the law"; "end" can mean "the goal, aim, purpose" or it can mean "termination"; in reality, Christ is both—He was the goal/purpose of the law (Gal. 3:19-25), and in Him the law was terminated (Col. 2:14; Eph. 2:13-16); only through Christ (not the law!) is the righteousness of God attained.
3. **Plan of salvation** = It was not Paul's intention to list the full plan of salvation, but he does mention "hearing" (v. 14, 17, 18), "believing" (v. 9, 10, 11, 14, 16), "confessing" (v. 9, 10), "calling" (v. 12, 13, 14); "calling" embraces repentance and baptism (Acts 2:21+38; 22:16); God's salvation is conditional (not unconditional) and is not attained by faith alone.

1. While Paul's Jewish friends had zeal, what did they lack?

2. What known fact (not a fictitious tale) must one "believe in your heart" in order to be saved?

3. How is the love and patience of God depicted in the last verse?

Verse for Meditation and Prayer: **Romans 10:17**

"So then faith comes by hearing, and hearing by the word of God."

Romans 11

Helpful Notes:

1. **Election no longer of works** = God's election of those who are "in Christ" is conditional (Eph. 1:3-4; Rom. 6:3-4); it is made available by His grace, and it cannot be earned by man, through works of the law of Moses (3:27-28; 7:4), works of human merit (Eph. 2:8-9) or legalistic works of any kind (Rom. 2:20, 28); nevertheless, obedient faith (i.e., works of faith) is essential to obtain grace (Jas. 2:14-26; Heb. 5:8-9).
2. **Olive tree** = Paul uses the image of an olive tree to illustrate the relationship between the Jews and Gentiles; the Jews are spoken of as branches broken off (due to their rejection) and the Gentiles as branches grafted in (due to their obedience); the Gentiles (the "you") are warned not to presume and the Jews are told that they can be restored.
3. **All Israel will be saved** = This is not affirming a nationwide conversion of Israel at the end of time; the word "so" is an adverb of manner (not time) and denotes that all of Israel who chose to be saved would be saved by obeying the gospel (10:12-17) and turning to the Deliverer (11:26-27) to have their sins taken away; salvation always requires obedience.

1. How can one receive "the goodness" of God?

2. What amazing attributes of God does Paul praise in verse 33?

3. What do the questions in verses 34-35 teach about the nature of God?

Verse for Meditation and Prayer: **Romans 11:33**

"Oh, the depth of the riches both of the wisdom and knowledge of God! How unsearchable are His judgments and His ways past finding out!"

Romans 12

Helpful Notes:

1. **Conformed** = The Greek word means "to form according to a pattern or mold; to fashion or shape one thing like another"; the word was used especially of things that are transitory, changeable or unstable; thus, God says not to fashion or shape ourselves after the pattern/mold of the world, with all of its wickedness; a Christian is to be holy.
2. **Transformed** = The Greek word is *metamorphoo*, from which we get our word "metamorphosis"; the word means "to change inwardly in fundamental character; to change into another form"; this inward change that finds expression in one's character and outward conduct can only be produced by spending time in the Word and being transformed into the image of Jesus Christ (2 Cor. 3:18).
3. **Members of one another** = All N.T. Christians are "members in one body," the church (12:4); this "one body in Christ" is made up of "many members," who have varying functions and abilities; not only do we belong to Christ (Acts 27:23; Gal. 5:24), we also belong to each other in His body.

1. According to verse 2, why should we be transformed?

2. What should we think about ourselves, according to verses 3 and 16?

3. What instruction in this chapter needs your attention the most?

Verse for Meditation and Prayer: **Romans 12:2**

"And do not be conformed to this world, but be transformed by the renewing of your mind, that you may prove what is that good and acceptable and perfect will of God."

June 29 Week 26, Day 5

Romans 13

Helpful Notes:

1. **Subject to governing authorities** = The Christian should stand out in his respect for others, including subjecting himself to civil authorities; in Paul's day, Nero Caesar was on the Roman throne (a most evil and inept ruler, who persecuted and killed Christians); rather than despise and rebel, Paul commanded to literally "arrange oneself under" them; this includes paying taxes to the government.
2. **God's minister** = Three times civil authorities are described in this way; their powers are ordained by God and are under His sovereign rule (Psa. 22:28); they are appointed by God (Dan. 2:21; 4:17, 25, 32) to maintain order, promote security, punish evildoers, etc.; to resist them (when their laws do not violate God's laws) is to resist and disobey God.
3. **Cast off, put on** = Christians are to cast away from self (a conscious, deliberate choice) all works of evil and thoughts of the flesh, and put on (a conscious, deliberate choice) the Lord and all things holy in His sight; this happens initially in baptism, but it is an ongoing process every day of life.

1. What should we do in order to not be afraid of civil authorities?

2. What debt do we "owe" to every person?

3. What "time" is it always for the Christian?

Verse for Meditation and Prayer: **Romans 13:14**

"But put on the Lord Jesus Christ, and make no provision for the flesh, to fulfill its lusts."

Mark Your Bible

1. **Romans 9:2**—"Have" is in the present tense, emphasizing the constant turmoil in Paul's heart for his fellow Jews who were lost.
2. **Romans 9:11**—The word "election" is not regarding their salvation; God chose Isaac over Ishmael and Jacob over Esau as part of His sovereign "purpose" to redeem man through Abraham's seed.
3. **Romans 9:13**—The words "loved" and "hated" are merely idioms that express preferred choice of one over another.
4. **Romans 9:15**—The "on whomever I will have mercy" includes the Gentiles (Isa. 55:7).
5. **Romans 9:21**—The "vessel for honor and dishonor" is not regarding salvation or eternal destiny, as if God made some to be saved and some to be lost. In the context, it has to do with God using His creations for purposes consistent with His overall purpose.
6. **Romans 9:22**—The Jewish nation ("the vessels of wrath") had prepared ("fitted") themselves for destruction through their own sin.
7. **Romans 9:23-24**—God's new Israel, the church ("the vessels of mercy") was eternally purposed to be composed of Jews and Gentiles.
8. **Romans 9:30-33**—"The law" of Moses could not bring about true righteousness; only obedient faith in Christ Jesus can do that.
9. **Romans 10:5-7**—God's plan of righteousness by faith does not require doing the impossible, like keeping the law perfectly. Rather, it is grounded in the perfect righteousness of Christ's sacrifice.
10. **Romans 10:11-13**—Underline the words "whoever" and "all" and connect with "no distinction." God shows no partiality (2:11; 3:22).
11. **Romans 10:14**—"Hearing" must be done critically, not passively. A "hearer" must listen carefully and examine critically what is said.
12. **Romans 10:16**—Circle "obeyed" and "believed"—God uses these words synonymously. They are also interchangeable with "calls" (v. 13) and "heard" (v. 18). Bible faith is more than mere mental assent. It involves submission and obedience.

(continued on next page)

Mark Your Bible

13. **Romans 10:16, 20**—Regardless of what modern critics might allege, God says that Isaiah wrote chapters 40-66 of his prophecy.
14. **Romans 10:19**—Those "who are not a nation" were the Gentiles.
15. **Romans 11:5**—The "remnant" were the first-century Jewish converts. The number was comparatively small to the whole population. Draw a line to "some of them" who are saved in verse 14. There would not be a massive conversion of Jews at any time.
16. **Romans 11:7-10**—Hearts are hardened by the choices they make to defy the demands of God. God makes the demands and then God permits the exercise of free will. God does not actively or arbitrarily harden; man does that on his own.
17. **Romans 11:11, 14**—The salvation of the Gentiles provoked "some" Jews (who had rejected Christ) to come back and obey Him.
18. **Romans 11:20, 22**—Salvation is conditional. One must "stand firm" (perfect tense) and "continue" (present tense) with God.
19. **Romans 11:22**—Whether one is a recipient of God's "goodness" or His "severity" is dependent on how man responds to His Word.
20. **Romans 11:25**—"The fullness of the Gentiles" noted the fulfillment of God's plan for salvation among the Gentiles, which involves the fullness of the Christian age. The Jews would remain hardened against the Christ until His return at the end of time. In the meantime, only "some" would be saved by obeying His commands.
21. **Romans 11:32**—Even though God has allowed His people to be shut up in disobedience, He still longs to extend His mercy to all who will stop disobeying Him.
22. **Romans 11:30-32**—Underline the four uses of "disobedient" or "disobedience." Faith and obedience are tied together in this book.
23. **Romans 11:36**—God is the source ("of Him"), the agency ("through Him") and the goal ("to Him") of all things.
24. **Romans 12:1-21**—With the exception of two verbs of instruction, all verbs of instruction to Christians in this chapter are in the present tense, denoting ongoing, habitual action. Christianity is your life!

Mark Your Bible

25. **Romans 12:1**—As "a living sacrifice," we recognize we are owned by God (1 Cor. 6:19-20) and are giving to Him what is already His.
26. **Romans 12:1**—The sacrificial life of a Christian is best understood as our "spiritual service" (ASV), rather than "spiritual worship" (ESV). The Greek word is not *proskuneo* (bow, kiss towards, worship) but *latreuo* (to serve, carry out religious duties). All of life should be service to God, but not all of life is worship.
27. **Romans 12:9**—There is a clearly discernible standard by which to know the difference between "evil" and "good"—i.e., God's Word!
28. **Romans 12:10**—"Be kindly affectionate" is a compound Greek word *philostorgos*—*philos* (friend) and *storge* (love for family, parents, children)—representing a tender, dear, devoted affection.
29. **Romans 12:14**—The verb "Bless" *(eulogeo)* means "to speak well of, to invoke blessings upon a person."
30. **Romans 12:20**—The "coals of fire" represent the shame and remorse experienced by an enemy who is rebuked with kindness.
31. **Romans 12:21**—The Greek word for "overcome" means "to conquer, prevail, be victor." (See Proverbs 17:13.)
32. **Romans 13:1-2**—When a government's ordinances violate the law of God (Ex. 1:15-17; Acts 4:20; 5:29), then a Christian must obey God. But where there is no violation of God's laws, civil government is to be obeyed.
33. **Romans 13:4**—Capital punishment is Divinely sanctioned (see also Gen. 9:6; Ex. 21:12-29; 22:18-20; Lev. 20:10-14; Num. 35:31-33).
34. **Romans 13:5**—We must obey civil authorities in order to know that we are right with God (i.e., "for conscience' sake").
35. **Romans 13:8**—Christians live on a higher plain. The underlying principle of their subjection to government is their love for others.
36. **Romans 13:11-12**—The fleeting nature of time and the imminent nature of "the day" of Christ's return must motivate us to work.
37. **Romans 13:14**—"Make no provision" is literally "give no forethought to." The allurements of the flesh must not find a home in our hearts.

July 1 Week 26, Day 7

Day of Reflection

Take time today to reflect on the five chapters that you read this week. You may choose to read all five chapters again, in one sitting, or certain parts of them. Take time today to answer at least one of these questions below. You may or may not write anything down—you can choose to write or simply reflect.

1. What personal application do I need to make from the chapters I have read this week?

2. How can these five chapters help draw me closer to Jesus?

3. What words, phrases or verses in these chapters do I want to go back and study more in depth?

4. What questions do I have about what I have read this week on which I need to do some further Biblical research?

Week 27

July 2-8

July 2	Read Romans 14
July 3	Read Romans 15
July 4	Read Romans 16
July 5	Read 1 Corinthians 1
July 6	Read 1 Corinthians 2
July 7	Mark Your Bible
July 8	Day of Reflection

Prayer for this week:

"Heavenly Father,
give me courage and strength this week
to live Your Word every day!"

Romans 14

Helpful Notes:

1. **Difference between doctrine and opinion** = It is essential to understand that this section of Scripture is not dealing with matters of doctrine, which are fixed teachings of Christ, which must be obeyed regardless of any person's wishes (Acts 5:29; Gal. 1:6-9); this section is dealing with matters of opinion, which are personal and expedient matters, and are not matters of law; in doctrine, there must be unity; in opinion, there must be liberty; in all things, there must be love.
2. **Stumbling block** = Christians must take responsibility for their words and actions, and be careful not to cause a weaker brother (one who has less spiritual knowledge and understanding) to stumble, including violating his own convictions in regard to expedients; we must help him to grow.
3. **Violate conscience** = If one does a right thing but believes it to be wrong (i.e., he doubts, and thus the act is "not from faith," violating his conscience), he sins; one's conscience (i.e., his very soul) must be carefully guarded, but it must be properly trained in God's Word to know and do right.

1. Without a single exception, what is every knee and every tongue going to do on the day of judgment?

2. What three concepts within the kingdom of God (i.e., the church) need special attention?

3. For what two things must we pursue (verse 19)?

Verse for Meditation and Prayer: **Romans 14:13**

*"Therefore let us not judge one another anymore,
but rather resolve this, not to put a stumbling block or
a cause to fall in our brother's way."*

July 3 Week 27, Day 2

Romans 15

Helpful Notes:

1. **Written for our learning** = The Old Testament is no longer a binding law upon man today, but there are hundreds of lessons that we can learn from it, which can generate perseverance, encouragement and hope in our lives today; the O.T. can increase our faith in and love for our amazing God.
2. **One another** = This is a reciprocal, reflexive pronoun, which emphasizes the responsibility of each party to equally engage in the required action in the direction of and for the good of the other party or parties; to be "like-minded toward one another," to "receive one another" and to "admonish one another" is the responsibility of each Christian toward every other Christian.
3. **The God of** – Paul describes four qualities of God in this chapter—the God of patience/endurance (v. 5), the God of comfort/encouragement (v. 5), the God of hope (v. 13) and the God of peace (v. 33); God is the ONLY source of these things in our lives; as we fulfill our responsibilities to each other in Christ, our God supplies us with all that we need.

1. In our responsibility to "receive one another," who is our ultimate example for having received us?

2. Although he was a Jew, to what people did God send Paul to be a minister? What challenges do you think he faced?

3. Where did Paul make it his aim to preach?

Verse for Meditation and Prayer: **Romans 15:5**

"Now may the God of patience and comfort grant you to be like-minded toward one another, according to Christ Jesus."

Romans 16

Helpful Notes:

1. **Churches of Christ** = Paul refers to a group of local congregations (perhaps around Corinth, where he was) as "churches of Christ"; this is a Scriptural designation for the Lord's people but is not intended to be its only title or name; it designates the body of people who are owned by Christ, by means of the purchase of His blood (Acts 20:28; Eph. 1:7).
2. **Divisions contrary to the doctrine** = The Bible places a great emphasis on the purity of the doctrine of Christ (cf. 2 John 9-11; Matt. 15:8-9; Gal. 1:6-9); those who would divide the body of Christ through false teachings or pushing their own opinions or traditions must be "watched out for" and not permitted to have any influence inside the church.
3. **Obedience** = The book of Romans, which places great emphasis on faith, emphasizes the essentiality of obedience to the will of God in order to be saved; a form of the word "obey" is found 11 times in the book, and it begins (1:5) and ends (16:26) stressing "obedience of faith"; truly one becomes and remains a Christian through faithful obedience.

1. Paul sent greetings to 26 people in Rome (24 by name), and he had never been there. What lesson can we apply from that?

2. What two actions must faithful Christians take toward those who cause divisions and offenses contrary to the doctrine?

3. What is a Christian's relationship to "good" and "evil" (v. 19)?

Verse for Meditation and Prayer: **Romans 16:17**

"Now I urge you, brethren, note those who cause divisions and offenses, contrary to the doctrine which you learned, and avoid them."

July 5 Week 27, Day 4

1 Corinthians 1

Helpful Notes: ** See Brief Introduction to First Corinthians on page 637.*

1. **The church of God** = There is no single "name" given for the Lord's church in the New Testament; it is called "churches of Christ" (Rom. 16:16), "the body of Christ" (1 Cor. 12:27), etc.; these are all designations of the nature and ownership of the church; the church belongs to God, for He "purchased" it with "His own blood" (Acts 20:28), and there is only one church that belongs to Him (Eph. 4:4+1:22-23).
2. **No divisions** = Jesus prayed that all believers would be "one" (John 17:20-21), in His "one" church (Eph. 4:4), teaching His "one faith" (Eph. 4:5), without addition or subtraction (Rev. 22:18-19); God will not accept ANY divisions; the authority of Christ demands that we "all speak the SAME thing"—such will lead to a division-less church!
3. **The message of the cross** = The preaching of Christ's death and resurrection is too simple for some and too offensive for others; thus, it is deemed "foolishness" in the eyes of those who rejected it; but it demonstrates both the "power" and the "wisdom" of God to save mankind.

1. According to verse 7, what should we be doing regarding the second coming of Christ?

2. What are the two ways in which the message of the cross is viewed by man?

3. According to the last verse, what should be our real focus?

Verse for Meditation and Prayer: **1 Corinthians 1:10**

"Now I plead with you, brethren, by the name of our Lord Jesus Christ, that you all speak the same thing, and that there be no divisions among you..."

July 6

Week 27, Day 5

1 Corinthians 2

Helpful Notes:

1. **Preaching is about substance** = Paul told the church that his preaching was not focused on "excellence of speech" (being a dynamic speaker), nor was it based upon "the wisdom of this age" (based upon human reasoning); his preaching focused on "Christ and Him crucified" and was based on "the wisdom of God"; that is the same preaching needed today.
2. **The things God has prepared** = While verse 9 is often quoted at funerals, the verse is not talking about heaven; in the context, man could have never imagined or known the eternal purpose of God made possible through Jesus Christ—all mankind being offered forgiveness of sins "in Christ" and the abundant spiritual blessings found only in His church.
3. **Verbal inspiration** = Verses 10-13 explain and affirm the verbal inspiration of the Bible: (1) only the Spirit of God knows the mind of God; (2) inspired men ("us/we") received the Spirit of God, who revealed the mind of God to them; (3) the inspired men put into "words" (now in your Bible) that which the Spirit taught them.

1. What was the one thing that Paul was "determined to know" (and declare) in his preaching?

2. From where did the "wisdom" that Paul preached originate?

3. What did Paul say would be the end of the wisdom and the rulers of the age?

Verse for Meditation and Prayer: **1 Corinthians 2:2**

"For I determined not to know anything among you except Jesus Christ and Him crucified."

Mark Your Bible

1. **Romans 14:1**—"Doubtful things" are matters of opinion.
2. **Romans 14:1**—The difference between the "weak" and the "strong" (15:1) is their level of spiritual knowledge and maturity. All Christians should be growing in these areas and not remain weak. The position or understanding of the weak must be respected, but it must not be allowed to control, rule and disrupt.
3. **Romans 14:3**—Some did not know that Christ made all meats permissible in the new covenant (Mark 7:19; Acts 10:9-16; 1 Tim. 4:3).
4. **Romans 14:8-9**—Christ is Lord and has authority, not us. All that we do must strive to foremost please the Lord!
5. **Romans 14:8**—It is important to remember, as we deal with others in the church who are weaker, that "we are [all] the Lord's."
6. **Romans 14:10-12**—Underline the words "all," "every" and "each." Every person will appear before Christ, bow before Him and give an account of his life. There are not exceptions.
7. **Romans 14:13, 15, 20, 21**—Draw a line from the words "destroy" to the words "stumbling," "offense," "stumbles." We overthrow (destroy) the faith of people when we cause them to stumble. Note also that a child of God can be destroyed (i.e., can fall away).
8. **Romans 14:20**—Keep "all things are pure" in context. It does not mean every sinful thing under the sun is now pure. It is talking about matters of opinion, specifically meats (v. 2, 14).
9. **Romans 14:21**—The word "wine" is from the Greek *oinos,* which can mean fermented or unfermented beverage.
10. **Romans 15:1**—"Weaker" Christians have scruples, failings, weaknesses when it comes to understanding the difference between essentials and nonessentials. Those who are stronger are responsible for being patient and bearing with them as they grow and mature.
11. **Romans 15:6**—Christians must think the same thing and speak the same thing. Speaking different things does not glorify God.

(continued on next page)

Mark Your Bible

12. **Romans 15:8-12**—Paul quotes four O.T. passages to prove that the unity of and peace among Jews and Gentiles was to be found only in the church. This is not yet future. This is right now.

13. **Romans 15:16**—One is "sanctified" by obeying the "truth" (John 17:17; Eph. 5:26). There is no direct operation of the Holy Spirit.

14. **Romans 15:19**—Illyricum is present day Croatia and Bosnia (former Yugoslavia). Paul's ministry had spanned 1,400 miles. His main concern is that he had "fully" (underline it) "preached the gospel."

15. **Romans 15:25-27**—The Gentile Christians felt themselves "debtors" to the Jewish Christians. Having received the "spiritual" blessing of the gospel through the Jews, they wanted to provide "material" blessings and relief in response.

16. **Romans 15:30**—The Greek for "strive together" literally means "to agonize together." Paul yearned for strong, passionate, fighting for him in their prayers. He believed in prayer—in fervent prayer!

17. **Romans 15:32**—Little did Paul know that he would arrive there four years later as a prisoner and be locked up for two years.

18. **Romans 16:1**—Cenchrea was the eastern port of Corinth.

19. **Romans 16:1**—Phoebe was "a servant of the church." There is no Biblical evidence that she was a "deaconess." The Greek *diakonos* can be translated "deacon," but it is most often translated generically as "minister" or "servant" (which it was of Jesus in 15:8). Being a "helper" (v. 2) is not the same as holding a leadership position.

20. **Romans 16:5, 14, 15**—Rather than having church buildings, the church met in homes. Perhaps verses 14 and 15 indicate there was more than one congregation in Rome.

21. **Romans 16:16**—This was a common greeting in that culture. The emphasis is on keeping it "holy" in the church.

22. **Romans 16:19**—In 1:8, their "faith" was spoken of, and here their "obedience" is known. The words are used interchangeably.

Mark Your Bible

23. **Romans 16:20**—Christ crushed Satan at the cross (Gen. 3:15). Here may be a reference to God crushing the efforts of the false teachers (cf. 2 Tim. 3:8-9) or likely to the ultimate victory of Christ and His people over Satan in the end (Matt. 25:41; Rev. 20:10). "Shortly" or "soon" can be translated "speedily" or "quickly" (Luke 18:8).

24. **Romans 16:22**—Paul often used an amanuensis (secretary or scribe) to whom he dictated the words for the letter (1 Cor. 16:21; Gal. 6:11; Col. 4:18; 2 Thess. 3:17).

25. **1 Corinthians 1:1**—This is probably the Sosthenes who was "the ruler of the synagogue" (Acts 18:17), likely Crispus' successor (18:8).

26. **1 Corinthians 1:2-10**—Mark six times the word "Lord" is used. "Jesus is Lord" is the theme of the book. The word is found 70 times in the book.

27. **1 Corinthians 1:2**—"Saints" are those who have been "sanctified" (set apart, made holy) "in Christ" as part of His "church."

28. **1 Corinthians 1:8**—"The end" is not necessarily referring to the end of time but to the completion or fulfillment of a goal reaching its "end" (see John 13:1)—i.e., keeping these Christians sound in faith.

29. **1 Corinthians 1:10**—Underline or highlight this verse. It is key.

30. **1 Corinthians 1:13**—In order to be "of Christ," two things are necessary: (1) Christ must be "crucified for you"; (2) you must be "baptized in the name of" Christ. Baptism is essential for salvation.

31. **1 Corinthians 1:17**—Paul was not minimizing the essentiality of baptism for salvation. He was minimizing the administrator of the baptism, especially since these Christians were elevating and identifying with those who baptized them. The work of a preacher is to preach, which includes the essentiality of baptism. If Paul wasn't sent to baptize, then why did he baptize people? Context is key!

32. **1 Corinthians 1:21**—Salvation was for those who believed and obeyed the gospel's requirements, including baptism (Acts 18:8).

(continued on next page)

Mark Your Bible

33. **1 Corinthians 2:5**—The faith of Christians and the Lord's church is not built on men but on the wisdom and power of God.

34. **1 Corinthians 2:7-16**—The "us" and "we" in these verses were the inspired men who received the revelation from the Spirit of God.

35. **1 Corinthians 2:10**—The Holy Spirit is God! As God, He is omniscient and, therefore, "searches" (i.e., knows) "all things."

36. **1 Corinthians 2:13**—Underline the word "words." The Spirit did not reveal thoughts or feelings, but the actual words to say/write.

37. **1 Corinthians 2:14-15**—The "natural man" considered Divine revelation to be foolish and chose to rely on the wisdom of the world instead, by which he would never have access to the mind of God.

Day of Reflection

Take time today to reflect on the five chapters that you read this week. You may choose to read all five chapters again, in one sitting, or certain parts of them. Take time today to answer at least one of these questions below. You may or may not write anything down—you can choose to write or simply reflect.

1. What personal application do I need to make from the chapters I have read this week?

2. How can these five chapters help draw me closer to Jesus?

3. What words, phrases or verses in these chapters do I want to go back and study more in depth?

4. What questions do I have about what I have read this week on which I need to do some further Biblical research?

Week 28

July 9-15

July 9	Read 1 Corinthians 3
July 10	Read 1 Corinthians 4
July 11	Read 1 Corinthians 5
July 12	Read 1 Corinthians 6
July 13	Read 1 Corinthians 7
July 14	Mark Your Bible
July 15	Day of Reflection

Prayer for this week:

"Heavenly Father,
help me to draw closer to You as I am reading."

1 Corinthians 3

Helpful Notes:

1. **No other foundation** = Jesus Christ is both the chief cornerstone (Eph. 2:20) and the only foundation of the church; He promised, "I will build my church" (Matt. 16:18); men may exalt themselves to "start a church" or may elevate others as "the head of the church," but Christ alone, and His teachings, are the solid foundation; a church built upon human wisdom is not the Lord's church.
2. **Anyone's work** = Paul speaks about building upon the foundation of Christ and to be aware of differences in one's "work"; the word "work" is being used for one's converts to Christ (see 9:1); some converts (who are durable like gold) will endure and make it to heaven; some converts (who are weak like straw) will not endure but be burned; the teacher will "suffer loss" of the convert but still be saved himself.
3. **The temple of God** = Many metaphors are used in Scripture for the church, including God's temple; God dwells in His temple/church (the people), both individually and collectively; His church must remain holy in service to the Lord and not allow false teaching or carnality to destroy it.

1. What caused these Christians to be carnal and not spiritual?

2. When we teach the gospel, who will take care of the growth of the church?

3. What metaphors are used in verse 9 to describe Christians?

Verse for Meditation and Prayer: **1 Corinthians 3:11**

"For no other foundation can anyone lay than that which is laid, which is Jesus Christ."

1 Corinthians 4

Helpful Notes:

1. **Faithful stewards** = Everything we have has been received from God (v. 7), including the opportunity to work and serve Christ; the work, the teaching, the words all belong to Christ, and not us; rather than be concerned about what others think of us (v. 3), our only concern should be what the Lord thinks (v. 4); we must be found faithful in His sight.
2. **Beyond that which is written** = It is sometimes easy to use human wisdom as a standard, but Christians must always use God's "written" Word as our standard; the authority of God's Word and the limitations of God's Word must be respected and obeyed; not only should we not "go" beyond what is written, we should not even "think" beyond it.
3. **Teach everywhere** = Paul did not alter his teaching to fit certain peoples or cultures; Paul taught the same "ways" (in doctrines and practices) everywhere that he went (4:17; 7:17; 14:33; 16:1); likewise, we are not to add to, take from, modify or seek to update anything in God's Word (Rev. 22:18-19; Gal. 1:6-9); we must teach only the oracles of God (1 Pet. 4:11).

1. What will our Judge reveal when He comes?

2. Whose praise should we want on the day of judgment?

3. Rather than "shame" his readers, why did Paul say that he wrote "these things"?

Verse for Meditation and Prayer: **1 Corinthians 4:6**

"Now these things, brethren, I have figuratively transferred to myself and Apollos for your sakes, that you may learn in us not to think beyond what is written..."

1 Corinthians 5

Helpful Notes:

1. **Withdraw fellowship** = When there is unrepentant sin in the church, the church must take action; the terms used in this chapter are: "be taken away from among you" (v. 2), "deliver such a one to Satan" (v. 5), "purge out the old leaven" (v. 7), "not to keep company with" (v. 9, 11), "not even to eat" (v. 11), "judge" (v. 12), "put away from yourselves" (v. 13); church discipline requires separation from sin.
2. **May be saved** = Withdrawing fellowship is not the man-made "excommunication"; church discipline has a purpose for the individual—to save his soul; the design is for the person "to learn" the seriousness of his sinful state (1 Tim. 1:20), to "be ashamed" of it (2 Thess. 3:14), to "destroy" his fleshly lusts and to be saved on the day of judgment; church discipline is an act of love toward one who is loved.
3. **Little leaven** = Church discipline also has a purpose for the church—to keep it pure and to prevent the spreading of sin; sin is a growing, spreading, infecting entity that can affect "the whole lump" (i.e., the church) if left unpurged.

1. Instead of being ashamed of the sin in the congregation, how had the Corinthian church responded to it?

2. What would happen to a congregation if it allowed unrepentant sin to remain in its midst?

3. Why would eating with such a person be forbidden?

Verse for Meditation and Prayer: **1 Corinthians 5:5**

"Deliver such a one to Satan for the destruction of the flesh, that his spirit may be saved in the day of the Lord Jesus."

July 12 Week 28, Day 4

1 Corinthians 6

Helpful Notes:

1. **Brother against brother before unbelievers** = Paul was not saying that Christians should not utilize civil protections or allow a church member's criminal behavior to go unrestrained; however, Christians need to be mindful of their influence upon non-Christians and avoid disgracing the cause of Christ in public; it would be better to take the high road and "accept wrong" than to hurt the church.
2. **Unrighteous living has consequences** = The ultimate Judge will not permit those living in sin to enter into heaven; the "unrighteous" are those who practice that which is sinful in the eyes of God, whether among those who refuse to obey the gospel or among Christians who practice ungodliness.
3. **Such were some of you** = Some of the Christians "were" (imperfect, denoting ongoing behavior in the past), before their conversion, actively involved in sin; it was by choice and not something over which they had no control; but they were no longer living that lifestyle, because (1) they repented, changing their mind and direction regarding sin, and (2) they were baptized to be washed from those sins.

1. What impact could it have on the Lord's church for Christians to be fighting against each other in court?

2. What three things happened when they were baptized (v. 11)?

3. Why do we need to glorify God in our bodies?

Verse for Meditation and Prayer: **1 Corinthians 6:20**

"For you were bought at a price; therefore glorify God in your body and in your spirit, which are God's."

1 Corinthians 7

Helpful Notes:

1. **The present distress** = Context is so critical; Paul mentions in verse 26 that the church in that day was facing (and going to be facing) a temporary period of "distress," "trouble" (v. 28) or opposition against the faith; some of the instructions he gives in this chapter regarding certain choices and actions must be understood in light of that "present distress."
2. **A spouse is not to depart** = The general and universal marital law of our God is that once a couple is married (who both had a Scriptural right to marry), neither one is to "depart" or "divorce" the other (7:10-11); if either of them do depart, there are only two options: remain unmarried or be reconciled (still considered married in God's eyes); Jesus gave only one exception for the innocent party (Matt. 19:9).
3. **Remain in the state in which called** = This ONLY applies to an external condition or state that is NOT inherently sinful (such as circumcision or slavery); this is NOT teaching that one in an unscriptural (i.e., sinful) marriage can remain in that marriage upon conversion (6:9-11 already denied that), anymore than a homosexual or polygamist could "remain."

1. If someone divorces their spouse, what two options do they have?

2. According to verse 19, what is it that really matters?

3. How long are a husband and wife bound to each other?

Verse for Meditation and Prayer: **1 Corinthians 7:11**

"But even if she does depart, let her remain unmarried or be reconciled to her husband. And a husband is not to divorce his wife."

Mark Your Bible

1. **1 Corinthians 3:1-4**—Christians must grow in Christ, not behaving as immature, worldly men, who are self-seeking and divisive.
2. **1 Corinthians 3:5**—"Ministers" (NKJV) are "servants" (NASB), from the Greek *diakonos*. They are not to be exalted and revered. They are "not anything" (v. 7) but laborers for God (v. 9).
3. **1 Corinthians 3:12**—Some converts are like "gold, silver, precious stones"—they will endure the trials of life and remain faithful. Some converts are like "wood, hay, straw"—they will not endure the trials of life and will not remain faithful.
4. **1 Corinthians 3:15**—This is not teaching "once saved, always saved." The expression "suffer loss" is reference to one's converts not making it to heaven. The expression "will be saved" refers back to the teacher, who will still be saved in heaven himself, based upon his own life (v. 8). The "work" is a convert (9:1).
5. **1 Corinthians 3:16-17**—This context is about the church (as a whole) being the temple of God. Each individual Christian's body being the temple of God is discussed in 6:19-20.
6. **1 Corinthians 3:21**—We must put our allegiance in God and not in man. When we do that, all of God's blessings are ours equally.
7. **1 Corinthians 4:1**—The Greek word for "servants" in this verse literally means "under-rowers." Paul saw himself as an underling, a subordinate, and serving at the pleasure of the Master.
8. **1 Corinthians 4:2**—"Stewards" are managers of another person's property. It must be used wisely for the owner's glory.
9. **1 Corinthians 4:7**—Underline "what do you have that you did not receive?" Everything we have is from God (Jas. 1:17).
10. **1 Corinthians 4:8-13**—Paul used irony and sarcasm to convince their factious leaders to stop boasting in themselves.

(continued on next page)

Mark Your Bible

11. **1 Corinthians 4:15**—Paul was their "father" in the faith. He had "begotten" them by teaching them the gospel. One is "born again" by "obeying" the "word of God" (1 Pet. 1:22-23). The teaching of the gospel is God's power to save (Rom. 1:16)—not the teacher and not a direct operation of the Holy Spirit upon one's heart.
12. **1 Corinthians 4:19**—Underline "if the Lord wills." This is the only way we should plan or do anything (Jas. 4:15).
13. **1 Corinthians 5:3**—Not all judging is wrong. In fact, judging properly (according to God's righteous standard) is commanded and essential to remain pure (John 7:24; see 1 Cor. 5:12b).
14. **1 Corinthians 5:4**—Church discipline is to be exercised (by the authority of Christ, not man) by the whole church and involves a public, formal procedure when the church is assembled together.
15. **1 Corinthians 5:5**—"Delivering to Satan" is the act of withdrawing the church's fellowship from him and turning him back over to the realm of the devil, where he has determined to live. The church is simply following the lead of Christ (v. 4), for God does the same toward His people who turn to sin (Rom. 1:24-28; Acts 7:42).
16. **1 Corinthians 5:7-8**—In the O.T., the Jews were to remove all leaven for Passover; in the N.T., Christ is our Passover, who requires us to remove the leaven of wickedness and keep focused on truth.
17. **1 Corinthians 6:2**—Saints "judge the world" through their preaching, their condemnation of sin and their godly living (see Heb. 11:7).
18. **1 Corinthians 6:3**—In like manner, the faithful and godly lives of Christians will pass judgment on the angels who sin, as well.
19. **1 Corinthians 6:9**—God's marriage laws are applicable to alien sinners and not just Christians.
20. **1 Corinthians 6:9-11**—One may not continue to live in sin when he becomes a Christian. He must repent and discontinue whatever sin he was engaged in before (including sinful sexual relationships).

Mark Your Bible

21. **1 Corinthians 6:9**—Two different Greek words are used for homosexuals, pertaining to both the active and the passive partners.
22. **1 Corinthians 6:11**—It is in baptism when one is washed in the blood of Jesus (Acts 22:16), set apart for a holy purpose (Eph. 5:26) and absolved of all guilt from sin (Rom. 6:3-4, 17-18).
23. **1 Corinthians 6:12**—It was either a common saying that "All things are lawful for me," or Paul was reminding them that all actions are within one's power to control. Nothing sinful is ever lawful.
24. **1 Corinthians 6:18**—Sexual sin has physical and psychological affects unlike any other sin—flee from it and overcome it.
25. **1 Corinthians 6:19**—As the Holy Spirit dwells in the temple/church as a whole (3:16-17), He dwells in each Christian upon baptism (Acts 2:38; Gal. 4:6; Rom. 8:9).
26. **1 Corinthians 7:1**—This is an idiom for sex (Gen. 20:6; Prov. 6:29).
27. **1 Corinthians 7:2**—God designed and confined sex to marriage.
28. **1 Corinthians 7:8**—Keep in context of the "present distress" (v. 26).
29. **1 Corinthians 7:10**—"Not I but the Lord" means the Lord dealt with this while on the earth (Matt. 5:32; 19:9).
30. **1 Corinthians 7:12**—"I, not the Lord" is not Paul's opinion, but it is a specific matter that the Lord did not specifically address while on the earth. Everything Paul wrote was God-given (1 Cor. 14:37).
31. **1 Corinthians 7:14**—The unbelieving spouse is living within the purifying/sanctifying influence of the Christian spouse, which gives them a better life and may lead to their conversion. The same blessing extends to children who have a Christian parent.

(continued on next page)

Mark Your Bible

32. **1 Corinthians 7:15**—Remarriage is not under discussion in this verse; Paul is not giving another exception for divorce and remarriage. Jesus gave only ONE exception (Matt. 19:9). The Greek perfect tense on "not under bondage" emphasizes he/she is not now and never has been under this bondage. It cannot apply to the marriage bond. Rather it indicates the Christian was never enslaved to force himself on his mate and never obligated to renounce his relationship with Jesus, in order to chase the unbeliever who departs.
33. **1 Corinthians 7:27-28, 36-38**—Keep in context of "present distress."
34. **1 Corinthians 7:39**—A widow was free to remarry but only "in the Lord." This expression usually denotes a Christian (Rev. 14:13; 2 Cor. 12:2). If Paul had married, it would only be to a "sister" (1 Cor. 9:5). If Paul and widows were to marry Christians, what about us? (This is the first time remarriage is discussed in the chapter.)

Day of Reflection

Take time today to reflect on the five chapters that you read this week. You may choose to read all five chapters again, in one sitting, or certain parts of them. Take time today to answer at least one of these questions below. You may or may not write anything down—you can choose to write or simply reflect.

1. What personal application do I need to make from the chapters I have read this week?

2. How can these five chapters help draw me closer to Jesus?

3. What words, phrases or verses in these chapters do I want to go back and study more in depth?

4. What questions do I have about what I have read this week on which I need to do some further Biblical research?

Week 29

July 16-22

July 16	Read 1 Corinthians 8
July 17	Read 1 Corinthians 9
July 18	Read 1 Corinthians 10
July 19	Read 1 Corinthians 11
July 20	Read 1 Corinthians 12
July 21	Mark Your Bible
July 22	Day of Reflection

Prayer for this week:

*"Heavenly Father,
Your approval is all that matters to me!
Help me to live pleasing to You!"*

1 Corinthians 8

Helpful Notes:

1. **Knowledge puffs up** = Sometimes knowing something can cause one to have an inflated ego; however, any arrogance proves that he does not know as much as he could or should know; knowledge must be balanced with humility and love, and when it is not, the knowledge is useless and will prove to be an obstacle to further growth and true effectiveness.
2. **Conscience** = A person's conscience is that inner sense of oughtness that drives him to do what he believes to be right or to avoid what he believes to be wrong; in the process, it either accuses him or excuses him, in his own mind (Rom. 2:5); this inner faculty is unique to human beings; it is a sin to violate one's own conscience (Rom. 14:23) or the conscience of another (1 Cor. 8:12-23); it is essential that the "knowledge" guiding the conscience be trained by God's Word.
3. **Sin against others is sin against Christ** = We must be ever mindful of our influence on others (Matt. 18:6; Mark 9:42) and our action or inaction toward others (Matt. 25:40, 45); if we sin against another, causing him to sin, we sin against Christ Himself; this is not a matter to be taken lightly.

1. How can we learn to balance knowledge and love?

2. With true knowledge, what do we "know" about an idol?

3. To whom must our greatest devotion be directed in all things?

Verse for Meditation and Prayer: **1 Corinthians 8:13**

"Therefore, if food makes my brother stumble,
I will never again eat meat, lest I make my brother stumble."

July 17 Week 29, Day 2

1 Corinthians 9

Helpful Notes:

1. **Live from the gospel** = Paul spent most of this chapter defending his apostleship and his right, as a preacher of the gospel, to receive financial support; he provided compelling evidence from his peers, the Old Testament, everyday workers, priests of the temple, etc.; yet, he did not take support from Corinth, lest his efforts be made void by these critics; for Paul, his main "reward" was just to preach the gospel.
2. **All things to all men** = Paul did not become a sinner, nor did he violate any law of God; he did not conform himself to the world (in violation of Romans 12:2); Paul simply adapted himself (without compromise) to the setting and people in which he found himself (sacrificing some of his liberties), in order to save souls; that was always his goal!
3. **Discipline my body** = In striving to reach heaven (the ultimate race with the ultimate prize), "self-control in all things" is essential (Gal. 5:16-25); without controlling one's body with its passions, a child of God can become "disqualified" in the race and not receive the prize of heaven.

1. What law did God give about muzzling an ox and why?

2. For what reason was Paul striving to "endure all things"?

3. How does the "crown" for which we compete compare with the crown obtained in human contest?

Verse for Meditation and Prayer: **1 Corinthians 9:27**

"But I discipline my body and bring it into subjection,
lest, when I have preached to others,
I myself should become disqualified."

1 Corinthians 10

Helpful Notes:

1. **Happened as examples** = We would not know about the actions (good or bad) of O.T. characters if God did not record them for us in the Bible; Paul says that they are recorded as an "example" (Greek *tupos* meaning "pattern, model") to instruct us in how to please the Lord; seeing others fail helps to warn us to not fail in the same ways.
2. **Tempted beyond able to bear** = This is often misquoted to say that "God will not put more on me than I can handle"; the verse is about temptation to sin; God will stop temptation from exceeding my ability to handle it, and one way He does that is by providing a way of escape; God does not tempt us (Jas. 1:13), but He helps us through it (Heb. 2:17-18).
3. **Communion** = The word emphasizes that, when the church partakes of the sacred elements the Lord's Supper every Lord's Day, they are communing with Jesus Christ, who communes "with" us (Matt. 26:29) ; those in idol worship commune with demons; when we "all partake," we enjoy a unique oneness in the body of Christ (with Him and with each other), which should never be taken for granted.

1. In what way does Paul show that "God is faithful"?

2. Besides myself, whose good do I need to look out for?

3. Based upon what principle could Paul say that the Christians could eat any meat (10:25-26)?

Verse for Meditation and Prayer: **1 Corinthians 10:31**

"Therefore, whether you eat or drink, or whatever you do, do all to the glory of God."

1 Corinthians 11

Helpful Notes:

1. **The head** = Verse 3 presents the Divine order of authority (not a cultural matter but an eternal principle of God); the relationship between woman and man is likened to the relationship between Christ and the Father; woman is not inferior to man, any more than Christ is inferior to the Father, but they each have different roles in the Divine plan; subjection does not mean inequality; God's order must be respected.
2. **Come together** = Paul uses this expression five times in this chapter to denote their "come-together assembly" on the first day of the week; the purpose (as noted by the infinitive of purpose) of the first-day-of-the-week assembly was "to eat the Lord's Supper" (11:20, 33); since the church was to assemble "every first day of the week" (16:1-2), they were to partake of the Lord's Supper every Sunday (Acts 20:7).
3. **Unworthy manner** = "Unworthy" is an adverb (which modifies a verb) and not an adjective (which would modify a noun); the emphasis is not on a person being "worthy" to partake but on the manner in which he partakes being worthy—a "worthy manner" involves (1) discerning the Lord's body and (2) examining himself.

1. Because the church had changed the Lord's Supper from what it was supposed to be, what was the result among them?

2. Jesus said to "do this" (i.e., the Lord's Supper) in what?

3. What do we need to be "discerning" in the Lord's Supper?

Verse for Meditation and Prayer: **1 Corinthians 11:29**

"For he who eats and drinks in an unworthy manner
eats and drinks judgment to himself,
not discerning the Lord's body."

July 20

Week 29, Day 5

1 Corinthians 12

Helpful Notes:

1. **Miraculous, spiritual gifts** = Chapters 12-14 discuss this topic: the existence of these gifts (ch. 12), the expiration of these gifts (ch. 13), the exercise of these gifts (ch. 14); these were miraculous abilities (i.e., beyond one's natural ability) that were all given by the Holy Spirit when an apostle laid hands on a Christian (Acts 8:14-18); no gifts were better than others, as all gifts were bestowed by God for the proper functioning of His church.
2. **One body, many members** = The word "body" is found 18 times in this chapter, always preceded by the definite article "the" or the word "one" (five times); Christ only has "one body" (Eph. 4:4), which is His church (1:22-23); His body is composed of those who are "saved" (Acts 2:38-47); while there is great variety among the members, each one is needed and dependent on the others to function as God designed.
3. **Baptized into one body** = Water baptism is the only means by which one enters "into one body" (i.e., "into Christ" and "into His death" [Rom. 6:3-4, Gal. 3:27)]); one learns and is motivated to be baptized by the teaching of the "words" of the Spirit within the gospel (Eph. 5:26; Tit. 3:5; John 3:3-5).

1. Who decided what miraculous, spiritual gifts each Christian received in the first century?

2. How does Paul emphasize that all members are needed?

3. How should all members react when one member suffers?

Verse for Meditation and Prayer: **1 Corinthians 12:13**

"For by one Spirit we were all baptized into one body – whether Jews or Greeks, whether slaves or free – and have all been made to drink into one Spirit."

Mark Your Bible

1. **1 Corinthians 8:1**—*Agape* love will seek to build someone up, rather than put them down or arrogantly show superior knowledge.
2. **1 Corinthians 8:6**—God, the Father is the "Father of all things," and Christ is the agent through whom all things were created (John 1:3; Col. 1:16). There is NO other deity to whom we own any loyalty!
3. **1 Corinthians 8:11**—How many of His rights and privileges did Christ give up for His brethren? We need to learn from Him.
4. **1 Corinthians 8:11**—A Christian can fall away and perish.
5. **1 Corinthians 8:13**—My brother must be more important to me than my rights and privileges. But, I must also make it a priority to help to train a weaker brother to grow, mature and know truth.
6. **1 Corinthians 9:1**—A qualification to be an apostle was to have "seen Jesus Christ our Lord" (Acts 1:21-22). There can be no "apostles" today.
7. **1 Corinthians 9:5**—If Paul were to "take along" a wife, as the other apostles did, Paul stated she would be "a believing wife" (or more literally, "a sister, as a wife"). He would only marry a Christian.
8. **1 Corinthians 9:5**—Of all the names to specifically identify as being married, Paul said that Cephas/Peter had a wife. Perhaps God put this in the Bible to disprove the notion that Peter was the first Pope.
9. **1 Corinthians 9:17**—Paul saw his labor as being "entrusted" with a work that was not his but belonged to his Master in heaven. Thus, he longed to do nothing but preach the gospel—a reward in itself.
10. **1 Corinthians 9:19, 20, 21, 22**—Underline the five times the word "win" is used, then connect them all to the word "save" in verse 22.
11. **1 Corinthians 9:24**—The word "run" is a present imperative, emphasizing urgent and continuous action.
12. **1 Corinthians 9:26**—Paul was striving for heaven with absolute confidence (2 Tim. 4:8), pressing diligently for the prize (Phil. 3:14).

(continued on next page)

Mark Your Bible

13. **1 Corinthians 9:25**—The Greek word for "competes" is *agonizomai.* You can see the English "agonize" in it. It means "to contend, fight, struggle, engage in a contest; to fully expend all energies and to rigidly deny all passions." Heaven will surely be worth it all!
14. **1 Corinthians 9:27**—Even the apostle Paul could fall away.
15. **1 Corinthians 10:1-10**—Underline "all," "most" and "some" to see the contrast of "all" who were blessed and what "some" did."
16. **1 Corinthians 10:2**—By being immersed/surrounded by water above and beside them in the Red Sea, the Israelites entered into a new relationship with Moses, devoting themselves to his leadership.
17. **1 Corinthians 10:8**—There is no contradiction with Numbers 25:9, where it says that 24,000 died. This verse just says that 23,000 of them died in "one day."
18. **1 Corinthians 10:11**—"The ends of the ages" had come upon first-century Christians. It is simply the Christian age, the concluding dispensation of human history.
19. **1 Corinthians 10:12**—Calvinism's "perseverance of the saints" (i.e., once saved, always saved) is absolutely false. Anyone can fall.
20. **1 Corinthians 10:21**—How can anyone try to justify participating in unscriptural acts of worship with manmade religious groups?
21. **1 Corinthians 10:23**—It was either a common saying that "All things are lawful for me," or Paul was reminding them that all actions are within one's power to control. Nothing sinful is ever lawful.
22. **1 Corinthians 10:31**—Underline "whatever you do, do all to the glory of God." This is the overriding goal of everything we do!
23. **1 Corinthians 10:32-33**—We must consider the influence that our actions have on others, lest we ever jeopardize their salvation.
24. **1 Corinthians 11:2**—This is not a reference to "traditions of men" but to good "traditions" given by God (cf. 2 Thess. 2:15).

Mark Your Bible

25. **1 Corinthians 11:2-16**—This was a cultural practice within the Graeco-Roman culture that is not duplicated in our culture today. What they would "judge" (11:13) to be "proper" or "shameful" (11:6) is not the same in our day. To them, the covering/veil symbolized a woman's submission to male authority (11:10)—the veil was not a hat or small piece, but was a full veil that covered the entire face/head. To remove it symbolized rejection of male authority, which was equivalent to shaving the head—an act done by women of ill-repute (11:5-6).
26. **1 Corinthians 11:8-9**—God created men and women in a Divine order and with clear distinctions put in place by God.
27. **1 Corinthians 11:11-12**—The two genders were designed by God to complement each other and to have interdependence.
28. **1 Corinthians 11:20**—They were supposed to be coming together to eat the Lord's Supper, but that was not their purpose. Thus, Paul did "not praise" them in this (11:17).
29. **1 Corinthians 11:20-21**—Circle, connect and notice the difference between the suppers they were eating—"Lord's" versus "own."
30. **1 Corinthians 11:25-26**—The expression "as often as" indicates a known frequency—which was every first day of the week (16:1-2). It was not a temporal institution initiated by the Lord.
31. **1 Corinthians 12:3**—While the Spirit led some teaching in the first century, He instructs today through His completed revelation that is written in the Scriptures (Eph. 6:17).
32. **1 Corinthians 12:10, 28, 30**—The Corinthian Christians had elevated speaking in tongues as the best gift, but Paul lists it last every time.
33. **1 Corinthians 12:13**—"Made to drink" is a metaphor that refers to "all" Christians receiving the non-miraculous gift of the Holy Spirit upon one's baptism (Acts 2:38; Gal. 4:6; 1 Cor. 6:19-20).

(continued on next page)

Mark Your Bible

34. **1 Corinthians 12:18**—God made the human body (Psa. 139:14) and "set" each part in place according to His amazing design.
35. **1 Corinthians 12:22-24**—God is concerned about the "weak," "less honorable" and "unpresentable" parts of His body/church (draw lines connecting those); therefore, we should be, as well.
36. **1 Corinthians 12:25**—God wants NO division in His church (1:10).
37. **1 Corinthians 12:31**—"The more excellent way" is "love" in chapter 13.

Day of Reflection

Take time today to reflect on the five chapters that you read this week. You may choose to read all five chapters again, in one sitting, or certain parts of them. Take time today to answer at least one of these questions below. You may or may not write anything down—you can choose to write or simply reflect.

1. What personal application do I need to make from the chapters I have read this week?

2. How can these five chapters help draw me closer to Jesus?

3. What words, phrases or verses in these chapters do I want to go back and study more in depth?

4. What questions do I have about what I have read this week on which I need to do some further Biblical research?

Week 30

July 23-29

July 23	Read 1 Corinthians 13
July 24	Read 1 Corinthians 14
July 25	Read 1 Corinthians 15
July 26	Read 1 Corinthians 16
July 27	Read 2 Corinthians 1
July 28	Mark Your Bible
July 29	Day of Reflection

Prayer for this week:

*"Heavenly Father,
thank You for giving me everything that I need
in the Bible!"*

July 23 Week 30, Day 1

1 Corinthians 13

Helpful Notes:

1. ***Agape* love** = The Greeks had a variety of words for "love," but the noblest of all was *agape* love; this love was not based upon or motivated by emotion, but it was a deliberate commitment to sacrifice self and actively work (not just a feeling) in the best interest of others—unconditionally (no matter who they are or what they do) and unselfishly (without seeking personal gain); this is the love that God has for us, the love we are to have for God, and the love we are to have for all mankind.
2. **That which is perfect has come** = This is not the return of Christ—keep it in context; the miraculous, spiritual gifts (introduced in chapter 12) provided "part" of what early Christians needed in a part-by-part revelation of the N.T.; the "perfect" came when the New Testament was "completed" (the meaning of the Greek *teleion*) and was no longer being preached in "parts" (the "parts" and miraculous gifts ceased).
3. **Done away** = The miraculous, spiritual gifts would "fail," "cease," "vanish away," be "done away" and be "put away" when the "complete" N.T. was written, for they would no longer be necessary; they would have fulfilled their purpose.

1. What did Paul say it would sound like if he spoke without love?

2. What quality of love needs your attention the most?

3. What does *agape* love "never" do?

Verse for Meditation and Prayer: **1 Corinthians 13:13**

"And now abide faith, hope, love, these three; but the greatest of these is love."

1 Corinthians 14

Helpful Notes:

1. **Edification** = A form of the words "edify" or "edification" is found seven times in this chapter, which focuses on the assembly of the church; the word literally has to do with "a building or building a house" and came to mean "building up"; there is an interpersonal purpose of the church assembling and that is to encourage and build each other up.
2. **Understand** = The NKJV has the words "understand" or "understanding" nine times in this chapter, which focuses on what happens in the assembly; there are different Greek words behind these English words, which emphasize "hearing," "thinking," "the mind" and "understanding;" the assembly is not a place for confusion (v. 33); rather, everything must be understandable (and done "decently and in order," v. 40), so that it is edifying.
3. **The commandments of the Lord** = Paul never wrote his own opinions or ideas; everything that he wrote was given to him by God; when you read his writings in the Bible, they are truly (and only) the commandments of the Lord.

1. While the Corinthian Christians elevated speaking in tongues, which gift did Paul tell them to especially pursue?

2. What three things result from preaching God's Word (v. 3)?

3. Why would God spend a whole chapter regulating (in detail) what happens in His assemblies?

Verse for Meditation and Prayer: **1 Corinthians 14:40**

"Let all things be done decently and in order."

July 25 Week 30, Day 3

1 Corinthians 15

Helpful Notes:

1. **The gospel** = The word gospel is from the Greek *euangelion* and means "good news"; the gospel involves (1) facts to be believed: Jesus died, was buried and was raised from the dead (15:1-4); (2) commands to be obeyed (Mark 16:15-16); (3) promises to be enjoyed (Acts 2:38; Eph. 1:3-7); the gospel is what saves man from sin (when he meets its conditions) and will continue to save him, as he continues to hold fast to it.
2. **Christ is risen** = Our faith is founded on historical, proven facts (15:1-4); the tomb of Jesus was empty (Matt. 28:1-6); He "was seen by" hundreds of witnesses (15:5-8); this message was faithfully preached by men who endured personal loss, persecution and death (these men knew if the resurrection was a hoax or not); the fact that Jesus was raised from the dead guarantees that we will be raised from the dead.
3. **All will be changed** = The resurrected body will be incorruptible, immortal, bear the image of heaven, will be like Jesus (1 John 3:2), will be different from the earthly body but still identifiably tied to it (15:38), will be ready for eternity.

1. Why did Paul consider himself "the least of the apostles"?

2. What warning does Paul give about evil companions?

3. What reason exists that faithful Christians should fear death?

Verse for Meditation and Prayer: **1 Corinthians 15:58**

"Therefore, my beloved brethren, be steadfast, immovable, always abounding in the work of the Lord, knowing that your labor is not in vain in the Lord."

July 26 Week 30, Day 4

1 Corinthians 16

Helpful Notes:

1. **Collection** = As a part of their first-day-of-the-week gathering for worship, the Christians were to give; this was a universal command/order; "each" Christian who had received income was to give in proportion to what he had earned; this was to be put into the treasury (as they lay by in store) and not kept at home for some later collection; this was the authorized manner of financing the works of the church.
2. **The first day of the week** = The first day of the week has great significance to N.T. Christians (for it was the day that Christ was raised and the day that the church was established), and it is the day that they always assemble to break bread and worship God (Acts 20:7); the Greek in this verse indicates for this to happen EVERY first day of the week.
3. **Devoted to ministering** = The family of Stephanas had "set themselves" (ASV) or "devoted themselves" to ministering/serving their fellow Christians; the KJV says that they "addicted themselves"; the word means "to place in order, arrange, appoint"; they did not wait to be asked to serve; they appointed themselves to serve others and were addicted to it.

1. Why do you think God does not demand a "tithe" in the New Testament but says to give as we "prosper"?

2. Paul told the Christians, "Let all that you do be done in _________."

3. What did Paul say was to happen to the "anyone" who "does not love the Lord Jesus Christ"?

Verse for Meditation and Prayer: **1 Corinthians 16:13**

"Watch, stand fast in the faith, be brave, be strong."

2 Corinthians 1

Helpful Notes: ** See Brief Introduction to Second Corinthians on page 638.*

1. **Saint** = The Greek word for "saints" (*hagios*) fundamentally means "separated," and is usually defined "holy, sanctified, set apart"; therefore, "saints" are those who have been separated from the world and into a sanctified relationship with Christ, which takes place in baptism (Eph. 5:26); these are living persons (contrary to modern dogma) who are members of the church (Rom. 1:7; 1 Cor. 1:2; Phil. 1:1; 4:21-22).
2. **Comfort** = A form of the word "comfort" (in noun or verb) is found 10 times in verses 3-7; the verb *parakaleo* is a compound word that literally means "call to one's side," indicating a call to come and be present and help; God is the "God of all comfort" (coming to our side to help), and He expects us to come alongside and help one another; the Greek word is also translated "encourage, exhort, plead, etc."
3. **All promises of God are "Yes"** = God keeps His promises, for our "God is faithful"; specifically "all" of the promises (i.e., 332 O.T. prophecies) that God made concerning the Christ have "all" been fulfilled with a resounding "Yes!"

1. While these brethren were questioning Paul's apostleship, how did Paul say that he became an apostle?

2. What kind of comfort do we need to offer others?

3. When bad things happened to Paul, he learned to "not trust" in self but to "trust" in who?

Verse for Meditation and Prayer: **2 Corinthians 1:3**

"Blessed be the God and Father of our Lord Jesus Christ, the Father of mercies and God of all comfort."

Mark Your Bible

1. **1 Corinthians 13:1**—Paul is speaking in hypothetical (and even hyperbolical) language to prove a point. There is no explanation of "the tongues of angels" or any suggestion that man spoke such.
2. **1 Corinthians 13:1-3**—Paul emphasizes that it does not matter what a person says (v. 1), has (v. 2) or does (v. 3); if it is not motivated by and accompanied by *agape* love, it is all useless.
3. **1 Corinthians 13:2**—These were miraculous levels of spiritual gifts, including a miraculous level of faith (12:9).
4. **1 Corinthians 13:3**—Even if he was burned at the stake, such courage would profit him nothing if not done in love.
5. **1 Corinthians 13:4-7**—There are 15 qualities of *agape* love listed—seven positive qualities to practice and eight negative qualities to avoid. Each of these requires our attention and development.
6. **1 Corinthians 13:12**—In its infancy, the church needed the miraculous gifts, but maturity would develop when they had the full and complete New Testament and no longer relied on the miraculous.
7. **1 Corinthians 13:12**—Seeing only "part" of God's revelation is like looking in a brass mirror, but seeing the "complete" revelation would be a clear, crisp, sharp, face-to-face view of God's will.
8. **1 Corinthians 13:13**—All three would "abide" (present tense, emphasizing ongoing activity) after the spiritual gifts had been "done away." Faith and hope would find their culmination at the end of time, but love would endure and abide forever and ever in heaven.
9. **1 Corinthians 14:1**—Miraculous, spiritual gifts were only available to first-century Christians and are not available to us today.
10. **1 Corinthians 14:1**—Prophesying can involve both forthtelling (predicting future events) and foretelling (imparting God's truth).
11. **1 Corinthians 14:2**—When no one understands a person speaking in tongues (because there is no interpreter), what he says is a "mystery." He only "speaks mysteries" when no one translates.

(continued on next page)

Mark Your Bible

12. **1 Corinthians 14:2**—The word "unknown" found in the KJV has no basis in the Greek text. It should not have been put in the Bible.
13. **1 Corinthians 4:4, 5, 12, 19, 23, 28, 33, 34, 35**—The word "church" is found nine times in this chapter—sometimes in reference to "the people" who make up the church and sometimes in reference to "the assembly" of the church. Essential to the very nature of the church is the assembly. To be His church is to assemble regularly.
14. **1 Corinthians 14:6, 9, 10, 11**—Connect the words "tongue(s)" and "language(s)." Tongues in the Bible were real, known languages.
15. **1 Corinthians 14:13-14, 27-28**—God required that any foreign language spoken must be interpreted, in order for everyone to understand. If people could not understand the language and there was no interpreter, the speaker was to keep silent.
16. **1 Corinthians 14:22-23**—There is no way to teach truth with words (or mere sounds) that are not intelligible and understandable.
17. **1 Corinthians 14:26**—God lays down rules for exercising spiritual gifts, and it does not involve "each one" selfishly doing as he pleases in the assembly. "Each one" is rebuked in 1:12 and 11:21, and is rebuked here for stepping outside God's regulations. (There is no support here for solos or choirs. This verse is condemnation, not permission.)
18. **1 Corinthians 14:32**—The spirits of these men were under their control. They could follow the rules and keep silent at any time.
19. **1 Corinthians 14:33**—All of the congregations of the Lord's church were taught and guided by the same inspired truths.
20. **1 Corinthians 14:34-35**—Women were not prohibited from all speaking in the assembly, for all Christians are to "speak to one another" in congregational singing (Eph. 5:19; Col. 3:16). The general principle—"It is shameful for women to speak in church"—applies to speaking in a way that subordinates the man to her and violates the principle of subjection (Gen. 3:16; 1 Tim. 2:8-14).

Mark Your Bible

21. **1 Corinthians 15:4, 13-20**—The words "rose" and "risen" are in the Greek perfect tense, emphasizing an action in the past that remains permanent in the present. Christ was raised and remains raised!

22. **1 Corinthians 15:20-23**—"Firstfruits" means "to make a beginning." Jesus' resurrection is a guaranteed promise of a future harvest.

23. **1 Corinthians 15:24**—One must be in Christ's kingdom (i.e., His church) in order to be delivered to heaven at the end of time.

24. **1 Corinthians 15:25**—Christ reigns right now (present tense verb). The Jews' rejection of Christ did not postpone His reign for a future 1,000-year period (as premillennialists assert). He is reigning now!

25. **1 Corinthians 15:28**—In eternity, Christ will, in some sense, "be subject" to the Father. This perhaps indicates something that He forever relinquished by becoming a human and dying on our behalf. In some way, He will continue to be identified with us.

26. **1 Corinthians 15:29**—This must have something to do with the context of denying the resurrection. Paul changes pronouns to talk about what "they" do, perhaps indicating some unauthorized practice. Or perhaps it is talking about being baptized in hopes of being raised and reunited with loved ones later. Whatever the meaning, the point is, why do this if there is no resurrection? We don't have to know what this verse is talking about to know Paul's point.

27. **1 Corinthians 15:35-38**—There is continuity between the thing planted and the new plant, even though we cannot understand fully the process. However, the new plant (i.e., the new body) will be entirely different from the earthly, corruptible body of flesh.

28. **1 Corinthians 15:39**—Animals and humans have been proven scientifically to be different flesh. That could not be if evolution was true and our existence was tied to a single, rudimentary source.

29. **1 Corinthians 15:46-49**—These verses are nonsensical if heaven will actually be on earth. These verses prove that doctrine to be false.

(continued on next page)

Mark Your Bible

30. **1 Corinthians 15:51**—"All" will be changed, including the dead (15:35-41) and the living (15:50-54).
31. **1 Corinthians 15:57**—"Gives" is in the present tense, emphasizing that we are presently enjoying a victorious relationship with Christ.
32. **1 Corinthians 15:58**—The verbs "be" and "abounding" are present tense, emphasizing the need for ongoing, continuous action.
33. **1 Corinthians 16:1**—What Paul taught in one church, he taught everywhere (4:17; 7:17; 14:33). The gospel is universally applicable.
34. **1 Corinthians 16:5**—Macedonia is just north of Corinth.
35. **2 Corinthians 1:1**—Achaia was the region of southern Greece, which also had congregations in Athens and Cenchrea (Rom. 16:1).
36. **2 Corinthians 1:10**—Knowing that God had delivered (past tense) gives continuing confidence that He will deliver (future tense).
37. **2 Corinthians 1:24**—The word "stand" is in the Greek perfect tense, which emphasizes a past action (began to stand) with an abiding, present result (still firmly standing today).

Day of Reflection

Take time today to reflect on the five chapters that you read this week. You may choose to read all five chapters again, in one sitting, or certain parts of them. Take time today to answer at least one of these questions below. You may or may not write anything down—you can choose to write or simply reflect.

1. What personal application do I need to make from the chapters I have read this week?

2. How can these five chapters help draw me closer to Jesus?

3. What words, phrases or verses in these chapters do I want to go back and study more in depth?

4. What questions do I have about what I have read this week on which I need to do some further Biblical research?

Week 31

July 30-August 5

July 30	Read 2 Corinthians 2
July 31	Read 2 Corinthians 3
August 1	Read 2 Corinthians 4
August 2	Read 2 Corinthians 5
August 3	Read 2 Corinthians 6
August 4	Mark Your Bible
August 5	Day of Reflection

Prayer for this week:

"Heavenly Father,
my only hope is You!
Help me to remember that!"

July 30 Week 31, Day 1

2 Corinthians 2

Helpful Notes:

1. **Punishment** = This is a reference to the practice of church discipline, and it likely refers to the case in 1 Corinthians 5; the church was instructed to withdraw fellowship and put away the sinful brother, in order to save his soul (not crush him); while a rebellious minority in the church did not act, a loving majority did, and the brother had repented; church discipline is hard but it works; because it is commanded by God, it is necessary (not optional).
2. **Response to repentance** = When a brother has repented of sinful living, the church must respond quickly and purposefully; faithful Christians must (1) forgive, (2) comfort (help to encourage and strengthen), (3) reaffirm *agape* love through public actions of love and restoration; failure to do these things could cause his soul to be lost to the clutches of Satan again.
3. **Satan's devices** = The devil is shrewd, cunning and deceptive (Gen. 3:1; 2 Cor. 11:3, 14-15), and he has well-disguised traps (2 Tim. 2:26; Prov. 5:22); we must not give him an opportunity to operate (Eph. 4:27; 6:11), lest he outwit us and "seek to get more" (literally meaning of "take advantage").

1. What kind of responsibility do fellow Christians have for one another?

2. How often does God lead Christians "in triumph in Christ"?

3. The knowledge of Christ is like a fragrance, but how does it smell to different people?

Verse for Meditation and Prayer: **2 Corinthians 2:14**

"Now thanks be to God who always leads us in triumph in Christ, and through us diffuses the fragrance of His knowledge in every place."

2 Corinthians 3

Helpful Notes:

1. **New covenant** = A covenant is an agreement between two parties, and in the case of God's covenant, one of the parties is infinitely superior to the other; the new covenant was prophesied by Jeremiah (31:31-34), as one written on hearts, and stands in contrast with the law of Moses, which was, in part, written on stones; the new covenant is binding on all men today, as ratified by the blood of Christ (Heb. 9:15-17).
2. **The "end" of the old covenant** = In this context, the word "end" may have dual meaning: (1) the old covenant was abolished by the cross of Christ (Eph. 2:13-16; Col. 2:14), and came to an "end"; (2) the old covenant had a purpose, a goal, an end, which was to bring man to Christ (Gal. 3:19-25); Christ was the "end" of the old covenant in both ways.
3. **Veil** = The veil that Moses put over his face is taken and used metaphorically of a stubborn rejection that the Jews had toward Christ that hardened and "veiled" their understanding of who He really was; their preconceived Messianic ideas were incorrect, but they could not see beyond them.

1. Why could the Israelites not look steadily at Moses' face when he came off of Mount Sinai?

2. Why do some people still wear a "veil" (metaphorically) when they read the Bible and refuse to see the truth?

3. What is the "mirror" into which we look to emulate Christ?

Verse for Meditation and Prayer: **2 Corinthians 3:18**

*"But we all, with unveiled face, beholding as in a mirror
the glory of the Lord, are being transformed into the same image
from glory to glory, just as by the Spirit of the Lord."*

August 1 Week 31, Day 3

2 Corinthians 4

Helpful Notes:

1. **Treasure vs. earthen vessels** = The "treasure" in verse 7 is "the light of the gospel" in verse 6; the gospel is a treasure of immeasurable value (Matt. 13:44-46), teaching us about Christ and providing the means of salvation; God has given man (earthen vessels, who are like fragile, clay jars and of little intrinsic value) the responsibility of teaching His gospel; thus the glory is obviously in God and not in us!
2. **Outward vs. inward** = God draws a sharp distinction between one's physical body of flesh (the "outward" man) and one's eternal, in-the-image-of-God soul (the "inward" man); regardless of what happens to the outward body, the soul of man is separate (Matt. 10:28) and can/is strengthened by the Spirit of God through His Word (Eph. 3:16; 6:17).
3. **Temporary vs. eternal** = God draws a sharp distinction between material things of this earth which can be seen (and are temporary) and spiritual things from heaven which cannot be seen (and are eternal); while it is easy to focus on what we can see, we must focus more on things of eternal consequence.

1. For the sake of the gospel, whose "sight" was Paul most concerned about?

2. Rather than preaching "ourselves," what two things did Paul say they were preaching?

3. Even if it meant "death," what did Paul want from his life?

Verse for Meditation and Prayer: **2 Corinthians 4:7**

"But we have this treasure in earthen vessels, that the excellence of the power may be of God and not of us."

2 Corinthians 5

Helpful Notes:

1. **Judgment seat of Christ** = Judgment will take place before the "great white throne" (Rev. 20:11); Christ (the Son of Man, Matt. 25:31-32) will be our Judge, and every person who has ever lived will stand before Him; the standard of judgment will be His Word (John 12:48), comparing what we have done in the body to that standard; each person will be individually accountable before Him.
2. **New creation** = The key is to be "in Christ"; ONLY "in Christ" is the old life of sin and separation from God removed; "in Christ," one has a new relationship with Christ, a new life apart from sin, a new purpose, a new home and hope, a new way of living; there is only one way "into Christ," and that is through baptism (Gal. 3:27; Rom. 6:3-4), when one dies to sin and is raised to walk a new life.
3. **To be sin for us** = Christ "knew no sin" in that He never committed any sin (Heb. 4:15; 1 Pet. 1:19; 2:22), thus making Him the perfect, sinless sacrifice on our behalf; but Jesus did not become "sinful" or a "sinner" on the cross (and thus die in that state); He became our sin-offering (cf. Ex. 29:14), on which the Lord "laid" (Isa. 53:6) our sins for Him to "bear" (Heb. 9:28; 1 Pet. 2:24) for us.

1. What does Paul say that our spirit is doing within us, as it contemplates this earthly existence in light our heavenly home?

2. When the time comes that the Christian's spirit is "absent" from the body, where will the faithful Christian then be?

3. What does (or should) "the love of Christ" do to us and for us?

Verse for Meditation and Prayer: **2 Corinthians 5:21**

"For He made Him who knew no sin to be sin for us,
that we might become the righteousness of God in Him."

2 Corinthians 6

Helpful Notes:

1. **Commendable ministers of God** = Paul's critics sought to "blame" him and cause his converts to "stumble," which would impugn not only Paul but his work for the Lord; thus, Paul detailed his service to the Lord in three sets of information: (1) he presented 9 sufferings that he patiently endured, with the word "in" (v. 4-5); (2) he listed 9 qualities that sustained him through the sufferings, with the word "by" (v. 6-7); (3) he cataloged 9 paradoxes he had experienced, with the word "as" (v. 8-10).
2. **Unequally yoked** = A "yoke" involved a partnership or close relationship (as two animals in the same yoke, Deut. 22:10); Christians are not to enter into alliances with non-Christians (an unequal yoke) that can hinder their Christian walk and weaken or compromise their faith; just like light and darkness, Christ and the devil, a Christian and non-Christian are mutually exclusive in what really matters; this applies to various relationships, including marriage.
3. **Be separate** = Christians are to live a holy life (which means "separate," 1 Pet. 1:15-16); we are not to be "conformed" to the world (Rom. 12:2), pursue "friendship" with the world (Jas. 4:4) or "love" the "things" that are in the world (1 John 2:15-17); these instructions come from "the Lord" and with a promise (2 Cor. 6:17).

1. How did Paul describe himself and his companions in verse 1?
2. Having opened his heart to the Corinthian Christians, what did he plead with them to do toward him?
3. In verses 16-18, what "I will" promises does God make to His children, if they will maintain a holy relationship with Him?

Verse for Meditation and Prayer: **2 Corinthians 6:17**

"Therefore 'Come out from among them And be separate, says the Lord. Do not touch what is unclean, And I will receive you.'"

Mark Your Bible

1. **2 Corinthians 2:3**—Paul wrote First Corinthians so that the church would deal with sin before he arrived.
2. **2 Corinthians 2:4**—Paul had deep emotions for fellow Christians and was deeply troubled by sin in the church. The Greek word for "anguish" was also used for "prison, place of confinement." Here it literally involves a "compressing together" in a state of distress with a high degree of anxiety. His love was real, deep and overflowing.
3. **2 Corinthians 2:9**—Full obedience is the only acceptable obedience.
4. **2 Corinthians 2:10**—The withdrawing of fellowship was to be done in the presence of Christ (1 Cor. 5:4), and so was the restoration. This is what Jesus was talking about in Matthew 18:20.
5. **2 Corinthians 2:13**—Paul was anxious to hear a report from Titus about how things were going in Corinth.
6. **2 Corinthians 2:15**—"Being saved" and "perishing" are both present tense verbs indicating an ongoing process.
7. **2 Corinthians 2:17**—Paul's detractors (the "many") were hucksters, who handled the Word deceitfully for sordid, dishonest personal gain. They were adulterating the truth for their own advantage.
8. **2 Corinthians 3:3**—A transformed life is clear evidence of the power and love of God. It can be (and should be) evident to all.
9. **2 Corinthians 3:5**—No man is "qualified or adequate" (meaning of "sufficient") in and of himself to do the work of the Lord and transform lives. We must depend on God, who provides that sufficiency.
10. **2 Corinthians 3:5-11**—The two covenants are contrasted: the old covenant brought death and condemnation, the new brought life and righteousness. Both were from God, but the new was designed to excel much more in glory, as it was bought with Christ's blood.
11. **2 Corinthians 3:11**—The "what" that was "passing away" included the Ten Commandments, "engraved on stones" (v. 7), which included the Sabbath. The law of the Sabbath has been taken away.

(continued on next page)

Mark Your Bible

12. **2 Corinthians 3:17**—Jesus is the new covenant (i.e., "the Spirit" is the "new covenant" in verse 6). Thus, the new covenant of the Lord (v. 17b) provides liberty from the law, liberty from the veil of ignorance and liberty from sin.

13. **2 Corinthians 3:18**—From the word "unveiled," draw a line back to "veil" in verses 13, 14, 15, 16. The word "unveiled" in verse 18 is the Greek perfect tense, indicating an action in the past with abiding results. Christians understand the differences between the two covenants and are "unveiled" as they enjoy their freedom in Christ.

14. **2 Corinthians 3:18**—"Transformed" is from the Greek *metamorphoo* (see Romans 12:2). It means "to change inwardly in fundamental character." It is a present tense verb here, denoting a continual, ongoing growth, as one "beholds" (present tense) Christ in His new covenant and is constantly renewed into His image, looking more and more like Him, and less and less like our old self.

15. **2 Corinthians 4:4**—Jesus also called the devil, "the ruler of this world" (John 12:31; 14:30). He blinds people to the truth (3:14), but only those who choose themselves "not to believe."

16. **2 Corinthians 4:4**—Christ is the "exact likeness/image" of God (Heb. 1:3; Col. 1:15), not because He is a copy of deity but because He is actual deity, who came to this earth for us.

17. **2 Corinthians 4:8-10**—All verbs in these verses are present tense, denoting ongoing, sustained action. As continual as the persecutions were is how continual their victories and deliverances were.

18. **2 Corinthians 4:13**—Underline "we also believe and therefore speak." The stronger our faith, the more we will talk about Christ. If we do not speak about Christ, it is a reflection of our faith. Draw a line from the word "believe" to the word "knowing" in verse 14. A Christian faith is not a blind faith. It is based upon evidence.

19. **2 Corinthians 4:17**—Mark the contrast between "affliction" (which is "light" and "momentary") and "glory" (which is "weighty" and "eternal").

Mark Your Bible

20. **2 Corinthians 4:18**—The unambiguous contrast between the material universe and the eternal realm indicates that the material will not coexist with (or in) the eternal. Thus, there is no justification to teach that heaven will be on a renovated (thus, material) earth.
21. **2 Corinthians 5:1**—The word "know" is in the perfect tense, indicating a residing knowledge of absolute confidence. When Christians "walk by faith," it is not a blind faith or leap in the dark.
22. **2 Corinthians 5:1**—At death, the physical body will be "destroyed," which literally means "loosed down" ("torn down," NASB). At the same time, the spirit will "depart" (Phil. 1:23), which literally means "loosed up." Death is a separation (Jas. 2:26).
23. **2 Corinthians 5:1**—There is a clear distinction between the "earthly" body that we have for our earthly existence and the new "eternal" body ("habitation," v. 2) that will be given for our heavenly existence. The heavenly body is not going to live on earth.
24. **2 Corinthians 5:1**—The "building" is the resurrected body (1 Cor. 15).
25. **2 Corinthians 5:5**—As a "down payment" to show the certainty of our future home with God, He has "given us the Spirit" to make His home in us now (1 Cor. 6:19-20)—His "guarantee" or "pledge"!
26. **2 Corinthians 5:7**—Walking by faith is based upon Biblical evidence and walking according to Biblical authority.
27. **2 Corinthians 5:10**—We will be judged based upon what we have done "in the body." No one can do anything for us after we die to alter our eternal state. We will answer for how we have lived.
28. **2 Corinthians 5:15**—Christ did not just die for the elect (as some claim), but He shed His blood for all mankind (Heb. 2:9).
29. **2 Corinthians 5:18-19**—The "word of reconciliation" is the gospel, by which "the world" can be "reconciled" to God—i.e., brought back together with Him again (Rom. 5:9-10; Eph. 2:13).

(continued on next page)

Mark Your Bible

30. **2 Corinthians 6:1**—The fact that "the grace of God" can be received "in vain" proves the possibility of apostasy and that one can receive it and be lost again. It is conditional to receive it and retain it.

31. **2 Corinthians 6:14**—A Christian needs to marry a Christian (cf. 1 Cor. 7:39; 9:5; Matt. 6:33; Deut. 7:1-4).

32. **2 Corinthians 6:15**—"Belial" is the Hebrew word for "worthlessness" and is here applied to Satan.

Day of Reflection

Take time today to reflect on the five chapters that you read this week. You may choose to read all five chapters again, in one sitting, or certain parts of them. Take time today to answer at least one of these questions below. You may or may not write anything down—you can choose to write or simply reflect.

1. What personal application do I need to make from the chapters I have read this week?

2. How can these five chapters help draw me closer to Jesus?

3. What words, phrases or verses in these chapters do I want to go back and study more in depth?

4. What questions do I have about what I have read this week on which I need to do some further Biblical research?

Week 32

August 6-12

August 6	Read 2 Corinthians 7
August 7	Read 2 Corinthians 8
August 8	Read 2 Corinthians 9
August 9	Read 2 Corinthians 10
August 10	Read 2 Corinthians 11
August 11	Mark Your Bible
August 12	Day of Reflection

Prayer for this week:

*"Heavenly Father,
help me to search the Scriptures faithfully,
carefully and lovingly."*

August 6

Week 32, Day 1

2 Corinthians 7

Helpful Notes:

1. **Perfecting holiness** = Those who have been saved by the precious blood of Jesus ought to be motivated to further (even as Christians) "cleanse" themselves from "ALL filthiness" of carnal living and keep on (present tense) "perfecting holiness," which emphasizes that holiness in the sight of God is a continual and growing relationship; we can always do more to become more like God.
2. **Repentance** = Repentance is more than a feeling of sorrow or regret; repentance is a change of mind that leads to a change of conduct; true repentance is "produced" by "godly sorrow," which is a genuine, deep grief that one experiences toward his own sin in light of the sacrifice of Christ; thus motivated, true repentance prompts a change of life that results in salvation. Godly sorrow→ Repentance (change of mind)→Salvation from sin→Change of life.
3. **Worldly sorrow** = Not all sorrow produces genuine repentance; worldly sorrow stops at the sorrow and does not produce any meaningful or sustaining results—such as Judas (Matt. 27:3-5) and Herod Antipas (Mark 6:26-28), who sorrowed but not unto repentance, but rather unto "death" (eternal separation, Rom. 6:23).

1. Though Paul was experiencing other tribulations, the good news of the Corinthians' repentance filled him with what two things (v. 4)?

2. What is the difference between godly sorrow and worldly sorrow?

3. What did Titus remember about these brethren that increased his affections for them?

Verse for Meditation and Prayer: **2 Corinthians 7:10**

"For godly sorrow produces repentance leading to salvation, not to be regretted; but the sorrow of the world produces death."

2 Corinthians 8

Helpful Notes:

1. **Gracious gift** = The words "grace" and "gift" are used interchangeably in this context; in its basic form, the word "grace" means "favor"; grace is usually thought of in the gift of God's salvation to mankind, but man's generosity toward others (as here used), in response to God's grace, is also a "gift"; in this passage, the Gentile brethren in various congregations (Macedonia, Corinth, etc.) were extending "grace" (in a gift) to poor members of the church in Jerusalem (Rom. 15:26).
2. **Proof of your love** = God giving His Son to die in our behalf is the greatest gift ever given and is a clear demonstration of His love (8:9; John 3:16; Rom. 5:8); in response, man is able to demonstrate "the sincerity" or "proof" of his "love" by giving back to God every Sunday (1 Cor. 16:1-2) for "the ministering to the saints" (8:4).
3. **Providing things honorable** = A Christian must be ever conscious of how certain situations in which he finds himself look "in the sight of the Lord" and "in the sight of men," and he must endeavor always to be above reproach and avoid possible suspicion in how he handles matters; this is having regard for what is honorable.

1. How does Paul contrast the financial condition of the Macedonian brethren and the size of their gift?

2. While Paul was initially hesitant to take their gift, why did he finally accept it?

3. The Corinthian church had begun to collect their funds for the brethren in need "a year ago." What was Paul now asking them to do?

Verse for Meditation and Prayer: **2 Corinthians 8:9**

"For you know the grace of our Lord Jesus Christ,
that though He was rich, yet for your sakes He became poor,
that you through His poverty might become rich."

2 Corinthians 9

Helpful Notes:

1. **Purposes in his heart** = Regarding our giving every first day of the week, we are "to reach a decision beforehand, make up mind before" what we will give (which is the meaning of "purposes"); thus, we must prepare for our worship by choosing beforehand what we will give and committing to it; our heart responds to the love of God and decides in advance how to express love in return.
2. **The heart of the giver** = Money has an amazing pull on our hearts; God does not want us to give "grudgingly" (as if giving out of "pain, grief, sorrow or affliction"); money could make us think of our giving that way; God also does not want us to give out of compulsion or pressure; the Greek for "cheerful" is *hilaros,* which means "full of joy, gladness; happiness that is prompt to do anything"; our heart has every reason to give joyously!
3. **Indescribable gift** = The Greek for "indescribable" literally means "cannot be related or declared"; language fails in having the right words and minds fail in having the full capacity to truly understand the profound and amazing gift of Jesus Christ; in context, His gift ought to motivate us to give liberally and full of thanks.

1. Why does Paul use the agricultural illustration of sowing sparingly and sowing bountifully in this context?

2. Rather than limit us to a 10% tithe, how much does God want Christians to give today?

3. In liberal giving, not only are the needs and the service supplied, what is another (and the main) result?

Verse for Meditation and Prayer: **2 Corinthians 9:8**

"And God is able to make all grace abound toward you, that you, always having all sufficiency in all things, may have an abundance for every good work."

2 Corinthians 10

Helpful Notes:

1. **Boasting** = Paul uses the word "boast" or "boasting" repeatedly in these chapters, but he is not using the word in a sinful sense (like Rom. 1:30); while it can have a connotation of arrogant pride, it is used in these chapters as "an act of taking pride in something, or that which constitutes a source of pride"; specifically, Paul has been boasting about his brethren (i.e., bragging about them to other Christians), and because of vicious critics, he had to boast (by inspiration) of his right to be an apostle, but he did so humbly.
2. **Weapons of our warfare** = Christians are engaged in warfare against the devil and his evil forces, but they do not use manmade weapons; to win this spiritual battle, Christians have (as their weapons) the truth, righteousness, the gospel, faith, salvation, the Word of God, prayer, Christian love, etc. (Eph. 6:10-18; Rom. 12:19-21); with these weapons, we can analyze and dismantle false "arguments," unsound reasoning and rebellious thoughts with the "knowledge of God."
3. **Comparing is not wise** = Using others as our "measuring" rod and "comparing" our lives with the lives of others is "not wise"; there is only one standard that matters and that is what "God appointed"; it is the only universal, fixed, immutable standard.

1. For what purpose did Paul say that the Lord gave him "authority" as an apostle?

2. While Paul's critics were trying to destroy him in the eyes of the Corinthian church, what did Paul want for the church (v. 15)?

3. Rather than glory in self or our own supposed accomplishments, in whom does Paul say we should always glory?

Verse for Meditation and Prayer: **2 Corinthians 10:18**

"For not he who commends himself is approved,
but whom the Lord commends."

2 Corinthians 11

Helpful Notes:

1. **Godly jealousy** = Jealousy is a sin (Gal. 5:19-21), but Paul's deep affection (i.e., concern) for his brethren was a "godly jealousy," based upon their relationship with Christ; the church is married to Christ (Rom. 7:4; Eph. 5:22-33); since Paul had brought the Corinthian Christians into this marital relationship, he was "jealous" that they maintain a pure (uncontaminated) relationship with Christ until the end of time (pure doctrinally, morally, etc.).
2. **Robbed other churches** = Paul did not literally rob churches; however, since he was working with the church in Corinth, they should have been supporting him (1 Cor. 9:1-14; Gal. 6:6); but, because of these incessant, insatiable critics, he did not demand such support from Corinth and took it from other congregations; figuratively and facetiously, other congregations were being robbed.
3. **Satan transforms himself** = In the Garden of Eden, Satan appeared in the form of a serpent (v. 3), but on other occasions, he can appear as a messenger of truth and light (cf. John 8:44); the present tense on "transforms" (three times in verses 13-15) emphasizes this is the very character (i.e., ongoing behavior) of the devil; we must be ever vigilant of his deceptive ways and not falter.

1. How does Satan operate? What are his tactics?
2. How can we be on guard against Satan and his "ministers" transforming themselves into an appearance of righteousness?
3. Besides all of the physical traumas and perils Paul experienced, what was the "deep concern" that came upon him "daily"?

Verse for Meditation and Prayer: **2 Corinthians 11:2**

"For I am jealous for you with godly jealousy.
For I have betrothed you to one husband,
that I may present you as a chaste virgin to Christ."

Mark Your Bible

1. **2 Corinthians 7:5**—Paul's "deep concern" (cf. 11:28) for the brethren in Corinth "troubled [him] on every side." He endured various physical traumas, but his love for Christians surpassed any of that.
2. **2 Corinthians 7:5-7**—Note this is in Macedonia, where Paul had come when he "had no rest" and "did not find Titus" in Troas (2:12-13). Now, he "rejoiced" because of the report he received from Titus about the response of the church to his first letter.
3. **2 Corinthians 7:6**—The "downcast" is one who has a "relative inability to cope; lowly, undistinguished, of no account, of no degree; that which does not rise from the ground." God comforts them!
4. **2 Corinthians 7:12**—This is a reference to the incestuous man of 1 Corinthians 5 and his father.
5. **2 Corinthians 7:13**—The Greek for "refreshed" means "to cause someone to gain relief from toil; to cause to rest; to soothe, revive." Their repentance produced this result in those who were concerned about them. Christians care about each other's spiritual welfare.
6. **2 Corinthians 8:1**—The churches of Macedonia would have included the ones in Philippi, Thessalonica and Berea (Acts 16:12-17:12).
7. **2 Corinthians 8:5**—Circle the word "first." Christians can do much more when they "first" give themselves to the Lord (Matt. 6:33).
8. **2 Corinthians 8:9**—This verse summarizes the gospel. Jesus emptied Himself of the "riches" of heaven (Phil. 2:6-7; John 17:5)—not for Himself, but for us—so that we might be blessed with the richest treasures of this life (2 Cor. 4:7; Eph. 1:3-7) and the next (2 Pet. 1:11).
9. **2 Corinthians 8:14**—Christians help each other when they have the means to do so—it is a mutual blessing, when there is a need (Prov. 3:27; 2 Cor. 12:15). This has nothing to do with socialism.
10. **2 Corinthians 9:1**—The "ministering to the saints" was the financial gift being sent to the poor brethren in Jerusalem (draw a line to 8:4).

(continued on next page)

Mark Your Bible

11. **2 Corinthians 9:8**—Underline "God is able" and explore other verses that teach the same (Matt. 10:28; Rom. 16:25; Eph. 3:20; 2 Tim. 1:12; Heb. 2:18; Jude 24).
12. **2 Corinthians 9:8**—Underline the superlatives in this verse: "all" (3 times), "always," "abound," "abundance," "every."
13. **2 Corinthians 9:11**—Liberality in giving leads to thanksgiving.
14. **2 Corinthians 10:5**—The Word of God is that which captures errant thoughts and brings them back into the light of truth and obedience to Christ. While the context is about false teachers, application can be made to anyone's thoughts that are not aligned with God.
15. **2 Corinthians 10:7**—Paul's critics were making charges against him based on "outward appearance." Such superficial appraisal is never a reliable standard of judgment (1 Sam. 16:7; John 7:24).
16. **2 Corinthians 10:8**—Paul was made an apostle by "the will of God" (1:1); it was "the Lord" who invested him with "authority (cf. 13:10), which other apostles recognized about Paul (Gal. 2:7-10; 2 Pet. 3:15-16).
17. **2 Corinthians 10:12**—"Let another man praise you, and not your own mouth" (Prov. 27:2).
18. **2 Corinthians 10:17**—Only God deserves credit for our work!
19. **2 Corinthians 10:18**—My every effort should be to please God and not man (Gal. 1:10). It makes little difference if others approve.
20. **2 Corinthians 11:1**—Due to false apostles and false charges being made against him, Paul was forced to boast (which he calls "folly").
21. **2 Corinthians 11:3**—The "serpent" is Satan (Rev. 12:9).
22. **2 Corinthians 11:3**—There is a "simplicity" and "purity" "in Christ," of which we must not be ashamed or from which we must not be led astray. The doctrine of Christ alone will save (cf. v. 4)!

Mark Your Bible

23. **2 Corinthians 11:9**—"The brethren" is probably a reference to Silas and Timothy (Acts 18:5), and the gift may have been brought especially from the church in Philippi (Phil. 4:10-18), who was very generous.

24. **2 Corinthians 11:16**—Paul refers to himself as "fool" several times in this chapter. He is doing so because (1) that is how his enemies were identifying him, so he was "playing along," and (2) he was showing the irony of their senseless arguments and who he actually was in comparison to his critics (who were the real "fools"). These chapters are full of irony and a bit of sarcasm.

25. **2 Corinthians 11:22**—Paul's critics claimed to have greater credentials than Paul. Reluctantly, Paul continues to present his impeccable and nearly unmatched credentials, from a human standpoint.

26. **2 Corinthians 11:23-27**—Paul wrote this letter, chronologically, around Acts 20:1. There were still more imprisonments, scourgings, shipwrecks and perils to come. So this list is only partial.

27. **2 Corinthians 11:32-33**—Paul recounts what happened to him when the Jews sought to kill him in Damascus (Acts 9:23-25), and the governor was complicit in it. Paul's point? God took care of him!

August 12 Week 32, Day 7

Day of Reflection

Take time today to reflect on the five chapters that you read this week. You may choose to read all five chapters again, in one sitting, or certain parts of them. Take time today to answer at least one of these questions below. You may or may not write anything down—you can choose to write or simply reflect.

1. What personal application do I need to make from the chapters I have read this week?

2. How can these five chapters help draw me closer to Jesus?

3. What words, phrases or verses in these chapters do I want to go back and study more in depth?

4. What questions do I have about what I have read this week on which I need to do some further Biblical research?

Week 33

August 13-19

August 13	Read 2 Corinthians 12
August 14	Read 2 Corinthians 13
August 15	Read Galatians 1
August 16	Read Galatians 2
August 17	Read Galatians 3
August 18	Mark Your Bible
August 19	Day of Reflection

Prayer for this week:

"Heavenly Father,
You have been my refuge and strength
in difficult times! Thank You!"

August 13 Week 33, Day 1

2 Corinthians 12

Helpful Notes:

1. **Third heaven** = The exact meaning cannot be stated with certainty; that which seems to make the most sense is that "the first heaven" is the place where the birds fly (Gen. 1:20; Jer. 4:25), "the second heaven" is the place where the planets and stars are (Gen. 1:14; 22:17; Matt. 24:29), and "the third heaven" is the sacred place where God's throne and dwelling are (Matt. 6:9; 10:32; 16:17; 23:9).
2. **Thorn in the flesh** = To keep him from exalting himself above measure for what he had seen, Satan was permitted to inflict Paul with something that involved a certain pain, discomfort or suffering; the exact identity of this "thorn" is unknown, thus it is inappropriate to speak positively about it; some have suggested a physical malady, others have suggested the constant conflict with Judaizing teachers; we must not speak where the Bible is silent.
3. **Signs of an apostle** = Paul was not inferior to the other apostles, for he did "the signs" that only true apostles can do (and not the false apostles attacking him); there were some "signs and wonders and mighty deeds" that were peculiar to only these men, including imparting the miraculous, spiritual gifts through laying their hands on other Christians (Acts 8:14-20).

1. How was Paul able to endure his "thorn in the flesh"?

2. What did Paul say that he did "take pleasure" in? How could he take pleasure in such?

3. In describing the role of a parent, what did Paul say that he would gladly do for the souls of these brethren?

Verse for Meditation and Prayer: **2 Corinthians 12:9**

"And He said to me, 'My grace is sufficient for you, for My strength is made perfect in weakness.' Therefore most gladly I will rather boast in my infirmities, that the power of Christ may rest upon me."

2 Corinthians 13

Helpful Notes:

1. **Two or three witnesses** = This principle was established by God in the Old Testament and continued by Jesus (Matt. 18:16); the brethren in Corinth were playing with sin and were in need of discipline, but Paul would not discipline them on the account of "one witness" (Deut. 19:15); likewise, if his accusers were going to make any charge against him, it must follow this same criterion.
2. **In the faith** = One is either "in the faith" or he is not; "the faith" is used objectively here of the gospel system (Gal. 1:23; Jude 3) and being "in Christ"; there is a direct connection between Christ being "in you" (Gal. 2:20) and you being "in Christ/the faith" (2 Cor. 5:17); it is evident that one who is "in Christ/the faith" can so live that he would find himself outside of Christ/the faith; thus, there is the call to "examine" and "test" yourself to verify.
3. **Complete** = Twice (13:9, 11) Paul expresses his desire for the brethren to "be made complete"; the Greek words involve putting in order, repairing, mending, restoring back to a right arrangement; it involves the process of maturing to a condition where you properly function; "get yourself together and mature in your faith."

1. What warning did Paul issue to those brethren who had "sinned before" but had not repented?

2. By what objective standard or measurement can a Christian "examine" and "test" himself to ensure that he is "in the faith"?

3. What two things did Paul pray that these Christians would "do" in verse 7?

Verse for Meditation and Prayer: **2 Corinthians 13:5**

"Examine yourselves as to whether you are in the faith.
Test yourselves. Do you not know yourselves,
that Jesus Christ is in you? – unless indeed you are disqualified."

Galatians 1

<u>Helpful Notes:</u> ** See Brief Introduction to Galatians on page 639.*

1. **Defending apostleship** = As in the Corinthian correspondence, Paul is again offering a defense of his apostleship; this was not because Paul had his feelings hurt that people were rejecting his apostleship; to oppose his apostleship was to oppose "Jesus Christ and God the Father" (v. 1); if his enemies could discredit Paul, then they could discredit the message he was preaching and get people to follow their false doctrines instead.
2. **Pervert the gospel** = The Greek word for "pervert" means "to change, alter, distort into something of an opposite character"; this was not a little change but a wholesale corruption from the gospel of liberty to that of bondage, for the Judaizers were seeking to bind circumcision as a condition of salvation (Acts 15:1).
3. **Accursed** = The Greek word is *anathema,* which means "dedicated for destruction and under Divine curse, to be delivered to Divine wrath"; this is the strongest possible condemnation, and it is affirmed twice in these verses to sternly warn these Christians of the danger of altering and distorting God's Word; do not listen to or follow anyone who preaches any other gospel!

1. According to the beginning of this chapter, why did Jesus give Himself?

2. What/Who are the only two entities that we might seek to please? Which one was Paul seeking to please?

3. While the churches in Judea had not seen Saul in years, what were they continually hearing?

Verse for Meditation and Prayer: **<u>Galatians 1:9</u>**

"As we have said before, so now I say again, if anyone preaches any other gospel to you than what you have received, let him be accursed."

August 16 Week 33, Day 4

Galatians 2

Helpful Notes:

1. **Liberty vs. bondage** = Through Christ, mankind (esp. the Jews) had been made free from the yoke of the law of Moses and its requirements of circumcision, feast days, diet regulations, etc. (Acts 15:10); Judaizers were trying to enslave Christians (Jews and Gentiles) to the law of Moses in order to be saved; this is the whole focus of the book of Galatians: true liberty is found only in Christ.
2. **Hypocrisy** = Peter was acting one way with the Gentiles when the Jews were not around and then acting another way when the Jews came around—that's the very definition of a hypocrite; in Greek theater, actors spoke under masks, hiding their true selves; among Christians, this is out of line with the truth (v. 14), it is sinful (v. 17-18), and it can negatively influence others (v. 13b).
3. **Crucified with Christ** = The word "crucified" is in the Greek perfect tense, indicating something that happened in the past but has abiding results; in baptism, one crucifies the old man with its desires to serve sin (Rom. 6:3-6; Gal. 5:24), and he is now dependent on Christ to live as Christ directs in His Word; to attempt to be justified by the law nullifies this act and this grace.

1. Although we do not read his name in the book of Acts, who went with Paul to Jerusalem in Acts 15, along with Barnabas?

2. Why would Paul not yield to these false teachers, "even for an hour"?

3. According to the last verse, if man seeks to justify himself by returning to the Old Testament, what is the horrific result?

Verse for Meditation and Prayer: **Galatians 2:20**

"I have been crucified with Christ; it is no longer I who live,
but Christ lives in me; and the life which I now live in the flesh
I live by faith in the Son of God, who loved me and gave Himself for me."

Galatians 3

Helpful Notes:

1. **Purpose of the law** = God gives the purpose of the law of Moses: it was designed to expose sin (v. 19), making man conscious of sin and his need for a Savior (v. 22); it served as a "tutor to bring us to Christ" (v. 24), so that all men could be "justified by the faith of Christ Jesus"; the law was binding "till [Christ] should come" (v. 19), and now "we are no longer under" the Old Testament (v. 25).
2. **Baptized into Christ** = Christ was the Seed of Abraham, through whom all nations would be saved; as the fulfillment of that promise, God identifies the only means by which to get into Christ and the salvation He brings—"through faith" when one is "baptized into Christ"; there is no other way to enter into fellowship with Him, receive the forgiveness of sins and enjoy all spiritual blessings.
3. **All one in Christ Jesus** = In Christ, there is no distinction made in regard to salvation; all are equally saved and equally saved in the same manner; one's standing before God is not determined by race, gender or social position; the Jews needed to hear that the Gentiles were equal recipients of the promises of God and equal heirs of His salvation; the same applies today.

1. What did Christ do in order to redeem those who were under the old law?

2. What was the purpose of the Old Testament?

3. How can one be a recipient today of the promise to Abraham?

Verse for Meditation and Prayer: **Galatians 3:28**

"There is neither Jew nor Greek, there is neither slave nor free, there is neither male nor female; for you are all one in Christ Jesus."

Mark Your Bible

1. **2 Corinthians 12:1**—The Lord was the author of all of Paul's supernatural visions and the revealer of previously unknown truths.
2. **2 Corinthians 12:2**—Paul begins by speaking of himself in the third person, but then he identifies the "man" as himself.
3. **2 Corinthians 12:2**—"A man in Christ" is a Christian.
4. **2 Corinthians 12:2**—"Fourteen years ago" would have been 41-42 A.D., during the years when he was in Tarsus between Acts 9:30 and 11:25. The fact that he told no one about this before now reveals his humility and resistance to appear to be boasting.
5. **2 Corinthians 12:2**—Paul knew that his body and his spirit were distinct from each other.
6. **2 Corinthians 12:2-4**—Paul was taken to a "non-earthly" place. Heaven, where God dwells, is a "non-earthly" place. When we are "with the Lord" in eternity (2 Cor. 5:8; 1 Thess. 4:17), it will not be on a renovated earth.
7. **2 Corinthians 12:8**—This is similar to Jesus praying three times in Gethsemane for the cup to pass from Him (Matt. 26:44).
8. **2 Corinthians 12:9-10**—As Christians, our strength to endure trials and remain faithful is not in ourselves. It is in those times of difficulties that we realize that God is using those trials to make us stronger. It is His "strength" (v. 9) in which we should glory.
9. **2 Corinthians 12:14**—The first visit was in Acts 18, when the congregation was established. The second visit was a "sorrowful" visit mentioned in 2:1.
10. **2 Corinthians 12:20-21**—Repentance involves changing one's conduct and discontinuing works of the flesh. It is not just saying and planning to change; it requires actually making the change.
11. **2 Corinthians 13:4**—The words "weakness" and "weak" are meant by human standards and evaluation. Man may have viewed as "weak," but the power of God was at work.

(continued on next page)

Mark Your Bible

12. **2 Corinthians 13:5**—The words "examine" and "test" are both imperatives (commands) and present tense, which indicates the responsibility for regular, ongoing self-examination.
13. **2 Corinthians 13:8**—There is only one "truth." We must love the Lord and do only those things that are in the interest of the truth.
14. **2 Corinthians 13:10**—Three times in this letter Paul emphasized that he wanted to use his apostolic authority for "edification/ building up" (10:8; 12:19; 13:10). However, if they did not repent, his authority would be used sharply to tear down.
15. **2 Corinthians 13:14**—Paul longs for all three members of the Godhead to bless these Christians, if they would remain faithful.
16. **Galatians 1:1**—Man was neither the source nor the conduit of Paul's apostleship. It was purely Divine origin, not human.
17. **Galatians 1:6**—"Turning away" is a present middle verb, indicating an action they were taking for themselves and it was in progress (but not yet complete). The word was used for military defections.
18. **Galatians 1:9**—Circle the word "anyone." This still applies today.
19. **Galatians 1:12**—To prove the authenticity of his message, Paul affirmed that he received his teaching "through the revelation of Jesus Christ" (cf. Eph. 3:3-5). Perhaps this is what Paul was doing for 6-8 years in Cilicia and Syria (between Acts 9:30 and 11:25).
20. **Galatians 1:13**—"Persecuted" and "tried to destroy it" are both in the imperfect tense, indicating ongoing, unceasing activity.
21. **Galatians 1:17-18**—Between Acts 9:20-26 is three years when Paul was in Damascus and Arabia, but not visiting any apostles.
22. **Galatians 1:19**—This is not James the apostle but one of Jesus' brothers (cf. Matt. 13:55), who did not believe until after Jesus' resurrection (John 7:5; 1 Cor. 5:7; Acts 1:14). He became an influential leader in the Jerusalem church (2:9; Acts 15:13). He was not an "apostle" in the technical sense but in the sense of being "one sent" as a messenger (like Barnabas in Acts 14:14).

Mark Your Bible

23. **Galatians 1:21**—Paul went there in Acts 9:30 and remained 6-8 years.
24. **Galatians 1:23**—"The faith" is used in the objective sense of the distinctive body of doctrine, i.e., the gospel system (cf. Acts 6:7; Jude 3). Note "preached" in verse 11 and "preaches" in verse 23, then draw a line connecting "the gospel" (v. 11) with "the faith" (v. 23).
25. **Galatians 2:1**—Make a note that these events parallel the events in Acts 15, when there was a meeting in Jerusalem regarding the Gentiles' relationship to the law of Moses and N.T. Christianity.
26. **Galatians 2:1**—Fourteen years after Paul's conversion would have been 49-51 A.D., which was the timing of the Jerusalem meeting.
27. **Galatians 2:2**—"Those of reputation" appear to be the apostles and other church leaders in Jerusalem. Connect it with the "seemed to be" in verses 6 and 9, where James, Peter and John are singled out.
28. **Galatians 2:3**—Titus, a Gentile, was not circumcised because the law of Moses was not binding. Paul had circumcised Timothy, a Jew (Acts 16:3), merely as a matter of expediency but not due to law.
29. **Galatians 2:7-8**—Although to different audiences, Peter and Paul preached the same gospel, as evidenced by the fact that God "worked effectively" miracles through them (2 Cor. 12:12).
30. **Galatians 2:9**—Paul's apostleship had equal credibility from God.
31. **Galatians 2:9**—"The right hand of fellowship" denoted a treaty or compact of full endorsement. They were on the same level in Christ.
32. **Galatians 2:11**—This chapter dismantles any attempt to elevate Peter to a place of primacy. He "stood condemned" for his actions of showing prejudice (v. 18), which emphasized he was not infallible and was not living "straightforward" toward "the truth" (v. 14). Additionally, he was not elevated among the three "pillars" (v. 9).
33. **Galatians 2:16**—We are justified by an obedient faith (Jas. 2:14-26+ Gen. 22:1-19) when we are baptized into Christ (Gal. 3:27).

(continued on next page)

Mark Your Bible

34. **Galatians 2:18**—The law of Moses (and justification therefrom) had been torn down, yet Peter's actions were seeking to rebuild it.

35. **Galatians 2:20**—Circle the word "me" twice. This is personal.

36. **Galatians 3:6**—Abraham was accounted righteous with God before circumcision and before the law of Moses (neither is essential for such). He was also accounted righteous because of his obedient faith (Rom. 4:12; Heb. 11:8; Jas. 2:23), recorded fifteen years after God had called him. We are also justified by an obedient faith.

37. **Galatians 3:8**—It was God's plan all along to save the Gentiles.

38. **Galatians 3:10**—In order to be justified by the old law, it had to be kept perfectly in all things. Since no one could, they were "cursed."

39. **Galatians 3:13**—Christ purchased our release from slavery to sin (i.e., our "curse") by being made "cursed" for us on the cross.

40. **Galatians 3:16**—Underline God's definition of the "Seed" promise to Abraham—it was a promise of "Christ." The law of Moses could not invalidate this promise made before it existed.

41. **Galatians 3:19**—Circle the word "till," which denotes the temporary nature of the law, which was fulfilled and removed by Christ.

42. **Galatians 3:22**—"Scripture" is reference to the Old Testament. It shut up man on all sides, making him conscious of sin and his need for a Savior.

43. **Galatians 3:23-26**—Most uses of "faith" in these verses (and v. 14) have the Greek definite article, indicating "the faith" (the gospel).

44. **Galatians 3:24**—A "tutor" was a guardian or custodian who was responsible for escorting a child to his teacher and ensuring that he properly matured. After that, the tutor was no longer needed.

45. **Galatians 3:25**—Underline "we are no longer under a tutor." Christians are not amenable to the Old Testament!

46. **Galatians 3:27**—Circle the word "for." Verse 27 explains how you become a child of God in verse 26. Baptism into Christ is required.

Day of Reflection

Take time today to reflect on the five chapters that you read this week. You may choose to read all five chapters again, in one sitting, or certain parts of them. Take time today to answer at least one of these questions below. You may or may not write anything down—you can choose to write or simply reflect.

1. What personal application do I need to make from the chapters I have read this week?

2. How can these five chapters help draw me closer to Jesus?

3. What words, phrases or verses in these chapters do I want to go back and study more in depth?

4. What questions do I have about what I have read this week on which I need to do some further Biblical research?

Week 34

August 20-26

August 20	Read Galatians 4
August 21	Read Galatians 5
August 22	Read Galatians 6
August 23	Read Ephesians 1
August 24	Read Ephesians 2
August 25	Mark Your Bible
August 26	Day of Reflection

Prayer for this week:

"Heavenly Father,
help me to take what I read
and apply it to my life."

Galatians 4

Helpful Notes:

1. **Adoption as sons** = Christians have been adopted into the family of God by means of the new birth process (John 3:3-5); what a tremendous blessing to "no longer [be] a slave" (even of sin and the elements of this world) "but a son"; God's children have been given God's Spirit to dwell in them (4:6; Acts 2:38), to identify them as His children (Rom. 8:16) and His heir (Rom. 8:17; Gal. 4:7).
2. **The fullness of the time** = God sent Christ at just the right time (cf. Rom. 5:6), when everything was providentially ready; the Romans brought a wide-spread peace and tremendous transportation and communication systems; the Greeks provided a very precise, universally-spoken language; the Jews had prepared the world with the inspired Scriptures from God and their devotion to the one true God; God was in control, and the time had come.
3. **Two women, two sons, two covenants** = The two covenants (v. 24) are contrasted using an inspired allegory; Hagar and her son of the flesh, Ishmael, represent the old covenant given at Sinai that brings bondage; Sarah and her son of promise, Isaac, represent the new covenant sent forth from Jerusalem that brings freedom; additionally, as Ishmael persecuted Isaac, the Judaizers were persecuting the church; going back to the old law is foolish.

1. According to verses 4-7, why did God send forth His Son?

2. Why was Paul "afraid for" the Christians to whom he was writing?

3. Why do you think Paul said that he was "laboring in birth again" for these Christians?

Verse for Meditation and Prayer: **Galatians 4:4**

"But when the fullness of the time had come, God sent forth His Son, born of a woman, born under the law."

Galatians 5

Helpful Notes:

1. **Circumcision** = God instituted circumcision with Abraham as a "sign" in the flesh (among males) of a special covenant relationship with God (Gen. 17:11), which continued in the law of Moses (Lev. 12:3); Judaizers in the N.T. sought to bind the custom on Christians as a condition of salvation (Acts 15:1), but it was not required under the new covenant; to require such would "profit nothing," for it had no value in one's relationship with Christ (v. 6).
2. **Fallen from grace** = One cannot fall from a place he has never been, nor be "severed/estranged" from someone to which never joined; to go back to the old law for justification removed one from Christ, along with the grace and salvation that He offered; "once saved, always saved" is not taught in Scripture; this passage affirms the possibility and reality of apostasy.
3. **Walk in the Spirit** = Strong contrast is drawn between flesh and Spirit, and Christians are urged to "walk in the Spirit," be "led by the Spirit," bear "the fruit of the Spirit," "live in the Spirit" and "sow to the Spirit" (6:8); this has nothing to do with God's operation outside of or over our free will; the emphasis is on choosing to deny the flesh by choosing to submit to and live according to the revealed words of the Spirit in the Bible (Eph. 6:17).

1. How can you use this chapter to prove that a Christian can fall away and be lost?

2. In what command from the Old Testament is all of God's laws regulating man's conduct toward man summarized and fulfilled?

3. What part of the fruit of the Spirit needs your attention the most?

Verse for Meditation and Prayer: **Galatians 5:4**

"You have become estranged from Christ, you who attempt to be justified by law; you have fallen from grace."

August 22 Week 34, Day 3

Galatians 6

Helpful Notes:

1. **Restore** = It is possible for a Christian to be "overtaken in any trespass" and be lost eternally; rather than ignore him, push him aside or leave him to fend for himself, a faithful Christian is to continually take measures to restore him; the Greek word for "restore" was used of a surgeon setting a broken bone (doing so gently, and putting it back in its right, full place) or fishermen mending nets (Matt. 4:21); souls are at stake, and we must act.
2. **Bear burdens** = Christians have a responsibility to each other—the word "burdens" in verse 2 is a heavy, crushing weight that belongs to another; this burden could be physical or material hardships, but in context, it is probably spiritual (cf. 2 Cor. 1:8), as one helps another out of his "trespass"; Christians also have a personal responsibility before God—the word "load" in verse 5 is a smaller burden of personal obligation, like a soldier's backpack.
3. **The law of Christ** = Some people want to claim that the Jews were under the law of Moses, but Christians are not under law today; such is nonsense; we are under law today—a law that has been given by Christ (1 Cor. 9:21; Rom. 3:27; 8:2; Jas. 1:25; 2:8; Col. 3:17); if we are not under law, then we could never sin (Rom. 4:15); we have a responsibility to keep His commandments (John 14:15).

1. With the principle of sowing and reaping, how do our life choices here affect our eternal destiny?

2. To whom are we to give special attention in doing good?

3. If I truly glory in the cross of Jesus Christ and the salvation it brings, what will the world mean to me?

Verse for Meditation and Prayer: **Galatians 6:10**

"Therefore, as we have opportunity, let us do good to all, especially to those who are of the household of faith."

Ephesians 1

Helpful Notes: ** See Brief Introduction to Ephesians on page 640.*

1. **In Christ** = To be "in Christ" is to be in a proper relationship with Christ and in the exclusive domain in which God blesses His children with "all spiritual blessings," including adoption, acceptance, redemption, forgiveness, grace, inheritance, etc.; one who is "in Christ" is in "the body of Christ" (1 Cor. 12:13; Eph. 1:22-23); the only way "into Christ" is through baptism (Gal. 3:27; Rom. 6:3).
2. **Redemption** = The Greek word means "to release by paying a ransom" or "to buy back," and was used especially of slaves who were bought out of bondage; in our case, Christ is our Redeemer, who bought us out of bondage to sin with the purchase price of His own precious blood (1 Pet. 1:18-19; 1 Cor. 6:19-20); without the blood of Christ, we would be enslaved to sin forever.
3. **The body of Christ** = The church of Christ is described as the body of Christ, with Christ as its head; when one is baptized, he enters the "one body" (1 Cor. 12:13), with all of the other "many members" who have done the same (1 Cor. 12:12); the church/body is the fullness of Christ, indicating He has nothing outside of the church, for it is in the church alone where He "fills all in all."

1. Compare 1:6 with Acts 10:34-35. When are we "made accepted in the Beloved"?

2. Compare 1:7 with Acts 2:38 and Galatians 3:27. If "forgiveness of sins" is "in Him," can we enjoy that before being baptized?

3. How much authority does Jesus have?

Verse for Meditation and Prayer: **Ephesians 1:7**

"In Him we have redemption through His blood, the forgiveness of sins, according to the riches of His grace."

Ephesians 2

Helpful Notes:

1. **By nature children of wrath** = This does not teach total hereditary depravity; these people were "dead in YOUR trespasses and sins" (v. 1), indicating their personal sin (not an inherited condition), as they were, through their conduct, "fulfilling" their own fleshly desires; "were" is imperfect tense, middle voice, indicating they "kept on making themselves" children of wrath (indicating personal involvement); "nature" means their own "sustained habit," which became subject to Divine "wrath"; their own habitual practice of sin is in view, which has brought God's wrath on them.
2. **Grace** = The word means "favor that is not merited or deserved"; man is truly saved by God's grace, demonstrated at the cross, but His grace is not unconditional; it is extended to all men (Tit. 2:11) and made available through instruction (Tit. 2:12), when God's conditions are met (Gen. 6:8; Heb. 11:7; Rom. 5:1-2); making His grace conditional does not make it any less a "gift" that is undeserved, but a gift that must be received and properly accessed.
3. **Made both one** = Through His death on the cross, Christ brought Jews and Gentiles together in "one body," which is His church; He "reconciled" their differences and made "peace" by creating "one new man from the two"; thus, Gentiles ("afar off") and Jews ("near") "both have access" equally "to the Father"; they are "fellow citizens" in His kingdom and "members" of His church.

1. How have God's "mercy," "love," "grace" and "kindness" been manifested to us?

2. For what reason have we been "created in Christ Jesus"?

3. What kind of "hope" is there for those who are outside of Christ?

Verse for Meditation and Prayer: **Ephesians 2:13**

"But now in Christ Jesus you who once were far off have been brought near by the blood of Christ."

Mark Your Bible

1. **Galatians 4:1** – An underage child (a minor) has no more legal standing than a slave, until the time that he reaches maturity.
2. **Galatians 4:3** – Before Christ came, Jews and Gentiles both were in slavery to elementary forms of religion, which enslaved to sin.
3. **Galatians 4:4** – Jesus was fully Divine (God's "Son") and human ("born of a woman"). He had to be both to accomplish His mission.
4. **Galatians 4:6** – "Abba" indicated a tender, intimate relationship.
5. **Galatians 4:10** – In Christ is freedom from this Jewish custom.
6. **Galatians 4:11** – Apostasy is possible. Calvinism is not Biblical.
7. **Galatians 4:16** – Paul places a great emphasis on "the truth" in this letter (2:5, 14; 3:1; 5:7). There is no continued salvation apart from it.
8. **Galatians 4:19** – These Christians had failed to mature and their souls were in jeopardy. They needed to be conformed to Christ!
9. **Galatians 4:22-23** – The bondwoman is Hagar; her son is Ishmael. The freewoman is Sarah; her son is Isaac.
10. **Galatians 4:26** – "The Jerusalem above" is the church (Heb. 12:22-23), which is free from sin and bondage to the law "in Christ"!
11. **Galatians 4:28** – We are Abraham's seed (3:29) and free (4:31) in Christ.
12. **Galatians 4:30** – Don't follow what God has cast out! The law of Moses does not justify and is not to be blended with the gospel. It would be going back to bondage to revert to the law of Moses.
13. **Galatians 5:1** – Through the cross, Christ made us free from enslavement to sin and the old law (including circumcision)
14. **Galatians 5:1** – The "yoke of bondage" is the old law (4:3, 8-9; Acts 15:10). Paul said, "Stop subjecting yourselves again to it!"
15. **Galatians 5:3** – One cannot bring over any part of the O.T. that is not authorized in the N.T. To seek justification for one part of the

(continued on next page)

Mark Your Bible

law morally obligates one to keep the whole law. This applies to persons today who want to justify instrumental music in worship by appealing to the O.T. It obligates bringing over the whole law.

16. **Galatians 5:1-6** – Underline "Christ" four times. By turning to the old law, they were abandoning Christ and fellowship with Him.

17. **Galatians 5:6** – A Biblical faith is an obedient faith ("obeying the truth," v. 7). Faith is more than mere mental assent. True faith works, keeps God's commands and is motivated by love (John 14:15).

18. **Galatians 5:13** – The liberty we have in Christ is not a freedom to indulge in sin (1 Pet. 2:16). Rather, true liberty, governed by *agape* love, enjoys the freedom to do right, including "serving" (present tense) fellow Christians. A paradox: we have been freed to serve.

19. **Galatians 5:16** – The word "walk" denotes how one conducts his life.

20. **Galatians 5:17** – God's will is continually opposed to (present tense of "are contrary") to man's fleshly desires. Thus, Christians must endeavor daily to control fleshly impulses and walk with the Lord.

21. **Galatians 5:19** – "Lasciviousness" or "lewdness" is from the Greek *aselgeia,* which involves "indecent bodily movements, unchaste handling of males and females." Christians must practice self-restraint, even in sexual behaviors that do not involve intercourse.

22. **Galatians 5:21** – Underline "and the like." This list is not exhaustive. Anything similar to these things is included.

23. **Galatians 5:21** – These verses are written to Christians. A child of God can so live as to fall from grace and not enter heaven.

24. **Galatians 5:24** – Repentance is when one decides to die to the practice of sin and live for Christ. One crucifies the old man in baptism (Rom. 6:3-6; Gal. 2:20), and a Christian must keep him crucified.

25. **Galatians 6:7** – God cannot be outwitted by man, so don't treat Him or His Word with contempt. God's ways must be respected.

26. **Galatians 6:7-8** – Actions have consequences – a lesson for all of us.

Mark Your Bible

27. **Galatians 6:9-10**—The terms "doing good" and "do good" are in the present tense, emphasizing ongoing, habitual behavior.
28. **Galatians 6:16**—"Rule" is from the Greek *canon*, which emphasizes a standard body of doctrine which God expects us to obey.
29. **Galatians 6:16**—"The Israel of God" is the church today (God's holy nation, 1 Pet. 2:9), comprised of God's people who have devoted their lives to Christ (3:29; 4:28; Eph. 2:19). (See note on Romans 9.)
30. **Ephesians 1:3**—There are no spiritual blessings outside of Christ.
31. **Ephesians 1:4**—God's election/choosing is not unconditional. God chose the location—"in Him." He accepts those who obey Him (Acts 10:35) and chose (before creation) the ones who would be "in Christ" to be His people. (See the next point.)
32. **Ephesians 1:5**—The Greek word for "predestined" means "to mark out with a boundary beforehand." The key in these verses is "in Him." God marked out a boundary (i.e., the "in Him" relationship) and chose/elected in advance to save everyone who became His sons (through the new birth process, John 3:3-5), which would place them "in Christ." God elected and predestined a class of people (all who obeyed Him) and not arbitrary individual favoritism.
33. **Ephesians 1:10**—This is referring to the Christian age, in which the Lord's plan of salvation is now available, which, when it is obeyed, gathers all of God's people "in one...in Christ."
34. **Ephesians 1:11**—God's "will" is emphasized in verses 1, 5, 9, 11. One is blessed with God's "inheritance" when he obeys the "will" of God, and then God "works" His will to put him "in Christ." Man's salvation is and always has been conditional.
35. **Ephesians 1:13**—They were baptized in Acts 19:5.
36. **Ephesians 1:13**—The indwelling of the Holy Spirit is promised to those who obey (Acts 2:38), as a (1) verification of Divine sonship (Gal. 4:6) and (2) down payment/pledge of eternal inheritance.

(continued on next page)

Mark Your Bible

37. **Ephesians 1:14**—"The purchased possession" is the church (Acts 20:28) and Christians (1 Cor. 6:19-20). This is talking about the future "day of redemption" (4:30), when we are delivered from this earth.

38. **Ephesians 1:18**—"Being enlightened" came through miraculous revelation (supernatural "wisdom" and "knowledge," 1 Cor. 12:8), but it does not come miraculously today (1 Cor. 13:8-13). We have the "complete" revelation today in God's Word.

39. **Ephesians 2:1, 5**—"Dead" means being separated from God because of their own "trespasses and sins."

40. **Ephesians 2:2**—"The prince of the power of the air" is Satan.

41. **Ephesians 2:2**—"Sons of disobedience" had so given themselves over to rebellion that they belonged to it as its adopted children.

42. **Ephesians 2:4**—Circle "But God." We were dead in our own sin, "But God" loved us and saved us. That's powerful!

43. **Ephesians 2:6**—God's saving grace was accessed upon their baptism, when they were "washed of water" (5:26; cf. Tit. 3:5, 7) and "raised up" (cf. Col. 2:12-13; 3:1). Tie this in with verses 8-9.

44. **Ephesians 2:8-9**—Salvation requires God's part—His "grace" makes salvation a "gift," which is "not of ourselves" (literally, not out of us, as a source). Salvation requires man's part—faithfully submitting to Divine mandate, which is not merely belief in one's heart but full obedience to His will (Eph. 5:26; Tit. 3:5, 7).

45. **Ephesians 2:9**—Salvation is not accessed by works of man's design, lest man "boast" that he earned his salvation. But works commanded by God do save (Jas. 2:14-26), including belief (John 6:29). True "work" and "gift" are not mutually exclusive, for God conditions access to His grace ("gift") upon man's obedience ("work").

46. **Ephesians 2:13**—Circle "But now." The Gentiles were on the outside of all that mattered, "But now" they were "in Christ Jesus."

Mark Your Bible

47. **Ephesians 2:13**—Underline "by the blood of Christ." That is the essential key to salvation (1:7; 1 Pet. 1:19; 1 John 1:7; Rev. 5:9-10).

48. **Ephesians 2:14**—"The middle wall of separation" may refer to the divider wall in the temple area that kept the Gentiles out of the Jewish area, or perhaps to the veil of the temple being torn to give everyone access, or to just the general animosity between the two.

49. **Ephesians 2:14-16**—Circle the three occurrences of "one" in these verses. There is no support for denominationalism in Scripture.

50. **Ephesians 2:15**—The old law (Old Testament) is no longer binding.

51. **Ephesians 2:21-22**—The church is the temple of God (1 Cor. 3:16-17), where God dwells, and Christians are its "stones" (1 Pet. 2:5).

Day of Reflection

Take time today to reflect on the five chapters that you read this week. You may choose to read all five chapters again, in one sitting, or certain parts of them. Take time today to answer at least one of these questions below. You may or may not write anything down—you can choose to write or simply reflect.

1. What personal application do I need to make from the chapters I have read this week?

2. How can these five chapters help draw me closer to Jesus?

3. What words, phrases or verses in these chapters do I want to go back and study more in depth?

4. What questions do I have about what I have read this week on which I need to do some further Biblical research?

Week 35

August 27-September 2

August 27	Read Ephesians 3
August 28	Read Ephesians 4
August 29	Read Ephesians 5
August 30	Read Ephesians 6
August 31	Read Philippians 1
September 1	Mark Your Bible
September 2	Day of Reflection

Prayer for this week:

"Heavenly Father,
Your love amazes me!"

August 27 Week 35, Day 1

Ephesians 3

Helpful Notes:

1. **The mystery** = The mystery of Christ is not "mysterious," nor does it require gathering "clues" to unravel it; "mystery" simply refers to truth that was previously unknown because it had not yet been revealed, but now it can be understood because it has been unveiled; God's plan all along (i.e., the mystery) was for Gentiles to "be fellow heirs" (3:6), having equal access to and acceptance of the eternal blessings "in Christ" (Isa. 2:2; 11:10; Dan. 7:14).
2. **Understand** = Some claim that the Bible cannot be understood, yet Paul told these Christians that "when you read, you can understand my knowledge," and later commanded them to "understand what the will of the Lord is" (5:17); God's will is knowable (John 8:32) and understandable when it is read.
3. **Eternal purpose** = Scripture affirms that God possessed an eternal plan, which included sending Christ to shed His blood for sinful man (1 Pet. 1:19-21); equally a part of that plan was His church (3:10-11), which Christ purchased with His blood (Acts 20:28); the Jews' rejection of the kingdom was not a surprise to God (as some claim), nor was the church an afterthought (to await the kingdom at a later time); the church is God's kingdom (Matt. 16:18-19), which He purposed before time began (Isa. 2:2-4; Dan. 2:44).

1. According to the end of verse 6, how does one become a partaker of the promise that is in Christ?

2. How did Paul see himself, in comparison with other Christians? Why do you think that is?

3. What is God able to do?

Verse for Meditation and Prayer: **Ephesians 3:20**

"Now to Him who is able to do exceedingly abundantly above all that we ask or think, according to the power that works in us…"

Ephesians 4

Helpful Notes:

1. **One body** = This letter already has placed an emphasis on "one" (1:10; 2:14-16), the "body" (1:22-23; 2:16; 3:6) and the "one body" (2:16), and it gave the inspired definition of the "body"—it is the church (1:22-23); therefore, God is stating plainly that there is "one church" and only "one church" (as much as there is only one God, one Lord, one Spirit); denominationalism finds no justification.
2. **One baptism** = Holy Spirit baptism was administered by Christ twice (Acts 2 and 10), but it is not the "one baptism"; the "one baptism" is the water baptism of the Great Commission, which was to last until the end of the world (Matt. 28:19), being administered by man (Acts 8:38), of penitent believers (Mark 16:16; Acts 2:38), by immersion in water (Rom. 6:3-4), for the purpose of obtaining "the forgiveness of sins" (Acts 2:38; 22:16).
3. **The unity of the faith** = The word "till" is an adverb of time, noting that the miraculous gifts would exist until a specific point in time—when "all come to the unity of the faith"; this is not "when all people believe the same"; the word "unity" means "oneness" and is "in contrast to the parts, of which a whole is made up"; "the faith" is the gospel system (Gal. 1:23; Jude 3); thus, the miraculous gifts (i.e., the parts) would last until the "unity" of the N.T. revelation (i.e., the whole) was complete; there are no miracles today.

1. What can happen to the church when everyone does his part?

2. When someone "learns Christ," what does he "put off" and what does he "put on" in his repentance and baptism?

3. To whom does Paul tell us to not give place or opportunity?

Verse for Meditation and Prayer: **Ephesians 4:32**

"And be kind to one another, tenderhearted, forgiving one another, just as God in Christ forgave you."

Ephesians 5

Helpful Notes:

1. **Walk** = The word "walk" is used often to depict one's entire life and how he conducts himself on a daily basis; Scripture deals with this negatively, as in not walking according to the flesh (Rom. 8:4); and Scripture deals with this positively, as in walking in love, in light, in wisdom and worthy of God (Eph. 5:2, 8, 15; 4:1); the word is often used in the present tense, to denote a habitual lifestyle; one begins his walk with the Lord in baptism (Rom. 6:4).
2. **No fellowship** = There are activities (i.e., works) that are described as "darkness" because they are opposed to the will of God; any activity that is not in accordance with "the light" of Scripture is a deed of darkness, and Scripture commands Christians not to share in or participate in that activity but to be holy (5:7; 2 Cor. 6:14-7:1; 1 Pet. 2:9-12); instead, by our lives and using God's Word, we are to expose and reprove sinful activity, so that souls can be saved.
3. **Savior of the church** = While some minimize the importance of the church, Scripture shows that Christ is the "Savior of the body"; the only ones who are saved are in His body; His body is His church (1:22-23), and there is only one body/church (4:4), thus one must be in Christ's church to be saved and only those in Christ's church are saved (Acts 2:38-47); He will save no other body.

1. In this chapter, in what three things or ways are Christians to walk?

2. In verse 20, how often are we to give thanks and for what things?

3. What standard are husbands to follow in their love for their wives?

Verse for Meditation and Prayer: **Ephesians 5:1**

"Therefore be imitators of God as dear children."

Ephesians 6

Helpful Notes:

1. **Slavery** = The Bible does not endorse the practice of slavery but it provides instructions for its regulation among Christians who live in societies where slavery is found (Eph. 6:5-9; Col. 3:22-4:1; Phile. 1-25); while Scripture does not advocate the violent overthrow of slavery, it provided the seeds (like the Golden Rule, Luke 6:31) that helped to abolish it in most civilized nations.
2. **Spiritual warfare** = Christians are engaged in the "fight of faith" (1 Tim. 6:12; 2 Tim. 4:7) against the devil, his schemes and his evil forces (2 Cor. 11:3, 13-15; 2:11; Matt. 25:41); this is not a carnal, fleshly or political battle, but it is a battle for saving souls from the wicked one; victory comes through truth, righteousness, the gospel, salvation, the Word of God, prayer and perseverance.
3. **The sword of the Spirit** = Many claims are made that the Holy Spirit works in hearts and lives today by means of some direct operation, straight to the heart; Scripture teaches that the means by which the Spirit works is very simple—it is through the Word that He inspired men to write; by means of that universal truth, the Spirit is able to work on all people in exactly the same way.

1. What is the promise that comes to children who obey their parents?

2. "Whatever good anyone does," especially under difficult circumstances, who is it that takes notice and will reward?

3. Why did Paul want the brethren to pray for him? What application can we make of that to ourselves?

Verse for Meditation and Prayer: **Ephesians 6:10**

"Finally, my brethren, be strong in the Lord
and in the power of His might."

Philippians 1

Helpful Notes: ** See Brief Introduction to Philippians on page 641.*

1. **Appointed for the defense** = The word "defense" is from the Greek *apologia*, which involves a verbal defense, an eagerness to make a defense; the word "appointed" means "to be appointed, destined, put in place"; Paul recognized that the providence of God had placed him where he was (in a Roman prison) for the purpose of defending Christ and His gospel, and Paul was glad.
2. **Christ is preached** = This is often misunderstood and misused; there were some brethren who were "preaching Christ" but out of improper motives; still, they were preaching the truth; to "preach Christ" requires preaching His will and His doctrine (cf. 1 Thess. 2:13; 1 Pet. 4:11; 2 John 9-11), which these brethren were doing; there is no hint that they were preaching religious error or any doctrine different than Paul preached.
3. **To die is gain** = Paul was only living in order that he might serve Christ, and apart from that, his life had no meaningful purpose; thus, if/when he died, it would be "gain," for he would get to be "with Christ" (1:23), at home with the Lord (2 Cor. 5:8), away from all earthly trials (2 Tim. 4:6-8) and at rest (Heb. 4:9-11); the Bible calls this "precious" (Rev. 14:13) and "very far better" (Phil. 1:23).

1. What did Paul say about his prayers and these brethren?

2. Rather than be "ashamed" of Christ, what did Paul say would happen to Christ in his life, whether he lived or died?

3. If Paul continued to live, what result did he know would come from that?

Verse for Meditation and Prayer: **Philippians 1:20**

"According to my earnest expectation and hope that in nothing I shall be ashamed, but with all boldness, as always, so now also Christ will be magnified in my body, whether by life or by death."

Mark Your Bible

1. **Ephesians 3:1**—Paul was writing this letter from prison in Rome (6:20). He was imprisoned because of his service to Christ Jesus.
2. **Ephesians 3:3**—"Revelation" is from the Greek *apokalupsis*, which means "uncovering, unveiling." Christ revealed His plan to Paul (Gal. 1:12), so that Paul could reveal it to man.
3. **Ephesians 3:10**—The work of the church is to make known the wisdom of God to the world, which includes His plan of salvation.
4. **Ephesians 3:15**—All of God's people are in the same family, which means they're in the same church. Manmade denominationalism is foreign to the teaching of the New Testament.
5. **Ephesians 3:15**—God says there is a difference between the locale of heaven and that of earth. Heaven will not be on a renovated earth.
6. **Ephesians 3:17**—The Greek has the definite article "the" before faith; Christ may be said to make His home in hearts through "the faith" (i.e., the gospel) or through our personal faith in His Word.
7. **Ephesians 3:19**—The word "passes" is from the Greek *huperballo*, which means "to attain a degree which extraordinarily exceeds a point on a scale of extent; literally, to throw far beyond."
8. **Ephesians 3:20**—Circle "Him who is able." Our God is able!
9. **Ephesians 3:21**—To be "in the church" is to be "in Christ Jesus." One cannot be in one and not be in the other.
10. **Ephesians 4:1**—A Christian is "called" by the gospel (2 Thess. 2:14).
11. **Ephesians 4:3**—Preserving and maintaining unity (based on God's revealed will) is of utmost importance in the church (Psa. 133:1)!
12. **Ephesians 4:7-8**—Christians in the first century were endowed with miraculous gifts from Christ after His ascension.
13. **Ephesians 4:12**—Circle the word "for" in this verse to find the purpose of the miraculous gifts in the early church.

(continued on next page)

Mark Your Bible

14. **Ephesians 4:13**—The church reached its mature state (i.e., the fullness that Christ intended) when the revelation of the New Testament was completed (and the miraculous gifts ceased).

15. **Ephesians 4:14**—We must use the Bible (one of its purposes) to identify, avoid and warn of the "trickery," "cunning" and "deceitful" measures of those who are not holding to sound doctrine.

16. **Ephesians 4:16**—The church can only grow stronger (numerically and spiritually) when every person does his part in the church and everyone builds each other up through love and service.

17. **Ephesians 4:19**—"Callous" or "past feeling" means "to become so accustomed to something that one no longer feels pain or is bothered by the implications of his actions; dead to all feeling." Moral sensitivity vanishes when sin is permitted to reign (Rom. 6:12).

18. **Ephesians 4:30**—The Holy Spirit is "grieved" when one disobeys or rebels against the Spirit-given Word (6:17; Gal. 5:16; Isa. 63:10). But if one cannot fall away, what difference would this warning make?

19. **Ephesians 4:32**—Forgiveness is commanded by Christ (Luke 17:1-4) and exemplified by Christ (Luke 7:48; 23:34), and disobedience is condemned by Christ (Matt. 18:21-35). He is our standard!

20. **Ephesians 5:3**—"Uncleanness" is moral impurity and involves even the thinking and desires of one's mind, in the sexual realm.

21. **Ephesians 5:10, 17**—One learns what is acceptable and pleasing to the Lord when one understands what the will of the Lord is. Draw a line connecting these verses. One CAN and MUST understand the Bible (it is objective, not subjective), and therefore, one CAN and MUST do those things that please the Lord.

22. **Ephesians 5:14**—There are some who are asleep spiritually and are, therefore, separated from (i.e., dead) the Lord (cf. 1 Tim. 5:6).

23. **Ephesians 5:18**—The Greek for "do not get drunk" is an inceptive verb *(methusko),* marking the process. God forbids man to "grow drunk"; thus, He forbids man to drink, which starts this process.

Mark Your Bible

24. **Ephesians 5:19**—The reciprocal pronoun "one another" emphasizes that singing in worship is to be done by everyone to everyone. Singing is not a performance done by some for others.

25. **Ephesians 5:19**—Instrumental music is not authorized in New Testament worship. God authorizes congregational, acapella singing by specifying it here. The Greek *psallo* once meant "to pluck," but it did not have that meaning in N.T. times. God said the melody is specifically to be made in the heart. If instruments are commanded in this verse, then everyone must both sing and play. We must not add to God's Word! Man added instruments centuries later.

26. **Ephesians 5:22-33**—The husband-wife relationship is to mirror the Christ-church relationship. To suggest the roles given to husbands and wives is not acceptable today is to suggest the roles given to Christ and the church are not acceptable. God's laws for marriage transcend time and culture, which quoting Genesis 2:24 proves.

27. **Ephesians 5:26**—Christ "sanctifies" into His body/church those who are "cleansed." The cleansing takes place "by the washing of water" (which is water baptism) "with the word" (as commanded in the gospel). When one is baptized, he is "born of water and the Spirit" (John 3:5), and is then cleansed/saved/forgiven (Acts 22:16; 2:38), and is then sanctified and added to the church (Acts 2:38-47).

28. **Ephesians 5:27**—When Jesus returns, He will present the church to Himself in heaven as His holy body (cf. 1 Cor. 15:24). One must be in His church!

29. **Ephesians 6:1, 5**—Children need to obey parents and slaves need to obey masters in all ways that are consistent with God's Word but should never violate Divine law. God's law always comes first.

30. **Ephesians 6:4**—Biblical parenting involves training (discipline) to do what is right and admonition (instruction, warning, guidance) to avoid what is wrong (Prov. 22:6; 13:24; 19:18; 23:13; 29:15, 17).

(continued on next page)

Mark Your Bible

31. **Ephesians 6:5-9** – These verses have application to the employee-employer relationship. Underline "bondservants of Christ" and circle the three uses of "as," noting that our actions are to be done to Christ, as we are first servants of Christ, seeking to please Him.
32. **Ephesians 6:10** – "Be strong" is a present passive imperative. Passive emphasizes that we are to allow the Lord to strengthen us, recognizing that the sufficient strength is not found in us but in Him.
33. **Ephesians 6:10** – "Whole armor" emphasizes we must be completely ready for the devil's every attack.
34. **Ephesians 6:11-14** – Underline the three uses of "stand" and the word "withstand." Christians must stand firm against the devil, not yielding ground, not yielding truth and not yielding any souls.
35. **Ephesians 6:18** – Circle the word "praying." This is the weapon that is often overlooked. The present tense emphasizes constancy.
36. **Philippians 1:1** – A "bondservant" is totally surrendered to his master as a loyal subject, whose will is consumed in his master.
37. **Philippians 1:5** – The word "fellowship" or "partnership" (v. 7) is from the Greek *koinonia*, which can include financial participation.
38. **Philippians 1:9** – Biblical love is an educated, discerning-truth-from-error love and not an unguided, heart-felt, "anything goes" emotion.
39. **Philippians 1:12** – "Furtherance" literally means "to cut forward." Paul's hardships were actually advancing the gospel even more.
40. **Philippians 1:23** – The word "depart" literally means "to loose up." In his death, Paul's soul would be "loosed up" from his body, like a ship loosed from the dock (Jas. 2:26). The soul and body are distinct.
41. **Philippians 1:25** – Paul anticipated being released (Phile. 22); history supports that he was for a time and was able to preach further.
42. **Philippians 1:27** – The word "worthy," from the Greek *axios*, meant "corresponding in weight," as if on a balancing scale – "your conduct" on one side of the scale and "the gospel" on the other side.

September 2 Week 35, Day 7

Day of Reflection

Take time today to reflect on the five chapters that you read this week. You may choose to read all five chapters again, in one sitting, or certain parts of them. Take time today to answer at least one of these questions below. You may or may not write anything down—you can choose to write or simply reflect.

1. What personal application do I need to make from the chapters I have read this week?

2. How can these five chapters help draw me closer to Jesus?

3. What words, phrases or verses in these chapters do I want to go back and study more in depth?

4. What questions do I have about what I have read this week on which I need to do some further Biblical research?

Week 36

September 3-9

September 3	Read Philippians 2
September 4	Read Philippians 3
September 5	Read Philippians 4
September 6	Read Colossians 1
September 7	Read Colossians 2
September 8	Mark Your Bible
September 9	Day of Reflection

Prayer for this week:

*"Heavenly Father,
please open my heart as I study Your Word
and to make honest application."*

September 3 Week 36, Day 1

Philippians 2

Helpful Notes:

1. **Mind of Christ** = Paul commands Christians to have the mind of Christ; that mind (1) does not operate selfishly or arrogantly at all, (2) humbly holds others above self, considering them superior, (3) aims to be concerned for and meet the interests of others and not just self; this mind is perfectly exemplified in Christ and is to be habitually adopted by His people.
2. **Deity of Christ** = Jesus was always "existing" (present tense) in the very essence of God—before the creation of the earth, after the destruction of the earth, AND during His lifetime on the earth; while on this earth, Jesus was fully God (John 1:1-3, 14; Matt. 1:21) and equal with God (John 5:18); He voluntarily "emptied" Himself of some independent exercise of some Divine attributes, but He did not empty Himself of His deity (Col. 2:9); He gave up "glory" with the Father for the form of a servant (John 17:5), in order to die for all mankind; that is love (John 3:16)!
3. **Work out your salvation** = The present tense, middle voice indicates to "keep on making every effort to obtain for yourself"; this is not suggesting we can earn our salvation, but it emphasizes the human responsibility inherent in our salvation; man is not wholly passive in his salvation, but must exercise his free will to "obey" (at the beginning of the verse) God; while we are working, God is also working, but we can and will fall if we stop working.

1. How was the humility of Christ demonstrated?

2. Who did Paul say was "like-minded" to him?

3. In his work for Christ, what happened to Epaphroditus?

Verse for Meditation and Prayer: **Philippians 2:3**

"Let nothing be done through selfish ambition or conceit,
but in lowliness of mind let each esteem others better than himself."

Philippians 3

Helpful Notes:

1. **We are the circumcision** = Paul cannot be talking about physical circumcision here, as he teaches that physical circumcision is of no profit to one's relationship with Christ (Gal. 5:6; 6:15); Paul is talking about an inward circumcision of the heart (Rom. 2:28-29), which identifies those in the church as the spiritual/true Israel of God (Gal. 6:16); these worship according to the truth of the Spirit (Eph. 6:17; John 4:24), glory in Christ Jesus (and not the law of Moses) and put no confidence in the flesh to keep the law perfectly.
2. **One thing** = Past accomplishments do not matter and past mistakes do not have to define us; all that matters is fulfilling the purpose for which Christ converted us; our "one thing" focus is to simultaneously "keep on forgetting" things of the past and "keep on reaching" toward the goal of pleasing Christ and living with Him eternally.
3. **Citizenship in heaven** = As members of the kingdom of Christ, we are living as "resident aliens" here (as "strangers and pilgrims on the earth," Heb. 11:13; cf. 1 Pet. 2:11), for the heavenly country is our true home; this affects everything about our lives, for we are governed by the laws of that heavenly land, and we long for Jesus to return so that we can "go home."

1. How did Paul identify his strong "zeal" for the law of Moses??

2. Rather than seeking to be justified by his "own righteousness," what "righteousness" did he seek to attain?

3. Whose "pattern" of walking do we need to follow?

Verse for Meditation and Prayer: **Philippians 3:14**

"I press toward the goal for the prize of the upward call of God in Christ Jesus."

September 5 Week 36, Day 3

Philippians 4

Helpful Notes:

1. **Rejoice in the Lord always** = Remember that Paul was in a Roman prison when he wrote these words; thus, regardless of circumstances, Christians need to "keep on rejoicing" (present tense imperative) "always"; the reason we can do that is because of our relationship with Christ—being "in the Lord" should always bring us joy, when we focus on those things that truly matter!
2. **Be anxious for nothing** = This chapter is full of challenges! The word for "anxious" means "to draw the mind in different directions, to be of a divided mind"; when competing forces are working on our minds, it can create anxiety; the only solution for that is to put our full trust in and lay everything before the Lord (Matt. 6:25-34; Jas. 1:6-8), who is "the God of peace."
3. **Be content** = Contentment is to be "self-contained, self-sufficient"; it is a mindset and behavior that must be "learned," in adjusting to all circumstances (and extremes, Prov. 30:8-9) of life; it even involves learning how to responsibly handle "abundance"; Paul had learned the "secret" of contentment, and that was found in his relationship with and strengthening from Christ (v. 13).

1. What did Paul call his brethren in the first verse?

2. What four words are used for prayer in verse 6? (The word "prayer" is one of the four.)

3. Since much of sound mental health is based on the quality of one's thinking, on what things does God tell us to meditate?

Verse for Meditation and Prayer: **Philippians 4:6**

"Be anxious for nothing, but in everything by prayer and supplication, with thanksgiving, let your requests be made known to God."

Colossians 1

Helpful Notes: ** See Brief Introduction to Colossians on page 642.*

1. **Conveyed us into the kingdom** = Two past tense verbs are used in verse 13 ("delivered" and "conveyed"), both noting a completed action; at the very moment that Christians had been rescued from the darkness, they were transferred into Christ's kingdom; the kingdom is NOT yet future, as premillennialists contend; it is a present reality and all Christians are in it now (cf. Rev. 1:9), having been "born of water and spirit" in baptism (John 3:3-5).
2. **Created all things** = Jesus Christ is NOT a created being, for He Himself created all things; He existed before all things and He holds all things together; the Greek word for "firstborn" does not mean "first created," but is "expressing His priority to, and preeminence over, creation, not in the sense of being the 'first' to be born"; Christ has priority over creation, for He created it and has "preeminence" over it; He is the Creator, not a created being!
3. **Continue in the faith** = Obtaining salvation is conditional (Mark 16:16; Acts 2:37-38); retaining salvation is also conditional, based upon one's continuing faithfully "in the faith" and "not" being "moved away" from it; the reason that inspired men repeatedly urge Christians to "continue with the Lord" (cf. Acts 11:23) is because apostasy is possible and their souls (once saved) can be lost.

1. What are some things that Paul says (in his prayer) would be evidence that one is "walking worthy of the Lord"?

2. What is it that Christ must "have" in "all things"?

3. Why does Paul state that "we preach" Christ to "every man"?

Verse for Meditation and Prayer: **Colossians 1:18**

"And He is the head of the body, the church, who is the beginning, the firstborn from the dead, that in all things He may have the preeminence."

Colossians 2

Helpful Notes:

1. **Fullness of the Godhead** = In the human body (John 1:14), Christ possessed "all the fullness of the Godhead" (see also 1:19); the sum total of all Divine nature, power and qualities made its "dwelling" (present tense emphasizes continuous, uninterrupted) in Christ; even on this earth, He was "existing" (present tense) as deity (Phil. 2:6); He was no less "God" in His human form.
2. **Baptism is a work of God** = Often times, some religious folks will claim, "We are not saved by works and baptism is a work, so baptism is not necessary for salvation"; works of human merit certainly do not save (Eph. 2:9; Tit. 3:5), but works of God (i.e., those works "required and approved by God") certainly do; Jesus even identified "believing" as a "work" (John 6:29); being baptized is doing that which is commanded by God (Acts 2:38; 10:48), in order that the power of God might work to give new life (Rom. 6:4).
3. **Nailed to the cross** = The parallel text of Ephesians 2:14-16 helps to identify "the handwriting of requirements" as the law of Moses; it was "contrary to us," because it revealed sin but could not take away sin (Heb. 10:4); Paul says that when Jesus was nailed to the cross that the old law was "nailed to the cross" and it was "taken out of the way" (perfect tense, emphasizing a permanent removal which can never be presented again); the law of Moses is no longer binding and it never again will be binding.

1. Where are "all the treasures of wisdom and knowledge" found?

2. How could someone cheat or defraud you of your reward?

3. From where is "the body" of Christ "nourished and knit together"?

Verse for Meditation and Prayer: **Colossians 2:13**

"And you, being dead in your trespasses and the uncircumcision of your flesh, He has made alive together with Him, having forgiven you all trespasses."

Mark Your Bible

1. **Philippians 2:3-4**—These verses are a good definition of *agape* love.
2. **Philippians 2:8**—Jesus submitted to and obeyed the eternal will of God (Heb. 10:7; John 8:29).
3. **Philippians 2:8**—Crucifixion was reserved for the worst criminals and most worthless slaves. Jesus bore that curse for us (Gal. 3:13).
4. **Philippians 2:10-11**—Underline the words "every" and "should." In this life, each person "should" bow and confess voluntarily. On the day of judgment, "every" one "shall" by compulsion (Rom. 14:11).
5. **Philippians 2:12**—Faith alone does not save. Faithful obedience does.
6. **Philippians 2:14**—Complaining or grumbling is sinful (1 Cor. 10:10).
7. **Philippians 2:15**—God does not call us to be perfect, but to live "above reproach," so that a charge cannot rightly be laid against us.
8. **Philippians 2:17**—Paul's life was gradually being sacrificed for the good of his brethren's eternity, and it brought him joy on top of joy.
9. **Philippians 2:25**—The name Epaphroditus may have its origin in the pagan goddess Aphrodite. He had truly been converted.
10. **Philippians 2:30**—The term "not regarding his life" or "risking" or "hazarding" (ASV) was a gambler's term, indicating that he was willing to "take chances" with his life for the good of the church.
11. **Philippians 3:2**—Judaizers (i.e., those who seek to bind the law of Moses, particularly circumcision, as a condition of salvation) are the "dogs" and "evil workers," who glory in circumcision so much that they are "mutilating" the flesh for their own glory.
12. **Philippians 3:3**—Acceptable worship of God is regulated by the Word of God, given by the Spirit of God (John 4:24; Eph. 6:17).
13. **Philippians 3:7-9**—Underline two uses of "gain" and one "found"; mark three uses of "loss"; circle two uses of "all." There is no value in earthly "gains" if we do not fully "gain Christ"!

(continued on next page)

Mark Your Bible

14. **Philippians 3:8**—The word "rubbish" means "useless material, including excrement, dung, manure, garbage, kitchen scraps."

15. **Philippians 3:11**—The ultimate goal is to be raised to life at the end. Nothing else matters if we are not victorious in the resurrection.

16. **Philippians 3:18-19**—The Judaizers were "enemies of the cross of Christ," for they taught that one could be right with God through the law of Moses, which made Christ's death for nothing.

17. **Philippians 3:19-20**—Circle "their" at the end of verse 19 and "our" at the beginning of verse 20. There is the difference. Their mind is on "earthly things," and our mind is on "heaven." Those are two very different places and will never be the same.

18. **Philippians 3:20**—Faithful Christians "eagerly wait" for Christ to come from "heaven," where we will return (1 Pet. 1:3-5). Our heavenly home exists now and will not be on a renovated earth!

19. **Philippians 3:21**—This earthly body will be "changed" (1 Cor. 15:51-54) completely to be conformed to the same form as Christ's glorified body. "We shall be like Him" (1 John 3:2).

20. **Philippians 4:1**—"Stand fast" involves subjecting oneself willingly to the authority of Christ and refusing to be influenced by false teachers and false teachings.

21. **Philippians 4:3**—All that matters is if one's name is written in the Book of Life (Luke 10:20), but one could so live that his name could be blotted out (Rev. 3:5). This was a warning to these women.

22. **Philippians 4:6**—Circle the words "nothing" and "everything." That is the contrast of life. When we give "everything" to God, there is "nothing" to worry about!

23. **Philippians 4:7**—The word "guard" is a military term that involves a protection that acts like a garrison, keeping the enemy out.

24. **Philippians 4:8**—There is a direct connection between how a person thinks and how he lives (Prov. 23:7; Mark 7:21-22). We must intentionally place our minds on things that will lead us to heaven!

Mark Your Bible

25. **Philippians 4:13**—Circle the word "all." In this context, it has to do with contentment. In a broader application, it recognizes that our source of strength (for all things consistent with the will of Christ) comes from the Lord (Eph. 6:10; 2 Cor. 12:9-10).

26. **Philippians 4:15**—The "giving and receiving" could be referring to "debits and credits." The church in Philippi had become Paul's "partner" in the work, and they may have been receiving and distributing the support for his mission work.

27. **Philippians 4:19**—Circle "my God" and "all." That summarizes it.

28. **Colossians 1:5**—The Christian's "hope" is "laid up" (i.e., stored up, put away) "in heaven" (not on earth). Heaven will not be on earth.

29. **Colossians 1:5**—The truth is objective, not subjective.

30. **Colossians 1:7**—Epaphras may have established this congregation (4:12-13; Phile. 23).

31. **Colossians 1:9**—There was a heretical group forming known as Gnosticism, who claimed to have superior knowledge. Paul's prayer that the Christians might be "filled full of knowledge" may be anticipating this group, and instilling the truth that all true knowledge of God is found in His Word.

32. **Colossians 1:14**—Only those who are "in Christ" have forgiveness.

33. **Colossians 1:15**—Jesus is the very essence of God in the flesh—the "exact likeness" and actual deity on earth (Heb. 1:3; John 1:1, 14).

34. **Colossians 1:16**—All things were created "by," "through" and "for" Christ.

35. **Colossians 1:18**—Jesus was not the first one raised from the dead, but He has preeminence over death in that He was raised and "dies no more" (Rom. 6:9) and is "alive forevermore" (Rev. 1:18).

36. **Colossians 1:19**—All Divine attributes reside in Christ (see 2:9).

(continued on next page)

Mark Your Bible

37. **Colossians 1:23**—Jesus said that when the gospel was "preached in all the world...then the end will come" (Matt. 24:14), speaking of the destruction of Jerusalem, not the final end of the world. Paul says that the gospel was "in all the world" (1:6, 23).
38. **Colossians 1:27**—Our only hope of going to heaven is to have a proper relationship with Jesus Christ—He in us, and we in Him!
39. **Colossians 2:4**—Christians must always be on guard against false teachers and false doctrines who can look and sound so very persuasive (Matt. 7:15; 2 Pet. 2:1; 3:17).
40. **Colossians 2:7**—The word "rooted" is in the perfect tense, urging the Christians to become deeply and firmly rooted and to not move (cf. Mark 4:17; Col. 1:23).
41. **Colossians 2:8**—Extreme caution must be exercised as false teachers will use human philosophy and manmade traditions (Mark 7:3, 5) to capture and "take as prey" those who are not rooted in Christ.
42. **Colossians 2:11**—In baptism, "the body of sin" is done away with (Rom. 6:6). In a play on words, Paul says a "circumcision" takes place in baptism, when, by an act of "Christ," sin is removed.
43. **Colossians 2:12**—Baptism is a burial in water and a resurrection out of water. Sprinkling is not baptism.
44. **Colossians 2:12-13**—Sins are forgiven in baptism and one is made alive "in Christ." To claim that baptism is not essential for salvation is to claim that one can be made alive "outside" of Christ.
45. **Colossians 2:14-16**—Draw a line connecting "taken it out of the way" to "sabbaths." The Sabbath Day was "nailed to the cross."
46. **Colossians 2:17**—The things of the old law were a shadow (not the substance) of things to come (Heb. 10:1). Why would anyone want to go back to the shadow when we have the reality—Christ?
47. **Colossians 2:21**—Keep in context. This has to do with following the regulations, doctrines and traditions put in place by false teachers.

Mark Your Bible

48. **Colossians 2:23**—"Self-imposed religion" is literally "will-worship." It is defined as one who "by his own volition he worships what seems best, whether unbidden or forbidden; worship that one devises or prescribes for himself." To worship in a way that is not regulated by God is sinful (John 4:23-24; Lev. 10:1-3).

September 9 Week 36, Day 7

Day of Reflection

Take time today to reflect on the five chapters that you read this week. You may choose to read all five chapters again, in one sitting, or certain parts of them. Take time today to answer at least one of these questions below. You may or may not write anything down—you can choose to write or simply reflect.

1. What personal application do I need to make from the chapters I have read this week?

2. How can these five chapters help draw me closer to Jesus?

3. What words, phrases or verses in these chapters do I want to go back and study more in depth?

4. What questions do I have about what I have read this week on which I need to do some further Biblical research?

Week 37

September 10-16

September 10	Read Colossians 3
September 11	Read Colossians 4
September 12	Read 1 Thessalonians 1
September 13	Read 1 Thessalonians 2
September 14	Read 1 Thessalonians 3
September 15	Mark Your Bible
September 16	Day of Reflection

Prayer for this week:

"Heavenly Father,
help me to build
a firm and unwavering trust in You."

Colossians 3

Helpful Notes:

1. **Idolatry** = The word means "the worship of idols" or "the worship of that which is seen"; specifically, in the Bible, it refers to the worship of any entity or object other than the one true God, or it can refer to worshiping the true God by means of images; in this text, "covetousness" is said to be "idolatry," for having an unholy, insatiable (even slavish) greed for things puts those things in place of God, making them an object of worship; money and material things is a subtle danger not often recognized that can lead to sin.
2. **Singing** = The N.T. church is to sing "to the Lord" (He is the focus and the authority) in its worship; singing involves congregational unity in (1) "teaching and admonishing," which requires words to be sung that can be understood, (2) "to one another," involves reciprocal action of all worshipers present, (3) "psalms" [patterned like the O.T. psalms], "hymns" [songs of praise], "spiritual songs" [distinct from secular, songs that edify]; (4) "grace" and "thanksgiving"; (5) no justification for mechanical instruments.
3. **In the name of the Lord** = The authority of Christ must govern everything that Christians do or say individually and the church does or says collectively; this has nothing to do with a formal script to recite but an acknowledgement of and submission to Christ's supreme authority in all things (Acts 4:7-10; John 12:48).

1. When a Christian has died to his old life, where is his life hidden?

2. What reason does Paul give to put off sinful attitudes and actions?

3. What do Christians need to do "if anyone has a complaint against another"?

Verse for Meditation and Prayer: **Colossians 3:17**

"And whatever you do in word or deed, do all in the name of the Lord Jesus, giving thanks to God the Father through Him."

September 11 Week 37, Day 2

Colossians 4

Helpful Notes:

1. **Thanksgiving** = There is a great emphasis in the New Testament on being thankful (cf. Luke 17:11-19), and it is emphasized repeatedly in this letter; not only should we learn to "give thanks to God" (1:3, 12), but we should "abound" in it (2:7), make it an ongoing habit (3:15), make sure it is entrenched in "all" that we do (3:17), and saturate our prayers with it (4:2); let us never be guilty of being "unthankful" (2 Tim. 3:2).
2. **Redeeming the time** = The word here for "redeeming" means "to buy out completely for oneself, to corner the market, take advantage of"; it is used metaphorically of time to emphasize the need for Christians to make "the best use of the time" (ESV) and "the most of the opportunity" (NASB), for we recognize that our time is brief and limited (Jas. 4:14); when we fully devote ourselves to Christ, He will change how we use our time.
3. **Read the epistle** = The books of the New Testament were already being recognized as inspired documents, accepted as such and being collected (this was not done by a council hundreds of years later); the writings of the N.T. were to be for the benefit of all—all members of the church (read publicly) and all congregations (shared among them); this ought to urge us to "read" our Bibles.

1. How should our prayers be characterized?

2. How should our words be characterized?

3. What message was to be conveyed to Archippus, which we would do well to heed ourselves?

Verse for Meditation and Prayer: **Colossians 4:6**

"Let your speech always be with grace, seasoned with salt, that you may know how you ought to answer each one."

September 12 Week 37, Day 3

1 Thessalonians 1

Helpful Notes: ** See Brief Introduction to First Thessalonians on page 643.*

1. **Grace and peace** = Paul's common greeting employed common greetings of that day, composed of words with special meanings to Christians; "grace" was the common Greek greeting, and in Paul's letters, he was wishing God's favor upon them; "peace" was the common Hebrew greeting, and in Paul's letters, he was wishing God's overall well-being; these blessings only come "from God our Father and the Lord Jesus Christ" (Eph. 1:2).
2. **Election** = God's election of His people is not unconditional; before creation, God chose those who would be "in Christ" to be His elect ones (Eph. 1:3-11; 1 Pet. 2:9-10), but He elected the group (i.e., church) as a whole, not pre-selecting specific individuals to be or not in the elect; it is through acceptance and obedience of the "gospel" (v. 5) that one becomes the "elect" of God (v. 4).
3. **Wait for His Son from heaven** = The Greek word for "wait" (which is used here in the present tense) means "a sustained, eager and confident expectation" (this is not a passive sitting around); Jesus will be coming "from heaven," which is a place very distinct from earth; He is delivering (present tense) His people from "the wrath of God" prepared in hell for the disobedient (Rom. 2:5-8; 2 Thess. 1:8-9).

1. In the first verse, Paul says that those in "the church" are in who?

2. What did Paul remember about these brethren?

3. What was becoming widely known about this congregation?

Verse for Meditation and Prayer: **1 Thessalonians 1:10**

"... to wait for His Son from heaven, whom He raised from the dead, even Jesus who delivers us from the wrath to come."

1 Thessalonians 2

Helpful Notes:

1. **The gospel** = Paul uses the words "the gospel" four times in this chapter (2:2, 4, 8, 9); he had been "entrusted" to "speak" and "preach" the good news about Jesus Christ; he calls it the gospel "of God," because it had originated in the mind of God and he had received it from God; in the midst of conflict and persecution, Paul was determined to do nothing more or less than to preach the gospel (i.e., "the word of God," v. 13). What an example!
2. **The Word of God** = "The word of God" is, first of all, NOT "the word of men"; it did not come "by the will of man" or by man's devising (2 Pet. 1:21); "the word of God" does not "contain" the Word of God or "become" the Word of God, as some claim, nor is it a mixture of human and Divine thoughts; every bit of it is of Divine origin (2 Tim. 3:16-17); this verse affirms verbal inspiration.
3. **You in the presence of Jesus** = The hope and joy that kept Paul going (even when hindered) was the thought of his brethren being ready for and present in the face of Jesus when He returns; the thought of them not being ready made him "afraid" (Gal. 4:11); another part of Paul's hope and joy is to personally see them there in the presence of Jesus and to be reunited with them (this text teaches both reunion and recognition beyond this life).

1. What three things did Paul say that he did "as a father"?

2. How did these Gentile brethren become "imitators" of their Jewish brethren in Judea?

3. Who kept Paul from going back again to Thessalonica?

Verse for Meditation and Prayer: **1 Thessalonians 2:13**

"For this reason we also thank God without ceasing, because when you received the word of God which you heard from us, you welcomed it not as the word of men, but as it is in truth, the word of God..."

September 14 Week 37, Day 5

1 Thessalonians 3

Helpful Notes:

1. **Perfect what is lacking** = The word for "perfect" means "to complete, mature, put in proper order, cause to function well"; there were some things about the "faith" of these brethren that were deficient and Paul wanted to come back to properly prepare and equip them; this is a need that we all have—to continually develop and mature our faith, so that we can do even more.
2. **Blameless** = "Blameless" does not mean "perfect and without mistake"; we all make mistakes; the word denotes one who lives above reproach and, when he makes mistakes, he properly handles those mistakes and makes them right; no charge or indictment can rightly be laid at his feet that he has done a wrong and not sought to make it right; a life of "holiness" is his goal.
3. **With all His saints** = The word "saints" (Greek *hagioi*) means "holy ones" and could be a reference to angels (Matt. 25:31; 2 Thess. 1:7); or, more likely, it is a reference to the spirits of His people who have departed from this life; He will bring those spirits with Him (those who have died "in Jesus," 4:14) to be reunited with their resurrected, spiritual bodies (1 Cor. 15:35-57).

1. Why did Paul send Timothy back to Thessalonica?

2. What report did Timothy bring back to Paul from Thessalonica?

3. In what two things did Paul pray that their love would increase and abound?

Verse for Meditation and Prayer: **1 Thessalonians 3:13**

"So that He may establish your hearts blameless in holiness before our God and Father at the coming of our Lord Jesus Christ with all His saints."

Mark Your Bible

1. **Colossians 3:1**—Those who are "raised with Christ" are those who have been "buried with Christ in baptism" (2:12).
2. **Colossians 3:1-2**—We are to persistently focus our attention and desires toward heaven "above"—following the standard given from heaven, seeking to please the Lord in heaven, longing to spend eternity with the Lord in heaven. Note that heaven is "above" where Christ is right now—heaven will not be on earth.
3. **Colossians 3:1**—"The right hand" was an expression used of a position of the highest, exalted honor and power (Rev. 17:14; 19:16).
4. **Colossians 3:3**—"Died" involves the decision of repentance to separate ourselves from the ways of this world and to bury the old man of sin in baptism (Rom. 6:2-6).
5. **Colossians 3:7**—These Christians "once lived in" sin (an imperfect tense verb denoting ongoing sinfulness). This included "living in " fornication (v. 5). Fornication is all forms of unlawful, sexual intercourse, which includes adultery. Adultery is not a one-time sin that is committed at the marriage and initial sexual union, but it is a perpetual sin for the duration of the relationship.
6. **Colossians 3:10-11**—"In Christ," no cultural barriers should separate us. We are all a new man "created" in "the image" of Christ.
7. **Colossians 3:13**—"Bearing with" means to hold oneself back.
8. **Colossians 3:22-25**—Draw a line connecting "God," "the Lord" (3 times) and "Master" (4:1). He must be our focus when facing unfortunate circumstances.
9. **Colossians 4:1**—We all have a "Master in heaven" to whom we will give account for how we have treated others. In Christ, masters and slaves are on the same level (2:12; 3:11; Gal. 3:28).
10. **Colossians 4:4**—Speaking God's Word as we "ought to speak" involves the right content, deep respect, proper attitude and courage.

(continued on next page)

Mark Your Bible

11. **Colossians 4:5**—We must ever be mindful of our influence on others. Also, this emphasizes a difference between those who are "outside" of Christ and those who are "inside."

12. **Colossians 4:9**—Onesimus was a runaway slave whom Paul had converted to Christ. The book of Philemon is written to his master. But Paul does not refer to him as a slave but as "one of you."

13. **Colossians 4:11**—The word "comfort" here is from the Greek *paregoria,* which means "a soothing, solace." A form of the term was used of medicines that would sooth, lessen pain or allay irritation.

14. **Colossians 4:12**—The Greek word for "laboring" is *agonizomai,* which involved "agonizing, wrestling, struggling, striving." Epaphras was doing this "fervently" in his "prayers" for the brethren.

15. **1 Thessalonians 1:3**—True "faith" and "love" are faithfully engaged in "work" and "labor" for the Lord. Faith and love are not mutually exclusive from work and labor. They are inseparable.

16. **1 Thessalonians 1:5**—Paul's preaching was accompanied by miracles (2 Cor. 12:12; Heb. 2:3-4), which confirmed the message that he was preaching.

17. **1 Thessalonians 1:6-7**—In following Paul's example, the church became a model/pattern for other Christians in Greece. We often do not know when others are seeing and following our example.

18. **1 Thessalonians 1:8**—The Greek word for "sounded forth" means "an echoing thunder or blasting as a trumpet." The Word of God reverberated from these Christians into "every place."

19. **1 Thessalonians 1:9**—The Gentiles realized that their idols were dead but the God of heaven was "the living and true God." Thus, they "turned" (1) away from their idols and (2) toward God. This was a picture of their full conversion to Christ (see Acts 15:3).

20. **1 Thessalonians 2:4, 6**—Underline "not as pleasing men" and "nor did we seek glory from men." Paul's motivation was not to please others or to receive praise himself. It was to please and praise God!

Mark Your Bible

21. **1 Thessalonians 2:7, 11**—Paul pictures himself as both "a nursing mother" and an instructing "father" with the brethren, helping them to development from spiritual infancy through spiritual maturity.

22. **1 Thessalonians 2:9**—Paul uses the word "labor" (hard, exhausting, strenuous work) and "toil" (involving painful struggle and hardship) to describe his work. He may have been making tents at night (Acts 18:3), so that he could preach during the day.

23. **1 Thessalonians 2:12**—"Calls" is in the present tense, denoting continual activity. God is constantly "calling" us into heaven.

24. **1 Thessalonians 2:13**—While other passages state that God "works in" His people (Eph. 3:20; Phil. 2:13), this text states that it is "the word of God" that "effectively works" (present tense, indicating ongoing) in His people. The two thoughts are synonymous.

25. **1 Thessalonians 2:14**—Those in the "church" are those who are "in Christ Jesus." If you're "in Christ," you're in His church, having entered by baptism (Rom. 6:3-4; 1 Cor. 12:13).

26. **1 Thessalonians 2:16**—God will permit people to press on in their sin until they reach a certain point of depravity, extending His mercy (cf. Gen. 15:16; Dan. 8:32; Matt. 23:32). But justice eventually comes.

27. **1 Thessalonians 3:2, 5, 6, 7, 10**—Paul talks about their "faith" five times in this chapter. Draw lines connecting them. Their faith was his greatest concern. True faith will "stand fast in the Lord" (v. 8).

28. **1 Thessalonians 3:3-4**—Christians "know" (used twice) that they will suffer for their faith (2 Tim. 3:12). But, it is worth it!

29. **1 Thessalonians 3:5**—The devil can tempt Christians to the point that they abandon their faith and are lost. Christians must resist!

30. **1 Thessalonians 3:11**—The compound subject in this verse—(1) our God and Father and (2) our Lord Jesus Christ—has a singular verb ("direct"). This emphasizes the equality of Jesus (in His deity) with the Father and the unity that exists between the Father and the Son.

Day of Reflection

Take time today to reflect on the five chapters that you read this week. You may choose to read all five chapters again, in one sitting, or certain parts of them. Take time today to answer at least one of these questions below. You may or may not write anything down—you can choose to write or simply reflect.

1. What personal application do I need to make from the chapters I have read this week?

2. How can these five chapters help draw me closer to Jesus?

3. What words, phrases or verses in these chapters do I want to go back and study more in depth?

4. What questions do I have about what I have read this week on which I need to do some further Biblical research?

Week 38

September 17-23

September 17	Read 1 Thessalonians 4
September 18	Read 1 Thessalonians 5
September 19	Read 2 Thessalonians 1
September 20	Read 2 Thessalonians 2
September 21	Read 2 Thessalonians 3
September 22	Mark Your Bible
September 23	Day of Reflection

Prayer for this week:

"Heavenly Father,
I long for Jesus to return and
take me home with Him forever."

September 17 Week 38, Day 1

1 Thessalonians 4

Helpful Notes:

1. **Sanctification** = The Greek word *hagiosmos* denotes a condition of holiness, into which certain people have been set apart; sanctification involves being (1) set apart from the world and not conformed to it (Rom. 12:1-2), and (2) set apart unto God for the sacred purpose of serving Him; one is initially sanctified by God's truth (John 17:17) when he obeys it through baptism (Eph. 5:26; 1 Cor. 6:11), and then he must continue to live a sanctified life, which is "the will of God."
2. **Dead in Christ** = There are only two groups of people in the context of verses 14-17: (1) the dead in Christ and (2) the alive in Christ; those who are outside of Christ (dead or living) are not in this context; the "dead in Christ" are faithful Christians who have died before the return of Christ; they will rise "first"—first before the living Christians are "caught up"; Scripture teaches there will be only one simultaneous resurrection of the just and the unjust (Acts 24:15; John 5:28-29) on the "last day" (John 6:54).
3. **Caught up** = The premillennial doctrine of the rapture is not taught in any Scripture, including this one; Christ's return will be both visible and audible (shout, voice, trumpet); it will not be silent or in secret; on that last day, the dead will be raised, then the living will be "caught up" with the dead "in the clouds to meet the Lord in the air"; Jesus will never step foot on this earth again.

1. What did Paul urge them to do in their love for one another?

2. Who is Jesus going to bring with Him when He returns?

3. What are we supposed to use to comfort one another?

Verse for Meditation and Prayer: **1 Thessalonians 4:17**

"Then we who are alive and remain shall be caught up together with them in the clouds to meet the Lord in the air. And thus we shall always be with the Lord."

1 Thessalonians 5

Helpful Notes:

1. **The day of the Lord** = The expression "the day of the Lord" is used throughout Scripture regarding a judgment of God coming upon a people; in this context, it is the final judgment of God at the end of time upon all people (2 Pet. 3:10); as Jesus Himself taught, it will come suddenly, unexpectedly and unpredictably, like a thief (Matt. 24:43-44), without a warning or any signs at all.
2. **Sober** = The Greek word *nepho* is often used of being "sober-minded" or "self-controlled"; the word can mean to "be free from every form of mental or spiritual 'drunkenness'"; in a physical sense, the word signifies "to be free from the influence of intoxicants"; alcohol and drugs have an "influence" on our bodies and our minds (even in small quantities); God calls us to be "free."
3. **Abstain from every form of evil** = As one "tests" or examines all things by the standard of God's Word, he is to "abstain from" (Greek *apecho* means "avoid contact with or use of something; keep away, avoid, hold or keep oneself from") "every form of evil"; the New Testament identifies numerous evils (i.e., sins) in the eyes of God, and the admonition here is to resist every kind of evil, whether one specified or anything "like" it (Gal. 5:21b), including those things that have an "appearance of evil" (KJV).

1. What two illustrations are used to describe the suddenness and unexpectedness of the timing of Christ's return?

2. As Christians strive to live a holy life to be prepared for Christ's coming, what should we be doing for each other (verse 11)?

3. What must we do for our elders, who are "over us in the Lord"?

Verse for Meditation and Prayer: **1 Thessalonians 5:2**

"For you yourselves know perfectly that the day of the Lord so comes as a thief in the night."

September 19 Week 38, Day 3

2 Thessalonians 1

Helpful Notes: * *See Brief Introduction to Second Thessalonians on page 644.*

1. **Rest** = The Greek word for "rest" here is different than other verses about heaven; the Greek *anesis* means "relief from something onerous or troublesome; relief from anxiety, tension, conflict, suffering; liberty, relaxation, easing"; as they had suffered "with" Paul, they would be given rest "with" Paul; what a motivation!
2. **Vengeance** = God's vengeance is an act of the righteous Judge (2 Tim. 4:8) administering Divine justice (Rom. 2:2); it is not an emotional outburst, like that of a human, nor should it be described as vindictiveness or revenge; God holiness demands that sin be punished; in God's justice, each person receives what he deserves (Rom. 1:32; 2:5-6) and what he chooses for himself (Rom. 9:22); the word "repay" in verse 6 indicates that punishment is reaping what one sows (deal out "tribulation [v. 4], receive "tribulation" [v. 6]).
3. **Eternal destruction** = Contrary to false teaching today, the word "destruction" does not mean annihilation or extinction; the ASV and ESV use the word "suffer," and suffering implies actual consciousness; Jesus tied the word "everlasting" with "punishment" (Matt. 25:46), which means "infliction of suffering or pain in chastisement; enduring torment"; the word "destruction" means "ruined state, loss of well-being; misery"; same word is used of Moab being destroyed by Babylon, but not extinguished (Jer. 48:8).

1. What was happening with the "faith" and "love" of the brethren?

2. What will happen among "His saints" at Jesus' return?

3. What part of Jesus' second coming are you looking forward to the most?

Verse for Meditation and Prayer: **2 Thessalonians 1:9**

"These shall be punished with everlasting destruction from the presence of the Lord and from the glory of His power."

2 Thessalonians 2

Helpful Notes:

1. **The falling away** = God foretold that "first" (before the return of Christ, thus after the writing of Paul) there would be "the apostasy" (NASB) or "the falling away"; the use of the definite article pointed to a definite rebellion and defection against God, His will and His pattern for N.T. Christianity (Acts 20:28-31; 1 Tim. 4:1-3; 2 Tim. 4:1-4); there has certainly been a great apostasy from the Lord and His church, as one reflects on the current condition of "religion" that claims the name of "Christ" in our world.
2. **Love of truth or believe a lie** = Both of these are choices that men make; in order to be saved (from sin and in eternity), one must truly "love" and "believe" the truth (make that choice); if one rejects the truth and has "pleasure in unrighteousness," then he will "believe the lie" (make the choice); God will not force truth on anyone (see "Mark Your Bible" note for 2 Thessalonians 2:11).
3. **Called by the gospel** = The word "called" is used frequently in the New Testament, and many folks use it to teach that God somehow verbally or orally calls people through whisperings of the Holy Spirit; this passage clearly teaches that man is "called" to ("chosen for") salvation (v. 13) "by our gospel" (v. 14); God's calling is always through the gospel (Rom. 10:14; 1 Cor. 1:18, 21).

1. What false doctrine were some teaching in Paul's day (v. 2)?

2. What does someone need to "love" in order to be saved?

3. In the midst of trials and impending persecution, what do Christians need to remember that God has given us (v. 16)?

Verse for Meditation and Prayer: **2 Thessalonians 2:14**

"To which He called you by our gospel,
for the obtaining of the glory of our Lord Jesus Christ."

2 Thessalonians 3

Helpful Notes:

1. **Withdraw** = The Greek word means "to keep one's distance, keep away, to shrink from a person"; it involves avoiding fellowship and social contact—not "keeping company" (v. 14; 1 Cor. 5:11); the present tense indicates an ongoing action, not just a one-time act; this is a "command" (an authoritative order) given to the whole church ("you, brethren") to be carried out by the authority of Christ (1 Cor. 5:4) without partiality ("every brother who") toward those who abandon inspired instructions (cf. 2:15).
2. **Walk disorderly** = This was a military term denoting those who are "not keeping rank, insubordinate, unruly, out of step"; this applies to "every brother" ("anyone," v. 14) who "walks out of step" with God's Word and "does not obey" (v. 14); the word "walks" (v. 6) and the word "obey" (v. 14) are in the present tense, denoting an ongoing, habitual sinfulness, not just a one-time sin.
3. **Admonish as a brother** = The Greek *noutheteo* literally means "to put in mind"; it means "to counsel about avoidance or cessation of an improper course of conduct; to warn"; the wayward member from whom the church has withdrawn fellowship is not our enemy; he is a lost brother, who needs to feel the shame of his sin through a discontinuance of social contact and regular warnings.

1. Why did Paul want the brethren to pray for him?

2. Why does God place such a strong emphasis on working?

3. Why does Scripture teach us to withdraw fellowship from brethren who have strayed? What if we do not practice it?

Verse for Meditation and Prayer: **2 Thessalonians 3:14**

"But we command you, brethren, in the name of our Lord Jesus Christ, that you withdraw from every brother who walks disorderly and not according to the tradition which he received from us."

Mark Your Bible

1. **1 Thessalonians 4:1-2**—Pleasing God involves "commandments." These are not commandments from men but "through the Lord Jesus." This is the only way that we know how "to walk" with God.
2. **1 Thessalonians 4:3**—Being set apart unto God involves continually abstaining from all unlawful sexual acts outside of marriage, regardless of what the world thinks. Fornication was so prevalent in the Greek world that it was part of their very religion.
3. **1 Thessalonians 4:4**—A Christian must learn to master his own body (Rom. 6:19; 1 Cor. 9:27) and keep it pure (1 Cor. 6:18-20)!
4. **1 Thessalonians 4:7**—"Uncleanness" has to do with moral impurity that stains the soul in the eyes of God.
5. **1 Thessalonians 4:8**—When people today reject the call to sexual purity and the sacred use of the body, they are rejecting God.
6. **1 Thessalonians 4:11**—Christians must not be meddling busybodies in other people's business (2 Thess. 3:11; 1 Pet. 4:15; 1 Tim. 5:13).
7. **1 Thessalonians 4:11-12**—A Christian must work and take personal responsibility for himself, learning to be self-sufficient.
8. **1 Thessalonians 4:13**—"Fallen asleep" is an idiom for death, and it is reference only to the body and not the soul (Dan. 12:2; John 11:11, 43). The soul does not sleep (Ecc. 12:7; Jas. 2:26), but the soul is conscious after death (Rev. 6:9-11; Luke 16:19-31; Phil. 1:23; Luke 23:43).
9. **1 Thessalonians 4:13**—Those who have "no hope" are those who die outside of Christ.
10. **1 Thessalonians 4:14**—Our living hope is founded upon the historical fact of Jesus' death and resurrection (1 Pet. 1:3; 1 Cor. 15:3-4). Circle "even so." We are as certain of the future as we are of the past.
11. **1 Thessalonians 4:17**—When we ascend from this earth, we will "always be with the Lord." There will be no return to this earth once we depart and it is destroyed (2 Pet. 3:10-13).

(continued on next page)

Mark Your Bible

12. **1 Thessalonians 5:1**—It is not possible to know "the times and the seasons" of the return of Christ. Jesus did not know when He was on this earth (Matt. 24:36). Paul did not know. We do not know.
13. **1 Thessalonians 5:3**—Upon Jesus' "sudden" and unexpected return, there will be "no escape" (2 Thess. 1:6-10) and no second chances.
14. **1 Thessalonians 5:5**—The expression "sons of" means to be "characterized by" (cf. 1 John 1:5; John 8:12; Eph. 5:8).
15. **1 Thessalonians 5:7**—The two words "drunk" in this verse are two different Greek words. One is for "the state or condition of being drunk" (*methuo*). To reach that state or condition of drunkenness involves *methusko,* which is an inceptive verb that marks "the process of getting drunk." God condemns the state of drunkenness (Gal. 5:21) and drinking that leads to it (Eph. 5:18; Prov. 20:1).
16. **1 Thessalonians 5:9**—The word "appoint" has nothing to do with Calvinism's predestination and a premillennial tribulation. God did not save us (v. 8) in order that we might experience His wrath (or condemnation), but He saved us to deliver us from His wrath (1:10) and receive eternal salvation in heaven. Obtaining it is up to us.
17. **1 Thessalonians 5:10**—Jesus "died for us" so that we should "live together with Him" now and in eternity (4:17).
18. **1 Thessalonians 5:19**—In the first century, one might "quench the Spirit" by not using his miraculous gift. Today, one can "quench the Spirit" by living a life contrary to the teachings of the Word.
19. **1 Thessalonians 5:20**—"Prophecies" are the teachings of God's Word (whether in prediction or prescription). This could have application during the days of miraculous prophetic activity, and/or it could apply today to those who "make nothing of" (literal definition of "despise") or disregard the teaching of God's truth.
20. **1 Thessalonians 5:23**—Paul's focus was on the "whole" of man being "completely" sanctified by God and ready for the coming of Christ. He may have simply been focusing on the inward man and outward man (cf. 2 Cor. 4:16-18) without intent of absolute distinc-

Mark Your Bible

tion. Often "spirit" and "soul" are used interchangeably in Scripture. If they are to be understood separately, the "spirit" is the imperishable part of man made in the image of God (Gen. 1:26) and the "soul" is the life force within the body (Acts 20:10). Again, Paul may not be distinguishing them in this verse.

21. **2 Thessalonians 1:5**—It is not that anyone is "worthy" of heaven. But those who endure persecution for His name and remain faithful through it all will be admitted into (found "worthy") the heavenly kingdom. We need to walk "worthy" now (v. 11) to be deemed "worthy" (by His grace) then.

22. **2 Thessalonians 1:7**—Jesus will be revealed "from heaven" (cf. Acts 1:11; 1 Thess. 1:10). We are going to "heaven" (1 Pet. 1:4). Heaven will not be on a renovated earth. That is non-sensical.

23. **2 Thessalonians 1:8**—This is why the Great Commission is so important! One must know, believe and obey God to be saved and avoid eternal punishment in hell (Heb. 5:9; Matt. 7:21-23).

24. **2 Thessalonians 1:9**—The worst part of hell is being separated from God for all eternity (Matt. 7:23; 8:12; 25:41), having rejected all chances and second chances, and suffering utter abandonment.

25. **2 Thessalonians 2:2**—The word "spirit" is used here for a "teacher" (1 John 4:1).

26. **2 Thessalonians 2:3**—There is no way today to confidently identify "the man of lawlessness." Many have tried. There is no justification for teaching this is some mystical person to appear right before the return of Christ, also called (as is claimed) the "Antichrist." If the two are connected, John said that "many antichrists have come" and are "now already in the world" (1 John 2:18; 4:3), and Paul said that "the mystery of lawlessness is already at work" (2 Thess. 2:7). The Bible does not specifically identify for us "what he is" or "who he is," and we need to be satisfied with that.

(continued on next page)

Mark Your Bible

27. **2 Thessalonians 2:3**—"The son of perdition" means that he is characterized by or belongs to destruction. He is "the perishing one," who is destined to be destroyed (cf. John 17:12).

28. **2 Thessalonians 2:4**—This is not necessarily the physical sanctuary but an indication of the exaltation made to the place of God.

29. **2 Thessalonians 2:6**—Again, Scripture does not identify for us the one who "restrains." To speculate is just that—speculation. These brethren knew (v. 5). And Paul's point was that God is in control. At the proper time, God will allow things to unfold. Trust God.

30. **2 Thessalonians 2:7-9**—Satan was already at work and was deceiving many. While we do not know the details, the confidence all Christians need is in verse 8—the Lord will defeat and bring to naught all lawlessness and wickedness at "His coming."

31. **2 Thessalonians 2:11**—There is a common idiom used in Scripture that puts the active voice for the passive, stating that God actively does something, when He is simply permitting it. God respects man's free will—if man wants to "believe the lie," God will allow it. God is said to have hardened Pharaoh's heart, when it was actually Pharaoh who hardened his heart in response to God's law. "Lies" are contrary to God's nature, but He allows man to make a choice. (See other uses of this idiom: Jer. 4:10, Ezek. 20:25, Matt. 6:13.)

32. **2 Thessalonians 2:13**—God chose classifications of people who would be saved—all who obey His will are chosen to be saved.

33. **2 Thessalonians 2:13**—Sanctification involves (1) God's part (the Word given "by the Spirit") and (2) man's part (obeying the Word).

34. **2 Thessalonians 2:15**—These are not the traditions of men (Matt. 15:1-9). These are inspired instructions given by God in His Word (cf. 3:6; 1 Cor. 11:2). There was a body of authoritative Christian doctrine already being compiled (i.e., the N.T. books) and shared.

35. **2 Thessalonians 3:3**—Circle the word "But." Man might be faithless but God never is. God is always faithful and will take care of you.

Mark Your Bible

36. **2 Thessalonians 3:5**—"The love of God" could refer to His love for me or my love for Him. "The patience of Christ" could refer to having patience in serving Christ or to Christ's patience toward me.

37. **2 Thessalonians 3:6**—See 2:15. These are God's traditions, not man's.

38. **2 Thessalonians 3:10**—The present tense verbs emphasize that a Christian's "continued" unwillingness to have "ongoing" employment should result in "ongoing" hunger. Working and taking responsibility for one's self is a Scriptural principle from the very beginning (Gen. 3:19).

39. **2 Thessalonians 3:14**—To "note" means to "put a tag on that man." He is to be identified to the whole church (in a loving manner). This is not an "elders' only" action or something done in private. It is to be done "when you are gathered together" (1 Cor. 5:4). The present tense indicates a continued mark until there is repentance.

40. **2 Thessalonians 3:14**—"Do not keep company" is in the present tense, emphasizing an ongoing activity (or ongoing cessation of activity). "Keep company" means "to mix up together, associate with," which would include eating together and social contact (1 Cor. 5:11).

41. **2 Thessalonians 3:14**—The purpose is not to kick him out of the church and condemn him forever to hell. The purpose is to place wholesome pressure on him to create a sense of shame and a desire to do right. This is done to save his soul (1 Cor. 5:5) and to maintain the purity of the church (1 Cor. 5:6).

42. **2 Thessalonians 3:17**—Paul used an amanuensis to actually pen his letters (cf. Rom. 16:22), but he told the brethren how to discern if a letter was truly from him. There would be a distinguishing mark of genuine authenticity—a salutation in his own handwriting.

September 23 Week 38, Day 7

Day of Reflection

Take time today to reflect on the five chapters that you read this week. You may choose to read all five chapters again, in one sitting, or certain parts of them. Take time today to answer at least one of these questions below. You may or may not write anything down—you can choose to write or simply reflect.

1. What personal application do I need to make from the chapters I have read this week?

2. How can these five chapters help draw me closer to Jesus?

3. What words, phrases or verses in these chapters do I want to go back and study more in depth?

4. What questions do I have about what I have read this week on which I need to do some further Biblical research?

Week 39

September 24-30

September 24	Read 1 Timothy 1
September 25	Read 1 Timothy 2
September 26	Read 1 Timothy 3
September 27	Read 1 Timothy 4
September 28	Read 1 Timothy 5
September 29	Mark Your Bible
September 30	Day of Reflection

Prayer for this week:

"Heavenly Father,
help me to put Your church first
in my life every day."

September 24 Week 39, Day 1

1 Timothy 1

Helpful Notes: ** See Brief Introduction to First Timothy on page 645.*

1. **Sound doctrine** = The term "sound doctrine" is found only in Paul's letters to Timothy and Titus, where preachers are commanded to preach only and tolerate only "sound doctrine"; first, note the emphasis on "doctrine"—there is an objective body of truth that must be our standard in all things; second, the Greek word for "sound" is the origin of our word "hygiene"—the word means "healthy," and also "free from error"; we must teach and accept "no other doctrine," which leads to spiritual health.
2. **Mercy** = The Greek word for "mercy" (*eleos*) means "kindness or concern expressed for someone in need"; it can often be translated "pity, compassion"; sometimes the explanation and differentiation between "grace" and "mercy" has been stated as: "Grace is receiving what you don't deserve; mercy is not receiving what you do deserve."
3. **Good warfare** = Christians are engaged in a spiritual warfare against the devil, against his forces of evil, against false doctrine, against false ideas that permeate humanity; as we fight this battle between good and evil, we must be fully armed (Eph. 6:10-18) and seeking to bring man's thoughts into captivity by the Word of God (2 Cor. 10:4-6); this is an ongoing battle (1 Tim. 6:12; 2 Tim. 4:7).

1. What did Paul say was "the purpose of the commandment" that "they teach no other doctrine"?

2. Once God's grace and mercy saved Paul, where did He place him?

3. Why did Paul say that Christ had shown longsuffering to him?

Verse for Meditation and Prayer: **1 Timothy 1:15**

*"This is a faithful saying and worthy of all acceptance,
that Christ Jesus came into the world to save sinners,
of whom I am chief."*

1 Timothy 2

Helpful Notes:

1. **Prayers** = Paul mentions four types of prayers in verse 1: "supplications" are urgent requests to meet a need; "prayers" involve devotion and expressing one's dependence upon God; "intercessions" are petitions on behalf of another; "thanksgivings" allow us to express gratitude for all the blessings He bestows; these prayers are not only to be made for ourselves but "for all men."
2. **One Mediator** = A "mediator" is literally "a go-between," who "mediates between two parties to remove disagreement or reach a common goal"; Jesus is uniquely qualified, for He can equally relate to both sides (Divine and human); the identification of Christ as the "one" and only "Mediator" excludes Mary as the "Mediatrix" or any saints who have already died (as is claimed).
3. **Men** = There are two different Greek words used for "men" in this context; in verse 4, God desires all "men" to be saved (the Greek *anthropos* is generic for all mankind); in verse 8, God desires that "the men" pray everywhere (the Greek *aner* means "male exclusively, in contrast to female"); obviously women are permitted to pray to God (1 Cor. 11:5; Acts 12:12); this is addressing public prayers wherever Christians assemble, that the men are to lead those prayers and, therefore, direct all acts of worship to God.

1. What is the stated reason that God wants us to pray for all rulers?

2. How can we follow God's rules without becoming bitter?

3. What are the four godly virtues in which women need to "continue"?

Verse for Meditation and Prayer: **1 Timothy 2:4**

"Who desires all men to be saved
and to come to the knowledge of the truth."

September 26 Week 39, Day 3

1 Timothy 3

Helpful Notes:

1. **Bishop** = "Bishop" comes from the Greek word *episkopos,* which literally means "over-seer"; these men are responsible for the oversight, superintendency and rule of the church (under the authority of Christ, of course); these men are the "elders" and "pastors" of the church (terms used interchangeably in Acts 20:17, 28; 1 Pet. 5:1-2; Tit. 1:5-7); there was always a plurality of these men serving in a local congregation (Acts 14:23; Phil. 1:1); there is no Biblical authority for one bishop to serve over several congregations or for any person to be called an "archbishop."
2. **Deacon** = "Deacon" comes from the Greek word *diakonos,* which is usually translated in its generic meaning of "servant, minister"; when used in its special sense, *diakonos* denotes those men who serve in an official role in the church (Phil. 1:1), following the oversight of the elders but being over a work (Acts 6:3).
3. **The house of God** = The church of Christ is denoted by various metaphors (such as body, kingdom, temple, etc.); the word "house" or "household" here is a reference to "family" (mark the same word in verses 4, 5, 12); the church is not a building, but it is the family of God; we must behave properly (as He instructs) in God's family; God has no children outside of His family.

1. What qualification is there for the children of an elder?

2. What do deacons who "have served well" "obtain for themselves"?

3. What does Paul summarize in the last verse of the chapter?

Verse for Meditation and Prayer: 1 Timothy 3:15

"But if I am delayed, I write so that you may know how you ought to conduct yourself in the house of God, which is the church of the living God, the pillar and ground of the truth."

1 Timothy 4

Helpful Notes:

1. **Depart from the faith** = "The faith" (with the definite article) is the objective body of truth (i.e., the gospel, Gal. 1:11+23), which is "obeyed" in order to be saved (Acts 6:7); there is only "one faith" (Eph. 4:5) given by the Lord (Jude 3); it is possible (and here predicted) that one can "fall away" (a meaning of "depart") by choosing to rebel against God's will; apostasy is possible.
2. **Exercise toward godliness** = "Godliness" literally means "to be well devout," and denotes a deep devotion and piety (an awesome respect), characterized by a sustained God-ward attitude, that strives to do what is well-pleasing to God; the word "exercise" (Greek *gumnazo,* from which we get "gymnasium") is a present tense imperative emphasizing the need to constantly train with rigorous self-discipline in order to reach the goal of godliness.
3. **The gift WITH the hands of the eldership** = "Gift" can refer to a miraculous gift of the Spirit or an appointment to a leadership position; given "by prophecy" indicates that prophecy accompanied its bestowal somehow; it is evident that Timothy received a miraculous gift only "through" (Greek *dia*) the laying on of Paul's hands (2 Tim. 1:6; cf. Acts 8:14-18), but the gift in 4:14 was given "with" (Greek *meta*) the elders' hands, likely referring to a public endorsement of the elders for a special ministry (cf. Acts 13:2-3).

1. According to God's Word, what do we need to do before we eat?

2. The "promise" that comes with exercising godliness involves what two facets of life?

3. In what areas was Timothy (and Christians today) to be an example?

Verse for Meditation and Prayer: **1 Timothy 4:8**

"For bodily exercise profits a little, but godliness is profitable for all things, having promise of the life that now is and of that which is to come."

September 28 Week 39, Day 5

1 Timothy 5

Helpful Notes:

1. **Widows indeed** = There are four classes of widows in this chapter: a widow with family (5:4, 8, 16), a widow who lives for pleasure (5:6), a younger widow (5:11-15), and a widow indeed; the "widow indeed" is to be especially honored (which denotes special care physically and emotionally, and even financially), for she has no Christian family to see to her needs, she has God first in her life, she is over 60 years old, she was a faithful wife, and she has done good works in the church (5:3, 5, 9-10).
2. **Provide for own** = The word "provide" involves "giving careful thought beforehand," in order to properly care for and provide for needs; the primary responsibility for the care of family members in need is their own family; families who do not take care of those in their "own family" are said to repudiate and disown "the faith" and have become worse than a non-Christian in the eyes of God.
3. **The Scripture** = The Greek word for "Scripture" (*graphe*) emphasizes that which has been "written"; God's people identified the inspired documents as they were written and began collecting them and distributing them; in verse 18, Paul quotes from the O.T. (Deut. 25:4) and the N.T. (Luke 10:7) and calls both (equally) "Scripture" and inspired; the present tense "says" emphasizes the sacred Scripture, written in the past, has continual authority.

1. How are we to treat older and younger members of the church?

2. Why do you think God gives so much attention to widows throughout Scripture?

3. What are some things that each Christian can do for widows?

Verse for Meditation and Prayer: 1 Timothy 5:8

"But if anyone does not provide for his own,
and especially for those of his household,
he has denied the faith and is worse than an unbeliever."

Mark Your Bible

1. **1 Timothy 1:1**—It is likely that Paul converted Timothy to Christ (Acts 16:1-3; 1 Cor. 4:17; Phil. 2:22; 1 Tim. 1:18; 2 Tim. 1:2; 2:1).
2. **1 Timothy 1:6**—Paul said that some have "strayed" and "turned." Apostasy is very possible, as emphasized in these letters to Timothy (1:19-20; 4:1-3; 5:15; 6:10, 20-21; 2 Tim. 2:18; 4:4).
3. **1 Timothy 1:10**—Circle "any other thing." God's list of sins is not exhaustive or as specific as it could be. "Any thing" like this that is "contrary to sound doctrine" is also sin (cf. "such things," Gal. 5:21).
4. **1 Timothy 1:13**—Lack of knowledge of God's will is not an excuse and does not negate the sinfulness (cf. Acts 23:1; 26:9). Paul thought he was doing God's will, but he was wrong. Fortunately, God's grace and mercy were extended to him.
5. **1 Timothy 1:13-15**—God will forgive any sinner who repents and obeys His will. God does not show partiality (Acts 10:34-35).
6. **1 Timothy 1:16**—Some want the Greek word *eis* in Acts 2:38 (translated "for") to mean "because of." If it means to be baptized "because" one already has the forgiveness of sins in Acts 2:38, then it means to believe "because" one already has eternal life in this verse.
7. **1 Timothy 1:18**—God was behind the choosing of Timothy as Paul's helper (Acts 16:1-3).
8. **1 Timothy 1:19**—Underline "the faith." There is an objective faith, i.e., the gospel. Throughout the letters to Timothy and Titus, there is a repeated emphasis on "the faith," "the truth," "the doctrine," "the word," etc. Underline each one when you come across it.
9. **1 Timothy 1:20**—The church had withdrawn fellowship from these men (see 1 Cor. 5:1-5, 13), in an effort to save their souls.
10. **1 Timothy 2:1, 4, 6**—Underline three uses of "all." God has a universal interest and love for all mankind. That does not mean that all are universally saved. Salvation requires personal choice, but God did not arbitrarily decree any to be lost against their will.

(continued on next page)

Mark Your Bible

11. **1 Timothy 2:4**—In order "to be saved," one must "come to the knowledge of the truth." This verse provides the means by which salvation is to be attained—one must know the truth (John 8:32).
12. **1 Timothy 2:6**—Calvinism teaches "limited atonement," that Jesus only died for "the elect." God says that Jesus died for all (Heb. 2:9).
13. **1 Timothy 2:6**—"Ransom" is a price paid in the place of or in behalf of another, purchasing the release of those who obey the truth.
14. **1 Timothy 2:8**—The word "everywhere" emphasizes wherever Christians and congregations assemble—whether in Sunday worship or in a group home Bible study.
15. **1 Timothy 2:8**—The emphasis is on the "holy" lives and proper attitude of the men leading in worship. A posture is not being dictated.
16. **1 Timothy 2:9**—The outward adornment should reflect the inward character of godliness. The extremes of "overdressed" (shamefully lavish) or "underdressed" (shamefully sexually provocative) must be avoided, lest she become a distraction in worship.
17. **1 Timothy 2:11**—This is not total silence (for women are to sing, Eph. 5:19), but a submissive attitude of attentiveness and receptiveness, under the authority of the men in the assembly (1 Cor. 11:3).
18. **1 Timothy 2:12**—A woman is not to teach publicly or in any way to exercise authority over the man in the assemblies of the church (cf. 1 Cor. 14:34-35). This does not prohibit all teaching (Tit. 2:3-4; Acts 18:26; Col. 3:16).
19. **1 Timothy 2:13**—Circle the word "For," an explanatory conjunction, providing the historical reasons (Biblical foundation) for these respective roles—the creation order and the woman leading humanity into sin by being deceived. This proves that these roles are universal and perpetual ("everywhere," v. 8), from the beginning of time until the end. This was NOT a temporary or cultural matter.
20. **1 Timothy 2:15**—This could mean (1) woman brought the Savior into the world or (2) her domestic role is her most rewarding place.

Mark Your Bible

21. **1 Timothy 3:1**—Being an elder/bishop is a position of work and service in the church, not a promotion or reward for deacons.
22. **1 Timothy 3:2**—"Must" emphasizes that all of these qualifications are required. They are not optional. The present tense of "must" emphasizes the men must continue to meet these qualifications.
23. **1 Timothy 3:3**—The word for "given to" literally means "near, beside." He must not come under the allure or influence of alcohol.
24. **1 Timothy 3:4-5**—How a man "rules" (leads, manages, heads) his own family will indicate how he will do the same for the church.
25. **1 Timothy 3:6-7**—Even elders must be watchful for "the devil."
26. **1 Timothy 3:8**—Some conjecture that deacons can be given to "a little" wine, just "not much." The same concept is found elsewhere in Scripture. Using that logic, would it be permissible to engage in "a little" ("not much") wickedness (Ecc. 7:17; Jas. 1:21), sin (Rom. 6:12), the world (Rom. 12:2), debauchery (1 Pet. 4:4) or adulterous desires (2 Pet. 2:14). "Not much" does not justify even "a little."
27. **1 Timothy 3:11**—The wives of the elders and deacons must also meet God's qualifications.
28. **1 Timothy 3:15**—God's church must support and remain steadfast in God's truth. His truth is essential, immutable and foundational.
29. **1 Timothy 4:1**—"Latter times" is a reference to the final dispensation—the Christian age (cf. Acts 2:16-17; 2 Tim. 3:1)
30. **1 Timothy 4:1**—"Spirits" are teachers (1 John 4:1), and in this case, "false teachers" who are seducing.
31. **1 Timothy 4:1**—"Doctrines of demons" could be a reference to false doctrines in general or the adoration of "dead saints," as "demons" represented the spirits of those who had died.
32. **1 Timothy 4:2**—The Greek for "seared" is the origin of our English "cauterize." The conscience had become calloused and numb.

(continued on next page)

Mark Your Bible

33. **1 Timothy 4:1-3**—Paul was predicting specific seeds of Catholic dogma and corruption.
34. **1 Timothy 4:4-5**—All animals were now clean under the new covenant (Acts 10:15; Mark 7:19) and could be eaten, if preceded by thanksgiving and prayer.
35. **1 Timothy 4:10**—In prospect, God wants all to be saved, so Jesus died for all. In reality, only those who believe and obey are saved.
36. **1 Timothy 4:12**—The Greek word for "youth" denoted males up to 40 years old. Timothy was probably in his mid-30s.
37. **1 Timothy 4:12-16**—The verbs "be an example," "give attention," "meditate," "give yourself," "take heed" and "continue" are all present tense imperatives, denoting continuous, ongoing behavior.
38. **1 Timothy 5:9**—"Taken into the number" involves being "enrolled" or "put on a list." Such was an indication of receiving support (even full support) from the church.
39. **1 Timothy 5:11**—The word "refuse" has to do with not putting younger widows "on the list" of "enrollment" (v. 9) for support.
40. **1 Timothy 5:17**—Elders who have proven an established diligence in their work for the church should receive financial support. All elders are worthy of honor, but laborers are worthy of compensation.
41. **1 Timothy 5:19**—Being able to establish a matter based upon the plurality of credible witnesses has been a long-time principle demanded by God (Deut. 17:6; 19:15; Matt. 18:16).
42. **1 Timothy 5:20-22**—These verses are in the context of instruction to the evangelist regarding elders in the church.
43. **1 Timothy 5:23**—This was instruction to Timothy regarding a personal, medical issue that he was frequently suffering. Rather than drinking water only (which was contaminated with impurities), Timothy was told to also mix "a little wine" in it for a medical remedy. This was not license for social, moderate drinking. (The Greek word *oinos* can mean fermented or unfermented.)

Day of Reflection

Take time today to reflect on the five chapters that you read this week. You may choose to read all five chapters again, in one sitting, or certain parts of them. Take time today to answer at least one of these questions below. You may or may not write anything down—you can choose to write or simply reflect.

1. What personal application do I need to make from the chapters I have read this week?

2. How can these five chapters help draw me closer to Jesus?

3. What words, phrases or verses in these chapters do I want to go back and study more in depth?

4. What questions do I have about what I have read this week on which I need to do some further Biblical research?

Week 40

October 1-7

October 1	Read 1 Timothy 6
October 2	Read 2 Timothy 1
October 3	Read 2 Timothy 2
October 4	Read 2 Timothy 3
October 5	Read 2 Timothy 4
October 6	Mark Your Bible
October 7	Day of Reflection

Prayer for this week:

"Heavenly Father,
help me count my blessings
and not take any for granted."

October 1 Week 40, Day 1

1 Timothy 6

Helpful Notes:

1. **The good fight of the faith** = Paul told Timothy to "fight" (Greek *agonizomai*), which involved an intense struggle, whether in a military or an athletic sense; in either setting, the command was to exert strenuous effort to win at all costs; "the faith" is worth fighting for, as false teachers were leading "some" away from "the faith" (4:1; 6:21); the use of two definite articles emphasizes there is "one fight" (for the Lord and His cause) and "one faith."
2. **Good confession** = The Greek word for "confess" is *homologeo,* which literally means "to speak the same thing"; before one is immersed into Christ, he must "confess" his faith in Jesus Christ (cf. Acts 8:37; Rom. 10:9-10); when one "confesses" the deity of Jesus Christ, he is confessing (i.e., "speaking the same thing") what Jesus Himself confessed before Pilate (John 18:36-37).
3. **Potentate** = God is the "only Potentate" (or "Sovereign," NASB); the term denotes God's exclusive right to rule and reign over the Universe, for He is the Supreme Power that created all things and maintains authoritative ownership of all things (Psa. 24:1; Deut. 10:14); therefore, to Him "be honor and everlasting power."

1. What does the love of money cause people to do?

2. What did Paul tell Timothy to "pursue"?

3. Rather than trust in his riches, what are the rich to do?

Verse for Meditation and Prayer: **1 Timothy 6:10**

"For the love of money is a root of all kinds of evil,
for which some have strayed from the faith in their greediness,
and pierced themselves through with many sorrows."

October 2 Week 40, Day 2

2 Timothy 1

Helpful Notes: * *See Brief Introduction to Second Timothy on page 646.*

1. **Ashamed** = Paul uses the word "ashamed" three times in this chapter (1:8, 12, 16); the word means "the feeling of shame arising from something that has been done"; there is no shame to be felt or experienced regarding the gospel (v. 8), suffering for the gospel (v. 12) or of brethren in the gospel (no matter their condition, v. 16); our faith and confidence should be in Christ and the glory of the gospel.
2. **Immortality** = The word means "the state of not being subject to decay"; our mortal bodies are subject to decay, but our spirit will not see or experience death or decay—it will exist forever; the body, while "sown in corruption," will be "raised in incorruption" (1 Cor. 15:42) and this "mortal" will put on "immorality" (15:53).
3. **Pattern of sound words** = "Words" emphasizes that God's revelation to man was verbally inspired in actual "words" (not thoughts, ideas or feelings); "sounds words" are spiritually "healthy" in the eyes of God, for it is His objective body of truth; "pattern" emphasizes that the revealed will of God in the Bible is our standard to follow in all things—we are under Christ's law (1 Cor. 9:21; Rom. 8:2), and we must obey it as our pattern in all things.

1. Where did Paul say that Timothy's "genuine faith" came from?

2. To what did Paul tell Timothy that he needed to "hold fast"?

3. Why did Paul want the Lord to grant mercy to Onesiphorus and his family?

Verse for Meditation and Prayer: **2 Timothy 1:12**

"For this reason I also suffer these things; nevertheless I am not ashamed, for I know whom I have believed and am persuaded that He is able to keep what I have committed to Him until that Day."

2 Timothy 2

Helpful Notes:

1. **Salvation in Christ Jesus** = It is essential to understand that "every spiritual blessing" is "in Christ" (Eph. 1:3), including one's "salvation" (2 Tim. 2:10); since salvation is "in Christ," then only those who are "in Christ" have salvation; the N.T. makes it very plain that the only way "into Christ" is to be "baptized into Christ" (Rom. 6:3; Gal. 3:27); baptism is absolutely essential to obtain salvation and to enter into Christ; there are no exceptions.
2. **Rightly dividing the word of truth** = "Rightly dividing" is from a Greek word that was used of cutting a path in a straight direction, so that a traveler may go directly to his destination; so the word means, "guide the word of truth along a straight path"; the emphasis is on handling and teaching the Scripture accurately; this obviously (and strongly) implies that there is only one way to cut a straight path with the Scripture and all other ways are in error.
3. **Flee** = The English word "fugitive" finds its origin in the Greek word *pheugo;* it means to "avoid" or "flee from" something rapidly, due to its potential danger; elsewhere in this chapter, Paul warned to "shun," "depart" and "avoid" certain foolish and sinful activities; a Christian must guard himself against threats and dangers to his soul; the Christian life is a not a passive existence.

1. What three metaphors does Paul use to describe the work of a faithful Christian (especially a faithful preacher) in verses 3-6?

2. As part of the solid foundation of God, what is one thing "the Lord knows"?

3. What are some qualifications of "a servant of the Lord"?

Verse for Meditation and Prayer: **2 Timothy 2:15**

"Be diligent to present yourself approved to God,
a worker who does not need to be ashamed,
rightly dividing the word of truth."

2 Timothy 3

Helpful Notes:

1. **The last days** = Simply, "the last days" is used in the N.T. as a synonym for the Christian age; Peter said that "the last days" began on the day of Pentecost (Acts 2:16-17+Joel 2:28; see also Heb. 1:2); in 2 Timothy 3:1-5, Paul describes "the perilous times" that would be coming in the last days (characterized by evil and wicked deeds), and Paul told Timothy to "turn away" from it; Timothy could only obey that command if he was living in the last days (and he was).
2. **Inspiration of God** = The word "inspiration" is from the Greek *theopneustos,* which literally means "God-breathed"; God revealed to inspired men (2 Pet. 1:20-21) His will in inspired "words" (1 Cor. 2:10-13); the word "Scripture" means "written," thus that which is God-breathed is not feelings or thoughts that man had, but the very words that are "written" in the Bible (both Old Testament and New Testament are verbally inspired), and as a Divine source demands, that which is written is free from all error.
3. **Complete** = The Scriptures are complete (2 Pet. 1:3; Jude 3), thus, the man of God is "complete" with Scripture, being able to meet all of its demands; with Scripture, man is "thoroughly equipped" (i.e., completely outfitted) with all that he needs—the perfect passive verb emphasizes the permanent nature of the Scripture having been given by God; man is complete with Scripture and will receive no additional revelation from God (as such is not needed).

1. How can someone "always be learning" but never gain knowledge?

2. What had Timothy possibly witnessed in Lystra (Acts 14:19-20)?

3. For what is Scripture profitable?

Verse for Meditation and Prayer: **2 Timothy 3:16**

"All Scripture is given by inspiration of God,
and is profitable for doctrine, for reproof, for correction,
for instruction in righteousness."

2 Timothy 4

Helpful Notes:

1. **Evangelist** = The Greek word *euangelistes* is tied to *euangelion*, which is translated "gospel"; some have suggested that an evangelist is a "gospelizer" (the word "evangelism" has its roots here); the word is a compound of *eu* ("good") and *angelos* ("messenger") —a messenger of good; an evangelist proclaims the good news of Christ and how to be right with Him.
2. **Crown of righteousness** = The Greek word for "crown," *stephanos*, is the crown of victory, symbolizing triumph; it is not earned, but it is the reward for those who live the righteous life desired by the Lord; the crown/reward is not only a reward for righteousness but the crown/reward itself consists in righteousness (2 Pet. 3:13).
3. **Heavenly kingdom** = The word "kingdom" is used synonymously in the N.T. with the church (Matt. 3:2; 4:17; 16:18-19; Col. 1:13; Rev. 1:9); the word is also used of heaven itself, where the church/kingdom will be delivered at "the end" (1 Cor. 15:24); the heavenly kingdom is the final and eternal state of the Lord's kingdom (4:1; Matt. 25:34; 2 Pet. 1:11), where Christians will share the victory with Christ (2:12); note carefully that the Bible calls this the "heavenly kingdom," not an earthly, millennial kingdom.

1. What three metaphors are used to describe the action necessary in faithfully living the Christian life (verse 7)?

2. While his friends abandoned Paul at his first defense, who was with him?

3. For what reason did Paul say the Lord strengthened him?

Verse for Meditation and Prayer: **2 Timothy 4:7**

"I have fought the good fight,
I have finished the race,
I have kept the faith."

Mark Your Bible

1. **1 Timothy 6:2**—The Greek word for "despise" is *kataphroneo*, which literally means "to think down upon or against someone." Christians are not to "think down upon" anyone, especially our brethren, even if we think they should be doing something different.
2. **1 Timothy 6:4**—The Greek word for "obsessed" (*noseo*) was a medical term which described one who was "preoccupied with or so morbidly interested" in something that it made him sick.
3. **1 Timothy 6:9**—All verbs in this verse are in the present tense, denoting that continual pursuit of riches leads one to keep falling into temptation and to keep drowning in destruction.
4. **1 Timothy 6:9-10**—Circle and connect the words "many" (v. 9) and "all" (v. 10) and "many" (v. 10). Being obsessed with money leads one in the wrong direction.
5. **1 Timothy 6:10**—The "affection" (*phileo*) for money (not just money itself) is "a" root (not the only root) of all kinds of "evils" (plural).
6. **1 Timothy 6:10**—"Greediness" leads one away from the true God to another "god/idol" (Col. 3:5).
7. **1 Timothy 6:14**—The "keep" here is not just about obeying but is more about preserving the integrity of the gospel that was under attack, for the very nature of the gospel is that it is without spot.
8. **1 Timothy 6:20**—The word "committed" was a banking term for making a "deposit." The gospel had been deposited into Timothy's hands/trust, and he was commanded to defend and protect it.
9. **2 Timothy 1:5**—"Genuine faith" is literally "non-hypocritical." There was nothing feigned or fake about his faith. It had been tried, tested and proven (see 1 Peter 1:7).
10. **2 Timothy 1:5**—Contrast Ahaziah's mother (2 Chron. 22:2-4).
11. **2 Timothy 1:6**—This was a miraculous gift imparted by the hands of an apostle (cf. Acts 8:18; 19:6). See note on 1 Timothy 4:14.

(continued on next page)

Mark Your Bible

12. **2 Timothy 1:6**—The fact that Timothy was urged to "stir up" the miraculous gift within him emphasizes that the gifts did not take control of the one who possessed them (as some charismatics claim today), but the gifts were in subjection (cf. 1 Cor. 14:32).

13. **2 Timothy 1:9**—Human generated works do not exclude obedience to commands given by God to "do" His works. "Works" prescribed by God are essential to salvation (John 6:27-29; Jas. 2:14-26).

14. **2 Timothy 1:10**—The word "abolished" can mean "render inoperative, powerless, ineffective." Jesus removed "the sting of death" (1 Cor. 15:55-56) in His resurrection, when He abolished man's enslavement to the "fear of death" (Heb. 2:15; cf. Rev. 1:18).

15. **2 Timothy 1:12**—The words "know," "believed" and "persuaded" are all in the Greek perfect tense, indicating something that started in the past but has firm results still abiding in the present.

16. **2 Timothy 1:12**—"What I have committed" was a banking term that involved "property entrusted to another." It could be translated "my deposit." Paul deposited his soul, his life, his future, his all.

17. **2 Timothy 2:1**—God's "grace" is "in Christ Jesus," therefore, God's grace cannot be accessed outside of Christ Jesus. One is "baptized into Christ" (Rom. 6:3; Gal. 3:27), therefore, one must be baptized in order to receive God's grace.

18. **2 Timothy 2:11**—We died to sin when we repented and were baptized (Rom. 6:2-4). That's when we began to "live with Him."

19. **2 Timothy 2:12**—This is not talking about the premillennial 1,000-year reign. This is our ultimate salvation in the final state of glory, in which we share the victory of Christ (4:8, 18; Rev. 3:21).

20. **2 Timothy 2:13**—This clearly teaches the possibility of apostasy.

21. **2 Timothy 2:17**—The Greek word for "cancer" is *gangraina,* which was a disease involving severe inflammation, which could become a destructive, spreading ulcerous condition leading to death (like gangrene or cancer). This is what false teaching is.

Mark Your Bible

22. **2 Timothy 2:20**—There are different types of members in the church: (1) faithful, godly members ["gold and silver"] who honor God by their lives; (2) false-teaching troublemakers ["wood and clay"] who dishonor God and weaken the church (cf. 1 Cor. 3:10-15).

23. **2 Timothy 2:25**—Repentance is a "gift" of God (cf. Acts 11:18), just as salvation is a "gift" of God (Eph. 2:8). Both are opportunities given by God, which require a response and obedience from man.

24. **2 Timothy 3:3**—The Greek word for "unloving" is *astorgos,* which takes the negative *a* and combines it with "family love" (*storgos*). The word means to be "without natural affection" (ASV), being void of tender love parents and children have for each other. One result of such a condition is abortion—murdering one's own child.

25. **2 Timothy 3:5**—The verb "turn away" is an imperative (command), in the present tense (emphasizing continuous action) and in the middle voice (denoting acting toward oneself). Paul was commanding Timothy, "Keep turning yourself away at all costs!"

26. **2 Timothy 3:6**—"Gullible" indicates being spiritually weak, immature and easily distracted and led astray.

27. **2 Timothy 3:12**—Underline this verse. Persecution should be expected, since the Christian life stands in glaring contrast to the darkness engulfing the world. Sin is condemned by a righteous life, which will cause the darkness to lash out against the light.

28. **2 Timothy 3:15**—The Greek word for "childhood" is *brephos,* which can include the unborn (Luke 1:41, 44), a newborn (Luke 2:12, 16) or a young child (Mark 9:21). All are equally human and all can be taught about God, Jesus and the great Bible stories.

29. **2 Timothy 3:15**—One cannot know how to be saved "in Christ Jesus" except through knowledge of the Holy Scriptures.

30. **2 Timothy 4:1**—The return of Christ is called His "appearing," which emphasizes that it will be visible, open and apparent (not a "secret rapture," as is often taught).

(continued on next page)

Mark Your Bible

31. **2 Timothy 4:2**—Preaching the Word is an urgent command, which involves convicting of sin, condemnation of sin and encouragement to faithful living. This instruction necessitates great patience.

32. **2 Timothy 4:3-4**—Even in the church, some develop an intolerance for the sound doctrine of Christ (the one pure gospel), so they collect teachers who scratch their felt-needs and they abandon the substance of the one true faith. We see this happening today.

33. **2 Timothy 4:6**—Paul likened his situation to the drink offering of the O.T., which was often poured out before the offering of various sacrifices (Ex. 29:40; Lev. 23:13; Num. 4:7; 15:5, 7, 10; 28:7). Paul knew that he was dying in God's service, that the sacrificial action was now commencing, and he found pleasure in that.

34. **2 Timothy 4:6**—The word "departure" literally means "to loose up," likely referring to his soul "loosing up" from his body at his death (Phil. 1:23; 2 Cor. 5:8). The soul and body are distinct (Jas. 2:26).

35. **2 Timothy 4:7**—All the verbs in this verse ("have fought," "have finished," "have kept") are in the Greek perfect tense, which denotes past action with abiding results. Paul is looking back over his Christian life, at the full commitment he made, and recognizing that his life is now coming to an end.

36. **2 Timothy 4:9**—About 6-8 years earlier, Demas was a "fellow laborer" of Paul (Phile. 24; cf. Col. 4:14). Now he has "loved this present world" and "forsaken" the Lord. Apostasy is very possible.

37. **2 Timothy 4:11**—About 20 years earlier, Mark was not useful to Paul when he turned back on the first missionary journey (Acts 13:13; 15:36-41). Now he is "useful." Mark must have grown and matured. (This Mark wrote the gospel account called "Mark.")

38. **2 Timothy 4:17**—"The mouth of the lion" may refer to deliverance from death at his first trial, although death was still imminent.

39. **2 Timothy 4:20**—Miracles had a purpose (i.e., to confirm the message preached, Mark 16:20; Heb. 2:3-4). They were not designed for or used for personal benefits.

Day of Reflection

Take time today to reflect on the five chapters that you read this week. You may choose to read all five chapters again, in one sitting, or certain parts of them. Take time today to answer at least one of these questions below. You may or may not write anything down—you can choose to write or simply reflect.

1. What personal application do I need to make from the chapters I have read this week?

2. How can these five chapters help draw me closer to Jesus?

3. What words, phrases or verses in these chapters do I want to go back and study more in depth?

4. What questions do I have about what I have read this week on which I need to do some further Biblical research?

Week 41

October 8-14

October 8	Read Titus 1
October 9	Read Titus 2
October 10	Read Titus 3
October 11	Read Philemon
October 12	Read Hebrews 1
October 13	Mark Your Bible
October 14	Day of Reflection

Prayer for this week:

"Heavenly Father,
thank You for giving me a church family!"

October 8

Week 41, Day 1

Titus 1

Helpful Notes: * *See Brief Introduction to Titus on page 647.*

1. **God cannot lie** = The essence and nature of God is truth; He is called "the God of truth" (Deut. 32:4; Isa. 65:16), who "keeps truth forever" (Psa. 146:6); every "word" He speaks is "truth" (John 17:17; Psa. 119:160); thus, God is free from all deceit; it is against His nature (and thus "impossible," Heb. 6:18) for God to lie; thus, when He promises "eternal life," the promise is sure.
2. **Set in order, appoint elders** = There was something "lacking" in the churches in Crete—they did not have elders; Titus was to "set in order" the church and "appoint elders in every city"; every congregation needs a plurality of qualified men to serve as elders (Acts 14:23); appointing them is certainly a process that requires teaching, training and preparing the men and the congregation.
3. **Exhort and convict** = A foundational qualification for an elder is that he must "continually hold fast the faithful word"; he must know the Word (through diligent study) and "be able" to use the Word to (1) recognize false teachings and (2) battle false teachings; he must "exhort" (urge, encourage, instruct) and "convict" (rebuke, refute and correct error) those who oppose truth; he must do this for the furthering and preservation of the pure gospel, and especially for the safety and preservation of the flock of God.

1. Why would Paul call Titus "a true son"?

2. What were the false teachers doing with entire families?

3. How was it evident that these false teachers did not really "know God," as they professed?

Verse for Meditation and Prayer: **Titus 1:2**

"In hope of eternal life which God, who cannot lie, promised before time began."

Titus 2

Helpful Notes:

1. **Sound doctrine** = Healthy and pure doctrine is essential for the church to be properly organized, to properly worship, etc.; but healthy and pure doctrine is also essential for each Christian's daily life of service to the Lord; one cannot properly or acceptably live for Christ without conforming his mind, heart, choices and activities to the sound doctrine of Christ.
2. **God's grace** = Several key truths are taught here about grace: (1) grace is Divine favor that is undeserved; (2) only through God's grace can one have "salvation"; (3) God's grace has been made available to "all men" (contrary to Calvinism's "limited atonement"); (4) God's grace is conditional (contrary to Calvinism's "unconditional election"), for it "teaches" man various Divine instructions to obey; (5) God's grace was extended to man when Jesus "gave Himself for us"; (6) God's grace gives us hope.
3. **Zealous of good works** = Christ died on the cross to redeem and purify His people, but it was not merely for them to possess a redeemed and purified status; Christ died so that His own special people would be "zealous" (i.e., "earnestly committed, exceeding enthusiastic") for all that God has prescribed as "good works" (embracing obligations toward God and all mankind).

1. What does the grace of God teach us to "deny"?

2. In what ways does the grace of God teach us to "live"?

3. For what does the grace of God teach us to "look"?

Verse for Meditation and Prayer: **Titus 2:14**

"Who gave Himself for us,
that He might redeem us from every lawless deed and
purify for Himself His own special people, zealous for good works."

Titus 3

Helpful Notes:

1. **Works of righteousness** = There are different kinds of "works" discussed in the N.T.; two major kinds are highlighted in this chapter; verse 5 emphasizes that we are not saved "by works of righteousness that we have done"; these are actions initiated and implemented by human ingenuity and merit (cf. Eph. 2:8-9; 2 Tim. 1:9); a human system or plan of "works" will not save, but that does not mean that there are no works necessary for salvation; "works" that are a required response to God's commands are essential to salvation (John 6:27-29; Jas. 2:14-26).
2. **Washing of regeneration** = The Greek word for "washing" involves the whole body; "regeneration" means "new birth, born again"; thus, there is a parallel here with John 3:5 (the new birth into the kingdom), 1 Corinthians 12:13 (baptism into the one body), Ephesians 5:26 (cleansed with the washing of water); each of these passages also emphasizes the work of the "Spirit" through "the word" to create faith and lead to obedience; this is a clear reference to baptism, which does "save us" (1 Pet. 3:21).
3. **Maintain good works** = We must be "ready for" and "maintain good works" (3:1, 8, 14; cf. 1:16; 2:7); "maintain" means "to be busy with, take the lead in, practice regularly"; in all three verses, the present tense verbs indicate ongoing action; we are "created in Christ Jesus for good works" (Eph. 2:10), as prescribed by God.

1. What can lead one away from foolish hatefulness (verses 3-4)?

2. How does Paul describe the divisive man?

3. What is one reason given to learn to maintain good works?

Verse for Meditation and Prayer: **Titus 3:5**

"Not by works of righteousness which we have done,
but according to His mercy He saved us, through the
washing of regeneration and renewing of the Holy Spirit."

Philemon

Helpful Notes: ** See Brief Introduction to Philemon on page 648.*

1. **Onesimus** = From the information in the short letter, it is apparent that Onesimus was Philemon's runaway slave, who had "wronged" and likely stolen from Philemon before fleeing; Roman slaves were not considered a person but a thing, a tool, a piece of property with no rights to life or liberty (and runaways were even more worthless); God never desired or condoned slavery, but He provided regulations for His people to observe.
2. **Receive** = Paul's appeal to Philemon was to "receive" him as Paul's "own heart," to receive him as Philemon would "receive" Paul, and to receive him "forever" as "a beloved brother"; the word "receive" denotes receiving one into the family circle and not as a slave; seeing slaves as "beloved brothers in the Lord" is the concept that conquered slavery in civilized society.
3. **Perhaps** = By using the word "perhaps" (v. 15), Paul sees a distinct possibility of God's providence at work in Onesimus finding Paul in a Roman prison and being converted to Christ, so that Philemon and Onesimus could now be brothers "in the Lord"; the accounts of Joseph and Esther in the O.T. show that God can use events to bring good out of evil (Gen. 45:5, 8-9; 50:20), but without overriding anyone's free will or condoning evil in any way; we know that God is at work (Rom. 8:28), even if we don't know how.

1. Instead of issuing a command as an apostle, how did Paul appeal to Philemon?

2. Why did Paul not just keep Onesimus with him?

3. What did Paul tell Philemon to do about any debt Onesimus owed?

Verse for Meditation and Prayer: **Philemon 16**

*"No longer as a slave but more than a slave –
a beloved brother, especially to me but how much more to you,
both in the flesh and in the Lord."*

Hebrews 1

Helpful Notes: ** See Brief Introduction to Hebrews on page 649.*

1. **The Son** = Being called God's "Son" does not make Jesus inferior or a descendant; the expression "son of" was often used in Scripture to depict the nature of a person (Mark 3:17; John 17:12; Eph. 5:6); being God's "Son" makes Him equal with God (John 5:18; 10:30-33; Phil. 2:6); when Christ "spoke," it was God speaking (1:1-2; John 12:48-50); the first four verses of Hebrews 1 exalt Christ as deity, and then the next nine verses use the O.T. to prove it.
2. **Better** = The word "better" is used thirteen times in the book of Hebrews to emphasize the ultimate superiority of Christ, His new covenant and Christianity over all things pertaining to the old covenant (the law of Moses); the purpose of such emphasis was to prevent Christians of a Jewish background, who were weak in the faith, from returning to an inferior and obsolete system.
3. **Ministering spirits** = Christ is far superior to angels in so many ways, for He is the King on the throne and angels are merely ministering spirits; angels are sent out by the King to "minister" (serve and care on behalf of) God's people; it is unknown what they do and how they do it, but it is refreshing to know that the Lord takes such interest in us and created heavenly beings for this purpose.

1. What is Jesus' reaction to "righteousness" and "lawlessness"?

2. How does the writer contrast the creation with the Creator?

3. What is one work of angels, according to verse 14?

Verse for Meditation and Prayer: **Hebrews 1:3**

"Who being the brightness of His glory and the express image of His person, and upholding all things by the word of His power, when He had by Himself purged our sins, sat down at the right hand of the Majesty on high."

Mark Your Bible

1. **Titus 1:2**—Eternal life is spoken of in the N.T. as a present possession (John 3:36) and a future blessing (Mark 10:30; cf. 1 Tim. 4:8).

2. **Titus 1:3**—First, note that God's will was presented through the preaching of His Word (Rom. 10:14). It was not "manifested" by a direct operation of the Holy Spirit. Second, note that what Paul spoke was "His [God's] Word" and not Paul's (cf. Gal. 1:11-12).

3. **Titus 1:4**—There is only "one faith" (Eph. 4:5), not many! Paul (a Jew) and Titus (a Gentile) enjoyed that "common faith" together.

4. **Titus 1:5, 7**—An "elder" is a "bishop." Draw a line connecting.

5. **Titus 1:6**—To be an elder, a man must have children who are Christians and lived faithfully while at home. The father is not responsible for the choices of his children after they leave home.

6. **Titus 1:10**—The Greek word for "insubordinate" means "refusing submission to authority; rebellious; not subject to rule." There will be individuals in the church like this, which is the reason "for" (first word in the verse) the qualifications that God gave.

7. **Titus 1:13**—The reason that God gives to "rebuke" these unruly, deceptive and corrupting brethren is not to get rid of them but "that" (word of purpose) "they may be" (present tense, denoting ongoing activity) "sound in the faith." The purpose was to save them.

8. **Titus 1:15**—This verse is often misused. It simply means that to those who are pure/cleansed (having obeyed Christ, 1 Pet. 1:22; 1 Cor. 6:11), "all things" that the Jews once considered unclean (i.e., foods, vessels, etc.) are now "pure" (and not ritually unclean).

9. **Titus 2:3**—The Greek word for "slanderer" is *diabolos,* the word for "devil" (Matt. 4:1, 5, 8, 11), and it means "accuser." The devil is the chief slanderer; thus, to engage in slander or gossip is to be aligned with the devil and his ways. (The NASB has "malicious gossips.")

10. **Titus 2:4**—The word for "love" of husbands and children is *philos,* which is a genuine, warm affection.

(continued on next page)

Mark Your Bible

11. **Titus 2:5**—The Greek word for "chaste" is the primary word for "holy" (*hagnos*). Young women must learn (thus being taught) to be holy and pure in all areas of their lives (their words, their choices, their habits, their behavior with others, their modesty, etc.).
12. **Titus 2:5**—We should all live our lives with this goal: that the Word of God may not be spoken against due to our activity or inactivity.
13. **Titus 2:8**—By maintaining a "pattern of good works" and "sound speech," a Christian can cause an opponent to be ashamed. "Ashamed" literally means "to turn in," meaning "to turn one upon himself and so produce a feeling a shame." Godly living causes those in darkness to reflect on themselves and hopefully to change.
14. **Titus 2:10**—The word "adorn" is from the Greek *kosmeo* (origin of English "cosmetics"), which means "to arrange, to put in order so as to appear to be neat and well organized; to cause something to have an attractive appearance." Our lives must not distract from the doctrine of God! Even more, they must bring "luster" to it.
15. **Titus 2:11-12**—The grace of God teaches. Therefore, in order to obtain the grace of God, we must obey whatever it teaches.
16. **Titus 2:13**—The single definite article "the" and the conjunction "and" emphasize that the two nouns refer to the same person. Jesus Christ is (1) our great God and (2) our Savior. The deity of Christ (as both and equally God and Savior) is emphatically affirmed.
17. **Titus 3:1**—Christians are to be "subject" (literally, "arrange under") and honor government rulers (cf. Rom. 13:1-7; 1 Pet. 2:13-17) up to the point that their demands contradict God's will (Acts 5:29).
18. **Titus 3:4**—The Greek word for "love" is *philanthropia*, highlighting God's genuine, affectionate concern for fallen humanity.
19. **Titus 3:5**—Circle the word "but." God Himself contrasts "works of [human] righteousness" (which do not save) with "the washing of regeneration" (baptism), which does save.
20. **Titus 3:5, 7**—Draw a line from "saved" in verse 5 to "justified" in

Mark Your Bible

verse 7. To be "saved" is to be "justified"—the terms are used synonymously. We are "saved" by baptism and "justified" by grace. Thus, God's grace saves us at the point of our baptism. Grace and obedience are not counter to each other, but complement each other.

21. **Titus 3:8**—"Believed" is a comprehensive and summary term for full obedience to God's plan of salvation (cf. Acts 16:34).

22. **Titus 3:10-11**—The Greek word for "reject" literally means "to ask aside," and can be translated "reject, avoid, having nothing more to do with." Church discipline is to be exercised against those who cause divisions in the church (1:11; cf. Rom. 16:17; Prov. 6:19).

23. **Philemon 1, 9**—While Paul's body was a prisoner of Rome, his soul belonged to (was "hidden" and locked up in, Col. 3:3) Christ.

24. **Philemon 2**—"Lord Jesus Christ" is not like a first, middle and last name. "Lord" emphasizes His authority. "Jesus" emphasizes His saving work. "Christ" emphasizes that He is the O.T. Messiah.

25. **Philemon 6**—The Greek word for "sharing" or "fellowship" is *koinonia,* which often references financial contribution, even generosity (Rom. 15:26; 2 Cor. 9:13; Heb. 13:16).

26. **Philemon 9**—Paul was in his 60s, which was more "aged" in that time, especially with all that he had endured.

27. **Philemon 10**—Onesimus is called a "faithful and beloved brother" in Colossians 4:9. Philemon lived in Colossae, thus Onesimus is mentioned in that letter, to identify him to the church as a brother.

28. **Philemon 10**—Paul had converted Onesimus to Christ. He is called "my son" (cf. 1 Tim. 1:2; 2 Tim. 1:2; Tit. 1:4). Paul had "begotten" him "through the gospel" (1 Cor. 4:15; 1 Pet. 1:23).

29. **Philemon 11**—This is a play on words. Onesimus' name means "profitable." He is now living up to his name. Philemon's name means "affectionate." Paul wants him to live up to his name, too.

30. **Philemon 12**—Rome is 1,200 miles from Colossae.

(continued on next page)

Mark Your Bible

31. **Philemon 16**—In the letter, underline "receive" (v. 12, 15, 17), "brother" (v. 7, 16, 20) and "in the Lord" (v. 16, 20). Each of these is used three times in the book to emphasize what is most important —the brotherly relationship in the church here and now, and the "forever" joy of that relationship in heaven together.

32. **Philemon 18**—Even after one becomes a Christian, previous wrongs must be made right, wherever such is possible and Biblical.

33. **Philemon 19**—Paul may have converted Philemon, also.

34. **Philemon 22**—Paul believed in the power of prayer, and he believed that he would be released from his Roman prison soon. History indicates that he was released for a time. He wrote 1 Timothy, Titus and 2 Timothy during that time. Then, he was imprisoned in Rome again and for the final time (2 Tim. 4:6-18).

35. **Hebrews 1:1**—The word "prophet" means "one who speaks forth." God inspired certain men as "prophets" (in both the O.T. and N.T.) to speak forth His Word. Some was foretelling, but all forthtelling.

36. **Hebrews 1:2**—"Last days" is used in the N.T. as a synonym for the final age—the Christian dispensation; Peter said that "the last days" began on the day of Pentecost (Acts 2:16-17+Joel 2:28).

37. **Hebrews 1:2**—"Heir of all things" means He owns all things.

38. **Hebrews 1:2**—Jesus created all things (John 1:3; Col. 1:16). Therefore, He Himself is not a created being.

39. **Hebrews 1:3**—Jesus is the exact likeness of God, bearing the exact nature/essence of God (John 10:30; 14:9; Col. 1:15). He is God!

40. **Hebrews 1:3**—As our High Priest (a main thrust of this book), Jesus offered Himself as a sacrifice to cleanse/purify us from our sins.

41. **Hebrews 1:4**—The Jews placed a great emphasis on angels, especially in the giving of the law (Acts 7:53; Gal. 3:19), even giving reverence to them (Col. 2:18). Such was improper, and they needed to learn the absolute superiority of Jesus over angels in every way. Since the new law came through Christ, it was superior to the old.

Mark Your Bible

42. **Hebrews 1:5**—Jesus being "begotten" of God involved His incarnation (John 3:16), but more so His resurrection and enthronement in heaven (Acts 13:30-34) and His work as High Priest (Heb. 5:5).

43. **Hebrews 1:6**—Jesus as "the firstborn" denotes His prominence and superiority over all things (Col. 1:15, 18). It emphasizes His "firstness" and priority over everything and is not about order of birth.

44. **Hebrews 1:6**—Angels are created beings who worship God. Jesus is the Creator who is worthy of worship.

45. **Hebrews 1:10-12**—Jesus is Jehovah, who is eternal. He is over creation, He was before creation, He will be after creation is destroyed.

46. **Hebrews 1:13, 3**—Sitting at "the right hand" is the place of highest honor, authority and rule. Jesus Christ is reigning right now over His kingdom (and no angel is), and is not waiting for a future so-called "millennium" to reign.

October 14 Week 41, Day 7

Day of Reflection

Take time today to reflect on the five chapters that you read this week. You may choose to read all five chapters again, in one sitting, or certain parts of them. Take time today to answer at least one of these questions below. You may or may not write anything down—you can choose to write or simply reflect.

1. What personal application do I need to make from the chapters I have read this week?

2. How can these five chapters help draw me closer to Jesus?

3. What words, phrases or verses in these chapters do I want to go back and study more in depth?

4. What questions do I have about what I have read this week on which I need to do some further Biblical research?

Week 42

October 15-21

October 15	Read Hebrews 2
October 16	Read Hebrews 3
October 17	Read Hebrews 4
October 18	Read Hebrews 5
October 19	Read Hebrews 6
October 20	Mark Your Bible
October 21	Day of Reflection

Prayer for this week:

"Heavenly Father,
all that you have done for me is truly amazing!
Thank You!"

October 15 Week 42, Day 1

Hebrews 2

Helpful Notes:

1. **Miracles, wonders and signs** = These three terms are often used interchangeably of the supernatural activities of God; "miracle" emphasized the nature of the activity—a supernatural, mighty work of power; "wonder" emphasized the reaction or effect—man stood in awe; "sign" emphasized the design—intended by God to demonstrate or prove something; the early Christians had miraculous "gifts of" (noting the source) "the Holy Spirit" (1 Cor. 12:4-11).
2. **Fear of death** = Christians no longer need to fear death; in Christ's death, He rendered the devil inoperative, powerless and ineffective (meaning of "destroy"); Satan introduced death and exercised dominion over it because of sin, but Jesus' death took that fear away (2 Tim. 1:10); the devil operates on limited power today (1 Cor. 15:25-26), and no Christian need fear death, for through it, man finds the Lord (1 Cor. 15:55-56; Phil. 1:21-23; 2 Cor. 5:8).
3. **Merciful and faithful High Priest** = Jesus being our High Priest is a major theme of this book—He sacrificed Himself for us and He intercedes for us now; "merciful" emphasizes that He knows what it is like to be human and He sympathizes; "faithful" emphasizes that He is reliable and dependable and we can have full confidence in Him to help us and to keep His Word.

1. Why do we need to "give the more earnest heed" to God's Word?

2. Why was Jesus made for a time "a little lower than the angels"?

3. Why did Jesus have to be "in all things...made like His brethren"?

Verse for Meditation and Prayer: **Hebrews 2:9**

"But we see Jesus, who was made a little lower than the angels, for the suffering of death crowned with glory and honor, that He, by the grace of God, might taste death for everyone."

Hebrews 3

Helpful Notes:

1. **Christ built all things** = The writer states and argues the law of causation—every effect must have an adequate cause; no house or nation springs into existence by itself (nor does a universe); design demands a designer; the builder of all things is God, and God (as emphasized in this context) is "Christ Jesus" (v. 1); Christ created all things (John 1:3; Col. 1:16), making Him superior to Moses.
2. **Departing from the living God** = A Christian can fall away and be lost, otherwise this warning has no meaning; verse 12 addresses "brethren" (those fully in Christ), and warns that "any" of them could slip into "unbelief" and "fall away" (ESV) from God; such apostasy would lead to eternal punishment (10:27, 30-31); lapsing back into Judaism (or a former life of sin) will cause one to be lost.
3. **Exhort** = The Greek word for "exhort" is *parakaleo,* which is a compound word that literally means "call to one's side"; in this verse, it is a present tense imperative, indicating an urgent and ongoing need for continuous action (which is further underscored by the word "daily"); exhortation can prevent apostasy, therefore, we must pay attention to our brethren and call them alongside and encourage them to remain steadfast in their faith and service.

1. How does the writer prove Jesus is greater than Moses?

2. For what purpose does the writer use the example of the Israelites?

3. What can we do to help someone to not fall away from the Lord?

Verse for Meditation and Prayer: **Hebrews 3:12**

"Beware, brethren, lest there be in any of you an evil heart of unbelief in departing from the living God."

October 17

Week 42, Day 3

Hebrews 4

Helpful Notes:

1. **Rest** = The word "rest" is used in three ways in this chapter: (1) the rest God promised to Israel in Canaan (v. 3, 5), (2) God's cessation from creating work on the seventh day (v. 4), (3) but the emphasis of this chapter is on the "rest" that awaits God's faithful in heaven; the "rest" Christ offers in heaven is superior to the "rest" to which Joshua led Israel in the Promised Land; everything about Christ and what He has to offer is superior to the old covenant.
2. **Sympathize** = The Greek word is *sumpatheo,* which literally means "to suffer with"; the word involves a compassion, when one is "touched with the feeling" (ASV) of another; how uplifting to know that the heart of Jesus is touched by our frailties and weaknesses, for He knows what it is like to be human.
3. **Without sin** = While Jesus knows what temptation is like (Matt. 4:1-11; 1 John 2:15-17), He never yielded to temptation and, thus, never sinned; this point is emphasized throughout the N.T. (7:26; 9:14; 2 Cor. 5:21; 1 Pet. 2:22; 1 John 3:5), for a sinless sacrifice of the Christ is the only means of obtaining salvation from our own sins; Christ defeated Satan in every way that he could be defeated.

1. What do we need to do in order to enter the rest of heaven that God has for us?

2. How powerful is God's Word in our lives?

3. What do we find when we "come boldly" to God's throne?

Verse for Meditation and Prayer: **Hebrews 4:15**

"For we do not have a High Priest who cannot sympathize with our weaknesses, but was in all points tempted as we are, yet without sin."

Hebrews 5

Helpful Notes:

1. **Perfected** = Keep this in context: Jesus was (and is) morally perfect in every way (He is God!), so the writer is not suggesting that He was imperfect or flawed; the context is about Jesus being our High Priest; He was "perfected" (completely qualified) to be our High Priest when He, as God, experienced suffering on our behalf and was "obedient" to the Father, even to the point of death.
2. **Eternal salvation** = Jesus is the sole source (and cause) of "eternal salvation," which man so desperately needs; note that Jesus' salvation is (1) eternal in duration (in contrast to the temporal/annual salvation the Jews experienced), (2) universal in prospect (available to "all"), (3) conditional (only extended to those who "continually [Greek present tense] obey Him"); God's promises are always conditional—man must submit and obey Him as God!
3. **First principles** = These are the basic, beginning elements of Christianity (like the ABCs), some of which are described in 6:1-2; first principles are essential and must be fortified, but Christians must grow to "maturity" and become "teachers" by studying the deeper elements (i.e., the solid food) of God's Word, so that they can properly discern "good and evil," "truth and error"; otherwise, their weak faith will cause them to fall away (6:6).

1. How does Jesus differ from the high priests under the old covenant?

2. Why were there some things "hard to explain" for the writer? Was it because the subject was hard or for another reason?

3. How is one described who only partakes of the milk of the Word?

Verse for Meditation and Prayer: **Hebrews 5:9**

"And having been perfected, He became the author of eternal salvation to all who obey Him."

October 19 Week 42, Day 5

Hebrews 6

Helpful Notes:

1. **Impossible to renew to repentance** = Some people wonder if this means that they are lost forever and they can never, ever come back and be saved; the word "renew" is the leading verb, and the two present tense participles ("crucifying" and "put") show contemporaneous action with "renew"; while people continually "crucify" the Son of God and continually "put Him to an open shame," they cannot be renewed (it is "impossible"); but if they will stop doing that, then they could repent and be restored.
2. **Fallen away** = Some who deny the possibility of apostasy deny that the individuals in this chapter were ever saved; Scripture says they were "enlightened" (converted out of darkness), "tasted" God's "gift" (of salvation), were "partakers of the Holy Spirit," "experienced" the riches of God's Word and the Christian age; no description could have more thoroughly depicted that these were converts to Christ; verse 6 says that after they were saved, they had "then fallen away"; one cannot fall from where he has not been.
3. **Unchangeable** = God is "immutable"—He does not change, for His very nature is unchangeable; thus, when God makes a promise, it is "impossible for God to lie"; the integrity of His character guarantees that every purpose He has and every promise He makes will happen just as He designed it, without change.

1. What can we do to press on to maturity as a Christian?

2. How can we help those who have fallen away to come back?

3. What is the Christian's "anchor of the soul"?

Verse for Meditation and Prayer: **Hebrews 6:19**

"This hope we have as an anchor of the soul, both sure and steadfast, and which enters the Presence behind the veil."

Mark Your Bible

1. **Hebrews 2:1**—"Drift away" in the Greek literally means, "to flow by." Like a boat that lets loose its anchor and gradually drifts away, so can one gradually drift from the gospel (even through "neglect," v. 3) and be lost. Apostasy is possible and warned about frequently.
2. **Hebrews 2:2**—"The word spoken through angels" is the law of Moses (Acts 7:53; Gal. 3:19).
3. **Hebrews 2:2**—All the disobedient will be punished.
4. **Hebrews 2:3-4**—These verses are key and should be underlined. The purpose of miracles in the Bible was to "confirm" (i.e., authenticate, establish, put something beyond doubt) that which was being "spoken," for God would "bear witness" through the miracles that what was being spoken was from Him (Mark 16:20; John 3:2). Since we have the completed revelation of God today (2 Tim. 3:16-17; 2 Pet. 1:3; Jude 3), miracles are no longer needed or happening.
5. **Hebrews 2:5**—"The world to come" is a reference to the Christian age (not a millennial age). The contrast was being made between the old covenant and the new covenant ("the world of which we speak"), to show the new covenant to be superior.
6. **Hebrews 2:6-8**—The "him" in these verses is mankind.
7. **Hebrews 2:9**—There is no "limited atonement," as Calvinism teaches. Jesus did "taste" (i.e., experience to the full) death "for" (Greek *huper,* "in behalf of, for the benefit of") "everyone." No exceptions!
8. **Hebrews 2:11**—We become "brethren" with Jesus when He sets us apart and makes us holy in the "one" family (upon our baptism, Gal. 3:26-27).
9. **Hebrews 2:12**—The Greek word for "assembly" is *ekklesia,* which is the word for "church." Built within the word "church" is the fundamental element of assembling together. The church is not the church without the assembly.
10. **Hebrews 2:12**—Jesus sings with us in the worship assembly.

(continued on next page)

Mark Your Bible

11. **Hebrews 2:18**—The Greek word for "aid" is a compound word, *boetheo*, which literally means "run to a shout." Like a parent who runs to the cry of a child, so Jesus runs to the cry for help, when His brethren are tempted, as He (1) can sympathize and (2) He is able.
12. **Hebrews 3:1**—Jesus is called an "Apostle" because He was "one sent forth"—"sent" by God to die on the cross (John 4:34; 6:38).
13. **Hebrews 3:3**—Jesus is superior to Moses; therefore, the new covenant (of Christ) is superior to the old covenant (of Moses).
14. **Hebrews 3:6**—We are the "house" of Christ, which is His church (1 Tim. 3:15; 1 Pet. 2:5). Being His house/church is conditional.
15. **Hebrews 3:6**—Perseverance is key to this book, for it is key to the Christian life. A Christian can forfeit his salvation if he does not hold "firm to the end." "Once saved, always saved" is not Biblical.
16. **Hebrews 3:7, 13, 15**—Underline the word "today." This matter is urgent. It requires action "today" and every day.
17. **Hebrews 3:6, 7, 12, 13, 14, 15**—Circle the words "if," "lest" and "beware." Salvation is conditional. Constant self-evaluation is necessary, recognizing the danger of falling away from God.
18. **Hebrews 3:7**—What Scripture says is what "the Holy Spirit says" (cf. 1 Tim. 4:1; 2 Pet. 1:20-21). Therefore, whatever the Spirit says to us today is through the written Word (10:15-17; Eph. 6:17).
19. **Hebrews 3:8**—This is a reference to Israel in the wilderness of Sinai, as they murmured and doubted God, even after seeing His power.
20. **Hebrews 3:11**—God's "wrath" is His measured and just retribution against sin. It is not a human, emotional outburst of uncontrolled anger. It is the holy God punishing the unholiness of sin (which is a violation of His Divine law).
21. **Hebrews 3:12-13**—Circle the two uses of the word "any."
22. **Hebrews 3:12-19**—Note this downward spiral: deception→sin→ hardened heart→unbelief→falling away→death.

Mark Your Bible

23. **Hebrews 3:18-19**—Those who did "not obey" were the same as those who did "not believe." Biblical belief is obedience (John 3:36).
24. **Hebrews 4:1, 11, 14, 16**—The writer uses the phrase "let us" 13 times in this book. It is not only an expression of exhortation and urgency, but it also shows empathy by including the writer in it.
25. **Hebrews 4:1**—There is a need for a healthy (reverential) fear of failure and the consequences that follow from disobeying God.
26. **Hebrews 4:1, 11**—Circle the words "any" and "anyone."
27. **Hebrews 4:1**—It is possible to "come short" of heaven. The perfect tense is used, emphasizing an abiding failure to reach the goal.
28. **Hebrews 4:2**—To be effective, the Word of God must be mixed or united by faith with an obedient response to it. The wise man not only "hears" God's Word, He does it (Matt. 7:24-27; Jas. 1:21-25).
29. **Hebrews 4:3**—Those who have "believed" are those who have "obeyed." Draw lines connecting those terms in 3:18, 19; 4:3, 6, 11.
30. **Hebrews 4:9**—This verse is not suggesting Christians observe the Sabbath. It is using the Sabbath figuratively (while it was literal in Genesis 1) of a "rest from labors" that awaits Christians in heaven, just as God rested on the seventh day (v. 10; cf. Rev. 14:13).
31. **Hebrews 4:12**—God's Word is "living" (i.e., it is not a dead document; it is from the living God and continually begets spiritual life). It is "powerful"—from the Greek word *energes,* denoting that it is effective to accomplish its intended purpose (cf. Isa. 55:10-11).
32. **Hebrews 4:14**—In this verse, the writer reaches the main theme of the book—the high priesthood of Jesus, who opened heaven to us. As sinners, we desperately needed (and need) someone to intercede before the holy God for us (to remove and continue to remove sin).
33. **Hebrews 4:14**—Our "confession" is our pledge of faithful obedience to the Lord.

(continued on next page)

Mark Your Bible

34. **Hebrews 4:16**—The word "come" is in the present tense, emphasizing to come regularly and often before God in prayer. It is also in the middle voice, denoting that we are to come ourselves (not needing any other mediator or intercessor than Jesus Himself).

35. **Hebrews 5:1, 4, 5**—Jesus did not "glorify Himself" as High Priest but was "appointed" by God, proving He was qualified.

36. **Hebrews 5:5**—Jesus was "begotten" of God in His incarnation (John 3:16) and in His resurrection and enthronement (Acts 13:33).

37. **Hebrews 5:7**—This verse depicts the suffering of Jesus in Gethsemane and Golgotha, when He cried out with silent and then loud weeping. He was "heard" (Psa. 22:24) and God raised Him from the dead. Jesus could not be High Priest without His death (by means of sacrificing Himself) and His resurrection—both are key.

38. **Hebrews 5:8-9**—As Jesus "learned obedience," we must "obey Him" to be saved. Draw a line from "obedience" to "obey." Being saved by "faith alone" is not taught in Scripture.

39. **Hebrews 5:11**—The word "dull" means "slow, sluggish, lazy." Spiritual apathy will lead to weakness as a Christian, for there is no growth. Spiritual growth requires "hearing the Word of God" diligently and daily (Rom. 10:17; Acts 17:11) with an "honest and good heart" (Luke 8:15).

40. **Hebrews 5:12-14**—Christians need to mature in their faith, so that they can become teachers and help others to discern good and evil.

41. **Hebrews 6:1**—"Perfection" is growing to spiritual maturity, pressing forward from the first principles to deeper faith.

42. **Hebrews 6:5**—"The age to come" is the Christian age (see 2:5).

43. **Hebrews 6:7-8**—Those who are saved can fall away, be lost and be sentenced to eternity in hell.

44. **Hebrews 6:12**—Inheriting the promises of God (i.e., heaven) requires perseverance/endurance in faith-filled service. One must avoid becoming lazy or sluggish (see 5:11).

Mark Your Bible

45. **Hebrews 6:17-18**—The "two immutable things" are God's "promise" and His "oath." Both are unchangeable and guaranteed.

46. **Hebrews 6:19**—The "hope set before us" (v. 18) is our "immutable" promise, thus it is "sure and steadfast." "Behind the veil" is where the holy of holies was, where God dwelt. Our hope is in heaven.

47. **Hebrews 6:20**—A "forerunner" clears the way for others follow behind him. Jesus entered "the Holy Place" (9:12) and opened "a new and living way" for us "through the veil" (10:19-20). He did it "for us," so that we could enter heaven to be with Him. When we "enter" heaven, we will enter where Jesus has already entered as our "forerunner." There is no way that heaven can be or will be on a renovated earth.

Day of Reflection

Take time today to reflect on the five chapters that you read this week. You may choose to read all five chapters again, in one sitting, or certain parts of them. Take time today to answer at least one of these questions below. You may or may not write anything down—you can choose to write or simply reflect.

1. What personal application do I need to make from the chapters I have read this week?

2. How can these five chapters help draw me closer to Jesus?

3. What words, phrases or verses in these chapters do I want to go back and study more in depth?

4. What questions do I have about what I have read this week on which I need to do some further Biblical research?

Week 43

October 22-28

October 22	Read Hebrews 7
October 23	Read Hebrews 8
October 24	Read Hebrews 9
October 25	Read Hebrews 10
October 26	Read Hebrews 11
October 27	Mark Your Bible
October 28	Day of Reflection

Prayer for this week:

*"Heavenly Father,
please help me to open my heart to Your Word
and put my whole trust in You!"*

Hebrews 7

Helpful Notes:

1. **Melchizedek** = When Jesus entered into heaven forever, He became a High Priest "according to the order of Melchizedek" (6:20); Melchizedek was both a king (of Salem—of righteousness and peace) and a priest (of the Most High God); his priestly functions were not determined by his genealogy and his "term limit" as a priest was not limited to a certain period of time; Melchizedek's priesthood was, therefore, like Jesus' priesthood: royal, righteous, peaceable, personal and eternal.
2. **Scripture spoke nothing** = Moses said "nothing" about someone from Judah being priest; some would suggest, then, that the silence of Scripture is permissive; but it is obvious that the silence is prohibitive, as the law had to be changed for the priesthood to be changed; if one argues today in favor of a practice on which Scripture is silent (ex: mechanical instruments in worship), it would require changing God's law to accommodate; we have no right to act outside of (without) God's authority; His silence is prohibitive.
3. **Intercession** = In His role as High Priest, Jesus always and continually lives for the purpose to continually make intercession for His people (two present tense verbs so emphasize); the Greek for "intercession" means "to make an earnest request, to appeal to someone"; Jesus is making petitions and pleading with God on our behalf; as High Priest, He stands between man and God.

1. What priestly tribe paid tithes to Melchizedek through Abraham?

2. To change one part of the law means what about the rest of the law?

3. In verses 26-27, how was Jesus' sacrifice for sins different?

Verse for Meditation and Prayer: **Hebrews 7:25**

*"Therefore He is also able to save to the uttermost
those who come to God through Him,
since He always lives to make intercession for them."*

Hebrews 8

Helpful Notes:

1. **Not be priest on earth** = Because Jesus was not from the priestly tribe of Levi, He could not be priest on earth; Scripture clearly affirms that the Messiah was to serve as priest and as king simultaneously (Zech. 6:12-13; Psa. 110:1-7); therefore, this simultaneous reign (as priest and king) was not on earth but in heaven; thus, the premillennial doctrine of the earthly reign of Christ contradicts the Bible and is false and untenable.
2. **The copy and shadow** = The Bible frequently employs "types" and "antitypes," where something in the O.T. serves as a "type" of an "antitype" in the N.T.; the antitype in the N.T. is the "true" (v. 2) or "heavenly things" (v. 5), and the type in the O.T. is "the copy and shadow," which has a shadowy outline foreshadowing the real substance (v. 5); the type is temporary and imperfect, while the antitype is permanent and perfect; why would anyone want to hang on to a shadow (O.T.) when he can have the real thing?
3. **Better covenant** = The first covenant (made with Israel at Sinai, Deut. 5:2) was designed by God to be preparatory for the new and temporary, thus it was removed by the death of Christ (Eph. 2:14-16; Col. 2:14-17); the "new" covenant is "better" (i.e., highly superior); note this contrast between the "old" and the "new": national vs. universal, stone vs. spirit, based on physical birth vs. based on spiritual birth, sins remembered vs. sins remitted, a copy vs. the real thing, repeated sacrifices vs. one sacrifice, animal's blood vs. Jesus' blood; why would anyone choose the old over the new?

1. What was the "something to offer" that our High Priest had?

2. Upon what was the "better covenant" established?

3. By using the word "new," what does that imply about "the first"?

Verse for Meditation and Prayer: **Hebrews 8:12**

"For I will be merciful to their unrighteousness,
and their sins and their lawless deeds I will remember no more."

Hebrews 9

Helpful Notes:

1. **Tabernacle** = The O.T. tabernacle represented the place where God would "meet" with His people; it was a "type" (a shadow, a copy, a prophetic preview) of the place where God would meet with His people in the N.T.; the "holy place" represented the church, God's house on earth (9:1-10), and the "holy of holies" represented heaven, God's eternal house (9:8, 11-12, 24; 6:19-20; 8:2); Amos prophesied of rebuilding the tabernacle, which is fulfilled in the church (Acts 15:14-17; Amos 9:11-12).
2. **Blood** = The word "blood" is a key word in this book; it is used 22 times, and 12 of those are in this chapter; the underlying principle that "life is in the blood" (Lev. 17:11) is applied spiritually to man's sinful condition; God required blood sacrifices to forgive sins (Heb. 9:22)—exchanging one life for another—but the blood of animals could not "take away sins" (10:4); Jesus had to shed "His own blood" to obtain "eternal redemption" for us (9:12).
3. **Testament, Testator** = The Greek word *diatheke* is usually translated "covenant" but is also translated "testament" (same thing); Jesus is the "testator" of His will—He laid down the conditions of His will, and He also had to die for His will to go into effect; "the promise of eternal inheritance" is found only in Christ's "New Testament," and one must submit to its conditions to receive it.

1. What had to happen in order for Jesus' new testament to have "force"?

2. What did Jesus have to do for us to have remission of sins?

3. What appointment awaits every person? And what is after that?

Verse for Meditation and Prayer: **Hebrews 9:15**

"And for this reason He is the Mediator of the new covenant, by means of death, for the redemption of the transgressions under the first covenant, that those who are called may receive the promise of the eternal inheritance."

Hebrews 10

Helpful Notes:

1. **Draw near** = Because of the redemptive and reconciliatory work of Christ on the cross and now in heaven (as our Great High Priest), we are able to "draw near" to God (7:19), with full access and "in full assurance of faith"; every Christian should find great comfort and joy in that, take full advantage of it and never "draw back" (instead of drawing near) from Christ (10:38-39).
2. **Hearts sprinkled** = The "conscience" is cleansed by "the blood of Christ" (9:14); as the blood in the old covenant was applied through sprinkling (9:13; 11:28; Ex. 29:21; Lev. 8:30), that imagery is adopted here to speak of the application of Christ's blood in cleansing us; the inspired writer affirms that the cleansing from sin takes place when "our bodies [are] washed with pure water" in baptism (Acts 22:16; Eph. 5:26; Tit. 3:5; 1 Pet. 3:21).
3. **Endurance** = The Greek word *hupomone* literally means "a remaining under" and carries a full meaning of "the capacity to hold out and bear up in the face of difficulty; patience, fortitude, steadfastness, perseverance"; endurance has a goal: "receive the promise" (v. 36), "an enduring possession" (v. 34), "great reward" (v. 35), "saving of the soul" (v. 39); however, lack of endurance (i.e., drawing back) has consequence: perdition (eternal punishment).

1. What made the efficacy of Christ's sacrifice so much better?

2. What did Christ open for us?

3. What "remains" for ones who turn from Christ and "sin willfully"?

Verse for Meditation and Prayer: **Hebrews 10:39**

"But we are not of those who draw back to perdition, but of those who believe to the saving of the soul."

October 26

Week 43, Day 5

Hebrews 11

Helpful Notes:

1. **Faith** = The Greek word *pistis* is defined by Greek scholars as having three main elements: (1) firm conviction, (2) trustful surrender; (3) obedience; it is not merely a mental assent or acceptance of truths; the Hebrews writer describes (rather than define) faith as having (1) full assurance and confidence (i.e., a foundation that underlies) and (2) inner conviction and persuasion (i.e., based upon objective evidence and not a leap in the dark); note that "by faith" in this chapter (used 18 times) is coupled with an active verb—Biblical faith is an obedient faith and this chapter proves it.
2. **Please God** = Four things are necessary to please God (according to verse 6): (1) must have faith, which leads to action; (2) must draw near (come) to God; (3) must believe God exists and that He rewards; (4) must diligently and continually seek God and His will.
3. **Faith in the promise of heaven** = A repeated emphasis in this chapter is on the "better" "city," "country," "homeland," "reward" that God had "promised" His faithful in "heaven"; while all of the faithful of old "died, not having received the promises" in this life, there is repeated emphasis that they "looked for" and could "see" the promises afar off, through the eye of faith; one day all God's faithful will enjoy that heavenly homeland together!

1. What confession did Abraham and his descendants make about their place on this earth?

2. What did Moses choose over "the passing pleasures of sins"?

3. What immoral resident of Jericho was spared destruction due to faithful obedience?

Verse for Meditation and Prayer: **Hebrews 11:6**

"But without faith it is impossible to please Him,
for he who comes to God must believe that He is,
and that He is a rewarder of those who diligently seek Him."

Mark Your Bible

1. **Hebrews 7:2**—The "tithe" was practiced by Abraham and then by the Jews under the Mosaic law. The N.T. does not require the Christian to "tithe" (i.e., demanding one-tenth) but to give as he "prospers" (1 Cor. 16:1) and as he "purposes" in his "cheerful" heart (2 Cor. 9:6-7).

2. **Hebrews 7:7**—That Abraham is referred to as "the lesser" and Melchizedek as "the better" emphasizes the superiority of Christ and His covenant over the old covenant (not morally, but in position).

3. **Hebrews 7:11, 19**—The law of Moses "made nothing perfect" in regard to one's relationship with God. Because the old covenant could not forgive sin permanently, man could not have deep or true fellowship with God. It took the blood of Christ for that.

4. **Hebrews 7:17**—There is great emphasis in this chapter on the life and priesthood of Jesus being "forever" (7:17, 21, 24), "continually" (v. 3), "endless" (v. 16) and "always" (v. 25). Truly, Jesus "lives"!

5. **Hebrews 7:18**—Verse 12 says that there was "a change of the law." In Christ, the law of Moses was "annulled." The Greek word means "set aside, abolish, abrogate; refusal to recognize the validity of something." The old law was broken down and abolished (Eph. 2:14-15), wiped out and taken out of the way (Col. 2:13-14).

6. **Hebrews 7:19**—Only because of Christ and His blood do we have "a better hope" and are we able to "draw near to God." That is the focus of the whole book. All Christians are priests and now have direct access to God through Christ (1 Pet. 2:5, 9; Rev. 1:6; 5:10).

7. **Hebrews 7:25**—Christ saves "to the uttermost," meaning He saves completely and for all time. His salvation is unchangeable!

8. **Hebrews 7:27**—"Once for all" is a key term in the book (used 11 times). Christ's sacrifice is for all time, is perpetually valid and is non-repeatable. (Compare that with "the faith" in Jude 3.)

9. **Hebrews 8:1**—The fact that Jesus is "seated" shows that He finished His earthly work and His sacrifice would never be repeated.

(continued on next page)

Mark Your Bible

There was no seat in the holy of holies for the high priest to sit.

10. **Hebrews 8:2**—The holy of holies in the tabernacle foreshadowed heaven. (See "Helpful Notes" for chapter 9.)
11. **Hebrews 8:5**—Moses was to make the tabernacle "according to the pattern." The O.T. tabernacle was a type of the N.T. church (the antitype). If the type had a pattern to which it had to conform, then the antitype (the church) must have a pattern to which to conform.
12. **Hebrews 8:7-8**—The "fault" of the O.T. was not in its design (for God designed it). The "fault" was that it could never completely remove sin, for the blood of animals could not take away sin (10:1-4; 9:15), and those under the covenant could not keep it perfectly. Thus, it could not bring its followers into perfect fellowship with God. The "first" was designed to prepare for the "second"!
13. **Hebrews 8:8**—Jeremiah prophesied that "the days are coming" (known as the "last days"), fulfilled in the Christian age.
14. **Hebrews 8:8**—New" implies the removal of the "old."
15. **Hebrews 8:8-10**—This new covenant would be made with Jews and Gentiles in the spiritual Israel, the church (Gal. 6:16; 3:29).
16. **Hebrews 8:10-11**—Rather than being physically born into a relationship with God and then taught later, the new covenant would be taught to the mind (for reasoning) and obeyed from the heart in order to be born into a relationship with God (Rom. 6:17; John 3:5). This could not involve infants until they matured to understanding.
17. **Hebrews 8:12**—Sins were remembered every year under the old covenant (10:3). They were never to be remembered under the new.
18. **Hebrews 8:13**—The word "made" is in the Greek perfect tense, emphasizing that God "made the first obsolete" in the past and it remains (permanently) obsolete still in the present.
19. **Hebrews 8:13**—In Jeremiah's day, the "old" covenant was "becoming obsolete," "growing old" and "ready to vanish away." When Christ died on the cross, it died also (Col. 2:14; Eph. 2:14-16).

Mark Your Bible

20. **Hebrews 9:7, 25-28**—A major contrast is between the high priest who had to offer the "blood of another" (9:25), "first for his own sins and then for the people's" (7:27) , with Jesus who offered "His own blood" (9:12) for the "sins" of others (9:26-28), not His own sins (4:15). Why would anyone go back to that old system?
21. **Hebrews 9:8**—The O.T. system could not provide access to "the Holiest of All" (i.e., heaven) until Christ, His blood and His new covenant came. That's the whole emphasis of the tabernacle.
22. **Hebrews 9:10**—The "time of reformation" was a medical term that literally meant "making straight" (like a broken limb). It is a reference to "the present time" (v. 9)—the Christian age—in which the inadequacies of the old covenant are made straight.
23. **Hebrews 9:11**—The "good things that have come" include the new covenant with full forgiveness of sins and full fellowship with God.
24. **Hebrews 9:12**—The phrase "once for all" is key in this book. Underline each use (7:27, 9:12, 26, 28; 10:10; cf. "one" in 10:12, 14).
25. **Hebrews 9:12**—Jesus obtained "eternal" redemption for His people, rather than "annual," which had to be repeated each year. His sacrifice never had to be repeated!
26. **Hebrews 9:15**—The sins committed under the old covenant were not fully forgiven until (and without) the death of Christ. His blood, in essence, flowed backwards to them and forward to us.
27. **Hebrews 9:24**—Jesus is not just in the presence of God now, He is there "for us," to give us access and intercede for us (7:25).
28. **Hebrews 9:26**—Man has existed (and needed redemption) since "the foundation of the world." Man did not come along billions of years later.
29. **Hebrews 9:26**—"The end of the ages" is "the last days" (1:2), the consummation of "these last times" (1 Pet. 1:20), representing the climax of history in the Christian age.

(continued on next page)

Mark Your Bible

30. **Hebrews 9:26**—The word "to" (in "to put away sin") is the Greek preposition *eis,* which always points forward (prospective), never backward to mean "because of" (apply to Acts 2:38).

31. **Hebrews 9:26**—The expression "put away" means to cancel, abolish (sins) and is the same word in 7:18 of the old covenant.

32. **Hebrews 9:28**—Jesus is not coming the "second time" to die for sins (again). He is coming to gather His people to eternal salvation.

33. **Hebrews 10:1, 3, 11**—The "same" O.T. sacrifices were "repeatedly" offered "continually year after year" because sins were remembered (simply passed over or atoned) "every year," however these sacrifices could "never take away sins." Jesus' "one sacrifice for sins forever" (10:12) was desperately needed! Underline these terms, and ask, "Which system is better? Why go back to the old?"

34. **Hebrews 10:4**—Underline this key verse.

35. **Hebrews 10:15**—"The Holy Spirit witnesses to us" today. The word "witnesses" is in the present tense, denoting continual, ongoing activity. What He "witnesses" today is what "He had said before." "Had said" is the Greek perfect tense, denoting past action with abiding results in the present. The Holy Spirit does not speak or witness to us today apart from the Bible but only through the Bible.

36. **Hebrews 10:24-25**—Apostasy is an ever-present danger (the whole point of this book). A chief function of the assembling of the saints is edification (1 Cor. 14:26). Neglecting the assembly was leading Christians to abandon their faith and fall away (then and now). Thus, the ever-present need to continually encourage one another.

37. **Hebrews 10:26**—When one turns from "the truth," he falls away, because there is no other system of salvation for him. Apostasy is not only very possible, it is too often a reality.

38. **Hebrews 10:29**—Those who fall away (such is possible!) will suffer a "much worse punishment" than death (v. 28). What could be worse? This argues for an eternal, conscious punishing ("a just reward," 2:2) of the unfaithful. Hell is not extinction or annihilation.

Mark Your Bible

39. **Hebrews 10:31**—It is desirable for a righteous person to "fall into the hand of the Lord" (2 Sam. 24:14). But it is terrifying and dreadful for an unrighteous person. The choice is up to each person. This context is addressing apostates, pleading with them to come back.
40. **Hebrews 10:39**—To "draw back" or "shrink back" is from a Greek word that involves hesitancy or timidity, in contrast to those who are earnestly committed. While shrinking back is not an option, neither is being neutral!
41. **Hebrews 11:3**—Evidence-supported faith recognizes that everything was "made" by something or someone (cf. Rom. 1:20). Every effect demands a cause. "The word of God" created all things out of nothing (Psa. 33:6, 9). "God said" is found ten times in Genesis 1.
42. **Hebrews 11:4**—The reason that Abel's worship was accepted by God and Cain's was not is because Abel worshiped "by faith," indicating that his worship was according to the Word of God (Rom. 10:17) and Cain's was not. How we worship matters to God!
43. **Hebrews 11:7**—Obedience passes judgment on man's disobedience. Light exposes darkness (John 3:19-21; Eph. 5:8-13).
44. **Hebrews 11:19**—Abraham was so set on obeying God that Isaac was already dead in his mind, which meant that when God stopped the sacrifice that He raised Isaac from the dead "figuratively."
45. **Hebrews 11:26**—The Greek word for "looked" means "to look away from all other objects in order to look only at one."
46. **Hebrews 11:39**—The faithful of old did not receive their reward in this life. They did not see the promised Messiah. But, through faith, they knew it was coming and they lived with and in that hope.
47. **Hebrews 11:40**—Being made "perfect" is a frequent term in this book (7:11, 19; 9:9; 10:1, 14). It is not moral sinlessness in view. It is having a perfect relationship with God, with full forgiveness of sins and full fellowship with God through Christ. Because of the blood of Christ, faithful of all ages are made perfect with God.

Day of Reflection

Take time today to reflect on the five chapters that you read this week. You may choose to read all five chapters again, in one sitting, or certain parts of them. Take time today to answer at least one of these questions below. You may or may not write anything down—you can choose to write or simply reflect.

1. What personal application do I need to make from the chapters I have read this week?

2. How can these five chapters help draw me closer to Jesus?

3. What words, phrases or verses in these chapters do I want to go back and study more in depth?

4. What questions do I have about what I have read this week on which I need to do some further Biblical research?

Week 44

October 29-
November 4

October 29	Read Hebrews 12
October 30	Read Hebrews 13
October 31	Read James 1
November 1	Read James 2
November 2	Read James 3
November 3	Mark Your Bible
November 4	Day of Reflection

Prayer for this week:

"Heavenly Father,
please help me to use the difficulties in my life
to grow stronger in my faith."

Hebrews 12

Helpful Notes:

1. **Chastening of the Lord** = Sometimes God allows hardships to come into a Christian's life (called "chastening" or "discipline"); while such is not pleasant, they can (and do) have positive purposes: gives evidence of our Father's love, shows we are His children, helps us to learn to submit to Him and honor Him, profits us to develop and increase in holiness and righteousness; hardships toughen us up in our character and in our service (Rom. 5:3-4; Jas. 1:2-4).
2. **Registered in heaven** = Verses 22-24 seem to merge the redeemed who are in the church presently on this earth with the redeemed who are already in heaven, stating that Christians have come to the heavenly Jerusalem and, at the same time, to Jesus and His blood; he states clearly that the honored ones in His "church" are "registered" or "enrolled" in heaven—their names are in the Book of Life (Luke 10:20; Phil. 4:3; Rev. 21:27); this forever answers the question of whether one must be in the church to go to heaven.
3. **Unshakeable kingdom** = The church of our Lord (i.e., the kingdom) "cannot be shaken"; "the gates of Hades shall not prevail against it" (Matt. 16:18), and it "shall never be destroyed" (Dan. 2:44); no matter what else happens around us to material things, the church "shall stand forever" (Dan. 2:44); we have (and are in) the indestructible kingdom now, and one day those who remain in His kingdom will be delivered to the Father (1 Cor. 15:24).

1. Who is the "great cloud of witnesses" for us to emulate?

2. As we endure hardships, who is our ultimate example to follow?

3. Seeing we are so blessed, how do we need to serve God (v. 28)?

Verse for Meditation and Prayer: **Hebrews 12:2**

"Looking unto Jesus, the author and finisher of our faith, who for the joy that was set before Him endured the cross, despising the shame, and has sat down at the right hand of the throne of God."

October 30

Week 44, Day 2

Hebrews 13

Helpful Notes:

1. **Marriage to be honored** = "Marriage is to be held in honor among all"; the Greek for "honor" involves something that is "of exceptional value; costly, precious; to be highly honored"; God created marriage and wants everything about His creation respected, especially the gift of sexual union that He designed only for a husband and his wife to enjoy; all sex outside of the husband-wife bond is sinful and will be judged by God.
2. **The fruit of our lips** = The Jews offered sacrifices of animals under the old covenant; under the new covenant, Christians offer various sacrifices of praise to God, some of which are done with our "lips"; in our assemblies, every worshiper uses his "lips" to sing praises to God (Eph. 5:19; Col. 3:16; 1 Cor. 14:15), which are an acceptable offering to Him (Psa. 54:6; 57:9); in fact, singing (from the lips) is the only authorized music in N.T. worship.
3. **Obey those who rule over you** = "Those who rule over" is better translated as "leaders"; the context of the verse points to "elders" in the church, and denotes mutual responsibility toward each other; members are to joyously "obey" (follow, being persuaded by) the eldership and yield to their authority; elders are responsible to "be alertly concerned about, to care for" (literally, "to chase sleep," to be sleepless) the church and each member, knowing that they will give an account on the day of judgment.

1. How tolerant is God of any sexual activity outside of marriage?

2. What has God promised that He will "never" do?

3. Like a worthless animal carcass, where did Jesus suffer for us?

Verse for Meditation and Prayer: **Hebrews 13:5**

"Let your conduct be without covetousness; be content with such things as you have. For He Himself has said, 'I will never leave you nor forsake you.'"

October 31 Week 44, Day 3

James 1

<u>Helpful Notes:</u> ** See Brief Introduction to James on page 650.*

1. **Temptation** = There is a difference between "trials" (v. 2) and "temptations" (v. 13); "trials" are outward persecutions due to living the Christian life; "temptations" are solicitations to the inner man to do evil; God does not tempt us, for He is holy and "of purer eyes than to behold evil" (Hab. 1:13); the tempter tempts us by exploiting our weaknesses and fleshly desires; God always provides a way of escape (1 Cor. 10:13) if we resist the devil (Jas. 4:7).
2. **Doers** = In His "word," God prescribes what He expects of us; it is not sufficient to know and respect those things; God commands us (present tense imperative) to "be" (exhibit, demonstrate yourselves continually) "doers" (consistently obedient); the one who "hears" the words of Jesus and "does" them is considered "wise" (Matt. 7:24-25) and will be "blessed" (Jas. 1:25; Luke 11:28).
3. **Perfect law of liberty** = The gospel of Christ (1) is "perfect"—from a perfect God, it is without defect and is all-sufficient to accomplish its purpose; (2) is "law"—Christians are under law, a rule of action (1 Cor. 9:21; Gal. 6:2); (3) provides "liberty"—freedom from sin (John 8:32), freedom from the old law (Rom. 7:4), freedom from the fear of death (Heb. 2:14-15; Rom. 8:1-2); let us be doers of it!

1. To what does James liken a person who doubts?

2. What will eventually happen to the rich man and his riches?

3. From where does every good thing in this life come?

Verse for Meditation and Prayer: **<u>James 1:25</u>**

"But he who looks into the perfect law of liberty and continues in it, and is not a forgetful hearer but a doer of the work, this one will be blessed in what he does."

James 2

Helpful Notes:

1. **Partiality** = Older translations had "with respect of persons," which captures more the literal meaning; "partiality" is showing "personal favoritism" and the Greek literally means "to receive one's face"; it is basing thoughts about a person and treatment of a person on that person's externals (their appearance, their ethnicity, their wealth, etc.); God does not do such (Acts 10:34; Rom. 2:11), and when we do, we commit sin (Jas. 2:9).
2. **Faith only** = Salvation by "faith alone" is a very common doctrine among denominations but it finds zero support in Scripture; faith is essential to salvation (Heb. 11:6; John 8:24), but Biblical faith is not merely a mental assent to information presented; Biblical faith is an obedient faith; without obedience, faith by itself is without "profit" (2:14, 16), unable to "save" (2:14), "dead" (2:17, 26), not seen (2:18), demonic (2:19), useless/barren (2:20), incomplete (2:22), not a friend of God (2:23), not able to justify (2:24-25).
3. **Works** = Many treat the word "works" with contempt today, but it is a word that God uses with great purpose; it is found 13 times in verses 14-26; the word "works" is used variously in the N.T. for (1) works of the law of Moses (Rom. 3:27-28), (2) works of human merit (Eph. 2:8-9), and (3) works as a proper response to the commands of God; this last category of works are essential for salvation (Jas. 2:14-26), as even faith is a work (John 6:27-29); what God commands, we must obey (i.e., "work") to be saved (Heb. 5:9).

1. What will judgment be like for those who show no mercy now?

2. What creatures believe but are not saved?

3. What does James say happens at death?

Verse for Meditation and Prayer: **James 2:24**

"You see then that a man is justified by works, and not by faith only."

November 2

Week 44, Day 5

James 3

Helpful Notes:

1. **Stricter judgment** = James is not telling Christians to not become "teachers"; Jesus commanded all Christians to be teachers (Matt. 28:19-20) and God censured certain Christians who were not maturing to the point of being teachers (Heb. 5:12-14); James is issuing a strong warning of the seriousness of teaching and the consequences of misleading the souls of others by teaching falsehoods; we must always teach the truth (Eph. 4:15; Gal. 1:8-9), for more severe judgments are upon those with more responsibility (Luke 12:48).
2. **Tame the tongue** = Some read that "no man can tame the tongue" and wrongly conclude, "Then I don't need to try; I can just let it fly"; that is not what James is saying, as the whole Bible condemns the improper use of the tongue (Prov. 6:16-19; Eph. 4:25-32); James 3 is written to urge Christians to control this little member in all things; while "no man can tame the tongue," GOD CAN!
3. **Wisdom** = The wisdom that comes from God is very different than the wisdom of the world; one finds the wisdom of God in His Word (Prov. 2:1-6) and by asking Him to help you find it in His Word and live it out (Jas. 1:5-8, 17); a person's wisdom is known and demonstrated by his works on a daily basis—there is a vast difference between one who is self-seeking and one who is meek.

1. What three large things are affected by relatively small things (verses 3-5)?

2. How is the mouth used inconsistently?

3. What is the result of having and following earthly wisdom?

Verse for Meditation and Prayer: **James 3:17**

"But the wisdom that is from above is first pure, then peaceable, gentle, willing to yield, full of mercy and good fruits, without partiality and without hypocrisy."

November 3 Week 44, Day 6

Mark Your Bible

1. **Hebrews 12:1** — Christians must "lay aside from themselves" any and all things that impede their Christian faith, especially sins that "obstruct, constrict and tenaciously cling" to them. Through training, runners learn to get rid of all entanglements to be successful.
2. **Hebrews 12:2** — The Greek word for "looking" means "to look away from all else in order to fix one's eyes on one thing." We cannot run our race with divided attention. Jesus must be our all!
3. **Hebrews 12:2** — The word "author" means "originator, founder; one who leads the way to follow," and the word "finisher" is "one who brings through to final attainment, to final goal at the end."
4. **Hebrews 12:2** — The word "faith" could be talking about our personal faith or the gospel or both.
5. **Hebrews 12:1-2** — Connect the word "before" in these verses.
6. **Hebrews 12:1-3** — Connect the words "endurance" and "endured" (twice) in these verses.
7. **Hebrews 12:5-10** — Underline and connect the words "sons," "son," "father," "fathers," "Father" and "He" in these verses. Hardships that we endure are (1) because of and (2) fortify our relationship with our Father. Similar to but even more than an earthly father for his children, our Father knows and wants what is best for us!
8. **Hebrews 12:6** — Note Revelation 3:19 next to this verse.
9. **Hebrews 12:14** — Circle "see the Lord." This is all that matters! We must pursue holiness every day, "lest" we fall short of seeing Him.
10. **Hebrews 12:15-16** — Underline and connect the three instances of "lest anyone/any." We must look out for ourselves, and we must also strive to help our brethren to ultimately "see the Lord" (v. 14).
11. **Hebrews 12:16** — The word "profane" could be translated "totally worldly," for this person has no interest in heavenly, godly matters. They have elevated the material and physical over the spiritual.

(continued on next page)

Mark Your Bible

12. **Hebrews 12:23**—"Firstborn" is plural (referring to the people) and not singular (referring to Jesus). Members of the church are "the firstborn ones," a position of special honor and privilege.

13. **Hebrews 13:1**—"Brotherly love" is from the Greek word *philadelphia.*

14. **Hebrews 13:2**—The Greek word for "hospitality" is *philoxenia* and literally means "love of strangers." "Entertained angels" is a reference to Abraham in Genesis 18:1-22; 19:1.

15. **Hebrews 13:3**—"In the body also" is a reminder (1) that we are subject to hardships also, and (2) that we need to hurt when others hurt and then seek to help them (1 Cor. 12:26; Rom. 12:15; Gal. 6:2).

16. **Hebrews 13:5-6**—We need to have faith-filled trust in the providence of God to take care of us, rather than put our faith and trust in money and the pursuit of money. Rely on God, not money!

17. **Hebrews 13:7**—These are "leaders" who faithfully taught the Word while alive. They died victoriously (Rev. 14:13). Imitate their faith.

18. **Hebrews 13:8**—What Jesus did for them and what they taught about Jesus is still true! He will do the same for you!

19. **Hebrews 13:10**—The Christian's "altar" was the sacrifice of Christ's body for our sin. Those who continue to hold to the O.T. cannot and will not enjoy the blessings of Christ. One cannot serve at the O.T. altar and the N.T. altar (Gal. 5:2-4)!

20. **Hebrews 13:20**—The old covenant was temporary and passed away. The new covenant (the focus of this book) is eternal! It is a better covenant, built upon better (and eternal) promises.

21. **James 1:1**—A "bondservant" is a voluntary slave, who has gladly given up his own will wholly to the will of another.

22. **James 1:2**—Christian "joy" is not determined by circumstances. "Fall" denotes an external and sudden entrapment in a difficult situation. We cannot control circumstances, but we can control our reaction. It is not a matter of "if" they will come, but "when."

Mark Your Bible

23. **James 1:3-4**—Endurance and steadfast perseverance are not developed in a vacuum; they require trials and adversities to be produced and strengthened. There are long-term benefits (Rom. 5:3-4).

24. **James 1:5-6**—Effective prayer must be persistent ("ask" is in the present tense), humble (ask "God," from whence all things come) and confident ("ask in faith with no doubting"). Note Matthew 7:7.

25. **James 1:6**—"Doubt" indicates one who is of a "divided mind" (see v. 8)—he is "uncertain and at odds with himself." This is the opposite of faith. Faith is an unwavering trust that God "can" (He is able) and God "will" (He is faithful) (Heb. 11:6; 2 Tim. 1:12).

26. **James 1:12**—The Greek word for "approved" involves "being genuine on the basis of testing; approved by test, tried and true." When a Christian has passed through the fire and come out pure in the eyes of God (1 Pet. 4:12-13), he will receive the "garland of victory" from God in eternal life (1 John 2:25; Tit. 1:2; 2 Tim. 4:8).

27. **James 1:12**—Love is manifested in obedience (John 14:15; 1 John 5:3).

28. **James 1:14**—"Drawn away" is from the Greek *exelko,* which means "to draw away out of, to lure forth out of." The word "enticed" is from *deleazo,* which means "to lure, beguile, entice, seduce, catch by bait." But, these are our "own" baits. The devil lures us forth into temptation by alluring us with our own lures.

29. **James 1:15**—"Desire" (i.e., temptation) is not sin, until it conceives/intends to do something and moves into action (then, it is sin).

30. **James 1:15**—"Sin" is singular in this verse. It only takes one sin to bring forth "death" (i.e., separation from God, Isa. 59:1-2). Sin will separate us from God now (1 Tim. 5:6) and eternally (2 Thess. 1:9).

31. **James 1:17**—God is immutable! He does not change! "Shadow of turning" could be an inspired reference to the earth's rotation. The Greek for "turning" did include "the revolution of the heavenly orbs." Whether that use is meant here or not, it is still valid.

(continued on next page)

Mark Your Bible

32. **James 1:18**—The gospel is responsible for our birth into spiritual life and into God's family (John 3:5; 1 Pet. 1:23; 1 Cor. 4:6).
33. **James 1:18-25**—Draw a line connecting "word" (at least 4 times) with the word "law" in verse 25.
34. **James 1:22-25**—Draw a line connecting "doers," "doer" (twice), "continues" and "does." Note the emphasis on active obedience.
35. **James 1:25**—"Continues" is in the present tense—ongoing action.
36. **James 1:27**—True, God-based religion shows (1) a caring interest in other people and (2) a devotion to personal purity in God's eyes.
37. **James 2:4**—Underline "evil thoughts" and connect it to the word "partiality." Showing partiality is evil!
38. **James 2:7**—The "noble name" by which we are called is the name of Christ—being called "Christians" (Acts 11:26; 26:28; 1 Pet. 4:16) is the most "beautiful" and the highest name we can wear.
39. **James 2:8**—The "royal law" is the same as the "perfect law of liberty" (1:25)—it is the gospel. It is "royal" because it has been given by the King. In obeying it, we become like the King (John 13:34-35).
40. **James 2:9**—Circle "you commit sin." You are a "transgressor." Partiality can go both ways: (1) prejudice AGAINST someone due to externals, or (2) preference FOR someone due to externals.
41. **James 2:10**—By breaking one law, one is condemned by the law, even if it is considered a "small" portion of the law. We must obey all of God's law, not just the parts that are easy or we like.
42. **James 2:14**—The Greek construction of the last question in the verse anticipates a negative answer. Faith without works cannot save!
43. **James 2:14-26**—Underline the word "works" in this section. It is found 13 times. Underline the word "faith" in the whole chapter. It is also found 13 times. Faith + Works = Salvation.
44. **James 2:19**—Underline "Even the demons believe—and tremble!" But they are not saved. What a powerful point!

Mark Your Bible

45. **James 2:21, 24, 25**—Underline the word "justified" in these verses. Man is "justified by faith" (Rom. 3:28; 5:1), and he is also "justified by works." The Bible does not contradict itself. It complements.

46. **James 2:22-23**—Abraham's faith was "accounted to him for righteousness." When? When his faith obeyed! When his (1) faith and (2) works were (3) "working together" (and not before), Abraham's faith was made "complete" and he was "justified" with God. Abraham was NOT justified by faith alone.

47. **James 2:24**—The only verse in the N.T. that talks about "justified" and "faith only" or "faith alone" has the word "NOT" before "by faith only." Man is NOT saved by faith alone!

48. **James 2:26**—Death is the separation of the spirit from the body. The body is what dies and is buried; the spirit does not die (Luke 16:19-31; Ecc. 12:7; 2 Cor. 5:8). Since the body dies when the spirit leaves, the body must begin to live when the spirit enters. There is life in the womb from the moment of conception, and that life comes from the presence of the spirit in the body from conception.

49. **James 3:3-5**—There is a contrast drawn in these verses. Put a box around "bits," "very small," "little" (twice). Circle "whole body," "so large," "great" (twice). Then underline "obey," "turn" (twice) and "desires." These last underlined words emphasize that, with help from God, we can control the little tongue (boxed words), which will have an impact on our whole lives (circled words).

50. **James 3:6**—The destruction that the tongue can cause is not heaven-sent; therefore, it is like it originates in the fires of Gehenna.

51. **James 3:7**—God gave man "dominion over" the animals of the earth (Gen. 1:26-27; 9:1-2). It is not the other way around.

52. **James 3:7-8**—It takes a lot of work to tame a wild animal; still, you keep an eye on it. The tongue must be kept under constant guard.

53. **James 3:14**—We must guard our hearts (Prov. 4:23; Mark 7:21-23).

54. **James 3:14-17**—Wisdom is also contrasted in 1 Corinthians 1:18-2:16.

November 4 Week 44, Day 7

Day of Reflection

Take time today to reflect on the five chapters that you read this week. You may choose to read all five chapters again, in one sitting, or certain parts of them. Take time today to answer at least one of these questions below. You may or may not write anything down—you can choose to write or simply reflect.

1. What personal application do I need to make from the chapters I have read this week?

2. How can these five chapters help draw me closer to Jesus?

3. What words, phrases or verses in these chapters do I want to go back and study more in depth?

4. What questions do I have about what I have read this week on which I need to do some further Biblical research?

Week 45

November 5-11

November 5	Read James 4
November 6	Read James 5
November 7	Read 1 Peter 1
November 8	Read 1 Peter 2
November 9	Read 1 Peter 3
November 10	Mark Your Bible
November 11	Day of Reflection

Prayer for this week:

"Heavenly Father,
I want to be Your friend!
Help me to live like that every day!"

November 5 Week 45, Day 1

James 4

Helpful Notes:

1. **Spiritual adultery** = The sin of adultery is one of the most vile in our minds and it is frequently on God's lists (Ex. 20:14; Gal. 5:19; 1 Cor. 6:9); God's people are married to Him (Ezek. 23; Hos. 3; Rom. 7:1-4; Eph. 5:22-33); they commit "adultery" when they break the marriage vow they made to God by being entangled with the world (cf. Jer. 3:20; Hos. 9:1); Christians must keep themselves separate from the world (2 Cor. 6:14-18; Eph. 5:11; Rom. 12:2; Matt. 6:24).
2. **Resist the devil** = Satan is real (not imaginary); Christians are engaged in war against him (Eph. 6:10-18), but they are not helplessly under his control; he can be successfully resisted (cf. 1 Pet. 5:9) with the Lord's help (1 John 4:4); resist the devil by drawing near to God through study of His Word (Psa. 119:11), prayer (Matt. 26:41) and fellowship with Christians (1 Cor. 15:33; Ecc. 4:12).
3. **Sin of omission** = Sins of commission are understood and easily identifiable (ex: lying, stealing, fornication, murder, etc.); we avoid "committing" these so that we do not "sin"; sins of omission are not as often considered, but they are equally sinful in God's eyes; doing nothing (when God has commanded me to act) is just as sinful as doing an act that God has commanded not to do; neglecting to do God's will is "sin" and will be judged (Matt. 25:42-45).

1. What will the devil do when we resist him?

2. What will God do when we humble ourselves before Him?

3. What should knowledge of the brevity of life cause us to do?

Verse for Meditation and Prayer: **James 4:14**

"Whereas you do not know what will happen tomorrow. For what is your life? It is even a vapor that appears for a little time and then vanishes away."

James 5

Helpful Notes:

1. **Be patient** = Two different words are used for "patience" in this book; the Greek noun *hupomone* is found in 1:3-4 and its verb *hupomeno* in 1:12 and 5:11—this word involves "endurance, steadfastness, perseverance in the face of trials, circumstances and things"; the Greek verb *makrothumeo* is found in 5:7-8—this word literally means "to be long-tempered" and involves bearing with and being patient with people (especially in this context, brethren).
2. **The prayer of faith** = There is a promise/guarantee to those who "call for the elders" to "pray" for the "sick" that they will be "healed"; this was in the day of miraculous gifts, when "healing" and a Divine measure of "faith" (1 Cor. 12:9) were given by God for Divine purposes (Mark 16:20; Heb. 2:3-4), including to elders ("pastors," Eph. 4:8-11); oil was symbolically used in some healings (Mark 6:13); thus, "the prayer of faith" was a miraculous power guaranteed to heal the sick; that does not exist today (1 Cor. 13:8-13).
3. **Save a soul from death** = There is only one "truth"; "any" Christian can "wander" from it (apostasy is possible!), and thus wander from Christ, who is "the truth"; any way that is opposed to "the truth" is "the error"; a Christian who has turned from God's way to "the error of his way" is "a sinner" and is lost; a fellow Christian who "turns him back" will save him from eternal death in hell (Rev. 20:14) through the blood of Jesus (1 John 1:7, 9).

1. What Bible character is a great example of perseverance?

2. What does it mean to "let your 'Yes' be 'Yes,' and your 'No,' 'No'"?

3. What Bible character is a great example of the power of prayer?

Verse for Meditation and Prayer: **James 5:16**

"Confess your trespasses to one another, and pray for one another, that you may be healed. The effective, fervent prayer of a righteous man avails much."

1 Peter 1

Helpful Notes: ** See Brief Introduction to First Peter on page 651.*

1. **Foreknowledge** = The Greek word is *prognosis* and means "knowing before"; "before the foundation of the world" (1:20), God determined to provide a plan of salvation that would involve the death of Christ; God chose (elected) those who are "in Him" (Eph. 1:4) to be His people (1 Pet. 2:9)—these are ones who "obey" Him (1:2, 22) through baptism (1:23); this was not arbitrary or unconditional election, denying man's free will; God chose a type of person (i.e., the obedient), a class of people (those "in Christ").
2. **Inheritance** = This word is often used in the N.T. of the "eternal inheritance" (Heb. 9:15) in heaven; inheriting the eternal "reward" (Col. 3:24) is only available to God's children; because God is our Father (Rom. 8:13-17), by means of the new birth process (having "begotten us," 1:3, 23), we can "inherit eternal life" (Matt. 19:29).
3. **Reserved in heaven** = Christians have "a living hope" (1:3) and that "hope...is laid up for you in heaven" (Col. 1:5); Scripture tells us that there is only "one hope" (Eph. 4:4), and that hope is in "heaven"—the place that Christ "entered...in the presence of God" when He ascended (Heb. 9:24; Acts 1:9-11) and "from which we eagerly wait" for Christ to "descend" (Phil. 3:20; 1 Thess. 4:16); "heaven" is the place where Christians have "laid up treasures" (Matt. 6:19-21); heaven will not be on earth!

1. How does Peter describe heaven?

2. In "obeying the truth," what is our responsibility to "one another"?

3. Why is God's Word called a "seed"?

Verse for Meditation and Prayer: **1 Peter 1:3**

"Blessed be the God and Father of our Lord Jesus Christ,
who according to His abundant mercy has begotten us again
to a living hope through the resurrection of Jesus Christ from the dead."

1 Peter 2

Helpful Notes:

1. **Living stones** = Jesus said, "I will build my church" (Matt. 16:18); His "church" (1 Tim. 3:15) is the "spiritual house" (1 Pet. 2:5), with Christ as the "chief cornerstone" (2:7) and the Lord dwelling therein (1 Cor. 3:16); Christians are "living stones" in His house; the word "living" is a present tense participle, denoting ongoing activity—as long as we are "living" for Him, we are part of His house.
2. **Priesthood** = All Christians (i.e., members of His house/church) are "priests" (Rev. 1:6; 5:10), part of His "holy priesthood" (1 Pet. 2:5)—set apart for His sacred service, and part of His "royal priesthood" (2:9)—given regal status because of our relationship with the King; as priests, Christians are authorized to worship God personally and directly, without the need of a human go-between.
3. **Sojourners and pilgrims** = The Greek word for "sojourner" means to be "an alien, a foreigner in a strange land, living in a place that is not his home"; the Greek word for "pilgrim" indicates a "temporary resident, only staying for a short time, a traveler away from his own people"; truly, for the Christian, "this world is not my home"; our citizenship is in heaven (Phil. 3:20), so we see this earth as only a temporary dwelling away from home.

1. What transition has taken place in the lives of God's people, according to verses 9-10?

2. What may result from living godly lives before ungodly observers?

3. What does Peter say is "commendable before God"?

Verse for Meditation and Prayer: **1 Peter 2:9**

"But you are a chosen generation, a royal priesthood, a holy nation, His own special people, that you may proclaim the praises of Him who called you out of darkness into His marvelous light."

November 9

Week 45, Day 5

1 Peter 3

Helpful Notes:

1. **Heirs together** = Each faithful Christian is an "heir of God" (Rom. 8:17), with his "hope" resting fully upon "the grace" to be revealed at Christ's coming (1 Pet. 1:13); a Christian husband and a Christian wife are "joint heirs," not only "with Christ" (Rom. 8:17), but with each other of "the grace of [eternal] life"; thus, the most important task for a husband and wife is to help each other get to heaven together!
2. **Always ready to give a defense** = The word "defense" comes from the Greek word *apologia,* which means "an eagerness to make a defense, particularly against charges presumed to be false"; such a defense uses reason and logic in arguing God's truth; a Christian must always be ready to defend the faith, which necessitates a growing knowledge of God's Word (the very basis of his hope).
3. **Preached to spirits in prison** = When Jesus died, He did go to Hades for three days (Acts 2:27), but there would have been no need to preach to spirits while in Hades, for the destiny of those in Hades is fixed (Luke 16:26); Peter is talking about the Spirit of Christ speaking through Noah (1:11; 3:20; 2 Pet. 2:5) to the "disobedient" in Noah's day while they were alive, but at the time Peter wrote, those disobedient spirits were now confined in Hades (but not when Christ preached to them through Noah).

1. What are we to return for insults, instead of more insults?

2. What do we need to do if we want to love life and see good days?

3. What does verse 12 tell us about the providential care of God?

Verse for Meditation and Prayer: **1 Peter 3:12**

"For the eyes of the LORD are on the righteous,
And His ears are open to their prayers;
But the face of the LORD is against those who do evil."

Mark Your Bible

1. **James 4:1** – The common source of all fights (between nations, church members or family members) is selfishness. The word "pleasure" is from the Greek *hedone* (origin of English "hedonism"). Our fleshly pleasures "wage war" (literally, serve as a soldier and carry on a campaign) against us (cf. 1 Pet. 2:11; Rom. 7:23).

2. **James 4:2-3** – Jesus taught, "Ask and you shall receive" (Matt. 7:7). What then if you "don't ask"? In order to "receive," we must (1) "ask" God (2) for the right things (3) in the right way (4) with the right motives (5) with confidence that He will answer.

3. **James 4:4** – It is impossible to be friends with the world and God at the same time. Loving the world and seeking to be loved by the world actually puts us at war with God and creates "hostility" toward Him. We become an "adversary" of God!

4. **James 4:6** – The verbs "resists" and "gives" are in the present tense, denoting that God "keeps on" doing these things.

5. **James 4:7-10** – There are ten Greek aorist imperatives in these verses, which are commands of urgency that require immediate action. Go through and mark each one.

6. **James 4:9** – This is not teaching that the Christian is not to have fun! Draw a line back to the words "sinners" and "double-minded" in verse 8. Sin is nothing to laugh at! Repenting and overcoming sin is something every Christian should take seriously!

7. **James 4:11** – This is not a censure of all judging of brethren (cf. John 7:24; 1 Cor. 5:12), but it is censure of using our words to slander another or to speak with an arrogant, unjustified reproach, as if creating new law (cf. Matt. 7:1). We need to speak where God speaks (1 Pet. 4:11), with love (Jas. 3:13; Eph. 4:15), but not presume to be God.

8. **James 4:13** – Next to this verse write Prov. 27:1; Luke 12:18-20.

9. **James 4:13-14** – Circle the words "a year" and "tomorrow" and connect with a line.

(continued on next page)

Mark Your Bible

10. **James 4:14**—The brevity of life is emphasized throughout Scripture with a variety of illustrations (Job 7:6-10; 9:25-26; 14:1-2; Psa. 39:5-6).

11. **James 4:15**—God's will must take precedence over ours (Matt. 26:39).

12. **James 4:15**—Paul was fond of saying, "If the Lord wills" (Acts 18:21; 1 Cor. 4:19; 16:7). He lived with "the Lord's will" in mind. We must use our time and opportunities for Him (Eph. 5:15-17).

13. **James 4:15**—"This or that" includes everything that we do.

14. **James 5:1-3**—Underline the word "your." Their trust was in riches (Mark 10:23-24). Riches are not evil, until that is one's focus of life.

15. **James 5:2-3**—Those who trust in riches are laying up treasures in the wrong place and will suffer the consequences (Matt. 6:19-21).

16. **James 5:4**—"The Lord of Sabaoth" is the Lord of hosts, emphasizing His might, majesty and sovereignty. He will avenge (with His armies) those who are wronged.

17. **James 5:6**—Christ is "the just" One (Acts 3:14; 7:52; 22:14), who did not resist their murderous efforts (1 Pet. 2:21-23; Isa. 53:7).

18. **James 5:8**—All persons in all times must live with (1) absolute certainty of the Lord's return (Matt. 24:36-39; 2 Pet. 3:3-13) and (2) constant preparedness by steadfast living (Matt. 24:42-44; Rev. 2:10).

19. **James 5:9**—Jesus is ready to forgive or ready to judge. You choose which response you want from Him (Rev. 3:20).

20. **James 5:13**—"Keep on praying" and "keep on singing." Both verbs are present tense imperatives. Keep on in good times and bad times.

21. **James 5:16**—There is no Biblical authority for "lay persons" to confess their sins to "clergy." The command here is reciprocal for all Christians, but confession need be only as public as the sin is.

22. **James 5:16**—The words "pray," "effective" and "avails" are all in the present tense, denoting ongoing action in each term. As we "keep on praying," the prayer "keeps on working effectively" and it "keeps on availing" and accomplishing much for us!

Mark Your Bible

23. **James 5:19-20**—The Bible clearly teaches that a Christian can so sin as to be lost eternally (see also Gal. 5:4; 2 Pet. 2:20-22; 1 Cor. 10:12).
24. **1 Peter 1:2**—God had an eternal plan to save man. The Spirit revealed it in His Word. Christ shed His blood to accomplish it. Man must obey to secure it. All four of these are taught in this verse.
25. **1 Peter 1:2**—We are "set apart" from the world and to God for His service through the Spirit-given Word (Eph. 6:17; 2 Thess. 2:13-14)
26. **1 Peter 1:3, 23**—We were "begotten" and "born again" through baptism—the new birth process (John 3:3-5). This involves two elements—the Spirit's teaching in the gospel (i.e., the Word of God) and man's obedience in the waters of baptism, when he is cleansed "with the washing of water by the word" (Eph. 5:26; cf. Tit. 3:5).
27. **1 Peter 1:5, 7, 13**—Underline and connect the word "revealed" and "revelation." When enduring persecution, setting one's sights on the return of Christ gives hope and determination to press on.
28. **1 Peter 1:6**—The "various trials " that "grieve" Christians are but "light affliction...for a moment" when compared to the "eternal weight of glory" that awaits (2 Cor. 4:17; cf. Rom. 8:18).
29. **1 Peter 1:6-7**—Trials of life are designed to test, strengthen and prove one's faith and are not punishment for sin.
30. **1 Peter 1:10, 12**—The "prophets...searched carefully" and the "angels desire to look into" the grace that we find in Christ through His gospel. How blessed we are to have what they longed for!
31. **1 Peter 1:11**—Christ was working in and through the O.T. prophets. This shows His deity and His eternal existence.
32. **1 Peter 1:12**—The "Spirit of Christ" (v. 11) is the "Holy Spirit" (v. 12). The Holy Spirit prophesied the events in the O.T. through prophets and preached the fulfillment in the N.T. through apostles.
33. **1 Peter 1:13**—"Gird up the loins" was necessary to do with one's long garment in those days in preparation for vigorous and rigor-

(continued on next page)

Mark Your Bible

ous activity. It is necessary for a Christian to take his life for Christ seriously, thus preparing his mind for action and for trials ahead.

34. **1 Peter 1:15**—One is "called" through the gospel (2 Thess. 2:14).

35. **1 Peter 1:15**—"Holy" (from the Greek *hagios*) means for the Christian to be "set apart from a life of sin and unto service to God."

36. **1 Peter 1:18-19**—The Greek word for "redeemed" (*lutroo*) means "to buy out of, to set free by payment of ransom," as in the price paid to free a slave. This reminder that Christ gave His "precious blood" to buy us and free us from the penalty of sin is the basis for holy living and godliness (1 Cor. 6:19-20).

37. **1 Peter 1:22-25**—Underline and connect the words "the truth," "seed," "the word of God," "the word of the Lord," "the gospel." The gospel truth is that which saves us when we obey it.

38. **1 Peter 1:23-25**—God's Word is indestructible (Matt. 24:35).

39. **1 Peter 2:1**—Circle the three uses of "all." A Christian is to make the definite and decisive act (so the verb tense emphasizes) to permanently put away from himself all forms of unrighteousness.

40. **1 Peter 2:2**—Peter had emphasized being "begotten" (1:3) and "born again" (1:23). New Christians are "newborn babes" in Christ, and thus "long for" (as a hungry baby) the spiritual milk (elementary principles, Heb. 5:12-14) of God's Word, which is the only means by which they can be nourished and "grow."

41. **1 Peter 2:2**—Underline the word "pure." The Greek word *adolos* literally means "without guile." Christians should only desire and accept God's "unadulterated" Word, without any contamination.

42. **1 Peter 2:7**—Again the Bible contrasts those who "believe" and those who are "disobedient." Biblical faith is an obedient faith. To believe is to obey. To not believe is to not obey.

43. **1 Peter 2:9**—The church is a spiritual nation of all people set apart unto the Lord, dedicated to His sacred purpose. The church is God's new nation, a new/spiritual Israel (Gal. 6:16; 3:29).

Mark Your Bible

44. **1 Peter 2:11**—The word "abstain" means to "hold oneself back" and is in the present tense, denoting constant, habitual action. The Christian must abstain from all "fleshly lusts" and "every form of evil" (1 Thess. 5:22). Where is the justification for any level of any behavior or any substance that God has forbidden?
45. **1 Peter 2:12**—"The day of visitation" is the day of judgment.
46. **1 Peter 2:13-17**—Christians are responsible to submit to civil authorities (national and local), as long as it does not violate the law of God (Rom. 13:1-7; Acts 4:19-20; 5:29).
47. **1 Peter 2:14**—There is significant emphasis on doing "good" in this chapter (2:12, 14, 15, 20; cf. 3:6, 11, 16, 17; 4:19). Underline these.
48. **1 Peter 2:21**—The Greek for "example" is *hupogrammos,* which literally means "to write under." It was used in teaching children to write, with the pattern at the top of the page to be copied (written under) at the bottom of the page. Christ is our pattern for imitation.
49. **1 Peter 2:21**—The word for "steps" means "footprints." Jesus marked out the path, showing us the footprints in which to walk.
50. **1 Peter 2:22**—The N.T. frequency emphasizes the sinlessness of our Savior (Heb. 4:15; 7:26; 9:14; 2 Cor. 5:21; 1 John 3:5; 1 Pet. 1:19).
51. **1 Peter 2:23**—The word "revile" means "abusive language, insult."
52. **1 Peter 2:23**—The three verbs in this verse regarding Jesus' actions are in the Greek imperfect tense, which emphasizes ongoing action in the past. Jesus "kept on not insulting," "kept on not threatening," "kept on committing Himself" to God. Jesus trusted God to "judge righteously" those abusing Him, and so should we.
53. **1 Peter 2:24**—Jesus was both the priest (offering the sacrifice) and the victim (being sacrificed). The altar for the sacrifice was a tree (a cross). He was a vicarious sacrifice, dying in our stead (Matt. 20:28; 1 Tim. 2:6; Isa. 53:11-12), bearing the penalty for our sins (Isa. 53:5-6; 2 Cor. 5:21) but not actually becoming a sinner (1 Pet. 1:19).

(continued on next page)

Mark Your Bible

54. **1 Peter 2:24**—By His death, our souls are saved/healed from sin.

55. **1 Peter 3:2-4**—A Christian woman will be careful not to overdress or underdress. Her "chaste" (pure, holy) conduct and her Christian character ("the hidden person of the heart") will ensure that her inward adornment will be manifested in her outward adornment.

56. **1 Peter 3:6**—"Calling him lord" simply means that she recognized that he was "the head" of their household (cf. Eph. 5:22-33).

57. **1 Peter 3:7**—Underline the word "likewise," then connect it to "likewise" in verse 1 ("likewise, be submissive"), and connect that to "be submissive" in 2:18 and "submit yourselves" in 2:13. There is a submission that even husbands must exhibit (cf. Eph. 5:21).

58. **1 Peter 3:15**—Instead of focusing on the outward threats, Christians need to consecrate Christ as the Lord whom they seek to please. Peter is referencing Isaiah 8:12-13. Isaiah speaks of hallowing Jehovah, while Peter applies the text to Jesus Christ. Thus, this is clear affirmation of the divinity of Christ. He is Jehovah.

59. **1 Peter 3:20**—"Waited" is in the imperfect tense, denoting continual, ongoing activity. God's longsuffering kept on and kept on waiting (for 120 years, Gen. 6:3) for man to repent (cf. 2 Pet. 3:9).

60. **1 Peter 3:20**—Underline "saved through water." The water was "the means by which" (Greek preposition *dia*) they were saved.

61. **1 Peter 3:21**—The word "antitype" is the "true likeness or reality" which the salvation of Noah's family through water represented. (See note in Hebrews 8.) Just as they were "saved through water," so also "baptism" (i.e., in water) "now saves us." Noah's family was saved from a sinful world into a new cleansed world (by means of water), and we are saved from sin (being outside of Christ) into a new life (now "in Christ") by means of baptism. The essentiality of baptism is inescapable.

62. **1 Peter 3:21**—The word "answer" (NKJV) or "appeal" (NASB) denotes an appeal or formal request to God for a good conscience, emphasizing that such is not enjoyed before baptism.

Day of Reflection

Take time today to reflect on the five chapters that you read this week. You may choose to read all five chapters again, in one sitting, or certain parts of them. Take time today to answer at least one of these questions below. You may or may not write anything down—you can choose to write or simply reflect.

1. What personal application do I need to make from the chapters I have read this week?

2. How can these five chapters help draw me closer to Jesus?

3. What words, phrases or verses in these chapters do I want to go back and study more in depth?

4. What questions do I have about what I have read this week on which I need to do some further Biblical research?

Week 46

November 12-18

November 12	Read 1 Peter 4
November 13	Read 1 Peter 5
November 14	Read 2 Peter 1
November 15	Read 2 Peter 2
November 16	Read 2 Peter 3
November 17	Mark Your Bible
November 18	Day of Reflection

Prayer for this week:

*"Heavenly Father,
please give me the strength to overcome
the devil and his temptations."*

November 12 Week 46, Day 1

1 Peter 4

Helpful Notes:

1. **Speak the oracles of God** = Those who teach are subject to a "stricter judgment" (Jas. 3:1), for the words spoken must be accurate and not mislead in any way; thus, Peter demands proper stewardship of God's gifts and responsibilities—whenever "anyone" (that's all-inclusive) "speaks" on behalf of God, he must speak "the very words of God," in complete harmony with Divine revelation, without addition, subtraction, modification or injection of any personal opinions (Rev. 22:18-19; Gal. 1:6-9; Matt. 15:8-9).
2. **Fiery trial** = Christians are going to suffer persecution (2 Tim. 3:12), but persecution, like fire, has a refining element that can actually be a blessing: it tests and proves the quality of one's faith, it strengthens one's faith and resolve, it identifies one with Christ, it separates the true followers from superficial ones, it brings an anticipation of eternal joy; trials will come, we choose how we handle them.
3. **The name "Christian"** = The name "Christian" was Divinely given to followers of Christ (Acts 11:26; cf. 26:28); it is an honor to wear His name, but it will bring reproach (v. 14) and attempts to shame the one who wears it; a Christian must (an imperative) glorify God by wearing this name and in the manner he wears it, without any embarrassment (Acts 5:41); there is no place to add to His name by a hyphenated designation of a religious group.

1. What is one thing the world thinks is "strange" about Christians?

2. What should Christians do when persecuted for being a Christian?

3. To whom must suffering Christians keep committing their souls?

Verse for Meditation and Prayer: **1 Peter 4:16**

"Yet if anyone suffers as a Christian, let him not be ashamed, but let him glorify God in that name."

1 Peter 5

Helpful Notes:

1. **Elders, overseers, shepherds** = The Greek word *presbuteros* is translated "elder, presbyter" and indicates an older man of maturity and wisdom; the Greek word *episkopos* is translated "bishop, overseer" and indicates the authority and responsibility of oversight and rule; the Greek word *poimein* is translated "shepherd, pastor" and indicates the work of caring, feeding and protecting the flock; these three Greek words and six English words identify the same qualified men (1 Tim. 3:1-7; Tit. 1:5-9) who "serve" (in plurality, Acts 14:23) to lead congregations of the Lord's church.
2. **Among** = The word "among" is significant (also in Acts 20:28) to emphasize that the eldership's authority (and activity in that capacity) is limited to the congregation of which they are a member (i.e., "among"); no bishop is over multiple congregations; it also teaches the autonomy of each congregation.
3. **Your adversary** = The Bible never depicts the devil in a favorable light or in any cute or funny comics; he is "continually antagonistic" toward us; the Greek word was also used in a legal sense of "one who brings a charge or accusation against"; he is our ferocious enemy and not our buddy; the terms "walks," "roaring" and "seeking" are all in the present tense, emphasizing his constant prowl and fierce stalking in hunger; be sober and alert always!

1. Rather than being "lords over the flock," what are elders to be?

2. What clothing do all Christians need to wear?

3. How can we successfully resist the devil?

Verse for Meditation and Prayer: **1 Peter 5:10**

"But may the God of all grace, who called us to His eternal glory by Christ Jesus, after you have suffered a while, perfect, establish, strengthen, and settle you."

2 Peter 1

Helpful Notes: ** See Brief Introduction to Second Peter on page 652.*

1. **All sufficient** = The Bible is inspired, infallible and inerrant; as such, it is also all-sufficient, meaning that it supplies us with "all things that pertain to life and godliness"; every need that we have in living for God has been supplied to us in "the knowledge" found in the Word of God; since Scripture gives us "all things," it is lacking nothing—if some revelation is not in Scripture, then it really did not give "ALL" things; the word "given" is in the perfect tense, indicating a past action with abiding results.
2. **Make your call and election sure** = The Bible never teaches "once saved, always saved"; Christians are to "be even more diligent" to "keep on, continually making" (present tense) their relationship with the Lord absolutely "sure"; this emphasizes that our salvation is conditional to obtain and remains conditional to maintain.
3. **Moved by the Holy Spirit** = Not one single word "of Scripture" was placed there by the "private interpretation" of any penman; the words that are in the Bible "never came by the will of man"; while God used man to write His Word, the words did not originate in the minds of the writers; those "holy men of God" were "carried along" by the Holy Spirit, like a sailing vessel is borne along by the wind (same word in Acts 27:15, 17); the men wrote precisely what the Spirit guided them to write (not their ideas).

1. What are the seven qualities we must add to our faith?

2. If we make our call and election sure, what will we "never" do?

3. How did the men of God know what to write?

Verse for Meditation and Prayer: **2 Peter 1:21**

"For prophecy never came by the will of man, but holy men of God spoke as they were moved by the Holy Spirit."

2 Peter 2

Helpful Notes:

1. **Ways vs. way** = False doctrines of the false teachers among the church are called "destructive ways" (plural); in contrast, they were blaspheming "the way of truth" (singular, v. 2), forsaking "the right way" (singular, v. 15) and turning from "the way of righteousness" (singular, v. 21); Isaiah prophesied about the "HighWAY of holiness" (singular, 35:8) and Jesus urged to walk "the narrow way" (singular, Matt. 7:13-14); there is only one "way" to please the Lord and only one "way" into heaven.
2. **Reserved** = As "heaven" is reserved for the righteous (1 Pet. 1:3-5), hell is reserved for the unrighteous (stated three times in this chapter); first, the unrighteous are themselves "reserved" under "punishment" for "judgment" (2:4, 9), meaning that upon death, they are "kept, held" in conscious punishment (in Hadean torments), awaiting final judgment; second, the place of punishment itself (i.e., "the blackness of darkness" of hell) has been reserved" (2:17), the perfect tense emphasizing a past action with abiding results.
3. **Apostasy** = The last four verses of this chapter are some of the plainest verses in the N.T. teaching (and warning about) the possibility of apostasy; those who "have escaped" the corruption of the world (cf. 1:4) through knowledge and obedience of the "the way of righteousness" and have been "washed" of their filth, can again be "entangled," "overcome," "turn from" and "return" to their sinful ways and be in "worse" condition than before.

1. How do false teachers "bring in" their "destructive heresies"?

2. What two O.T. characters were saved from an unrighteous world?

3. What two animals illustrate the repugnance of turning from God?

Verse for Meditation and Prayer: **2 Peter 2:9**

"Then the Lord knows how to deliver the godly out of temptations and to reserve the unjust under punishment for the day of judgment."

November 16 Week 46, Day 5

2 Peter 3

Helpful Notes:

1. **Longsuffering** = The Greek word is *makrothumia*, which literally means "long tempered," indicating "one who is long in coming to anger, exercising self-restraint in the face of provocation which does not hastily retaliate"; God is longsuffering because He does not want anyone "to perish" (2 Pet. 3:9); thus, His longsuffering (which waits and waits) is for our "salvation" (3:15).
2. **Earth completely destroyed** = Some have erroneously suggested that heaven will be on earth; God said that "the heavens" and the "earth" will "pass away" (come to an end, no longer be there), "melt" and be "dissolved," and be "burned up" (best scholarly evidence supports "burn down, burn up, burn utterly, consume"); John says, "there was found no place for them" (Rev. 20:11); heaven and earth are two different places (Matt. 6:10, 19-20); Jesus went to "prepare" heaven (John 14:2-3) and will return from there (Phil. 3:20-21) to take us where He "entered" (Heb. 6:20).
3. **New heavens and new earth** = This expression is found 4 times (Isa. 65:17; 66:22; 2 Pet. 3:13; Rev. 21:1), and every single usage is figurative language (not literal heaven or earth); the N.T. figuratively refers to heaven itself as a new environment or realm for God's people to live; "there was found no place" for the old (our first) environment (Rev. 20:11), for it had "passed away" (Rev. 21:1); the saved are promised to leave this earth and go to heaven (Phil. 3:20); it will be an all new dwelling place, not of this earth.

1. Was the flood a localized event or worldwide event? Prove it.
2. Why is God delaying the return of Christ, according to verse 9?
3. What manner of persons must we be to be ready for Christ's return?

Verse for Meditation and Prayer: **2 Peter 3:10**

"But the day of the Lord will come as a thief in the night, in which the heavens will pass away with a great noise, and the elements will melt with fervent heat; both the earth and the works that are in it will be burned up."

Mark Your Bible

1. **1 Peter 4:1**—The Greek word for "arm" emphasizes "to get something ready or to equip with something." The thoughts, purpose and motive of Christ in His suffering must be that which equips us.
2. **1 Peter 4:1**—"Has ceased" is in the Greek perfect tense, denoting an action in the past that remains set in the present. This does not mean that Christians do not sin. But when they embrace the mind of Christ, they are willing to suffer for Him, determining that they have "spent enough" time sinning and do not desire to sin anymore.
3. **1 Peter 4:3**—The last four sins listed in this verse all have to do with drinking: (1) overflow with wine (i.e., drunk); (2) riotous drinking parties, orgies or carousing; (3) drinking matches or binges; (4) idolatrous ceremonies that involve drunkenness and licentious orgies. God provides no justification for drinking intoxicating beverage and clearly denounces such repeatedly (Prov. 20:1; 23:29-35).
4. **1 Peter 4:4**—Christians do not participate in the overflowing whirlpool of sin and depraved behavior of ungodliness, and for such restraint, they will be mocked and ostracized (see Luke 6:22).
5. **1 Peter 4:6**—They were alive when the gospel "was preached" to them, but they were "dead" at the time of Peter's writing. The gospel was preached to them so that they could prepare for death.
6. **1 Peter 4:7**—"The end at hand" could be a reference to the destruction of Jerusalem and the final death blow to Judaism (Dan. 9:26; Matt. 24:13-14). The phrase "at hand" literally means "draws near"; thus, if it is a reference to the second coming, it is an emphasis on the certainty of the event while the timing is uncertain.
7. **1 Peter 4:9**—Christian hospitality is essential to the health of the church and expressing "fervent love for another." It is emphasized numerous times in the N.T. (Rom. 12:13; Heb. 13:2; 1 Tim. 3:2).
8. **1 Peter 4:10**—The "gifts" could have been miraculous, non-miraculous or both. Whatever one's gift, he needs to see it as a "gift from God" and employ it to serve the good of others, for Christ's sake.

(continued on next page)

Mark Your Bible

9. **1 Peter 4:15**—The Greek word for "busybody" is a compound word that literally means "an overseer over other people's affairs." This is a person who meddles in things that do not concern him. Such is frequently spoken against (1 Thess. 4:11; 2 Thess. 3:11; 1 Tim. 5:13).
10. **1 Peter 4:17-18**—This "judgment" likely refers to the impending destruction of Jerusalem, of which Jesus warned (Matt. 24:1-34). "The house of God" is the church (1 Tim. 3:15), God's people.
11. **1 Peter 4:17**—Underline "obey the gospel." The gospel must be both believed and obeyed in order to be saved (cf. 2 Thess. 1:8-9).
12. **1 Peter 5:1**—Peter identifies himself not only as an "elder" but "a fellow elder," indicating that he was not any higher than any other elder in the local congregation. Also note that he does not identify himself as a pope.
13. **1 Peter 5:2**—Elders exercise oversight in areas of expediency (matters of judgment). Doctrine has already been set by Christ.
14. **1 Peter 5:4**—The Greek word for "Chief Shepherd" is *archipoimen*. There is no Biblical authority to call any man an "archbishop." Jesus is the Arch-Shepherd and "Bishop of your souls" (2:25).
15. **1 Peter 5:5**—The word "elders" is probably being used in its generic sense for older, more mature Christians (cf. 1 Tim. 5:1).
16. **1 Peter 5:5**—The verbs "resists" and "gives" are both present tense, denoting continual activity. The Greek word for "resist" was a military term used for an army lined up to oppose and stand against.
17. **1 Peter 5:7**—Circle the word "all." The word "cares" is present tense, emphasizing a constant, ceaseless care for us.
18. **1 Peter 5:9**—The devil is the one responsible for "sufferings"!
19. **1 Peter 5:10**—The Greek word for "perfect" is used in Matthew 4:21 of fishermen mending their nets. God will put us back together, make us whole and useful in His service. Underline all four promises—God will bring us out of sufferings stronger than we went in!

Mark Your Bible

20. **1 Peter 5:13**—Peter refers to John Mark, who may have been a convert of Peter ("my son"). He was the cousin of Barnabas (Col. 4:10) and one of Paul's companions (Phile. 24). Church history indicates that Mark wrote the gospel account bearing his name with assistance from Peter.
21. **2 Peter 1:1**—Peter identifies himself humbly, not as "the Bishop of Rome" or the head of the church in any way.
22. **2 Peter 1:2, 3, 5, 6, 8**—The words "know" or "knowledge" are key words in this book. Underline and connect "knowledge" in these verses. That knowledge is available to us in Scripture.
23. **2 Peter 1:4**—We do not become "Divine" but those "in Christ" who faithfully dwell in His Word are "transformed" into His image and "partake" of His unique qualities, like holiness, mercy, love, patience, etc. (2 Cor. 3:18; Col. 3:10; Heb. 12:10).
24. **2 Peter 1:5, 10**—Underline "giving all diligence" and "be even more diligent," and then connect them with a line.
25. **2 Peter 1:5**—The word "add" or "supply" was a word used of a chorus and here of the grand harmony and symphony of these qualities "chorused" together. The word actually emphasizes that each quality grows out of the one preceding, perfects the one preceding and then makes possible the next one. They all work together.
26. **2 Peter 1:8, 10**—Circle the two uses of "if." Our salvation is conditional. When you read the word "if," ask yourself, "What if these conditions were not met?" God's words have meaning!
27. **2 Peter 1:9**—The word "shortsighted" is from the Greek *muopazo*, the origin of the English "myopia." The word involved "closing or contracting the eyes," so as to see only that which is near.
28. **2 Peter 1:11**—The word "kingdom" is often used of the church (Matt. 16:18-19; Col. 1:13; Rev. 1:9), and here it is used of the final, eternal phase of the kingdom in heaven (cf. Acts 14:22; 2 Tim. 4:18; 1 Cor. 15:24).

(continued on next page)

Mark Your Bible

29. **2 Peter 1:14-15**—Peter uses two metaphors to describe his death. First, he was going to "put off my tent." He refers to his body like a garment that he would take off, emphasizing the temporary nature of the outward body and the immortality of the inward soul. Second, his death is called a "decease" or "departure." The Greek word is *exodus*. His spirit was going to "exit" from his body (Jas. 2:26; 2 Cor. 5:8). Jesus used this same word about His death (Luke 9:31). Both metaphors emphasize that death is not a cessation of existence or an entrance into unconsciousness. Death is merely a transition from one place to another—like changing clothes or walking out of a building.
30. **2 Peter 1:17-18**—Peter records what happened on the mountain of transfiguration (Matt. 17:1-13).
31. **2 Peter 1:19**—The prophecies of God concerning the Messiah were "certified, guaranteed and made certain" (meaning of the Greek for "confirmed") by the events at the transfiguration.
32. **2 Peter 1:20**—Prophecy is not always foretelling the future. Prophecy is speaking for God, and the prophets spoke of events in the past, present and future. All words they spoke and wrote were from God.
33. **2 Peter 1:20-21**—Circle "no," "any" and "never." There are no exceptions. Every word of the O.T. and N.T are from God, not man.
34. **2 Peter 2:1**—Underline the words "among," "bought" and "destruction." This plainly indicates that some brethren "among" the church who had been "bought" by the blood of Christ can end up in the "destruction" of hell. Apostasy is possible.
35. **2 Peter 2:1**—There were "false" (Greek *pseudo*) prophets in the O.T. and "false" (*pseudo*) teachers in the N.T. "False" depicts their character (deceptive) and their message (not true). The "God of truth" (Psa. 31:5) has one "the word of truth" (2 Tim. 2:15). Everything else is "false" and leads to "destruction." No middle ground.
36. **2 Peter 2:1, 2, 3, 4, 6**—Underline and connect the words "destructive" and "destruction" with the word "hell." "Destruction" is not annihilation but eternal punishment in hell

Mark Your Bible

(Matt. 25:46), being eternally separated from God (2 Thess. 1:8-9).

37. **2 Peter 2:4**—The word for "hell" here is not *Gehenna,* of the eternal realm of punishment, but *Tartarus,* which is the place of torments in Hades—a temporal punishment until the day of judgment.

38. **2 Peter 2:6-7**—Homosexuality is identified by God as "ungodly" and "sensual conduct of the wicked" (ESV).

39. **2 Peter 2:7-8**—The filthy conduct of the wicked was continually "oppressing" Lot. The Greek is in a present passive participle. The word means "to cause distress through oppressive means; torment, wear out." At the same time, Lot was continually (imperfect tense) "tormenting" his own soul (active voice indicates) due to the unrestrained evil. Sin must not be taken lightly.

40. **2 Peter 2:9**—The word "knows" is the Greek perfect tense, indicating a permanent knowledge. The Lord has the knowledge, power and desire to deliver His people out of temptations. He always provides a way of escape (1 Cor. 10:13). How reassuring!

41. **2 Peter 2:12-13**—In destroying others, these false teachers destroy themselves, reaping their own "wages" (Rom. 6:23; Gal. 6:7).

42. **2 Peter 2:16**—The inspired apostles accepted and endorsed the talking donkey as authentic. Everything the Bible says is true.

43. **2 Peter 2:17**—The Greek word for "blackness" emphasizes the "darkest nether regions," "the gloom of the regions of the lost."

44. **2 Peter 2:19**—Sin is powerful! One is "enslaved to" (perfect tense denotes an abiding reality) anything or anyone he allows to master him and "overcome" him (perfect tense again). Jesus said that whoever keeps on committing sin "is a slave of sin" (John 8:34).

45. **2 Peter 2:20-21**—The words "worse" and "better" indicate a greater degree of punishment (cf. Luke 12:47-48; Heb. 10:28-29).

46. **2 Peter 3:2**—The conjunction "and" ties the O.T. and the N.T. together as being equally the verbally inspired "words" of God.

(continued on next page)

Mark Your Bible

47. **2 Peter 3:3**—"The last days" is a repeated expression in the N.T. referring to the Christian age (Acts 2:16-17; 1 Tim. 4:1; 2 Tim. 3:1).
48. **2 Peter 3:4**—They affirm that human history is recorded back to the beginning of the creation (not millions of years later).
49. **2 Peter 3:5-7**—"The word of God" is seen ten times in Genesis 1 when "God said." His Word created all things, including the "waters" that He "divided" and "gathered together" (Gen. 1:7-10). Those same waters (above and below the firmament) destroyed "the earth/world"—a universal (not local) flood. The "same [powerful] word" will universally destroy the earth with fire.
50. **2 Peter 3:8**—Circle the two uses of "as." The word means "like." This verse is NOT a formula (1 day=1,000 years). In context, it is a reminder that God's schedule is not man's schedule. He is eternal, not limited by time. He will keep His promise on His timetable. To take this out of context and make it literal is to create a pretext.
51. **2 Peter 3:9, 15**—Underline "longsuffering" in both verses and draw a line connecting them.
52. **2 Peter 3:9**—Circle the words "any" and "all." Those two words destroy Calvinism. God never willed (or predestined) any to be lost, and He did not send Jesus to die for only a select few.
53. **2 Peter 3:10**—"The day of the Lord" is the final day of judgment, which will commence with the certain and unexpected return of Christ.
54. **2 Peter 3:10**—There is no way to set a date or predict the timing at all of the coming of Christ. There will be no warning signs!
55. **2 Peter 3:11**—Circle the word "all." Nothing will be left!
56. **2 Peter 3:13**—The N.T. uses plain language. The earth is going to "pass away" (3:10-12; Matt. 24:35) and not "remain" (Heb. 1:11). We have an eternal dwelling place reserved in heaven (1 Pet. 1:4)—it is the "eternal kingdom" in "heaven," for which we await (2 Pet. 1:11; Phil. 3:20). Our present environment is called "heaven and earth,"

Mark Your Bible

and so is our future one—in heaven, away from this earth. There is no verse anywhere in Scripture that says the earth will be "refurbished," or that Jesus will ever stand or "reign" on the earth, or that anyone will inhabit the earth after it is destroyed. Scripture is plain.

57. **2 Peter 3:15**—What Paul wrote was not his own "wisdom" (cf. 1 Cor. 2:10-13; Gal. 1:10-12). It came from Christ.

58. **2 Peter 3:15-16**—Underline "written," "all his epistles" and "the Scriptures." Paul's writings are inspired Scripture, like "the rest" of the Bible.

November 18 Week 46, Day 7

Day of Reflection

Take time today to reflect on the five chapters that you read this week. You may choose to read all five chapters again, in one sitting, or certain parts of them. Take time today to answer at least one of these questions below. You may or may not write anything down—you can choose to write or simply reflect.

1. What personal application do I need to make from the chapters I have read this week?

2. How can these five chapters help draw me closer to Jesus?

3. What words, phrases or verses in these chapters do I want to go back and study more in depth?

4. What questions do I have about what I have read this week on which I need to do some further Biblical research?

Week 47

November 19-25

November 19	Read 1 John 1
November 20	Read 1 John 2
November 21	Read 1 John 3
November 22	Read 1 John 4
November 23	Read 1 John 5
November 24	Mark Your Bible
November 25	Day of Reflection

Prayer for this week:

"Heavenly Father,
thank You for hearing me when I pray!"

November 19 Week 47, Day 1

1 John 1

Helpful Notes: ** See Brief Introduction to First John on page 653.*

1. **Fellowship** = The Greek word *koinonia* means "participation, association, communion, close relationship, sharing in common (*koinos* means 'common')"; Christians get to enjoy fellowship with God (a close relationship) when we live in harmony with His will (1:3; 1 Cor. 1:9), and with fellow Christians when we together walk in harmony with God's will (1 John 1:3, 7); one must guard that fellowship closely and not extend it to those who "walk in darkness" rather than "the light" (2 Cor. 6:14; Eph. 5:11; 2 Thess. 3:6, 14-15).
2. **Cleanses** = The Bible often uses this expression for the cleansing from the defilement or the guilt of sin (Heb. 9:14; Eph. 5:26); in 1 John 1:7, the word "cleanses" is in the present tense, which emphasizes that God's cleansing of a faithful Christian's sins is continual, coinciding with the Christian's "continual walking" (present tense) in the light with Christ.
3. **Faithful** = The Greek *pistos* means "one in whom we can have full confidence; to be trusted, reliable"; this quality emphasizes God's superior integrity in His Word and steadfastness in His promises; "great" is His "faithfulness" (Lam. 3:23) in keeping His Word (2 Cor. 1:18; Heb. 10:23), in times of temptation (1 Cor. 10:13), in facing the devil (2 Thess. 3:3), in forgiving our sins (Heb. 2:17; 1 John 1:9); "If we are faithless, He remains faithful" (2 Tim. 2:13).

1. How did John know for certain that Christ was real?

2. What did John say was his purpose in writing these words?

3. What does God require of Christians in order to be forgiven?

Verse for Meditation and Prayer: **1 John 1:7**

*"But if we walk in the light as He is in the light,
we have fellowship with one another, and the blood of Jesus Christ
His Son cleanses us from all sin."*

November 20 Week 47, Day 2

1 John 2

Helpful Notes:

1. **Overcome the wicked one** = The nature of the devil is so vile that he truly is "the wicked one"; a Christian is able to "overcome" him because God is "greater" (4:4) and our "faith" in the greater God gives us "the victory" (5:4); a "strong" faith can only protect us from the wicked one and protect us from sinning against God when "the word of God abides in" us (2:14; cf. Rom. 10:17).
2. **Three methods of temptation** = The wicked one has been using the same temptation tactics from the beginning; we see the three used in the temptation of Eve (Gen. 3:6) and the temptation of Christ (Matt. 4:1-11): (1) lust of the flesh ("good for food," "stones become bread"), (2) lust of the eyes ("pleasant to the eyes," "all the kingdoms of the world"), (3) pride of life ("desirable to make one wise," "angels charge over you...bear you up, lest..."); Eve failed, but Christ succeeded because He quoted Scripture (Psa. 119:11).
3. **Antichrist** = Just let the Bible explain all we know: the Greek term *antikristos* is used 5 times in the N.T. (1 John 2:18, 22; 4:3; 2 John 7); he is NOT one specific, sinister person, NOR is he to appear right before Christ's second coming; John said "there are "many anti-christs" (not one) and that "even now" they had already "come" in John's day (2:18); it is a general designation for anyone who denies and rejects the plain evidence about the deity (or even humanity) of Jesus Christ in any age (then or now).

1. In God's eyes, where does one who "hates his brother" find himself?

2. What is "the promise" that God has "promised" to His children?

3. How can one "have confidence" at Christ's second coming?

Verse for Meditation and Prayer: **1 John 2:17**

"And the world is passing away, and the lust of it; but he who does the will of God abides forever."

1 John 3

Helpful Notes:

1. **Children of God** = The last phrase of chapter two speaks of being "born of" God (as does 3:9; 4:7; 5:1, 4, 18); one is "born of God" through the new birth process (John 3:3-5; Eph. 5:26; Tit. 3:5) and is then blessed by the love of God to be called a "child of God"; this is not something to take lightly, as it reflects a "manner (i.e., quality or kind) of love" that is immense, free, precious and eternal.
2. **Lawlessness** = "Sin" is from the Greek word *hamartia,* which literally means "missing the mark" (to veer away from what is right); "lawlessness" is from *anomia,* which literally means "against law" (to act contrary to law [sin of commission] or to fail to conform to law [sin of omission]); *anomia* is often translated "iniquity" (a transgression of the law); sin is NOT inherited, but something that a person "commits"; whoever "keeps on committing sin" (present tense) is a lawless person—no sin should be regarded lightly.
3. **Cannot sin** = Verb tenses are important and explanatory; in verse 6, "abides" and "does not sin" are present tense verbs, meaning "he who keeps on abiding in Him no longer makes a habitual practice of sin as in the past"; in verse 9, "been born of God" is perfect tense, emphasizing a past decision with a present determination; "does not sin," "remains" and "cannot sin" are present tense verbs, meaning "does not practice sin as a way of life because the Word keeps on abiding in him and he cannot stand to keep on living in sin as he did before"; verb tenses are critical.

1. Due to God's great love for us, what do we get to be "called"?
2. What is sin?
3. What answer is given for "why did [Cain] murder [Abel]?"

Verse for Meditation and Prayer: **1 John 3:16**

"By this we know love, because He laid down His life for us. And we also ought to lay down our lives for the brethren."

1 John 4

Helpful Notes:

1. **Test the spirits** = A human spirit resides in each person, and in this context, "spirit" stands for the person, and specifically for a "teacher" (whether a spirit/teacher of truth or a spirit/teacher of error, v. 6); John tells the Christians to put the teachers ("prophets") to the "test"; some early Christians may have had the miraculous gift of "discerning of spirits" (1 Cor. 12:10), but all Christians today can "test" teachers by comparing what they say with the teachings of God in Scripture (Acts 17:11; 2 Pet. 1:20-21).
2. **Love one another** = To "love one another" was taught by Christ (John 13:34-35; 15:9-17) as a "new" commandment, using His love as our measuring standard; loving one another is a prime identifying trait of a child of God (4:7), for one cannot love God and not love His brethren (4:20-21); loving as God loved us is unselfish, unconditional, self-sacrificing and seeks the best for the one loved.
3. **No fear in love** = Our love for God is brought to maturity (i.e., "perfected") by keeping His commandments and abiding in Him (4:12-16; 5:2-3); when we give ourselves to loving the Judge and expressing that love daily through obedience to His law, then we have "no fear" of judgment, but rather we have "boldness in the day of judgment," as we anticipate being judged by our Friend; but if we do not abide faithfully in His love, then there is a fear that anticipates punishment and the fear is "torment" in itself.

1. Why is it said that "He who does not love does not know God"?

2. Because "God so loved us," what "ought" we to do?

3. If I say that "I love God" but hate my brother, what am I?

Verse for Meditation and Prayer: **1 John 4:10**

"In this is love, not that we loved God,
but that He loved us and
sent His Son to be the propitiation for our sins."

November 23

Week 47, Day 5

1 John 5

Helpful Notes:

1. **Born of God** = It is essential to believe in both the deity and the humanity of Jesus Christ (which some in that day were challenging); some today read this passage and try to teach "salvation by faith alone"; verse 5 teaches that "whoever believes...is born of God"; in context, this book also teaches that everyone who "loves" (4:7) and "practices righteousness" (2:29) is "born of God"; obviously, "faith alone" does not make one a child of God, but a "faith working through love" that obeys God does (Gal. 5:6).
2. **Not burdensome** = The Greek for "burdensome" involves something that is "weighty or oppressive," and more specifically, "a source of difficulty or trouble because of demands made"; and God said that His commandments are NOT that; love for God lightens the load, seeing His benefits motivates the heart and overcoming the world makes victory all that one sees (cf. Matt. 11:28-30).
3. **Know have eternal life** = God wants His children to live confidently in this life concerning the next life; if we are living daily for Him and meeting His conditions (i.e., possessing and exhibiting an obedient faith that walks in the light of God's truth and confesses sin, 5:13; 1:7, 9), then we can "know" with certainty that we "have" (present tense) "eternal life"; we can lose that promise if we choose to stop meeting His conditions (2 Pet. 2:20-22; Jas. 5:19-20).

1. In addition to loving "Him who begot" us, who else do we love?

2. How does John define, "This is the love of God"?

3. Under whose sway or power does "the whole world" lie?

Verse for Meditation and Prayer: **1 John 5:13**

"These things I have written to you who believe in the name of the Son of God, that you may know that you have eternal life."

Mark Your Bible

1. **1 John 1:1**—This verse emphasizes Jesus' eternal nature, like John 1:1.
2. **1 John 1:1**—Jesus is the full expression of deity who gives life.
3. **1 John 1:1-2**—Jesus was not a spirit being, as some suggest. Not only was He seen, He was touched (John 20:25-28; Luke 24:39).
4. **1 John 1:5**—The Greek uses a double negative to double emphasize that there is "no, not one bit of darkness" in God.
5. **1 John 1:6, 7**—The word "walk" denotes the conduct of one's life.
6. **1 John 1:7**—The word "if" is used 5 times in the last 5 verses of this chapter. It introduces a condition. God's promises are conditional. It can go one way or the other, depending on if the condition is met.
7. **1 John 1:7**—The word "walk" is in the present tense, denoting an habitual, consistent pattern of life. It is not perfection, but it indicates one is trying his very best to walk faithfully in the Lord's will. As one "keeps walking" with the Lord, the Lord "keeps cleansing."
8. **1 John 1:7**—The "light" is staying true to God's Word (Psa. 119:105).
9. **1 John 1:7**—The same "blood" that cleanses in baptism (Acts 22:16) is the same "blood" that cleanses the Christian from sin.
10. **1 John 1:7, 9**—Circle the word "all" in both verses. All sin!
11. **1 John 1:9**—The word "confess" is from the Greek *homologeo,* which literally means "to say the same thing." When we "confess" our sin, we are saying the same thing that God says—this is a sin, it violates God's will, it separates me from God, it can condemn me to hell.
12. **1 John 2:1**—The Greek word for "Advocate" is *parakletos* and literally means "called to one's side." It described a person "who appears in another's behalf," and this verse was a technical term for a defense attorney who pleads one's case in the court of heaven. He alone is qualified for this role as "the righteous," who Himself never sinned, but appears "in the presence of God for us" (Heb. 9:24).
13. **1 John 2:2**—The doctrine of limited atonement is absolutely false!

(continued on next page)

Mark Your Bible

14. **1 John 2:2**—On the Jews' Day of Atonement, the high priest would sprinkle blood on the mercy seat (the lid of the ark of the covenant) (Lev. 16:14-15). (The Greek word for "mercy seat" is the word for "place of propitiation," Heb. 9:5). God's presence could only abide there (Ex. 25:22) if the blood was covering the people's sins. The blood of Christ is sprinkled on our hearts in baptism and faithful living (Heb. 10:22; 1 Pet. 1:2) to satisfy the consequences of our sins (Rom. 3:25; Heb. 2:17) and give us access to the presence of God.

15. **1 John 2:3-5**—Mark these three things: When we "keep on keeping [present tense] His commandments": (1) "we know that we know Him," (2) "the love of God has been completed and reached its goal," (3) "we know that we are in Him." In other words, we enjoy the most intimate relationship with our God when we obey Him!

16. **1 John 2:7-8**—John was not writing a "brand new" commandment that had never existed before, but the "old commandment" had a new measure, extent and quality to it—self-sacrifice (John 13:34).

17. **1 John 2:9-11**—The words "hates" and "loves" are both in the present tense, emphasizing ongoing behavior, and thus identifying a person's defining trait.

18. **1 John 2:15**—Worldliness leads to apostasy! One cannot love both the world and the Lord (Matt. 6:24; Jas. 4:4; 2 Cor. 6:14-18).

19. **1 John 2:17**—The one who "keeps on doing" (present tense) the will of God "keeps on abiding" (present tense) in heaven forever.

20. **1 John 2:18**—This helps to define "the last hour." John says that "it is" (present tense) "the last hour." In the N.T., the last hour stood for the final dispensation, the Christian age (Acts 2:16-17; Heb. 1:2).

21. **1 John 2:19**—One cannot go "out" if never "in." One cannot "continue" if he never "begins." These were once Christians (perhaps weak or superficial) who fell away (Matt. 13:20-21; 1 Tim. 1:19).

22. **1 John 2:20, 27**—The "anointing" was likely miraculous power from the Holy Spirit (1 Cor. 12:3-11) to discern truth from error (in order to recognize and refute false doctrines from the antichrists). With

Mark Your Bible

that miraculous gift, they would (in context) "know all things" they needed to know to discern truth and would not (in context) "need that anyone teach" them how to discern the error of the antichrists (or that the antichrists try to teach them their false doctrines).

23. **1 John 2:29**—The word "practices" is in the present tense, indicating a habitual activity. "Righteousness" involves (1) right-doing in relationship with man and (2) obedience to the commands of God. This kind of life provides evidence that one is a child of God.

24. **1 John 3:2**—We will not be deity, but we will somehow share His glory (Phil. 3:21) and be in full fellowship with the Father.

25. **1 John 3:3**—"Purifies" is in the present tense, denoting on ongoing need and activity, accomplished through faithful obedience (1 Pet. 1:22; 1 John 1:7, 9). Motivation for such is the "hope" of seeing Jesus.

26. **1 John 3:4-9**—Every instance of "sins" or "does not sin" or "cannot sin" in these verses is in the present tense, which denotes not a single sin or an occasional sin but a habitual practice or lifestyle of sin.

27. **1 John 3:5**—Jesus is qualified to "take away our sins" because He Himself had/has no sins (cf. Heb. 4:15; 7:26; 9:14; 2 Cor. 5:21).

28. **1 John 3:5, 8**—Jesus was "manifested" to (1) "take away our sins" and (2) "destroy the works of the devil." Draw a line to connect.

29. **1 John 3:8**—"All things were created" by Christ (Col. 1:16), which includes the devil. But "everything that He had made...was very good" (Gen. 1:31). So, the devil was not created evil, but some time at "the beginning," he rebelled against God. From then on, he has made it his mission to lead others into sin, to "slander" (so his name means) and make false accusations against God and His people.

30. **1 John 3:15**—Some sins are the seeds that lead to other sins (ex: Matt. 5:28). Some sins originate in the "heart" before they exhibit themselves in actions (Mark 7:20-23). But, both can be sinful. Hate has the spirit of a murderer and can lead to it (cf. Matt. 5:21-22), thus we must guard our hearts continually (Prov. 4:23).

(continued on next page)

Mark Your Bible

31. **1 John 3:18**—This verse is elliptical: "Let us not love *only* in word but *also* in deed." Christian love is a love of action!

32. **1 John 3:22**—See note on 1 John 5:14-15.

33. **1 John 3:23**—How shameful that many want to extract "believe" from this verse and from this context and teach salvation by "faith alone." Biblical faith is never merely a mental assent or trusting acceptance. An easy example to see that Biblical faith is equivalent to obedient faith is in John 3:36; Hebrews 3:18-19; 5:8-9. But, look in this context. The verse before (v. 22) teaches to "keep His commandments and do" (both present tense verbs). The verse after (v. 24) requires "keeping His commandments" (present tense). How could the verse in between teach "faith alone"? It does not!

34. **1 John 3:24**—As is the case throughout this book, the word "keeps" and the word "abides" are used in the present tense. As long as one "keeps on keeping God's commandments," that one "keeps on abiding in Him." The action is continuous and simultaneous.

35. **1 John 3:24**—The "how" and "what" of "the Spirit" being "given us" is not specified here—just the reality of it. We know today that it is not a direct operation of the Spirit, some direct illumination of truth or a working of miracles (1 Cor. 13:8-13; Eph. 4:8-13; Acts 8:14-18; 2 Tim. 3:16-17; 2 Pet. 1:3, 20-21; Jude 3). The Spirit works in us and through us by His Word (Eph. 6:17; Gal. 3:2), as we write it on our hearts (Psa. 119:11; Heb 8:10). The presence of the Spirit in our lives marks us (in the eyes of God) as one of His children (Rom. 8:14-17). Nothing else matters other than what God sees in us! The evidence that needs to be seen of the Spirit in our hearts is bearing the fruit of the Spirit in our daily lives (Gal. 5:23-24). That takes work.

36. **1 John 4:1-7**—Circle all uses of the phrase "of God" in these verses, then "of the world." There is a major difference. It begins with who one "hears" (mark that three times in verses 5-6). If one "hears" "truth," he can choose to believe and obey truth. If one "hears" "error," he cannot choose to believe and obey truth. This makes the "test" of every teacher critically and eternally important.

Mark Your Bible

37. **1 John 4:2-3**—There were false teachers of different sorts—some denying the humanity of Jesus (that deity ever truly and fully inhabited a human body, which means He could not have died for us) and others denying the deity of Jesus (that He was truly God, which made His death powerless for us). This "antichrist" philosophy was "already" present—it must be recognized and defeated.
38. **1 John 4:4**— God > Satan!
39. **1 John 4:9-10**—The vast, comprehensive and genuine nature of God's *agape* love for us existed prior to our love for Him and not based in any way on our love for Him (Rom. 5:8; John 3:16).
40. **1 John 4:10**—We get to "live through Him" now (John 10:10; Acts 4:12), and we get to "live through Him" eternally (1 John 2:25; 5:13).
41. **1 John 4:13**—See note on 1 John 3:24.
42. **1 John 5:1**—"Believes" is in the present tense, denoting a continual activity. Acceptable belief in the Bible always involves firm conviction that trustfully surrenders and obeys (John 3:36; Jas. 2:14-26). Belief on its own, without obedience, is demonic (Jas. 2:19).
43. **1 John 5:4**—True faith is able to constantly overcome (present tense) and constantly be victorious (present tense) over evil, as evidenced by resisting temptation (Jas. 4:7), avoiding the snares of the world (1 Pet. 2:11) and rejecting false doctrines (1 John 4:1).
44. **1 John 5:6, 8**—There are three solid and constant witnesses to the deity, Lordship and humanity of Jesus Christ—"water" (likely a reference to His baptism, at the beginning of His ministry, when the Father publicly acknowledged Him), "blood" (likely a reference to the cross, at the end of His ministry, when He shed His blood for our sins), and "the Spirit" (who has revealed "all truth" through the inspired writing of the Scriptures, which endures forever).
45. **1 John 5:11**—The promise of "eternal life" is conditional. One must be "in His Son" to have eternal life (Rom. 6:23; 2 Tim. 2:10). The only way "into Christ" is through penitent baptism (Rom. 6:3; Gal. 3:27).

(continued on next page)

Mark Your Bible

46. **1 John 5:14-15**—God wants us to have absolute "confidence" in prayer (cf. 3:21). In these verses, circle the word "if" and circle "because" in 3:22. Answered prayer is always conditional: (1) if "we keep His commandments" (3:22), (2) "if we ask according to His will," and (3) if "we know that He hears us," without doubting (Jas. 1:5-8). We have God's "will" given to us in Scripture, and it is always for our best interests (Deut. 6:24; 2 Cor. 12:7-10). We must trust God, in our prayers, to know better than we do how to answer. Some prayers are answered, "Yes"; some, "No"; some, "Not right now"; some, "Yes, but differently and even better."
47. **1 John 5:16**—All sins lead to death (Rom. 6:23), except when there is repentance (Luke 13:3; Rev. 2:5) and confession of sins (1 John 1:9). A sin for which one has repented and confessed does not lead to death. An unrepented and unconfessed sin leads to death.
48. **1 John 5:17**—There are sins of commission, when one "commits" an act that violates the law of God (3:4). There are sins of omission, when one fails to keep God's commandments (Psa. 119:172; Jas. 4:17). "All" sins of omission may be in view in this verse.
49. **1 John 5:18**—"Does not sin" is present tense, denoting one who does not continue to practice sin as a lifestyle (see 3:6, 9). Instead he "keeps himself" (present tense, ongoing activity), exercising self-discipline and maintaining his "walk in the light" (1:7).
50. **1 John 5:21**—"Idols" can be anything (or anyone) that takes the place of God or comes between us and God in our hearts or lives.

November 25 Week 47, Day 7

Day of Reflection

Take time today to reflect on the five chapters that you read this week. You may choose to read all five chapters again, in one sitting, or certain parts of them. Take time today to answer at least one of these questions below. You may or may not write anything down—you can choose to write or simply reflect.

1. What personal application do I need to make from the chapters I have read this week?

2. How can these five chapters help draw me closer to Jesus?

3. What words, phrases or verses in these chapters do I want to go back and study more in depth?

4. What questions do I have about what I have read this week on which I need to do some further Biblical research?

Week 48

November 26- December 2

November 26	Read 2 John
November 27	Read 3 John
November 28	Read Jude
November 29	Read Revelation 1
November 30	Read Revelation 2
December 1	Mark Your Bible
December 2	Day of Reflection

Prayer for this week:

"Heavenly Father,
I want to walk in Your truth!
Please help me to be faithful to You!"

2 John

Helpful Notes: ** See Brief Introduction to Second John on page 654.*

1. **Truth** = God's truth is an objective (not subjective) and fixed (not changing or changeable) standard that He has given to mankind in His Word (John 17:17); it can and must be known (v. 1; John 8:32) and continually (present tense) walked in (v. 4), emphasizing a mode of conduct that characterizes a person's life on a daily basis; "walking in truth" is a "commandment" from God (v. 4); truth should never be looked at negatively, when it is God's truth!
2. **The doctrine of Christ** = "Doctrine" is a Bible term and should be respected as such; the word "doctrine" simply means "teaching," and this is the "teaching" that comes from Christ (i.e., "all that I have commanded," Matt. 28:20) through inspired writers; this infallible standard must be respected, taught and demanded; nothing short of (or in addition to) should be accepted.
3. **Shares in evil deeds** = The Greek word for "shares" is *koinoneo* and means "to take part in, to partake, to participate"; to "share in their deeds" means "to be equally responsible for them"; if we in any way show approval for false doctrine, we join ourselves to it and to all that is associated with it (including the guilt of false teaching, cf. Rom. 1:32); God is serious about pure doctrine.

1. What caused John to rejoice greatly?

2. For what reason did John say to "look to yourselves"?

3. What is the result for those who go too far and do not abide faithfully in the doctrine of Christ?

Verse for Meditation and Prayer: **2 John 9**

"Whoever transgresses and does not abide in the doctrine of Christ does not have God. He who abides in the doctrine of Christ has both the Father and the Son."

November 27

Week 48, Day 2

3 John

Helpful Notes: * *See Brief Introduction to Third John on page 655.*

1. **Physical and spiritual health** = We often pray for the physical health of our brethren, but how much better would it be to pray for their spiritual health; John prayed that Gaius would "prosper in all things and be in health," but the measurement he desired in those areas was that they be "just as" (equivalent to) the health and prosperity of Gaius' soul; the health of the soul is infinitely (and eternally) more important (Mark 10:17-31; Matt. 6:33).
2. **Become fellow workers** = As John had warned in Second John about "sharing in the evil deeds" of false teachers by extending fellowship to them and showing approval, so the same concept follows here in reverse; by extending fellowship, showing approval and providing assistance to "workers of truth," we become "fellow workers for the truth" with them and with God.
3. **Imitate** = The Greek word for "imitate" is *mimeomai* and was used of a mimic or actor who would "mime" what another person was doing; the present imperative here calls for urgent and continued efforts to avoid mimicking anything that "is evil" and strive to perpetually mimic all that "is good," for in doing so habitually, one shows himself to be "of God" (i.e., influenced by God).

1. In what did John "have no greater joy"?

2. What sorts of things was Diotrephes doing against the brethren?

3. How can verse 11 be used in parenting children today?

Verse for Meditation and Prayer: **3 John 11**

"Beloved, do not imitate what is evil, but what is good.
He who does good is of God, but he who does evil has not seen God."

Jude

Helpful Notes: * *See Brief Introduction to Jude on page 656.*

1. **Contend** = The Greek word *epagonizomai* means "to exercise intense effort on behalf of something, involving intense struggle in a strenuous defense"; this is not some mild or passive effort, and God does not make this optional; God is appealing to His children to "wrestle...against spiritual hosts of wickedness" (Eph. 6:12) and "fight the good fight of faith" (1 Tim. 6:12).
2. **The faith** = The word "faith" is often used in a subjective sense in the N.T. for one's personal faith (ex: Rom. 10:17; Heb. 11:6); it is also used in the objective sense (with the definite article "the" usually preceding it), to designate the pure gospel (the universal, singular body of truth) given to mankind in God's inspired Word (Gal. 1:11+23; Acts 6:7; 1 Tim. 5:8); there is only "one" (Eph. 4:5).
3. **Once for all delivered** = The Greek adverb *hapax* means "pertaining to a single occurrence and decisively unique, of what is of perpetual validity, not requiring repetition," and should be translated "once and for all"; the same word is used for the sacrifice of Christ for our sins—"once for all" (Heb. 9:28; 1 Pet. 3:18); just as that was a single occurrence with perpetual validity, not requiring repetition or amendment, the same is true of Scripture (the gospel); there is NOTHING more to be delivered; it is final!

1. What does it mean that "the faith" was "once for all delivered"?

2. To what three characters did Jude liken the false teachers (v. 11)?

3. What four things "forever" belong to God (in the last verse)?

Verse for Meditation and Prayer: **Jude 3**

"Beloved, while I was very diligent to write to you concerning our common salvation, I found it necessary to write to you exhorting you to contend earnestly for the faith which was once for all delivered to the saints."

Revelation 1

Helpful Notes: * *See Brief Introduction to Revelation on page 657.*

1. **Keys to the book** = (1) It is a "revelation of Jesus Christ"—the Greek is *apokalupsis* (origin of English "apocalypse") and it means "an uncovering, unveiling"; (2) of "things which must shortly take place"—the time for the events of this book was "at hand/near" (1:3; 22:10), not thousands of years later; (3) "sign-i-fied"—the book is written in signs and symbols, not to be interpreted literally; (4) "to the seven churches of Asia"—it was written as a message of comfort and hope to first-century Christians under persecution and must have direct application and meaning to them.
2. **Alpha and Omega** = Alpha is the first letter of the Greek alphabet and omega is the last letter; Jesus is "the Beginning and the End" (v. 8), "the First and the Last" (v. 11, 17), "who is and was and who is to come"—He is the eternally existing one (John 1:1-2), and Rome is not; Jesus will take care of His people to the very end.
3. **Keys of Hades and of Death** = "Keys" signified authority to open; by means of His resurrection from the dead, Jesus had "all authority" over "all things"; "Death" is the state of the body upon its demise, and "Hades" is the conscious state/abode of the soul upon the death of the body; there is a distinction between body and soul; persecution may kill the saints, but Christ would raise them up.

1. What is the beatitude in verse 3?

2. While the Christians were being persecuted by a vile, earthly regime, what did they need to remember about their true King?

3. Write the names of the seven churches in Asia.

Verse for Meditation and Prayer: **Revelation 1:18**

"I am He who lives, and was dead, and behold,
I am alive forevermore. Amen.
And I have the keys of Hades and of Death."

November 30 Week 48, Day 5

Revelation 2

Helpful Notes:

1. **Letters** = Each of the seven letters follows the same basic pattern: (1) *Salutation* (from the Lord to the "angel" or messenger of the church, perhaps one sent to John or the minister of the congregation himself); (2) *Identification* (Christ's description of Himself, appropriate to the conditions of the church, using titles from chapter 1); (3) *Affirmation* (saying, "I know your works"); (4) *Commendation* (positive and praiseworthy virtues in the church); (5) *Condemnation* (complaints against or counsel for wrongs that needed to be corrected); (6) *Exhortation* ("He who has an ear, let him hear"); (7) *Exaltation* (a promise "to him who overcomes").
2. **Overcomes** = The word "overcome" is a key word in this book, written to Christians who were suffering severe persecution; the Greek word is *nikao,* which means "to win in the face of obstacles; be victor, conquer, prevail"; sometimes a Christian can feel overcome by sin, the devil, the world and life's circumstances, but with Christ's help (the one who overcame all), we can be victorious.
3. **Faithful until death** = The word "be" is in the present tense, urging continued faithfulness; He is not calling them to be "perfect or sinless," but to be steadfast in their daily walk with Him, enduring all things; "unto death" is not merely "up to the moment of death," but emphasizes "even if being faithful is the cause of your death"; the imperishable reward of eternal life awaits the faithful!

1. What did the church need to do to restore their first love?

2. What is the promise to those who are "faithful until death"?

3. What was the church in Pergamos doing well (in verse 13)?

Verse for Meditation and Prayer: **Revelation 2:10**

"Do not fear any of those things which you are about to suffer…
Be faithful until death, and I will give you the crown of life."

Mark Your Bible

1. **2 John 1**—John is probably merely identifying himself as "an older man" rather than an elder in the church.
2. **2 John 1**— "The elect lady" likely refers to a local congregation, with a greeting from another local congregation ("elect sister") at the end (v. 13). Or it could be a faithful Christian sister, whom he calls "lady" again in verse 5. The Greek word for "lady" is *kyria,* which may have even been her proper name (Kyria).
3. **2 John 1-4**—The word "truth" is found 5 times in these first four verses. Circle them and draw lines connecting them.
4. **2 John 4-6**—The word "walk" or "walking" is found 3 times in these verses. Underline them and draw lines connecting them. To "walk" emphasizes a person's regular manner of life, summarizing who they are, identifying their values and depicting their overall spiritual condition.
5. **2 John 4-6**—Underline and connect the four uses of "commandment(s)" in these verses.
6. **2 John 6**—God connects "love" and "walk" (present tense, sustained action) and "commandments." Love honors God's law and prompts one to keep God's commandments (1 John 5:3; John 14:15). Not keeping His commandments is an indication of a lack of true love for Him. Love and commandments are not mutually exclusive.
7. **2 John 7**—There were "many antichrists" deceiving and teaching false doctrines about Christ. (See notes in 1 John 2.) This was not some sinister personality to be revealed right before Jesus' return.
8. **2 John 8**—"Look to" is a present imperative, urging constant watchfulness and constant self-examination. There is personal responsibly to exercise. One must "work" in order to obtain his "reward" in heaven. If he does not work, he will "lose" his reward.
9. **2 John 9**—"Whoever" applies to "any" person and "every" person.
10. **2 John 9**—The word "transgresses" is better translated from the Greek word *proago* as "goes onward, takes the lead, goes too far."

(continued on next page)

Mark Your Bible

11. **2 John 9**—"Abide" and "abides" are both in the present tense, denoting ongoing activity. To "abide" in the doctrine of Christ means to faithfully remain in it and stay true to it, without veering to the right or left, adding or taking from it (Gal. 1:6-9; Rev. 22:18-19).
12. **2 John 9**—One cannot separate Christ from His doctrine.
13. **2 John 10**—The word "receive" involves "taking in and accepting." Hospitality and fellowship is not to be extended to false teachers.
14. **2 John 10**—The Greek word for "greet" is *chairo* and has at its root "rejoicing and being glad." There is no joy in false teaching. Specifically, in this verse, *chairo* means "wishing one well," showing approval of the one greeted or the doctrine they are teaching, desiring success for their efforts. Any doctrine that is not of Christ must not be endorsed or shown assistance or approval in way, and this extends to any and all persons who are advocating it. God is serious about His doctrine! There is only one and it must be guarded! No fellowship is to be extended; rather truth must prevail (Eph. 5:11).
15. **3 John 1**—Gaius was a common name in that day. There is no way to connect him with other men named Gaius in the N.T. John highly esteems this man, calling him "beloved" four times (v. 1, 2, 5, 11).
16. **3 John 1**—"Truth" or "the truth" is found 6 times in this book. Circle each one (v. 1, 3, 4, 8, 12). Truth is objective!
17. **3 John 2**—The "soul" is separate from the body (Matt. 10:28).
18. **3 John 3**—God's truth is objective! It is not relative! Each person is not his own truth or his own standard of truth! Circle the word "in"—one is either "in" the truth or "out of" the truth.
19. **3 John 4**—"My children" likely refers to John's converts or at least those whom he had spent time teaching God's Word.
20. **3 John 6-7**—Gaius was "faithfully" extending hospitality to Christians, and probably especially to traveling missionaries. He was "receiving" them and "sending them forward on their journey," which would have involved not only a place to stay but helping with money and supplies for the work.

Mark Your Bible

21. **3 John 9**—The Greek word for "preeminence" is *philoprotos* and literally means "fond of, loves being first." Diotrephes demanded having his way. Such could not be further from the spirit of humility that we are to emulate in Christ (Phil. 2:3-4).

22. **3 John 10**—The Greek word for "prating" means "to indulge in utterance that makes no sense; to talk nonsense about, disparage, babble." And the word is in the present tense, denoting a steady stream of unjust, senseless accusations.

23. **3 John 9-10**—All the verbs associated with Diotrephes in these verses are in the present tense, emphasizing his ongoing activity and the ongoing trouble he was to the church.

24. **3 John 11**—To not "see God" means that those persons are not truly acquainted with or in true fellowship with God (Matt. 5:8; 1 John 3:6).

25. **3 John 12**—When one faithfully "walks in the truth," then "the truth itself" approves and testifies on his behalf. Of course, the opposite is just as true (cf. 2 Thess. 2:12).

26. **Jude 1**—Christians have been "called" by the "gospel" (2 Thess. 2:14).

27. **Jude 1**—Those who are "kept for Jesus Christ" (NASB) are those who "keep [themselves] in the love of God" (v. 21). Draw a line connecting those two verses.

28. **Jude 3**—Underline this verse. It is key. (See "Helpful Notes.") Scripture was "delivered to the saints" (i.e., living Christians, Phil. 1:1). They immediately recognized the inspired writings, accepted them, collected them and compiled them (cf. 1 Tim. 5:18; 2 Pet. 3:16), hundreds of years before any council decided to vote on them.

29. **Jude 5**—The Israelites were "saved" by God and later "destroyed" by God due to their disbelief and disobedience (cf. Heb. 3:17-19). The Bible repeatedly teaches the possibility of apostasy.

30. **Jude 6**—There is zero evidence to support a claim that the angels cohabitated with women in Genesis 6. We must not teach something the Bible does not teach.

(continued on next page)

Mark Your Bible

31. **Jude 6, 13**—Just as heaven is "reserved" for God's faithful (1 Pet. 1:4), the same word is used here, revealing that hell is "reserved" for those who rebel against God and His will. The reservation (in both cases) is made by the choice of the individuals.

32. **Jude 7**—The Holy Spirit describes the homosexual sin of Sodom and Gomorrah (Gen. 19:4-11) as going "after strange flesh," to emphasize the unauthorized nature of this activity in the eyes of God. God said that homosexuality is "sexual immorality" and is "against nature" (Rom. 1:26-28). The destruction of these cities due to their homosexuality is set forth as an "example" for us today.

33. **Jude 7**—"Suffering" is a present tense verb, emphasizing that the sinful residents of Sodom and Gomorrah continue to suffer the punishment of eternal fire, even at the time of Jude's writing.

34. **Jude 9**—We don't know any more about this event than what is revealed in this verse. The Holy Spirit revealed it to Jude, thus we accept it and refuse to offer conjecture beyond what he says.

35. **Jude 14**—Some speculate that Jude quoted from the pseudepigraphal "Book of Enoch," suggesting that such implies that either the "Book of Enoch" is inspired or that Jude is not. But quoting from a secular source does not warrant either of those conclusions (see Acts 17:28 and Titus 1:12). However, there is no proof that Jude was quoting from this uninspired source. The Holy Spirit (cf. 2 Pet. 1:20-21) had Jude quote a prophecy of an O.T. character. That is what we know and that is all we need to know.

36. **Jude 15**—Circle the four uses of the word "all" and underline the four uses of "ungodly" in this verse.

37. **Jude 18**—"The last time" is the Christian age (Acts 2:16-17; 1 Tim. 4:1; 2 Tim. 3:1).

38. **Jude 20**—"Most holy faith" may be used here in the objective sense of "the faith"—the objective body of Divine truth.

39. **Jude 20**—Pray in harmony with the principles revealed by the Spirit in Scripture (Eph. 6:17).

Mark Your Bible

40. **Jude 21**—"Keep yourselves" is an imperative emphasizing that Christians must exercise diligence in "building" themselves up in the faith and keep the commands of God in order to keep themselves in the love of God (2 Pet. 1:10). Salvation is conditional to obtain and to retain, and it is possible to fall away and be lost.

41. **Jude 24**—The Greek for "keep" indicates that God "guards, protects and watches" those who "keep" themselves in His love (v. 21). He provides the resources needed to be kept by Him (i.e., the Bible, the avenue of prayer, the church family, the abundant blessings in Christ, the way of escape out of every temptation, the hope of heaven, etc.). With His help, we will "never stumble" (2 Pet. 1:10-11).

42. **Revelation 1:1**—This book was written to Christians, who were suffering severe persecution in the first century. As a message of comfort and hope, it had to have meaning to those brethren, and that is the understanding of the book that must be sought. Comfort came from knowing the events of victory described in the book "must shortly take place," not in a millennial age thousands of years later. The question that must be asked is: "What did it mean to them?"

43. **Revelation 1:1**—The book is written in signs. It is foolish to apply a literal understanding to symbolic language. This is key to remember. It is also imperative to not try to apply meaning to every single symbol. Read for the overall message, similar to parables. The overall message is one of triumph for God's people. That is the message those Christians needed to hear.

44. **Revelation 1:3**—There are seven beatitudes in this book (1:3; 14:13; 16:15; 19:9; 20:6; 22:7, 14).

45. **Revelation 1:3**—This book was a "prophecy" (cf. 10:11; 22:18-19). Prophecy is simply "speaking for another," and in this case, "speaking for Christ" (it is His revelation). These persecuted Christians were given full assurance that relief was on its way and victory was certain. Some events would be fulfilled in eternity, but their victory over Roman persecution was coming "shortly."

(continued on next page)

Mark Your Bible

46. **Revelation 1:3**—The first readers would "hear with understanding" exactly what John was writing. That is what matters.
47. **Revelation 1:4**—The primary audience were the seven churches of Asia. The number seven is symbolic in this book of perfection or completeness, which likely indicates these churches represent the entire church—a message of hope through them to all Christians.
48. **Revelation 1:4**—Asia was the western providence of Asia Minor.
49. **Revelation 1:4**—Seven was the number of perfection, used symbolically here to identify the Holy Spirit.
50. **Revelation 1:5**—While Christians were being persecuted by evil rulers and emperor worship was being demanded, they were reassured that Jesus is "the ruler over the kings" troubling them.
51. **Revelation 1:5**—"Love" is present tense. Jesus presently and continually loves us (don't forget that, persecuted Christians!) and "freed us from our sins by His blood" when we were baptized (Rom. 6:3-7).
52. **Revelation 1:6**—All Christians are priests (5:10; 1 Pet. 2:5, 9), made into "a kingdom of priests" (cf. Ex. 19:6), serving in His temple (1 Cor. 3:16), with direct access to God through the "blood" of Christ.
53. **Revelation 1:6, 9**—The kingdom is a present reality and those saved by the blood of Christ in baptism immediately become a part of His kingdom/church (John 3:3-5; Acts 2:41, 47). The kingdom is not yet to be revealed in the future (in a so-called "millennium")—Christians are in (and are) the kingdom now (Col. 1:13).
54. **Revelation 1:7**—Jesus will return in the exact manner that He went into heaven (Acts 1:9-11), "with clouds." It will not be done in secret. "Every eye will see Him," and his enemies will "mourn."
55. **Revelation 1:8**—The same eternal description is made of the Father in verse 4. Jesus is the "Almighty," meaning "all-powerful, omnipotent, sovereign Lord over all," and Rome is not.
56. **Revelation 1:9**—"Tribulation" is from the Greek word *thlipsis,* which means "pressing, pressure," and was used of grinding the

Mark Your Bible

wheat at the mill or of crushing the grapes in the wine press. The process was severe but the end result was pleasant and productive. John was in the tribulation right then.

57. **Revelation 1:9**—Patmos was not an island of paradise for retirees. It was a volcanic island where those exiled were forced into hard labor. Rome banished enemies and rebels to Patmos to punish them for refusing to worship the Roman emperor as "Lord and God." John was there because he would not abandon preaching "the word of God" or Jesus Christ, and neither should those Christians.

58. **Revelation 1:10**—"The Lord's Day" is the first day of the week, the day of worship for God's people. Jesus was raised from the dead on Sunday, which gave it significance to every Christian.

59. **Revelation 1:12**—The seven golden lampstands represent the seven congregations (v. 20), who were to be a light to the world.

60. **Revelation 1:13**—"The Son of Man" was Jesus (Dan. 7:13). Churches should take comfort that He is "in the midst." He "walks in the midst" of them (2:1), "knowing" and intimately aware of their struggles.

61. **Revelation 1:13**—The clothing described was reminiscent of the high priest (Ex. 28:4). Jesus is our Great High Priest (Heb. 4:14-16). Jesus is prophet (v. 1, 3), priest (v. 13) and king (v. 5).

62. **Revelation 1:14-15**—Jesus is described as God was in the O.T. (Dan. 7:9), with symbols emphasizing His omniscient wisdom (i.e., head, eyes), purity (i.e., white), strength (i.e., brass), authority over all (i.e., sounds of many waters, Ezek. 43:2).

63. **Revelation 1:16**—The "seven stars" represent the "seven angels" of the churches (v. 20). The simple meaning of the Greek word *angelos* is "messengers." These could have been representatives or ministers of the seven congregations, who were appointed to convey the messages from John to the churches (see 2:1, 8, 12, 18; 3:1, 7, 14). The initial message was that Christ is there in your midst, He knows what is happening and He is holding you in His hand.

(continued on next page)

Mark Your Bible

64. **Revelation 1:16**—The power, force and authority of His Word is represented in the sword (cf. Heb. 4:12; Eph. 6:17), and His majestic glory was like that of Moses at Sinai (Ex. 34:29-30) and of Jesus Himself at the transfiguration (Matt. 17:2).

65. **Revelation 1:17-18**—The present imperative carries the force of, "Stop being afraid" (prohibiting John and the Christians from continuing in an act in progress—i.e., fear). He continues to provide reasons. Jesus is in control. "I am the living One" (present tense) and "I am alive forevermore" (present tense). He is victorious over death and over the devil, and the saints will be victorious too!

66. **Revelation 1:19**—This may be an outline of the book: "the things which you have seen" may be the vision just received in chapter 1, "the things which are" may be the situation and conditions of the churches in chapters 2-3, and "the things which will take place after this" may be the prophetic revelations of chapters 4-22. Jesus wanted the Christians to know that He knew "the things which are" (happening to them right now) but that He was in control of "the things which will take place" shortly, as they triumph with Him.

67. **Revelation 2:1**—This book is addressed to seven actual congregations, who were suffering real problems in the first century. There were other congregations in the region of Asia (ex: Troas, Colossae, Hierapolis, etc.). Thus, the number seven (symbolic for completeness) must represent a message to the whole church. It had to be meaningful and helpful to them when they received it.

68. **Revelation 2:2**—The Greeks had multiple words for "know." A common one was *ginosko,* which meant "to take in knowledge, to come to know," thus a "knowledge by experience and progress." The word used by Jesus in each of the letters for "I know" is *oida,* which meant "complete, absolute, fullness of knowledge; knowing intuitively." Jesus knows all things.

69. **Revelation 2:2**—The Greek for "labor/toil" initially meant "a striking or beating," and it was used of toil that resulted in complete weariness and exhaustion, to the point of pain and great difficulty.

Mark Your Bible

70. **Revelation 2:2**—The Greek for "patience" was *hupomeno,* and it literally meant to "remain under." The church bore up under all kinds of burdens and difficulties, pushing through them, and they kept moving forward.

71. **Revelation 2:4**—Their original love, devotion and proper motive for worship and serving the Lord (including actively loving one another) had "fallen" and "grown cold."

72. **Revelation 2:5**—Repentance is not just something to do before baptism. Repentance is necessary for Christians who have strayed away from the Lord (Acts 8:22; Heb. 6:6). It involves a change of mind that leads to a change of life; it is emphasized twelve times in the book of Revelation and eight of those are in chapters 2-3.

73. **Revelation 2:5**—The "lampstand" was the church (1:20). A church can forfeit their right to exist as "Christ's church" and be disowned by Him if they stray from Him, His will and His purpose for them.

74. **Revelation 2:6**—The exact identification of the Nicolaitans is not known. There appears to be a connection with "the doctrine of Balaam" (2:14-15), which involved fornication and eating things offered to idols. There was a high level of self-indulgence among them, claiming that things done "in the flesh" did not affect one's "spirit/soul."

75. **Revelation 2:7**—Read, pay attention to and heed what the Holy Spirit says to all "the churches." This shows the universal scope of the book. It also warns against the deadly peril of spiritual apathy.

76. **Revelation 2:8**—Christians were constantly told that "Rome is eternal," but only Jesus is "the eternally existing one"—"the First and the Last." He had suffered, too, but there is life after death. (There is no condemnation or complaint against this congregation.)

(continued on next page)

Mark Your Bible

77. **Revelation 2:9**—Their "poverty" was no doubt due to the confiscation and pillaging of their property by the blasphemous Jews or the vicious Romans (an action taken against them because they were faithful Christians). Regardless, faithful Christians are "rich" (2 Cor. 8:9), for God "gives us richly all things to enjoy" (1 Tim. 6:17), which emphasizes our spiritual blessings over physical things.

78. **Revelation 2:9**—In speaking against Christ and His people, these Jews were disgracing their own name and were instruments in the hand of Satan, doing his bidding.

79. **Revelation 2:10**—The Lord does not promise escape from persecutions. Remember as you endure trials, the devil is the source of all of this. Eventually (keep reading the book), he will be defeated!

80. **Revelation 2:10**—"Ten days" is not a literal ten days (remember the book is written in signs, 1:1). The number 10 denotes human completeness—the time of the persecution will be severe but it is limited; it will come to an end, and in comparison with eternity, it is short (cf. 2 Cor. 4:17; Rom. 8:18).

81. **Revelation 2:11**—"The second death" is the eternal punishment and eternal separation from God in hell (see 20:14, 6; 21:8). The "wages" and end of sin is "death" (Rom. 6:23; Jas. 1:15), which is described in the Bible as separation (2 Thess. 1:9). Everyone will die (Heb. 9:27), but those who die outside of Christ will suffer a "second death" (separation) by being cast into hell.

82. **Revelation 2:12**—The sword represented the power, force and authority of His Word (1:16; Heb. 4:12). This can involve both protection for His people, as well as discerning judgment against those who taught or practiced or harbored error.

83. **Revelation 2:13**—Pergamos was the headquarters for emperor worship in that region, with altars there for sacrifices to the emperors, as well as a large altar to Zeus that looked like a great throne. There were other pagan temples there, also.

Mark Your Bible

84. **Revelation 2:13**—The Greek word for "martyr" is *martus,* and it essentially means "a witness." In this case, it was "one who witnesses at cost of life; one who bears witness by his death; one who crowns his testimony by giving his life for his faith."

85. **Revelation 2:14-15**—"The doctrine of Balaam" involved engaging in fornication and idolatry (Num. 25:1-2; 31:16). There was a general lifestyle of sexual promiscuity, but that was especially true in some forms of pagan worship, and large feasts to pagan gods were common. Many Christians were being pressed to compromise for their own safety.

86. **Revelation 2:17**—God took care of Israel with manna from heaven (Ex. 16:4, 15), and God will provide a banquet of spiritual sustenance that the world may not see and will not understand.

87. **Revelation 2:17**—The "white stone" was used variously in that time. The color white symbolized victory. A white stone was sometimes given in those days to someone acquitted by a jury in a trial, to a freed slave, to the winner of a race, to a warrior returning from victory in battle. Whatever the specific meaning, it was intended to emphasize victory and honor in standing for and with Christ.

88. **Revelation 2:20**—The exact identification of this false "prophetess" is not known. She was misleading, seducing and corrupting the church into fornication and idolatry (a recurring problem in the first century), following the doctrine of the Nicolaitans. The complaint against the church is that they were harboring and condoning. In verse 23, "her children" are likely "her followers."

89. **Revelation 2:26-27**—This is a reference to Psalm 2, which is a Messianic psalm. The picture is one of the Messiah triumphing over His enemy with the "rod" of His judgment and His people sharing in that victory with Him.

90. **Revelation 2:28**—"The morning star" is Jesus Himself (22:16). He is and will be their guiding light in the midst of darkness.

December 2 Week 48, Day 7

Day of Reflection

Take time today to reflect on the five chapters that you read this week. You may choose to read all five chapters again, in one sitting, or certain parts of them. Take time today to answer at least one of these questions below. You may or may not write anything down—you can choose to write or simply reflect.

1. What personal application do I need to make from the chapters I have read this week?

2. How can these five chapters help draw me closer to Jesus?

3. What words, phrases or verses in these chapters do I want to go back and study more in depth?

4. What questions do I have about what I have read this week on which I need to do some further Biblical research?

Week 49

December 3-9

December 3	Read Revelation 3
December 4	Read Revelation 4
December 5	Read Revelation 5
December 6	Read Revelation 6
December 7	Read Revelation 7
December 8	Mark Your Bible
December 9	Day of Reflection

Prayer for this week:

"Heavenly Father,
I long to worship You and glorify You,
for You alone are worthy!"

December 3 Week 49, Day 1

Revelation 3

Helpful Notes:

1. **The Book of Life** = The Book of Life is found several times in the O.T. and the N.T. (Ex. 32:32-33; Psa. 69:28; Dan. 12:1; Mal. 3:16; Luke 10:20; Phil. 4:3; Rev. 13:8; 17:8; 20:15; 21:27); it is God's record of those who belong to Him (cf. 2 Tim. 2:19); one has his name "registered in heaven" when he is baptized "into Christ" (Rom. 6:3-4; Gal. 3:26-27; Heb. 12:23); it is possible for one's name, once entered, to be removed from the book (Ex. 32:32-33; Rev. 3:5), which emphatically teaches the possibility of apostasy.
2. **Lukewarm** = The tri-cities of Hierapolis, Laodicea and Colossae were in close proximity, but their waters have been discovered to be very different; Hierapolis had hot springs and Colossae had cool springs; the water supplied to Laodicea was tepid mineral water; Jesus may have been using the differences in their waters to vividly depict His utter disgust for the spiritual condition of the church.
3. **Stand at the door and knock** = Some have misused this passage to apply to non-Christians, stating all they have to do is "open the door of their heart and invite Jesus into it"; keep this passage in context—Jesus is pleading with unfaithful Christians; "I stand" is the Greek perfect tense, emphasizing a past action with abiding results (He is still standing there!), and "knock" is in the present tense, emphasizing constant activity; to those who once had opened to Christ but are now closed, He is continually pleading.

1. What three names are written on Christ's redeemed?

2. What graphic thing was Jesus ready to do with the Laodiceans?

3. Why did Jesus say He was rebuking and chastening them?

Verse for Meditation and Prayer: **Revelation 3:20**

"Behold, I stand at the door and knock.
If anyone hears My voice and opens the door,
I will come in to him and dine with him, and he with Me."

December 4 Week 49, Day 2

Revelation 4

Helpful Notes:

1. **Throne in heaven** = This chapter, which begins the major portion of the book, gives its readers a glimpse into heaven to provide comfort and hope of victory, and the first thing seen in heaven (and the very center of the vision) is the throne of God; the word "throne" is found about 40 times in the book, emphasizing its central theme to the book; the throne symbolizes the sovereign rule of God (Psa. 47:8); these persecuted Christians needed to see God on His throne—He is still in control; He is omniscient, omnipotent and omnipresent; He has not abdicated His rule to Rome.
2. **Twenty-four elders** = Various identifications have been offered, such as a heavenly court of angels, denoting an order of angels (Isa. 24:23) or representing the order of priests (1 Chron. 24:7-18); perhaps they are best understood as representing God's people, with 12 from the O.T. (represented by 12 tribes/patriarchs) and 12 from the N.T. (represented by the 12 apostles); the number 12 was symbolic of organized religion or God's people (12x2=24).
3. **Four living creatures** = There are similarities with Ezekiel's vision (1:6-10) and Isaiah's vision (6:2-3), but there are differences; some identify these as the attributes of God; some see these as an exalted order of angels; others see them as creatures representing all of God's created creatures—wild animals, domesticated animals, humans and birds; whatever their meaning, they are constantly offering praise and adoration to God, for He alone is worthy.

1. What was opened to John?

2. What are the four living creatures singing in triplicate?

3. For what reason do the 24 elders say that the Lord is "worthy"?

Verse for Meditation and Prayer: **Revelation 4:11**

"You are worthy, O Lord, To receive glory and honor and power;
For You created all things, And by Your will they exist and were created."

December 5 Week 49, Day 3

Revelation 5

Helpful Notes:

1. **The Lion of the tribe of Judah, the Root of David** = A "Lion" represented strength and bravery, and in this context, a regal authority in fulfillment of prophecy (Gen. 49:9); the Lion would be from the tribe of Judah, which was also fulfillment of prophecy (Gen. 49:10; Heb. 7:14); Jesus came as a descendant of David, another fulfillment of prophecy (Isa. 11:1-10; Matt. 1:16); Jesus was both "the Root and the Offspring of David" (22:16), emphasizing His deity and His humanity; thus, this One alone was worthy to open the book and loose its seals.
2. **The Lamb of God** = Jesus is referred to as a "Lamb" 28 times in this book; Jesus was prophesied as a Lamb (Isa. 53:7; cf. 1 Pet. 1:19) and was identified by John the Baptist as "the Lamb of God" (John 1:29, 36); as the Lamb, He was "slain" for man's sins, but He was now "standing" (perfect tense, denoting permanence, having achieved redemption and now standing for His redeemed); without the atoning blood of the Lamb, God's people have no hope.
3. **Harps in worship** = Attempts have been made to use the presence of harps in heaven to justify mechanical instruments of music in worship today; remember that the book is written in figurative language; the "golden bowls of incense" are not literal, neither are the "harps" or a literal "lamb"; it is all symbolic language; they do not marry (Matt. 22:30) or eat (Rev. 7:16) in heaven, but that is not authority to bind or loose such today; keep things in context.

1. Who was found "worthy" to open the scroll and loose its seals?

2. How can Jesus be both a Lion and a Lamb?

3. According to the end of verse 9, who can be saved?

Verse for Meditation and Prayer: **Revelation 5:9**

"And they sang a new song, saying: 'You are worthy to take the scroll, And to open its seals; For You were slain, And have redeemed us to God by Your blood Out of every tribe and tongue and people and nation.'"

December 6 Week 49, Day 4

Revelation 6

Helpful Notes:

1. **Seals** = A seal was a unique mark of authenticity and authority and was used to protect the contents from unwarranted access and disruption; a seal could only be opened by the one with the proper authority to do so; with seven seals on the scroll, as each seal was broken, a part of the scroll was unrolled to reveal God's forthcoming dealings with men; the opening of the seals was for the announcing of the ultimate judgment and conquest of Rome.
2. **Four horsemen** = These are not literal horses or literal horsemen—remember that the book is written in signs (figurative language); the first four seals comprise a series (a similar vision is in Zechariah 6:1-8); horses are used in Scripture in connection with strength, terror, warfare and conquest (Isa. 30:16; 31:1; Job 39:22-28); the progression of the horsemen shows man's ongoing endeavor to live apart from God, in rebellion to His will, and the results thereof; Rome would not stand forever—her downfall is certain.
3. **Life after death** = The bodies of these martyrs "had been slain," and their souls had departed from the bodies to another realm (Jas. 2:26); note that death has occurred but these souls are still conscious, aware of their surroundings, remembering their past, able to speak and provided a place of rest; death is not cessation or even soul-sleep; the spirits of the dead are still very much awake and alert in their new environment (cf. Luke 16:19-31).

1. Why were the souls who John saw slain?
2. What did those slain souls want to know?
3. What assurance was given to those slain souls?

Verse for Meditation and Prayer: **Revelation 6:9**

"When He opened the fifth seal, I saw under the altar the souls of those who had been slain for the word of God and for the testimony which they held."

Revelation 7

Helpful Notes:

1. **Interlude** = This chapter is an interlude between the sixth and seventh seals to give reassurance to God's people; a Christian may wonder what would happen to them in the midst of the horrible judgment depicted in the first six seals, and this chapter provides two visions of the same people under differing circumstances: (1) God's faithful church on earth in the midst of persecution and (2) God's victorious church in heaven in the presence of God.
2. **144,000** = This is not a literal number, as the book is written in signs; the number 12 symbolized God's people (and sometimes organized religion, in general), which was then multiplied by itself for emphasis and then by 1,000, which symbolized absolute completeness; 144,000 represented all of God's people (i.e., all "the servants of our God," v. 3; cf. 1:1) while on the earth.
3. **Tabernacle over them** = The Greek word for "tabernacle" is *skene;* that word is taken and made into a verb in this verse: *skenoo;* the word means "to tabernacle, to dwell, to take up residence, to shelter"; in heaven, God's presence will be with His people forever and His eternal security will protect them and shelter them forever (see also 21:3).

1. For what reason were the four angels told to delay releasing the four winds on the earth?

2. In what have those in heaven been washed, in order to be made pure?

3. What will we get to do in heaven day and night?

Verse for Meditation and Prayer: **Revelation 7:15**

"Therefore they are before the throne of God,
and serve Him day and night in His temple.
And He who sits on the throne will dwell among them."

Mark Your Bible

1. **Revelation 3:1-2**—The church had a good reputation and looked good on the outside (they had "a name"), but on the inside, they "are" (present tense) "dead" spiritually, in the eyes of God. Even more, the few "things which remain" that are not yet dead are "ready" (present tense, "are on the verge of") "to die." Their "works" in the sight of God were "incomplete," for they apparently were good starters but not good finishers (cf. Gal. 5:7).
2. **Revelation 3:4**—"White" is used symbolically in the book of purity and/or victory. "Worthiness" is only possible through Christ when we submit to and obey the will of God—that's what makes us pure in the eyes of God and "worthy" of fellowship with Him.
3. **Revelation 3:5**—Jesus made this same promise in Matthew 10:32-33.
4. **Revelation 3:7**—Christ's identification at the end of the verse is a Messianic description from Isaiah 22:22. Only Christ has the "key" (which symbolizes authority) to open the door into the kingdom promised to David (John 3:3-5; Acts 4:12).
5. **Revelation 3:8**—There is no condemnation spoken against this church—only commendation.
6. **Revelation 3:8**—An "open door" in the N.T. was used in two ways: (1) as an opportunity to preach the gospel (Acts 14:27; 1 Cor. 16:9; 2 Cor. 2:12; Col. 4:3), and (2) as an admission into a place or state (Rev. 3:20; 4:1). Either one could be in view here, but it seems that Jesus is focused on their faithfulness in walking through open doors of service, even though they were of "little strength" (which is probably just an indication of their small size or ability).
7. **Revelation 3:10**—"Those who dwell on the earth" is used in this book as a reference to non-Christians (11:10; 13:8-12, 14; 17:8).
8. **Revelation 3:11**—In these letters, Jesus often said, "I will come to you" or "I am coming." These are expressions used of either blessing some (as a message of encouragement for doing right) or punishing others (as a message of warning for doing wrong), but He is not referencing His final coming at the end of time.

(continued on next page)

Mark Your Bible

9. **Revelation 3:11**—The Christians needed to work diligently to not lose their reward—obvious warning that a Christian can fall away and lose his eternal salvation.

10. **Revelation 3:12**—These could be a reference to being a strong member of the church (which is the Lord's temple, 1 Cor. 3:16; Eph. 2:20) or to being given a firm reward in heaven (the eternal holy place).

11. **Revelation 3:12**—Many pagan religions and even the emperor worship utilized marks or brands to identify adherents. If that is in view here, Jesus is reassuring these Christians that they have the greatest marks/brands of identification: (1) they are part of God's family (have His name on them), (2) they have citizenship in heaven (have the eternal city's name on them), and (3) they belong to Christ by means of redemptive purchase (they have His name).

12. **Revelation 3:14**—No commendation is given to this church.

13. **Revelation 3:14**—The word "Amen" comes from the Greek *amen.* It means "let it be so, truly," and as used here identifies Christ "as the ultimate affirmation, the authenticator of truth." This was a title reserved only for God, for He alone guarantees the truth.

14. **Revelation 3:14**—Jesus is not a created being or even the first created being. The Greek word *arche* here means "the origin, the active cause," denoting the means by which something came into being. A form of the word (*archegos*) is used in Hebrews 2:10 to identify Christ as the "Author" of salvation, obviously emphasizing He was the "Originator" of salvation. Likewise, Christ is the "Originator" (prime source, active agent) of "the creation" (which is affirmed elsewhere in the N.T.—John 1:3; Col. 1:16). Rome was often identified as being eternal and lasting forever, but the reality was that Jesus was the eternal one (John 1:1-3; 8:58).

15. **Revelation 3:16**—"Lukewarm" was used by Jesus to depict their spiritual condition—they were indifferent, unconcerned, uncommitted, unattached, lethargic, etc. Such was absolutely nauseating to Christ.

Mark Your Bible

16. **Revelation 3:17-18**—Jesus centered on three major commercial industries in Laodicea to emphasize the pitiful state of their souls. Laodicea was a banking center ("rich, wealthy, poor, gold"), manufacturer of fine, woolen garments ("clothed, shame, nakedness"), and a medical center known for their eye salve ("blind, eyes, see"). Of course, each had a spiritual application—enjoy the true riches of God, be washed and made pure in the blood of Christ, and open your eyes to see where you are and where God wants you to be.
17. **Revelation 3:19**—God rebukes and chastens His people because He loves them (Heb. 12:5-11) and wants them to grow to endure trials and be strengthened for greater service. Even in their present, sinful, rebellious condition, He still loves them!
18. **Revelation 3:19**—"Be zealous" is a present imperative, emphasizing the need for continuous action and giving urgency to repentance.
19. **Revelation 3:20**—Underline "anyone." Jesus would have been thrilled with even one response.
20. **Revelation 3:21**—Faithful Christians will share with Christ in the glory and triumph of His victory! We will not be made deity, but we will enjoy eternal fellowship with deity on His throne!
21. **Revelation 4:1**—"After these things" is a literary device used throughout the book to present the visions in their sequence.
22. **Revelation 4:1**—This is similar to the way Ezekiel's vision commenced (Ezek. 1:1).
23. **Revelation 4:1**—This "first voice" was the voice John heard in 1:10—the voice of Christ.
24. **Revelation 4:1**—The word "must" emphasizes that God is in control, which would provide encouragement to the persecuted saints.
25. **Revelation 4:2**—Caesar was on the throne in Rome, from whence came fear and terror and persecution. Seeing God on His throne, as the sovereign ruler over all, brings reassurance and excitement.

(continued on next page)

Mark Your Bible

26. **Revelation 4:2**—"I was in the Spirit" simply means that John was under the power and influence of the Spirit in what he was seeing.

27. **Revelation 4:2**—The fact that God is sitting on the throne emphasizes His reigning power and dominion, which Rome does not have.

28. **Revelation 4:3**—The exact meaning of the various stones is difficult to state with certainty, as John is describing a heavenly scene with earthly vocabulary. The overall picture is one of the absolute radiance and majesty of God. The "rainbow" was a sign of a covenant-making God, who provides hope and mercy for His faithful people.

29. **Revelation 4:4**—The "white robes" represent purity. The "crowns of gold" represent victory. (The word used is the "victor's crown.")

30. **Revelation 4:5**—The fullness of the power and sovereignty of the Almighty God are displayed (Ex. 19:16-20; Psa. 18:12-18; 77:18), demonstrating the very presence of God in that place.

31. **Revelation 4:5**—"The seven Spirits of God" is the Holy Spirit (1:4). The "seven" (perfect number) "lamps of fire" reflect the Spirit's role in bringing the light of God's truth (John 6:63; 16:7) to man (2 Pet. 1:20-21; 2 Tim. 3:16-17).

32. **Revelation 4:6**—The "sea of glass" was temporarily separating John from the throne, but later God's people "stand on the sea" (15:2), and ultimately the separating "sea" will be "no more" (21:1).

33. **Revelation 4:8**—This parallels the worship of the seraphim in Isaiah 6. Around the throne of God is constant worship, perhaps with representations of His entire creation (living creatures) glorifying Him.

34. **Revelation 4:10**—The whole heavenly court joins in the worship, perhaps representing redeemed humanity. Thus, all of the worship of all of God's creation is directed toward Him (and not Caesar).

35. **Revelation 4:10**—To "cast their crowns" is acknowledgement of God's complete sovereignty. While no crown is worthy to be worn around Him, the crown of victory has been given by Him. The redeemed will "reign" in a sense, but not in equality with God.

Mark Your Bible

36. **Revelation 4:11** — Only Jehovah is "Lord"! Only Jehovah is Creator! Only Jehovah is "worthy" of all praise — not Rome or Caesar!
37. **Revelation 5:1** — The O.T. prophets of Isaiah, Ezekiel and Daniel wrote of scrolls/books with seals. This was common.
38. **Revelation 5:1** — "Written on the inside and the back" may have indicated it was filled with importance or, more likely, that the message contained therein was complete. This scroll likely contained God's providential plans for the world yet to be unfolded.
39. **Revelation 5:1** — The word "sealed" is in the perfect tense, emphasizing (along with the number "seven," which symbolizes perfection/completion) how securely the book was sealed. Secured seals could only be opened by the one qualified with the proper authority to do so.
40. **Revelation 5:2, 4** — A "worthy" one would have the rank and qualifications necessary. Only such a one would have the ability to open.
41. **Revelation 5:3** — Only a Divine being would be capable of opening and directing events yet to come.
42. **Revelation 5:4** — The Greek word *klaio* indicates "weeping audibly," like a child who is hurt. It is in the imperfect tense, indicating continuous activity.
43. **Revelation 5:6** — "Horns" were a symbol of power, thus Jesus has perfect/complete power to overcome His enemies and defend His people. "Eyes" symbolize vision and wisdom, thus Jesus has perfect/complete/full vision that is ever vigilant for His people (Zech. 4:10), seeing and knowing all things in the lives of His people.
44. **Revelation 5:8** — Christ is deity and worthy of worship. The throne will later be called both "the throne of God and of the Lamb" (22:3).
45. **Revelation 5:8** — "Saints" are God's holy ones on this earth, who are members of His church (Rom. 1:7; Phil. 1:1). They are Christians.

(continued on next page)

Mark Your Bible

46. **Revelation 5:9**—The Greek word used for "new" here is *kainos,* which emphasizes a new kind (not "new" in point of time). This is a unique song, centered on the sacrifice of Christ and the redemption that He provides through His blood. That makes Him "worthy" of all praise!

47. **Revelation 5:9**—Christ purchased the church with His blood (Acts 20:28), into which "all nations" were to "flow" (Isa. 2:2-3). There is not any person or nation who cannot receive the benefits of the blood of Christ. It is for "every" possible person (Heb. 2:9).

48. **Revelation 5:10**—The "kingdom" is a present reality (1:9; Col. 1:13), not some yet-future hope. All of those in His church (v. 9) are in His kingdom (v. 10).

49. **Revelation 5:10**—All Christians are priests (1:6; 1 Pet. 2:5, 9). There is no specialized priesthood warranted or needed.

50. **Revelation 5:10**—God's people are redeemed now, in the kingdom now and reigning on earth now. This is not talking about some future millennial reign. They are worshiping Christ at His throne now and they are reigning with Him as part of His kingdom now. What a great message of encouragement and hope for those being tortured by a pagan ruler and kingdom!

51. **Revelation 5:11**—Christians need not fear the hosts of the Roman army. The heavenly host is greater—in number and might.

52. **Revelation 5:12**—There are seven traits worthy of praise in this verse. These are ascribed to Christ here and to the Father in 4:11; 5:13; 7:12. Jesus is Divine!

53. **Revelation 5:13**—"Under the earth" is likely a reference to the Hadean realm. Praise is offered equally and fully to both the Father and the Son. Nature is personified elsewhere in Scripture as praising God (Psa. 148:7-10).

54. **Revelation 5:14**—The word "said" is in the imperfect tense, indicating that they "kept saying over and over and over, 'Amen!'"

Mark Your Bible

55. **Revelation 6:1**—The announcement to simply "Come" was probably directed at the horsemen, to go ahead and ride across the stage of this drama. These horsemen were instruments of heavenly judgment, for "was given" to them their weapons, power and victory (6:2, 4, 8), showing the concession of the permissive will of God.

56. **Revelation 6:2**—"White" is a symbol of victory. A white horse was always a sign of a conqueror riding in triumphal march. This appears to be outside conquest, as the bow symbolized military power (Jer. 51:56; Psa. 46:9), but it was a weapon of the Parthian army and not Rome. Write, "The white horse of conquest."

57. **Revelation 6:4**—"Red" pictured bloodshed as a result of war. "Kill one another" probably signifies civil war, which would continue to lead to bloody persecution of Christians. Write, "The red horse of war."

58. **Revelation 6:5-6**—This is "The black horse of famine," which usually follows war. Everything is counted and weighed on the scales. A working day's wage (i.e., denarius) would be enough to buy just enough food for one man to eat in one day (i.e., a quart of wheat) or just enough cheap barley to feed his family for one day. Famine and starvation reigned. But the luxuries of oil and wine for the rich would flow freely for them. Christians would suffer economic persecution under Rome.

59. **Revelation 6:8**—On the heels of pestilence comes the "pale horse of death." There would be much death, and Hades would gather up the spirits of the dead. The graves and Hades would fill up due to every kind of calamitous death. Widespread devastation was coming but it would be limited, as only a portion of the earth is affected.

60. **Revelation 6:9**—God was going to judge Rome (as seen in the first four seals) for what is revealed in the fifth seal. A brazen altar of sacrifice was used at the tabernacle and the temple, and the blood of the victims was poured out at the base of the altar (Lev. 4:7). A figurative sacrificial altar is seen with bloody martyrs underneath.

(continued on next page)

Mark Your Bible

61. **Revelation 6:10**—"Those who dwell on the earth" is used in the book of Revelation to refer to those who are not God's people.

62. **Revelation 6:11**—They are given white robes of victory. They are provided "rest" (see 14:13), as they await reunion. Persecution would continue but God's providence is at work for His people. So, be patient and let God work His plan. These same souls are in 20:4.

63. **Revelation 6:12-14**—Each of these natural calamities is found in the O.T. with reference to God's judgment upon nations or cities (Psa. 102:25-26; Isa. 13:10-13; 34:4-5; 50:3; Jer. 4:23-28; Ezek. 32:7-8; 38:18-23; Joel 2:10-11, 28-31; Nah. 1:5). This sixth seal could represent a temporal judgment of God upon the nation of Rome (as these O.T. verses may show), or depict the second coming of Christ as "the great day of His wrath" (6:17) comes to completely and finally overthrow the enemies of Christ. Whichever of these two meanings it is, it is certain that God does not tolerate rebellion, He will defend His faithful people, and His judgment against evil will come.

64. **Revelation 6:15-16**—Seven classes of mankind represent all of the godless inhabitants of earth, from the highest to the lowest. All are seized with fear (Joel 2:1; Hos. 10:8).

65. **Revelation 6:17**—God's judgment is inescapable (Joel 2:11).

66. **Revelation 7:1**—The number "four" usually symbolized things of the earth, like the four points of a compass. The four winds here are symbolic of Divine retribution (Jer. 4:11-12; 18:17; 49:32, 36; Ezek. 5:2; 1:14; Psa. 106:27; Job 38:24; Isa. 41:16).

67. **Revelation 7:2-3**—One who had "the seal of the living God" on them indicated (1) ownership (they belonged to God, 2 Tim. 2:19) and (2) protection (from the wrath of God that was to come, Ezek. 9:4-6). This seal of ownership is later contrasted with the "mark of the beast" (13:16-17). Which seal/mark should a Christian want?

68. **Revelation 7:4-8**—Much controversy has surrounded these verses. As seen in the "Helpful Notes," the 144,000 is symbolic of all of God's people on EARTH (not heaven), who needed to be sealed

Mark Your Bible

with the ownership and protection of God during the coming storms of Divine judgment. John is not making a distinction between Jews and Gentiles. If these verses focus on the Jews who are saved, why are Abraham, Isaac and Jacob excluded? Why is the tribe of Dan excluded? Why is there a "tribe of Joseph"? Throughout the N.T., Israel is used as a type of the church, God's spiritual/ true "Israel of God" (Rom. 2:28-29; 9:6-8; 10:12; Gal. 3:29; 6:16). The 144,000 represent complete fullness of God's church (His new, spiritual Israel), who are protected by His seal to be brought safely through the tribulations.

69. **Revelation 7:9**—This "great multitude" is the same people as in verses 1-8, but now they are out of the world and in the very presence of God, "standing before the throne." The word "standing" is in the perfect tense, denoting now a permanent position. They had "overcome" and are now receiving His eternal promises.

70. **Revelation 7:9**—The "white" robes symbolized victory (and purity) and the palm branches symbolized joy and rejoicing.

71. **Revelation 7:10**—Salvation did not belong to Rome! The one "on the throne" was not Rome! The One "who sits on the throne" and to whom belongs "salvation" is "our God"! Circle "our."

72. **Revelation 7:12**—Everyone in heaven worships God with a sevenfold ascription of praise, beginning and ending with "Amen!" Each of the seven elements of this amazing doxology is preceded in the Greek with the definite article—"*The* blessing and *the* glory and *the* wisdom, *the* thanksgiving and *the* honor and *the* power and *the* might, Be to our God" for all of eternity. No one else is worthy!

73. **Revelation 7:14**—"Come out" is in the present tense, denoting a continual process, perhaps viewing Christians who are continually "coming out" of the tribulations of the world and into heaven.

74. **Revelation 7:14**—The "great tribulation" is not something at the end of time. They were already enduring it (1:2, 9; 2:10, 13; 6:9-11). It is a time of intense suffering and persecution.

(continued on next page)

Mark Your Bible

75. **Revelation 7:15**—The reward for the redeemed is that they will always be before the throne of God and always serving Him in glorious splendor. Rome demanded that the image of the emperor be worshiped (at least once a year). God's faithful who worship only Him on this earth will worship and serve Him personally (not a mere image of Him) forever and ever.

76. **Revelation 7:16**—The language of this protection is found in Isaiah 49:10. Momentary affliction here (2 Cor. 4:17) stands in stark contrast to the eternal weight of glory before God's throne.

77. **Revelation 7:17**—This language is borrowed from Isaiah 25:8. See also Psalm 126:5.

December 9 Week 49, Day 7

Day of Reflection

Take time today to reflect on the five chapters that you read this week. You may choose to read all five chapters again, in one sitting, or certain parts of them. Take time today to answer at least one of these questions below. You may or may not write anything down—you can choose to write or simply reflect.

1. What personal application do I need to make from the chapters I have read this week?

2. How can these five chapters help draw me closer to Jesus?

3. What words, phrases or verses in these chapters do I want to go back and study more in depth?

4. What questions do I have about what I have read this week on which I need to do some further Biblical research?

Week 50

December 10-16

December 10	Read Revelation 8
December 11	Read Revelation 9
December 12	Read Revelation 10
December 13	Read Revelation 11
December 14	Read Revelation 12
December 15	Mark Your Bible
December 16	Day of Reflection

Prayer for this week:

"Heavenly Father,
let me not be distracted by this world and
help me to focus fully on You!"

December 10 Week 50, Day 1

Revelation 8

Helpful Notes:

1. **Trumpets** = The seals of the last vision were used to hide things until they were opened; trumpets, however, are used to announce things, particularly warnings of impending judgment (Joel 2:1-11; Ezek. 33:3; Isa. 27:13); they often indicated God's intervention in this world's affairs (Ex. 19:16, 19); the seven trumpets here are for shouting warning and judgment on Rome and calling for immediate repentance; seven is symbolic of the completeness of the task.
2. **Incense of prayers** = The golden altar for incense stood outside the Most Holy Place and here it is "before the throne"; incense may not represent the prayers themselves but the intercession that Christ adds to the prayers (1 John 2:1; Heb. 7:25), which brings them to the throne of God as a sweet savor, pleasing to God and indicative of a forthcoming answer from Him; God heard the prayers of His suffering, struggling people, and He answered in verse 5.
3. **One third** = One third indicates the intentionally partial nature of these warning judgments upon wicked men (like the fractions in Zechariah 13:8-9), thus they do not represent the last and final day of God's judgment at the end of time; a large part (one third) is affected but it is not universal; the partial destruction is designed to give men an opportunity to reflect, repent and turn to God.

1. What imagery is used to depict the prayers of the saints ascending to God in heaven?

2. What name was given to the flaming meteor that fell in the fresh water?

3. What was the angel flying through heaven saying?

Verse for Meditation and Prayer: **Revelation 8:4**

"And the smoke of the incense, with the prayers of the saints, ascended before God from the angel's hand."

Revelation 9

Helpful Notes:

1. **The bottomless pit** = A "key" in this book symbolizes authority to open; demonic forces (in the form of demon-like locusts) come from the bottomless pit to fulfill God's purposes in punishing the persecutors of His people; "bottomless pit" is found seven times in this book and appears to refer to the intermediate dwelling place of wicked/fallen spirits (Luke 8:31; Rev. 20:1-3), paralleled with Tartarus (2 Pet. 2:4).
2. **Locusts** = Locusts were a devasting force (used as the eighth plague against Egypt, Ex. 10:1-20), usually traveling in huge swarms that appeared like oncoming dark clouds (read Joel 2:1-11); locusts usually destroyed vegetation, but here they are tormenting the enemies of Christ who did "not have the seal of God" (7:3-4). (See "Mark Your Bible" for 9:5-10.)
3. **Army of two hundred million** = This is the largest number in the book; the number is twice ten thousand times ten thousand, emphasizing a massive and complete number; they were released from the river Euphrates and set on killing; this may represent Rome's most dreaded enemy who they never fully conquered—the Parthians, who were just beyond the Euphrates and fought skillfully upon horses; this may symbolize the external invasion of an evil secular power that would be used in the hand of God to punish the oppressors of His people.

1. What arose out of the bottomless pit?

2. Who was protected from the army of locusts?

3. Although they worshiped idols, what could idols not do?

Verse for Meditation and Prayer: **Revelation 9:20**

"But the rest of mankind, who were not killed by these plagues, did not repent of the works of their hands, that they should not worship demons, and idols of gold, silver, brass, stone, and wood, which can neither see nor hear nor walk."

Revelation 10

Helpful Notes:

1. **Interlude** = As he did with the seals (in chap. 7), John inserts a pause or interlude in the drama between the sixth and seventh symbols in the series; the purpose of the interlude is to pause the building drama and to give strong reassurance to the people of God; in this interlude (10:1-11:13), there are four main symbolic pictures: the angel and the seven thunders (10:1-7), the little book (10:8-11), the measuring of the temple (11:1-2), and the two witnesses (11:3-13); Divine retribution is coming upon God's enemies, which will entail difficulties, but God's people are known and protected by Him, and the cause of Christ will be victorious.
2. **A little book** = This "little" book was to reveal part of God's purposes; the command to eat was similarly made to Ezekiel (Ezek. 2:8-3:4); the message from God would be "sweet" (joyful) to receive, but it would be "bitter" (tough) to deliver; some think the book contained the rest of the prophecies (starting in chapter 12), while others think it contained messages of sorrow and woe for those who have rejected God; whatever the content, John was to consume it, master it and continue preaching it.
3. **Seven thunders** = Thunder is symbolic in the book of warnings of Divine judgments (8:5; 11:19; 16:18); the number seven represents completeness; the message delivered must have been of complete and full warning of impending Divine wrath; nothing should be attempted to literalize the seven thunders.

1. Where did the mighty angel stand?

2. What was John told to do with the little book?

3. What affect would the little book have on John?

Verse for Meditation and Prayer: **Revelation 10:10**

"Then I took the little book out of the angel's hand and ate it,
and it was as sweet as honey in my mouth.
But when I had eaten it, my stomach became bitter."

Revelation 11

Helpful Notes:

1. **Measure the temple of God** = This is not the literal temple, as it was destroyed in A.D. 70, nor is this a supposed restored temple at the end of the world; the temple that Ezekiel measured was not a physical temple either (Ezek. 40); the temple is the true spiritual Israel—i.e., the church (1 Cor. 3:16; 2 Cor. 6:16; Eph. 2:21; 1 Pet. 2:5), the people of God; God's people were being measured for protection and deliverance (cf. Zech. 2:2), in the midst of persecutions and tribulations; this does not mean physical harm or death would not come to them, but God's hand was going to be over them.
2. **Three-and-a-half** = This is half of seven (which is completeness or perfection); so, three-and-a-half represents incompleteness, indefinite but limited; the incompleteness may not only represent the restlessness associated with the experience but also the inadequacies of the enemy of God to overcome His people; 42 months (11:2), 1,260 days (11:3; 12:6) and "a time, and times, and half a time" (12:14; cf. Dan. 7:25; 12:7) are all equivalent with 3.5 years; this was an indefinite time of turmoil, but it would not last forever.
3. **Two witnesses** = Rather than literal, the number "two" symbolizes strength; there is great strength in the Scriptures and in the church's witnessing/proclamation of them; even in the face of adversity, the militant spirit of true Christians and their publication of the gospel would remain strong and undeterred.

1. As a sign of protection, what did the angel tell John to measure?

2. When the kingdoms of this world fail, what do we know about the kingdom of Christ?

3. Upon whose power and reign should Christians focus?

Verse for Meditation and Prayer: **Revelation 11:15**

"Then the seventh angel sounded: And there were loud voices in heaven, saying, 'The kingdoms of this world have become the kingdoms of our Lord and of His Christ, and He shall reign forever and ever!'"

Revelation 12

Helpful Notes:

1. **Child** = The "male Child" is easily identified as the one "who was to rule all nations with a rod of iron" (v. 5); this is a quote from Psalm 2:9, which is Messianic and applies to Christ; His earthly life is depicted from His birth to His ascension, when He was "caught up to God and His throne"; Jesus was victorious over the devil, and His people will be also (v. 10-11).
2. **Woman** = Identifying the Child helps in identifying the woman; the woman is not the virgin Mary, as verses 13-17 will not apply to a single individual; some have identified her as the nation of Israel, who produced the Christ, and some have identified her as the church; it seems best to combine these and see the woman as symbolic of God's redeemed people, spiritual Israel (Gal. 4:26), as both the woman and her Child are targets of the devil's wrath; Scripture often depicts God's people and the church as a woman (Isa. 54:5-6; Jer. 6:2; 2 Cor. 11:2; Eph. 5:22-33); see her "offspring" in verse 17.
3. **Dragon** = The dragon is identified as "that serpent of old" (cf. Gen. 3:1-19), "the Devil and Satan"; the Greek word for "devil" (*diabolos*) means "slanderer, accuser," and the Greek word for "Satan" means "adversary"; his "red" color symbolizes the blood he will shed; the "seven heads" symbolize authority; the "ten horns" symbolize great power; the "seven diadems," worn by royalty, may symbolize his deception; the "tail" shows great strength.

1. What does Satan do to "the whole world," according to verse 9?

2. How do the persecuted overcome, according to verse 11?

3. What is it that Satan "knows that he has"?

Verse for Meditation and Prayer: **Revelation 12:11**

"And they overcame him by the blood of the Lamb and by the word of their testimony, and they did not love their lives to the death."

Mark Your Bible

1. **Revelation 8:1**—The seventh seal, seventh trumpet and seventh bowl are used as transition and preparation for what happens next.
2. **Revelation 8:1**—The silence represents a short delay in judgment, but silence always indicates that something is to come and is used as a dramatic effect of suspense, reverence and expectation. The silence may also be indicative that God silenced every other creature in heaven in order to hear the prayers of His saints on earth.
3. **Revelation 8:1**—"Half an hour" is not to be taken literally. It simply symbolizes a short period of time.
4. **Revelation 8:2**—The seventh seal unfolds the entire group of seven trumpets that are ready to sound.
5. **Revelation 8:2**—The "seven angels" here are different than other angels in the book. They have a special position and mission.
6. **Revelation 8:5**—Noises, thunder, lightning and earthquake are also associated with the seventh trumpet (11:19) and the seventh bowl (16:18). God's judgments are about to come.
7. **Revelation 8:6**—Not every detail in Revelation has a corresponding significance. Rather than trying to give meaning to every detail, focus on the whole picture being presented. God's people are under severe oppression of the vile Roman empire, and God is bringing about a destruction of these hostile forces and the triumph of His people. It is a drama unfolding, with devastating warnings and comforting revelations.
8. **Revelation 8:7**—Scientists at that time classified nature in four parts: land, sea, fresh water and heavenly bodies. The first four trumpets are figuratively (not literally) unleashing God's judgment upon nature, as a warning of judgments upon wicked men.
9. **Revelation 8:7-9:19**—History reveals the downfall of the Roman empire was due in large part to (1) natural calamities, (2) internal rottenness and (3) external invasion. The first four trumpets predict natural calamities, the fifth foretells internal rottenness and the sixth deals with external invasion.

(continued on next page)

Mark Your Bible

10. **Revelation 8:7**—The land was struck. This is reminiscent of the seventh plague upon the Egyptians (Ex. 9:24).

11. **Revelation 8:8**—The seas were struck. This is reminiscent of the first plague upon the Egyptians (Ex. 7:20-21). In the O.T., the movement or removal of mountains (or being on fire) always symbolized troublesome times (Psa. 46:2; Isa. 54:10; Ezek. 38:20; Mic. 1:4).

12. **Revelation 8:10-11**—The fresh water was struck. Wormwood water is used in the O.T. as a symbol of suffering or punishment for evildoing (Deut. 29:18; Prov. 5:4; Jer. 9:15; 23:15).

13. **Revelation 8:12**—The heavenly bodies were struck. This is reminiscent of the ninth plague upon the Egyptians (Ex. 10:21-23). This is figurative language, not literal. There are consequences for persecuting God's people. The purpose of these warnings is to call evil men to repentance and to prepare God's people for their deliverance (similar to the way the plagues were used in Egypt).

14. **Revelation 8:13**—The eagle was often a token of judgment (Matt. 24:28). "The inhabitants of the earth" is used throughout the book of Revelation of those earth-bound people who are rebellious, sinful and have rejected Christ as their Lord (3:10; 6:10; 11:10, etc.). The remaining three trumpets will announce the worst is coming.

15. **Revelation 9:1**—The first four trumpeted judgments were inflicted indirectly by means of natural forces, but the final three will be more personal and affect rebellious man directly.

16. **Revelation 9:4**—This is one reason that having "the seal of God" is so important (7:3-4).

17. **Revelation 9:5**—The number "five" symbolized limited power or incompleteness (so limited torment and not total devastation). "Five months" was also the lifespan of a locust.

18. **Revelation 9:6-10**—These locusts depict the torment inflicted by evil on the human spirit and conscience, and they show the power of sin. The nature of evil is to destroy and men often lead themselves to their own destruction. God wanted these people to repent.

Mark Your Bible

19. **Revelation 9:11** – The Hebrew "Abaddon" and Greek "Apollyon" both meant "Destroyer." Many have tried to identify him with a specific person, but such is futile. This likely symbolizes a hellish rottenness of internal corruption within Rome and among its corrupt rulers that ultimately led to the fall of the empire (and the deliverance of God's people).

20. **Revelation 9:17-19** – One should not get lost in the details or think that every detail has some symbolic meaning. These details have no prophetic or doctrinal significance, other than to add to the seriousness of the warning and the powerful impact of the drama.

21. **Revelation 9:20-21** – Here we learn that these judgments were (1) upon the evil world power (i.e., Christians might suffer from them in this life but not in the judgment), (2) designed to reassure Christians that Rome will never triumph over Christianity, and (3) punitive measures to get evil men to repent and turn to God. Unfortunately, the evil men did not repent but continued to engage in the worship of "demons" (i.e., idols, 1 Cor. 10:20).

22. **Revelation 10:1** – The rainbow connected this angel with the throne of God (4:3). Face shining like the sun and feet like pillars of fire symbolize how closely this angel has been with the presence of God and how seriously his message of Divine vindication must be taken.

23. **Revelation 10:2-3** – One foot on the sea and one foot on the land emphasizes that the message (his cry) is for the whole world.

24. **Revelation 10:4-6** – Whatever the seven thunders revealed was to be sealed up and kept secret (like visions in Daniel 12:4, 9). There would be no more warning – "delay no longer." The warning of the six trumpets was sufficient, repentance had not come and the time for retribution would not be delayed.

25. **Revelation 10:5** – This is similar to Daniel 12:7.

(continued on next page)

Mark Your Bible

26. **Revelation 10:7**—God's purpose is going to be completed. Rome cannot and will not thwart the plans of God for His church and for the redemption of mankind. The seventh trumpet would prove this to be true and open the way for God's purpose to be fulfilled.

27. **Revelation 10:11**—This would seem to indicate that the contents of the little book are the prophecies that John is yet to give in the rest of the book about "many peoples, nations, tongues and kings." Or, it is indicative that John had more preaching opportunities on the horizon.

28. **Revelation 11:1**—Understanding many of the symbols in this chapter is difficult, so one should be cautious in being dogmatic.

29. **Revelation 11:2**—The outer court represented those in the world and perhaps even unfaithful Christians who have fallen away.

30. **Revelation 11:3**—Sackcloth is a symbol of mourning and repentance (cf. Jonah 3:5-6).

31. **Revelation 11:4-6**—The vision in verses 4-13 of the two witnesses appears to divide into three parts (v. 4-6, 7-10, 11-13). At first (v. 4-6), the gospel would be preached with success. The vision of two olive trees and two lampstands comes from Zechariah 4. The church in its efforts to spread the gospel (represented in the strength of the two witnesses) will be the light to the world (the oil fueled the lampstand, perhaps indicating the Spirit's influence through the Bible to illuminate the world).

32. **Revelation 11:7-10**—The second part of the vision of the two witnesses (v. 7-10) shows a crushing force that comes against the two witnesses (the church preaching the gospel) and appears to have success in destroying it (at least temporarily). This represents the period of time in which the readers are living.

33. **Revelation 11:7**—The beast is a demonic force in league with Satan (coming from the bottomless pit of demonic spirits) but distinguished from Satan (20:10). The beast represents Rome and specifically the Roman emperor.

Mark Your Bible

34. **Revelation 11:8-9**—The crushing efforts of the Roman emperor against Christianity appear to be victorious and that the religion of Christ is dead, never to rise again. Sodom and Egypt symbolize the moral perversion and spiritual bondage of these evil people, who crucify afresh Christ and His work (cf. Heb. 6:6; 10:29). Three-and-a-half days is an indefinite but limited time (see "Helpful Notes"). This emphasizes the temporary nature of this extremely heinous persecution of the Christians.
35. **Revelation 11:10**—See "Mark Your Bible" for 3:10 and 6:10.
36. **Revelation 11:11-13**—The third part of the vision of the two witnesses (v. 11-13) shows the great triumph (which is just ahead) of the two witnesses (the church preaching the gospel) over the crushing persecution of Rome (the beast). God is more powerful than Rome and more powerful than any hostile force against God's people—God's people and the gospel will always be victorious.
37. **Revelation 11:11-12**—The enemies will see the revival of God's people and His cause (cf. Ezek. 37:10), and they will recognize that it was brought about by Divine power, for the Word of God cannot be chained (2 Tim. 2:9) or destroyed (1 Pet. 1:23-25; Matt. 24:35).
38. **Revelation 11:13**—A "tenth" may be symbolic of a small portion and 7,000 (7 [Divine completion] times 1,000 [a large sum or ultimate completeness by God]) must represent the complete number of those who needed to perish and did perish. This entire verse symbolically shows that this was an act of God in retribution for persecuting His people. Those who survived saw God's hand in it.
39. **Revelation 11:14**—The interlude is now over, which was designed as a message of Divine retribution against God's enemies, in order to reassure God's people that He will protect them and deliver them. After the fourth trumpet, three "woes" were to follow in the last three trumpets (8:13; 9:12). The seventh trumpet is the third woe.
40. **Revelation 11:15**—The seventh trumpet is transitional (see note on 8:1), leading to the next vision.

(continued on next page)

Mark Your Bible

41. **Revelation 11:15-19**—Some struggle with placing this section chronologically, since this is obviously an announcement of the final victory and triumph of Christ and His church/kingdom. Chapter 12 begins the second half of the book, so it may be that God has created parallel sections in the book (in the first half and then in the second half), which both look toward and work toward the end. Also, there are darker days ahead, as depicted in the second half of the book, so God is announcing the outcome of those days right here, before they are described. Going into the second half of the book and the dark days ahead, Christians could already know the outcome and remember what is coming—VICTORY!
42. **Revelation 11:15-17**—This is a picture of great triumph of Christ and His church. The "kingdoms of this world" had been broken under the hand of God, and HIS kingdom (His one kingdom) and NOT Rome will "reign forever and ever"! Rome is not eternal, but Christ is! Rome is not all-powerful, but Christ is! Rome is not the highest throne, but Christ's is! Rome's reign will not last forever, but Christ's will! Underline the last part of verse 15.
43. **Revelation 11:16**—Worship belongs to God, not Rome!
44. **Revelation 11:18**—This is a picture of the last judgment, when the rebellious nations (who have rebelled to their fullest extent against God) will receive the wrath of God, but God's faithful will be rewarded. God is sovereign—He rules over all!
45. **Revelation 11:19**—Because of the death of Christ on the cross, the veil into the very presence of God (the ark represented God's presence among His people) has been opened (Matt. 27:51; Heb. 10:20). The church (i.e., the temple of God, 1 Cor. 3:16; 2 Cor. 6:16) is victorious in God's eternal temple (see 1 Cor. 15:24-28; Heb. 12:26-28). God's promises in His covenant have not been forgotten but have been fully and gloriously realized! While it may appear sometimes that the enemy has won, Christians know that victory is ours!
46. **Revelation 12:1**—This begins the "second half" of the book (perhaps revealing the contents of the "little book," which John

Mark Your Bible

ate). A "great sign" and "another sign" (v. 3) "appeared in heaven" to show the Christians that the struggle in which they were engaged was started by Satan against God, and the Christians' present conflict was part of a greater conflict between God (with His forces that fought for everything that was right) and the devil (with his forces that fought for everything that was evil). The Christians were not alone in this battle. God was fully and personally engaged in the overthrow of their enemy—the devil and Rome. Christians will be victorious.

47. **Revelation 12:1, 3**—John reminds the readers, with the word "sign," that this revelation from Christ (the whole book) is written in symbolic language. The word also emphasizes that something quite marked and Divine is being presented.

48. **Revelation 12:4**—The stars here represent his angels under his charge.

49. **Revelation 12:5**—The "male child" is emphatic and literally reads "a son, a male child," perhaps to emphasize His strength and power as the One to "rule all the nations with a rod of iron." Christians need not fear Satan, as the Christ is more powerful.

50. **Revelation 12:5, 10**—Christ ascended into heaven to "His throne." This is depicted in Daniel 7:13-14. Upon Christ's death (Rev. 12:11; Acts 20:28), His resurrection (Acts 2:24-31), His ascension (Acts 1:9) and coronation (Acts 2:30-36), Christ's kingdom was established. Christ is reigning now (not in some future earthly millennium), which proves that the devil is not, as his power was stripped and limited by the blood of the Lamb (Heb. 2:14-15; Eph. 1:20-23).

51. **Revelation 12:6**—This represents God's providential care over His children, following the ascension of Christ and through all times of great trial. The persecution will be severe but it will be incomplete and limited in its time. (See "Helpful Notes" in Revelation 11 for 1,260 days, mentioned in 11:2-3 and again in 12:14.)

52. **Revelation 12:7**—Michael is called the "archangel" (Jude 9) and is seen defending Israel in Daniel 10:21; 12:1.

(continued on next page)

Mark Your Bible

53. **Revelation 12:7**—Contextually, this war in heaven breaks out upon the ascension of Jesus to His throne.

54. **Revelation 12:7-11**—This is NOT a recounting of the original fall of Satan. Keep it in context. By the enthroning of Christ in heaven, Satan was "cast out" and no longer permitted to accuse the saints before God (Rom. 8:33). The sacrificial blood of Christ (and His subsequent resurrection and coronation) for the sins of the world took Satan's greatest strength away from him (access to God to make accusations) and limited his power over man.

55. **Revelation 12:11**—Those who submit to Christ ("they")—this was speaking directly to the persecuted Christians in John's day—were able to and would continue to be able to overcome the devil by (1) what Christ did for them and (2) what they do for Christ. They loved the death of Christ more than they loved their own lives.

56. **Revelation 12:12**—Stripped of his greatest power (to make accusation directly to God), the devil will use every bit of his wrath to try to destroy mankind and the church, although he knows that he is now doomed to ultimate defeat. (See note on 8:13.)

57. **Revelation 12:14**—The devil relentlessly persecutes the church (v. 13), but God protects her. God told the Israelites that, in bringing them out of Egypt, "I bore you on eagles' wings and brought you to Myself" (Ex. 19:4). God will protect and nourish His people, even in the midst of great tribulation (He doesn't completely remove persecution), reminding them that the time will be indefinite but limited.

58. **Revelation 12:15-16**—Water is often used symbolically in the O.T. as a peril faced by God's people (Psa. 42:7; 124:4; Isa. 43:2), but God delivers through His providence (cf. Matt. 16:18b).

59. **Revelation 12:17**—Satan will go after other Christians, throughout the ages—whoever will "keep the commandments of God" and devote themselves faithfully to "the testimony of Jesus Christ."

Day of Reflection

Take time today to reflect on the five chapters that you read this week. You may choose to read all five chapters again, in one sitting, or certain parts of them. Take time today to answer at least one of these questions below. You may or may not write anything down—you can choose to write or simply reflect.

1. What personal application do I need to make from the chapters I have read this week?

2. How can these five chapters help draw me closer to Jesus?

3. What words, phrases or verses in these chapters do I want to go back and study more in depth?

4. What questions do I have about what I have read this week on which I need to do some further Biblical research?

Week 51

December 17-23

December 17	Read Revelation 13
December 18	Read Revelation 14
December 19	Read Revelation 15
December 20	Read Revelation 16
December 21	Read Revelation 17
December 22	Mark Your Bible
December 23	Day of Reflection

Prayer for this week:

"Heavenly Father,
thank You for giving me the power to
overcome trials and tribulations in life!"

December 17

Week 51, Day 1

Revelation 13

<u>Helpful Notes:</u>

1. **The beast of the sea** = The first beast represents the Roman emperor Domitian himself, who has been given authority and power by the devil (the dragon) to destroy Christians; the Roman emperor blasphemes God and demands to be worshiped as Lord and God; the pagan citizens worship him but the faithful Christians do not, which brings persecution and the sword.
2. **The beast of the earth** = The second beast represents some kind of priesthood (or strong arm, even a committee or official body) of the Roman emperor who enforces the worship of the first beast (Roman emperor) in each town, even making images to make it easier and universal for all to worship the emperor as "Lord and God"; he is referred to as "the false prophet" (16:13; 19:20; 20:10), which also denotes his religious affiliation.
3. **The mark of the beast** = Those who worshiped the beast were given a mark—which was the name of the beast or the number of his name; this mark represented the identifying mark of ownership of those who worship and follow the emperor (as the seal of God represented God's ownership and protection of His people, 7:2-4); faithful Christians could not (and would not) worship the beast, so they would not receive the mark, which in turn meant they suffered physically and economically, unable to buy and sell.

1. What did the world say in their worship of the beast?

2. What does it mean that Christ (the Lamb) was "slain from the foundation of the world"?

3. According to verse 10, what is needful for the saints?

Verse for Meditation and Prayer: **<u>Revelation 13:4</u>**

"So they worshiped the dragon who gave authority to the beast;
and they worshiped the beast, saying,
'Who is like the beast? Who is able to make war with him?'"

December 18 Week 51, Day 2

Revelation 14

Helpful Notes:

1. **Mount Zion** = Zion was the citadel of David in Jerusalem; the name was often used of Jerusalem as a whole, which was set on a mountain, thus "Mount Zion"; the name "Zion" was used in the O.T. to refer to God's faithful people (Mic. 4:1-7; Joel 2:32; Isa. 24:21-23; 40:1-9); it always represented victory; in the N.T., it is used in contrast to Mount Sinai, for it is "the heavenly Jerusalem, the city of the living God" (Heb. 12:22); it represents the throne and presence of God among His people and especially in heaven.
2. **Hell** = This is one of the most terrifying descriptions of hell in Scripture: (1) hell will be the experience of the "full strength" wrath of God; (2) hell will be a fully conscious torment with the intense punishment of fire and brimstone, reserved for the devil and his angels (20:10; Matt. 25:41); (3) hell will last "forever and ever"; (4) in hell, there will be "no rest day or night"; (5) hell's punishment will carry with it a full consciousness of just guilt, symbolized in this text by the presence (and consent) of Christ and His angels.
3. **Die in the Lord** = All will die, but not all will die "in the Lord"; one must enter "into Christ" through baptism (Rom. 6:3-4; Gal. 3:27), and then remain steadfast "in Christ" (Eph. 1:3, 7; 2:10; 1 John 1:7), in order to be "blessed" in death; death should not be something a Christian fears.

1. Instead of having the name of the beast as a mark, whose name did the Christians have on their foreheads?

2. How do we know hell will be a conscious punishment?

3. What is the promise for those who die "in the Lord"?

Verse for Meditation and Prayer: **Revelation 14:13**

"Then I heard a voice from heaven saying to me, 'Write: "Blessed are the dead who die in the Lord from now on." "Yes," says the Spirit, "that they may rest from their labors, and their works follow them."'"

December 19

Week 51, Day 3

Revelation 15

Helpful Notes:

1. **Bowls** = The seals were used to hide things until they were being opened; the trumpets were used to announce the warnings of impending judgment; now the announcing and warning are over; bowls are used to pour out and execute God's final judgment upon Rome; the number "7" symbolizes completeness, thus God's complete justice (wrath) was being brought against Rome.
2. **Plagues** = The term "plagues" would ring in the ears of John's readers; plagues were frequently used in the O.T. as instruments of punishment upon the wicked, and it would likely call to mind the ten plagues against the Egyptians, through which the enemy was afflicted but the people of God were delivered; the pouring out of these seven "last plagues" indicated that this will "finish/complete" God's just punishment of this vile nation.
3. **Tabernacle of the testimony** = This expression was used frequently in the O.T. for the tabernacle revealed and constructed at Mount Sinai (Ex. 38:21); it was given this name because it housed the ark of the covenant, in which were kept the Ten Commandments (Ex. 25:16; 32:15); the imagery of the Holy of Holies being "opened" in heaven was symbolic of the presence of God, from which the seven angels came to fulfill the will of God.

1. What were the seven angels bringing forth?

2. Who was standing on the sea of glass?

3. What is the gist of the song that the redeemed sing?

Verse for Meditation and Prayer: **Revelation 15:3**

"They sing the song of Moses, the servant of God, and the song of the Lamb, saying: 'Great and marvelous are Your works, Lord God Almighty! Just and true are Your ways, O King of the saints!'"

Revelation 16

Helpful Notes:

1. **Their just due** = The judgments of God are "true and righteous" (19:2; Gen. 18:25; Psa. 19:9); sin has consequences and will receive just punishment (i.e., what it deserves) for working against God and His will (1 John 3:4; Rom. 6:23); God is not "unjust" when He "inflicts wrath" (Rom. 3:3-9), for one "reaps" what he "sows" (Gal. 6:7); "all the nations that forget God" will "be turned into hell" (Psa. 9:17); man must not censure His righteous punishments.
2. **Blasphemed God** = Even though it would be obvious that God was the source of these punishments and had "power over these plagues," it is stated twice that the wicked recipients "did not repent" (16:9, 11), and three times it is stated that they "blasphemed God" (16:9, 11, 21) in the midst of the plague; their hearts were hardened and would not be moved; such is the nature of sin.
3. **Armageddon** = This is symbolic, not literal; Armageddon is the hill (elevated plain) of Megiddo in northwest Palestine where numerous decisive battles took place (ex: Egypt defeated Syria; Barak and Deborah defeated Sisera and Canaan; Gideon defeated the Midianites; Jehu killed Ahaz; Pharoah Necho killed Josiah); here it is not a specific location as it is a specific occasion; this is not a material, physical battle; it is the battle between righteousness and evil, between the forces of Satan and the forces of Christ, and Christ will be the victor (the actual battle is in chapter 19).

1. What did the angel of the waters say about God?

2. How bad was the pain of the fifth bowl that brought darkness?

3. What beatitude is stated?

Verse for Meditation and Prayer: **Revelation 16:15**

"Behold, I am coming as a thief. Blessed is he who watches, and keeps his garments, lest he walk naked and they see his shame."

December 21 Week 51, Day 5

Revelation 17

Helpful Notes:

1. **The great harlot** = This is a reference to the city of Rome, "that great city which reigns over the kings of the earth" (17:18); she was called "Babylon the Great, the Mother of Harlots" (17:5; cf. 18:5, 10), and she persecutes the saints (17:6; 18:20, 24); she is sitting on seven mountains (17:9), which is true of the city of Rome; she is a leading commercial power (18:3, 11-19); the first readers of this book would have recognized distinct references to the persecuting imperial Rome in the description of the harlot.
2. **The scarlet beast** = This is a reference to the Roman empire which supports the wicked city, and perhaps personified in a specific emperor (Domitian, the beast of the sea in ch. 13); the "names of blasphemy" may be the many gods of the empire; the seven heads are identified as the seven mountains (Rome sits on seven hills) and also as seven kings (see note for 17:10); the ten horns represent the ten kings and immense power of the empire (see note for 17:12).
3. **Overcome** = The focus of this book has repeatedly been upon the Christian who "overcomes"; the focus is now placed on the One who makes that possible—"the Lamb will overcome"; the Greek *nikao* means "to win in the face of obstacles; be victor, conquer, prevail"; Jesus Christ, the Lamb of God, the Lord of lords and King of kings, will overcome the beast and all those associated with him.

1. On what was the woman (i.e., Rome) drunk?

2. Who will overcome the forces of evil with the Lamb?

3. What words show the providence of God in verse 17?

Verse for Meditation and Prayer: **Revelation 17:14**

"These will make war with the Lamb, and the Lamb will overcome them,
for He is Lord of lords and King of kings;
and those who are with Him are called, chosen, and faithful."

Mark Your Bible

1. **Revelation 13:1**—The dragon is the one standing on the sand of the sea. He is the one giving power to the forthcoming beasts.
2. **Revelation 13:1**—Seven heads symbolize authority (seen as mountains in 17:9); ten horns symbolize great power (seen as ten kings in 17:12); ten crowns represent royalty, gained by deception, for each head bears a blasphemous name.
3. **Revelation 13:2**—This beast bears striking resemblance to the four beasts that Daniel saw come out of the sea (Dan. 7:1-8), the fourth one bearing ten horns represented Rome. This beast seems to combine all the brutality and evil of all four of Daniel's beasts into the evil persecution being unleased by Rome.
4. **Revelation 13:3**—Ideas vary on this but perhaps the "mortally wounded" was reference to the well-known myth in that day (not necessarily giving it credence) called "Nero *Redivivus*," which believed that Nero would return (either from death or from the land of the Parthians) and rule again (wounded but healed). Or it may simply refer to a Nero-type emperor reviving and intensifying the policies and persecutions of Nero (believed to be fulfilled in Domitian).
5. **Revelation 13:5**—See "Helpful Notes" for Revelation 11.
6. **Revelation 13:8**—See marking note for 3:10. "All who dwell on the earth" does not include Christians.
7. **Revelation 13:8**—Two truths are affirmed: (1) the Lamb was slain from the foundation of the world (planned from eternity, 1 Pet. 1:19-20; Eph. 3:10-11); (2) those who obey the commandments of the Lord and remain faithful were foreordained to have their names written in the Book of Life (21:27; 3:5; Phil. 4:3; Heb. 12:23; Eph. 1:4).
8. **Revelation 13:10**—The Lord does not desire for His people to take up the sword in their defense (Matt. 26:52), but to allow the Lord to mete out His justice and avenge His people (Rom. 12:19). Thus, He calls on His people to be patient and faithful (2:10; Heb. 10:35-39).
9. **Revelation 13:11**—The number two represents strength, which may show the force of this beast, but having

(continued on next page)

Mark Your Bible

fewer horns (i.e., more limited power) than the first beast (Roman emperor) himself. "Lamb" is a religious symbol. So, he shows himself outwardly to be religious but his messages are diabolical like the devil.

10. **Revelation 13:13**—These were pseudo prophets doing pseudo miracles—acts of deception. God does not allow false religions to do genuine miracles. These would be "lying wonders" (2 Thess. 2:9).
11. **Revelation 13:14**—The beast of the earth (the priesthood, enforcing group) had the duty of building images of the emperor, altars for his worship, and doing everything they could to enforce the state religion and the worship of the emperor. In forcing the people to worship the emperor, they identified those who did and punished those who refused.
12. **Revelation 13:15**—This priesthood caused the images of the beast to appear to speak, like ventriloquism, as if the emperor himself was speaking, demanding worship and calling upon rebels to be killed.
13. **Revelation 13:16**—Some heathen religions used brand-like marks to identify their adherents. For the Christian, worshiping the Roman emperor as Lord and God was blasphemy and was something they had to refuse at all costs (14:9-11; 16:2; 19:20; 20:4).
14. **Revelation 13:17**—When Christians refused to worship the emperor, they were in turn refused the privilege to buy and sell in the market place (and thus to feed their family).
15. **Revelation 13:18**—"The number of the beast" is "the number of a man," which is 666. Myriads of suggestions (even dogmatic claims) have been made to tie a specific person or name to this number (from Roman emperors in that day to the Pope to vile rulers in the modern era). All such attempts would seem very subjective (and some of them very forced) given our knowledge (i.e., limited knowledge) today. Perhaps it is as simple as considering that numbers in Revelation are symbolic. The number "6" represented evil, failure, imperfection (as one number short of seven, which is Divine perfection). This "mark of the beast" is contrasted with "the

Mark Your Bible

seal of God" that was given to "the servants of God" (7:3). Perhaps the number "6" in triplicate ("666") was simply meant to signify total evil, failure and imperfection to an extreme level. Whether this was embodied in a specific person (like the emperor/beast himself) or whether it was meant to symbolize evil in full rebellion against God, the point was that no Christian should do anything to bear this mark. Remain steadfast and do not give in, so that you can wear the "seal of God" and belong to Him!

16. **Revelation 14:1**—Chapter 14 is another interlude (like 7:1-17 and 10:1-11:13), following a very troubling scene, to give comfort and reassurance to God's faithful. The horrible scene in chapter 13 was of the beast standing on the earth and tormenting for 42 months (an indefinite but limited time of torment), and it gives way to this glorious scene of the Lamb standing on Mount Zion for all eternity, picturing the final triumph of the redeemed.
17. **Revelation 14:1**—The 144,000 represent the whole body of the redeemed. (See "Helpful Notes" in Revelation 7.) In chapter 7, they are on the earth, and in chapter 14, they are in heaven.
18. **Revelation 14:1**—Having the name of God "written on their foreheads" is in direct contrast to the unfaithful having the name of the emperor marked on their foreheads in 13:16-17. This "seal of God" (7:2-4) represented Divine identification and ownership.
19. **Revelation 14:2**—The three descriptions of the voice emphasize its overwhelming strength and beauty.
20. **Revelation 14:3**—This is a song of victory, a song of redemption, that only the body of the redeemed (the 144,000) know and understand, for they have been purchased "from the earth" by the blood of the Lamb (Acts 20:28; 1 Pet. 1:18-19; 1 Cor. 6:19-20).
21. **Revelation 14:4**—The redeemed of Christ are pure and unblemished (Eph. 5:25-27), because they have not engaged in spiritual fornication by worshiping the emperor or any of his idols. These have been loyal to the Lamb, having offered themselves as "firstfruits" sacrifices, set aside for God Himself (Ex. 23:19; 34:26).

(continued on next page)

Mark Your Bible

22. **Revelation 14:5**—They were "without fault" and "blameless" because the Lamb who redeemed them was "without blemish and without spot" (1 Pet. 1:19), making those who offered themselves to God to be like the sacrificial Lamb.

23. **Revelation 14:6-7**—The "everlasting gospel" is the eternal good news that is for all people of the earth, to call them to repent, turn to God from idols and worship the true Creator of all things, rather than obeying the command to worship the image of the beast.

24. **Revelation 14:7**—This verse is the turning point in the book. Up to this point, Rome has been punishing the people of God. Now, from this point forward, God's "judgment has come" upon Rome and they will be punished by God. Victory is assured to God's people!

25. **Revelation 14:8**—This is reminiscent of Isaiah 21:9. "Babylon" is here used to symbolize Rome. The announcement here is a prolepsis, which anticipates the future as if it were the present. The fall is described in chapters 17 and 18, but it is announced here before it happens. And it is spoken of in the past tense because of its absolute certainty in the eyes of God (similar to prophecies about the coming Christ, like Isaiah 53).

26. **Revelation 14:9-10**—This describes the horror if one were to give in to emperor worship in order to receive the mark and make life easier. The wrath of Caesar for not receiving the mark would be terrible, but the wrath of God for worshiping that image and receiving that mark would be even worse (cf. Matt. 10:28). The imagery of drinking a cup containing the wrath of God is from the O.T. (Jer. 25:15-16; 49:12; cf. 51:7-8). Those who become intoxicated by the wine of the world and turn from God will experience the "full strength" (undiluted, as they would often do with wine) "wrath of God."

27. **Revelation 14:12**—Endurance requires both continued faith and continued obedience to the commandments of God. One without the other will not produce steadfastness to Christ.

28. **Revelation 14:13**—The Greek word for "blessed" means "happy," as one who is spiritually rewarded. Those who worship the beast and

Mark Your Bible

bear his mark will not be "happy" in the next life (14:9-11). The Greek word for "rest" (*anapauo*) involves being "refreshed" and "gaining relief from toil." The Greek for "labor" (*kopos*) primarily denoted "a striking, beating," and came to mean "laborious toil under great adversity." (Read Matthew 11:28.) The Spirit gave a motivating reason to avoid hell (14:9-11) and a stronger motivation to strive for heaven through submission to God's will in "good works."

29. **Revelation 14:14**—This is reminiscent of Daniel 7:13-14 and is a reference to Christ. The "golden crown" is the crown of victory. The "sickle" is a symbol of Divine judgment (Joel 3:13; Mark 4:29).

30. **Revelation 14:15-16**—These verses may be depicting the harvest of the saints to be with the Lord (1 Thess. 4:14-17; Matt. 25:31-34). If this is viewed distinctly from verses 17-20, there is no thousand year separation between the two. They happen at the same time (Matt. 13:38-39; 25:31-34).

31. **Revelation 14:17-20**—These verses depict the harvest of the wicked. The symbol of the winepress for the wrath of God is used in Isaiah 63:2-4. "Ripe" (in verses 15 and 18) means that the plants are fully ready for harvest. The fully ripe grapes (i.e., those who are rebellious against the will of God and now deserving of punishment) were cast into the winepress to be utterly trampled by the wrath of God. (In 19:11-16, Christ treads the winepress.) This is similar to Genesis 15:16, when God was waiting for the iniquity of the Amorites to be "full" before punishment.

32. **Revelation 14:20**—The immense stream of blood emphasizes the large number of those who will be punished. The blood flows some 165-185 miles, which is obviously symbolic of the horror and completeness of God's judgment. The wicked will be punished.

33. **Revelation 15:2**—"Mingled with fire" may refer to the sea reflecting the judgments of God that are about to be poured out on man, or it may symbolize the trials through which the redeemed have come.

34. **Revelation 15:2**—In 4:6, the sea separated God from being approached. Here the redeemed are standing on

(continued on next page)

Mark Your Bible

it before the throne. In 21:1, the sea is "no more," giving way to intimate fellowship with the One on the throne.

35. **Revelation 15:2**—See "Helpful Notes" on Revelation 5 for "harps."

36. **Revelation 15:2-4**—As a very brief interlude, knowing that the bowls of wrath are about to be poured out, God's people are given a vision of the throne of God and of those who have already had "victory" over Rome. This is tremendous motivation and encouragement to remain faithful. Even if death overtakes because they did not bow down to Caesar, the scene in verses 2-4 awaits!

37. **Revelation 15:3**—The combining of "the song of Moses" and "the song of the Lamb" emphasizes the faithful of both covenants praising God together.

38. **Revelation 15:4**—The mention that "all nations" will "worship" before Him may refer to either (1) the redeemed will be made up of all nations or (2) the fact that at the judgment, every person will bow and confess to God (Rom. 14:11).

39. **Revelation 15:6**—Their apparel was that of the priests when they served at the tabernacle.

40. **Revelation 15:7**—This is a reminder that it is God who "lives forever and ever" and not Caesar or Rome.

41. **Revelation 15:8**—God's glory filling the sanctuary with "smoke" was found often in the O.T. (Ex. 40:35; 1 Kgs. 8:10-11; 2 Chron. 7:2-3; Isa. 6:4; Ezek. 10:4). The smoke was a symbol of God's powerful presence and shows that He is the source of the judgments coming forth. No one would be permitted to stop these judgments. The martyrs in chapter 6 had been told to wait, and now the wrath of God is filled and God's righteous purposes would be completed.

42. **Revelation 16:1**—There are similarities between the trumpets and the bowls, but the main difference is that the trumpets were warnings and calls to repentance, while the bowls are the actual punishments poured out when time for repentance has passed. The bowls are grouped as the seals and trumpets: four, two, interlude, one.

Mark Your Bible

43. **Revelation 16:2**—This resembles the sixth plague upon Egypt. This is great motivation to never want the mark of the beast.

44. **Revelation 16:3**—This resembles the first plague upon Egypt.

45. **Revelation 16:5**—God is the eternal, Almighty One! Rome is not! Rome was going to fall, and "Lord God Almighty" would prevail.

46. **Revelation 16:8**—The passive voice of "was given" suggests God was at work in this.

47. **Revelation 16:10**—Darkness symbolizes man's destruction and evil, standing opposite of God's truth and salvation. The word "darkened" is in the Greek perfect tense, emphasizing an abiding condition, not to be reversed.

48. **Revelation 16:12**—The way was prepared for enemies from the east (perhaps Parthians) to come against Rome.

49. **Revelation 16:13**—There is a brief interlude between the sixth and seventh bowl.

50. **Revelation 16:13-14**—The false prophet is the second beast of 13:11 (cf. 19:20; 20:10). Thus, these three allies of evil (the dragon [i.e., the devil]; the beast [i.e., the Roman emperor]; the false prophet [i.e., the unholy priesthood enforcing emperor worship]) send forth unclean spirits (i.e., spirits of demons) to deceive the kings of the world (through deceitful, lying wonders) to ally with Rome in battle. The "frogs" may symbolize their evil and false propaganda.

51. **Revelation 16:14**—The "great day of God" was an O.T. expression depicting a day of judgment and decisive battle (Jer. 30:7; Joel 2:11; 3:14; Amos 5:18; Zeph. 1:15). Similarly, the final day of judgment is called "the day of the Lord" (2 Pet. 3:10).

52. **Revelation 16:15**—With a gentle pause in the action, Jesus reassures the Christians and calls them to continued vigilance, purity and faithfulness. The verbs, "watches" and "keeps," are in the present tense, denoting ongoing activity. His coming is often likened to a "thief" (Matt. 24:36; 43; 1 Thess. 5:2; 2 Pet. 3:10).

(continued on next page)

Mark Your Bible

53. **Revelation 16:17**—"It is done" is in the perfect tense, emphasizing a permanent, unchanging state.
54. **Revelation 16:19**—The number "three" symbolized Divinity, which indicates that the overthrow of the city was by Divine power. The supposed supreme power of Rome would be toppled by God. (Rome is designated as "great Babylon.")
55. **Revelation 16:20**—The symbolic devastation to nature emphasizes the massive devastation. Mountains and islands were Rome's strongholds.
56. **Revelation 16:21**—Symbolically, the hailstones weighed about 100 pounds. That did not matter to hardened, wicked men. They continued to blaspheme God. The fall of Rome was due to three things: natural calamity, internal rottenness and external invasion. These are seen in the seven bowls of wrath.
57. **Revelation 17:1**—The Greek word for "judgment" is *krima,* which means "the sentence pronounced, a verdict, a condemnation." The events depicted in chapters 17-19 regarding the fall of Rome are the result of the "judicial verdict" already made by the righteous God.
58. **Revelation 17:1**—The "many waters" upon which Rome (i.e., the great harlot) "sits" are "peoples, multitudes, nations and tongues" (17:15), indicating Rome's vast territory and influence. "Sitting" refers to ruling over them. (This imagery was also used of ancient Babylon in Jeremiah 51:13.)
59. **Revelation 17:2**—Spiritual "fornication" is used to depict devotion to foreign gods and all the evil that came about as a result. "Inhabitants of the earth" and "those who dwell on the earth" is used in this book for the ungodly and does not include Christians.
60. **Revelation 17:4**—The "cup full of abominations" represented the moral impurities and ceremonies that accompanied idol worship.
61. **Revelation 17:5**—There was a Roman custom in which prostitutes who were in public brothels wore their names on their foreheads. The word "mystery" emphasizes this is to be taken symbolically.

Mark Your Bible

62. **Revelation 17:6**—This is an obvious reference to the persecution of Christians in the Roman empire. This is similar to what Jeremiah saw in ancient Babylon (Jer. 51:7). The word "drunk" is in the present tense, denoting a constant state of intoxication and thus a constant reality of persecution of the saints of God.

63. **Revelation 17:8, 11**—This may refer to the well-known myth in that day called "Nero *Redivivus*," which believed that Nero would come back to life. Domitian was, in effect, the reincarnation of the evil Nero, having revived and intensified his policies and persecutions.

64. **Revelation 17:8**—God's plan to redeem man was part of His eternal plan, but these had rejected that. (See note on 13:8.)

65. **Revelation 17:9-10**—The number "seven" in the "seven heads" and the "seven kings" should be understood symbolically, as representing emperors as a whole, rather than trying to count out and identify specific emperors at specific numbers.

66. **Revelation 17:12-14**—The ten horns are ten kings without a kingdom. "Ten" should be understood symbolically as complete, fullness of power. These may represent the vassal kings of the Roman provinces, who receive their authority from Rome but only rule for a short time. Their responsibility is to serve at the pleasure of the beast/emperor and obey his demands, particularly in opposing, fighting against and persecuting Christ and His people.

67. **Revelation 17:14**—"Lord of lords and King of kings" were titles given to God in the O.T. (Deut. 10:17; Psa. 136:2-3; Dan. 2:47) and are here given to Jesus. Jesus is God! He is Jehovah! He is eternal! The Roman emperor is not Lord of lords or King of kings or eternal! The victory of Jesus is certain, and so is the victory of His faithful.

68. **Revelation 17:16-17**—Through God's providence (to "fulfill His purpose," see Daniel 2:37-38; 4:17, 25, 32), the kings of the Roman provinces (once in subjection) would be Rome's undoing and have their part in her destruction (cf. Mark 3:25). The seeds of destruction are in every force of evil. Evil will be destroyed (even destroying itself), and Satan and his pawns will be defeated.

Day of Reflection

Take time today to reflect on the five chapters that you read this week. You may choose to read all five chapters again, in one sitting, or certain parts of them. Take time today to answer at least one of these questions below. You may or may not write anything down—you can choose to write or simply reflect.

1. What personal application do I need to make from the chapters I have read this week?

2. How can these five chapters help draw me closer to Jesus?

3. What words, phrases or verses in these chapters do I want to go back and study more in depth?

4. What questions do I have about what I have read this week on which I need to do some further Biblical research?

Week 52

December 24-30

December 24	Read Revelation 18
December 25	Read Revelation 19
December 26	Read Revelation 20
December 27	Read Revelation 21
December 28	Read Revelation 22
December 29	Mark Your Bible
December 30	Day of Reflection

Prayer for this week:

"Heavenly Father,
I long to spend eternity with You in heaven!
Help me to stay focused on that!"

Revelation 18

Helpful Notes:

1. **Babylon the great** = The ancient city of Babylon is used symbolically of Rome; this was first identified in 14:7-8, when judgment was turning from being inflicted by Rome to being announced against Rome; every description of "Babylon" in the book of Revelation (from sitting on seven hills [17:3, 9] to the massive empire of nations, commerce and trade [chap. 18]) aligns precisely with first-century Rome; thus, there would be great joy for the Christians to hear the loud announcement, "Babylon/Rome is fallen!"
2. **Come out** = Christians are always called to "come out" and to "be separate" from ungodliness and immorality around them (2 Cor. 6:17; Eph. 5:11), lest they be influenced by (1 Cor. 15:33) and become partakers in the sin (Rom. 1:32; 12:1-2; Gal. 6:1; 2 John 10-11), and the consequences of the wrongdoing fall on the Christians, as well; similar calls were made of God's people in the O.T. (Gen. 19:12-14; Num. 16:23-26; Isa. 48:20; Jer. 50:8; 51:6).
3. **One hour** = This is not a literal 60-minute timeframe, but it is used to symbolize and emphasize how quickly the fall will take place; it took years to build Rome to her great power and strength, but she will fall with great speed.

1. Why did God tell His people to "come out" of the ways of Rome?

2. What groups wept and mourned over the fall of Rome? Were they more concerned about her or themselves?

3. Why were God's people, apostles and prophets told to rejoice?

Verse for Meditation and Prayer: **Revelation 18:20**

"Rejoice over her, O heaven, and you holy apostles and prophets, for God has avenged you on her!"

Revelation 19

Helpful Notes:

1. **Hallelujah** = The four uses of this word in this chapter (v. 1, 3, 4, 6) are the only times it is found in the N.T.; the word is used often in Psalms; here the word is actually transliterated from the Greek, as the Greek word is *hallelouia*; the word is translated in the O.T., "Praise the LORD," or better, "Praise Jehovah"; all of heaven bursts into hymns of praise in this chapter.
2. **The marriage of the Lamb** = The marriage metaphor is used in the O.T. and the N.T. to depict the relationship between God and His people (Isa. 54:5-6; Jer. 31:32); in the N.T., the church is the bride of Christ (2 Cor. 11:2; Eph. 5:22-33; Matt. 25:1-13), for she is "married to" Christ (Rom. 7:4); in Revelation 19, the Lamb's "wife has made herself ready" (19:7), by having her garments "washed" and "made white in the blood of the Lamb" (7:14); the book of Revelation does not reveal to us the actual marriage itself.
3. **Worship God** = No angel is deserving of worship, and neither is any emperor; Domitian demanded that he be worshiped as "Lord and God," but there is only one "Lord and God"; only the God of heaven is Omnipotent—not Rome or Caesar; God alone is worthy of our worship; Christians must not be distracted by or threatened into behavior that takes glory away from the one true God!

1. While the readers were told to worship the emperor, what strong reminders are provided in this chapter about God?

2. Why do you think God describes the church as the "wife" of Christ?

3. Why do you think such a graphic scene of destruction is given?

Verse for Meditation and Prayer: **Revelation 19:6**

"And I heard, as it were, the voice of a great multitude,
as the sound of many waters and as the sound of mighty thunderings,
saying, 'Alleluia! For the Lord God Omnipotent reigns!'"

December 26 Week 52, Day 3

Revelation 20

Helpful Notes:

1. **A thousand years** = The book of Revelation is written in symbolic language; the numbers in the book are figurative, not literal; "ten" is a number for completeness, and "1,000" is an intensified multiple of ten, signifying ultimate completeness or perhaps merely a large number/sum for a long period of time; other Scriptures use "1,000" figuratively (Ex. 20:6; Job 9:3; Psa. 50:10; 90:4; 105:8; 2 Pet. 3:8); "1,000 years" is contrasted with "a little while"; the word "thousand" is used 30 times in Revelation and never is it literal.
2. **Binding of Satan for 1,000 years** = The term "bound" is sometimes used in the N.T. figuratively for restricting certain activities but still freedom in other areas (cf. Rom. 7:2); Jesus is "the strong man" in "binding" Satan (Matt. 12:29), and His death "disarmed" and triumphed over him (Col. 2:15), "destroying" the devil's "power" and his "works" (1 John 3:8; Heb. 2:14); yet Satan still roams as a roaring lion (1 Pet. 5:8); before Christ's death, Satan could accuse the saints and deceive the nations in carrying out global persecution to destroy Christianity (12:10; 20:3); Christ's death bound that power of the devil, and the gospel has free reign and power over him.
3. **Reign with Christ for 1,000 years** = The persons in view are those beheaded "souls" who were seen under the altar (6:9-11), and now they are seen reigning instead of being persecuted; they are on "thrones" because after their death, these martyrs are sharing with Christ in the blessedness and glory of His triumph (cf. Phil. 1:23).

1. Where will the devil be cast?

2. By what are the dead going to be judged?

3. What is "the second death"?

Verse for Meditation and Prayer: **Revelation 20:12**

"And I saw the dead, small and great, standing before God, and books were opened. And another book was opened, which is the Book of Life."

December 27 Week 52, Day 4

Revelation 21

Helpful Notes:

1. **New heaven and new earth** = The Bible (and Jesus Himself) makes a clear distinction between earth (where man dwells) and heaven (where God dwells and where the redeemed will spend eternity) (Matt. 5:34-35; 6:10, 19-21) and points to heaven (not earth) as our ultimate goal (John 14:2-3; Phil. 3:20; Col. 1:5; 1 Pet. 1:3-4; Heb. 6:20; 10:20); "the new heaven and new earth" is a figurative expression for describing the new environment of the saved in heaven; the Greek word for "new" (*kainos*) indicates a newness in quality or kind—the first heaven and earth (i.e., our material universe) will have "passed away" (Matt. 24:35; 2 Pet. 3:10-13), and there will be a new (and superior) kind of realm (i.e., heaven and earth) for us; see "Helpful Notes" for 2 Peter 3.
2. **The holy city, New Jerusalem, tabernacle** = The O.T. describes the city of Jerusalem as, "the city of God, the holy place of the tabernacle of the Most High" (Psa. 46:4), and the N.T. (in Rev. 21:2-3, Heb. 12:22-23) describes the victorious church with the same language; the "tabernacle" is a symbol of fellowship (i.e., where God and man meet), which emphasizes that God's presence is among His people (i.e., His church) in a special way for all eternity.
3. **The cube of heaven** = Heaven is described figuratively as a cube that is 12,000 furlongs on each side (or about 1,500 miles); the number is symbolic to impress a place of perfection and completion, with plenty of room for all of the redeemed.

1. What things will not be in heaven?

2. What people will not be in heaven?

3. Who are the "only" ones who will "enter" heaven?

Verse for Meditation and Prayer: **Revelation 21:27**

"But there shall by no means enter it anything that defiles, or causes an abomination or a lie, but only those who are written in the Lamb's Book of Life."

Revelation 22

Helpful Notes:

1. **Garden** = John sees a garden, reminiscent of Eden, symbolizing restoration of full fellowship with God, eternal enjoyment and supply of every need; three things are necessary to sustain life and they are all supplied here: (1) water (from the river/water of life), (2) food (from the tree of life with its fruits), (3) health (from the leaves of the tree of life); the curse enacted in Eden is removed; the repeated emphasis on "life" shows death is "no more" (21:4).
2. **Tree of life** = The tree of life was in the Garden of Eden, but access was blocked after man sinned (Gen. 2:9; 3:22, 24); this is a tree, according to the Greek construction, that "gives life," that is, "eternal life" (John 20:31); Jesus came to restore access to the tree (Rev. 2:7), so that the redeemed can partake of the tree of life in heaven's eternal paradise forever (Rev. 22:2, 14).
3. **I am coming quickly** = Time is emphasized in this chapter: "must shortly take place" (22:6), "I am coming quickly" (22:7, 12, 20), "the time is at hand" (22:10); keep in mind that time is often relative in prophecy (2 Pet. 3:8), but these statements indicate that Christ would fulfill the promises of this book and the events of this letter would soon begin to start unfolding (1:1), and once they started, they would happen quickly; once Christ's second coming arrived, that would happen suddenly and unexpectedly; everything in the book would not be immediately fulfilled, but the end is always said to be near, since each generation may be the last.

1. What will God's servants do while in heaven?

2. How will each person's "reward" be determined?

3. At the end of the chapter, what does John wish Jesus to do?

Verse for Meditation and Prayer: **Revelation 22:4**

"They shall see His face,
and His name shall be on their foreheads."

Mark Your Bible

1. **Revelation 18:1**—The announcement here of Rome's fall resembles O.T. announcements/prophecies of the fall of nations and cities: Babylon (Isa. 13; 21; 47; Jer. 50; 51), Nineveh (Nah. 3), Edom (Isa. 34), Tyre (Ezek. 26-27).
2. **Revelation 18:3**—The reason for Rome's destruction is that her wantonness, wealth and self-indulgence have corrupted her and the nations conquered and allied by her. Her fall is certain and just.
3. **Revelation 18:6**—The instructions to "repay her double" is given to God's angels, who will carry out His orders of justice.
4. **Revelation 18:6-7**—She is being punished in like kind and in proportion, "according to her works." Her pay is being doubled. (The wording is similar to the principle that Jesus gave in Matthew 7:2.)
5. **Revelation 18:7-8**—This language is borrowed from Isaiah 47:7-9. "Pride goes before destruction" (Prov. 16:18).
6. **Revelation 18:9-19**—Rome's power was built upon two major things: territorial conquest and trade expansion. Those two entities now stand in mourning over her fall: territorial conquest seen in her allies, "the kings of the earth" (18:9-10), and trade expansion is seen in two groups—"the merchants of the earth" (18:11-16) and "every shipmaster" and "sailor" (18:17-19).
7. **Revelation 18:12-14**—There are about 30 articles of trade mentioned, and they can be divided into seven groups: precious metals, beautiful cloth, every kind of wood and ornamented vessel, aromatic spices, articles of food, property, choice fruits.
8. **Revelation 18:19**—Casting "dust on their heads" was a sign of deep grief.
9. **Revelation 18:20**—God's people are called to "rejoice" over the fall of Rome. This vengeance is the punitive action of the Lord (not a personal vengeance), thus God's people are justified in rejoicing that God and His people have triumphed over evil (cf. Rom. 12:19).

(continued on next page)

Mark Your Bible

10. **Revelation 18:21**—Symbolizing the complete fall of Rome, so that she "not be found anymore," a great millstone was thrown into the sea. This is similar to Jeremiah 51:59-64.

11. **Revelation 18:22-23**—Three major things cease in Rome: amusement/social life (v. 22), industrial/business life (v. 22), home/domestic life (v. 23).

12. **Revelation 18:24**—After Rome fell and all of these things ceased, the blood of the martyrs was all that remained. This is the reason that Rome was destroyed. This is the reason that the glory of Rome vanished from the earth.

13. **Revelation 19:1-2**—The first "Hallelujah" praises God for the salvation He has brought from the great harlot, Rome. Underline "the Lord our God," as the "salvation and glory and honor and power" do not belong to Rome! The salvation here is from the persecutions of the vile empire. The reason for her judgment is stated again—she "corrupted the earth with her fornication" and she shed "the blood of His servants." It is not as much a rejoicing over the fall of Rome as it is a rejoicing over the triumph of righteousness.

14. **Revelation 19:3**—The second "Hallelujah" praises God for the absolute and eternal destruction of those who persecuted God's people. They will never rise again, as they are burning forever and ever. The rising smoke was mentioned earlier (14:11; 18:8, 9, 18).

15. **Revelation 19:4**—The third "Hallelujah" comes from the representatives of all God's people in heaven and the highest order of angels. Their short, "Amen! Hallelujah!" comes from Psalm 106:48.

16. **Revelation 19:5**—The "small and great" involves all levels of mankind, distinct from the heavenly beings. Those in the church on earth are called to praise God, regardless of economic, ethnic or education level.

17. **Revelation 19:6**—The fourth "Hallelujah" praises the Lord God Omnipotent who reigns. The reign of Caesars is temporary. The reign of God is eternal! He has not ever and will not ever stop reigning!

Mark Your Bible

18. **Revelation 19:7-8**—The fact that the bride (i.e., the church) has "made herself ready" emphasizes that there is personal responsibility. What has she done to make "herself ready"? She has kept her garments pure and white by "the righteous acts of the saints." Each Christian must have on a proper wedding garment at the feast (cf. Matt. 22:11), which is a garment washed and made white in the blood of the Lamb (7:9, 14), which occurs in baptism (Eph. 5:25-26) and is maintained through "righteous acts." Of course, this is "granted" by God as a gift, but it requires submission and obedience.

19. **Revelation 19:10**—The worship of angels was common (cf. Col. 2:18), but God alone is worthy of worship.

20. **Revelation 19:11-16**—Jesus has been depicted as Lion, Lamb and Judge. Now He is a Warrior. The "white horse" symbolizes victory. He has four names: (1) Faithful and True [emphasizing His nature and the trustworthiness of His Word, 1:5; 3:7, 14]; (2) mysterious name "that no one knew" [likely identifying an eternal nature that no one can understand]; (3) "the Word of God" [the full and complete revelation of deity to the world, John 1:1-3, 14; 1 John 1:1]; (4) "King of kings and Lord of lords" [there is no other, including any Roman emperor, 17:14].

21. **Revelation 19:12, 15**—Several marks, already mentioned in the book, identify Jesus: His eyes (1:14), His sword (1:16), His rule (12:5), His wrath (14:20).

22. **Revelation 19:11-21**—Chapter 16 foretold of the battle of Armageddon. Chapter 19 shows the results. Armageddon is not a material, physical battle; it is the battle between righteousness and evil, between the forces of Satan and the forces of Christ. The overriding thing that matters is that Christ is victorious and His enemy—all the forces of evil—are defeated.

23. **Revelation 19:13**—The blood in which the robe is dipped is not likely His blood but the blood of his enemies (Isa. 63:1-6).

(continued on next page)

Mark Your Bible

24. **Revelation 19:15** – The sword symbolizes His penetrating Word (Heb. 4:12), with which He will strike the nations and rule over them (2:27; 12:5; Psa. 2:9). Like with the sickle of chapter 14, Christ will visit His wrath upon the wicked world and tread upon them like grapes.
25. **Revelation 19:17** – The calling of the meat-eating birds to "the supper of the great God" is reminiscent of Ezekiel 39 (cf. Matt. 24:28).
26. **Revelation 19:20** – The beast of the sea (i.e., the Roman emperor) and the false prophet (i.e., the beast of the earth, the imperial priesthood who enforces the worship of the beast) will be thrown into hell.
27. **Revelation 19:21** – "The rest" denotes those who followed the beast and the false prophet. They will also be punished. Christ is victorious and Christ's people are victorious! They shall reign forever!
28. **Revelation 20:1** – A "key" represents authority to open and close. See "Helpful Notes" on Revelation 9 for "the bottomless pit." It is critical to realize that the key, the pit and the chain in this verse are ALL figurative. None of them are literal. This is true for other figurative things in the chapter, like dragon and thousand and years. Keep things in context.
29. **Revelation 20:1** – It is critical to remember that this whole book is written in figurative language (not literal), including this chapter. It is also helpful to note things that are not mentioned but are often taught today, such as: a reign on earth, David's literal throne on earth, rebuilding the temple, a throne in the city of Jerusalem in Palestine, Christ setting foot on earth, a 1,000-year reign of saints with Christ on earth either before or after His second coming, multiple resurrections of the dead, multiple judgments, etc.
30. **Revelation 20:3** – "A little while" is comparatively a short period of time. (See verses 7-10.) Even now, Satan still has power to deceive, but he apparently is restricted from inflicting a general persecution.
31. **Revelation 20:4** – After a martyr's death, he will experience a complete victory (1,000 symbolizes ultimate completeness) with Christ

Mark Your Bible

for a long period of time, as compared to the short, more limited time of their persecution. The focus is on the martyrs, not all dead. The reign is in heaven, not on the earth. The reign is in the present, not at the final judgment day. (This is life after death.)

32. **Revelation 20:4**—The book of Revelation depicts Christ as reigning before (1:9; 5:1-14), during (20:4) and after (20:11; 21:5; 22:16) the 1,000 years, which proves that they do not represent a literal 1,000 years of a literal reign on a literal earth over an earthly kingdom. All verses, especially this one, must be kept in their immediate, remote and Biblical context. Jesus began His reign at His ascension (Dan. 7:13-14; Acts 2:30-33), and His people are now part of His kingdom (Col. 1:13; Rev. 1:9).

33. **Revelation 20:5**—The triumph of the martyrs is called "the first resurrection." The "first resurrection" is not a reference to just the righteous just before an earthly reign of Christ. The Bible teaches that a general resurrection of "the rest of the dead" (20:5), in which all "the dead, small and great" (Rev. 20:12), the "good" and "evil" (John 5:28-29), "the just and the unjust" (Acts 24:15) will be raised in the same "hour" (John 5:28-29) on "the last day" (John 6:39-40; 11:24; 12:48), not separated by 1,000 years (or any years). Thus, the first resurrection is not the general resurrection. The "first resurrection" must be a symbolic way of describing that these martyrs had overcome (cf. 2:10-11), are enjoying relief from that horrible persecution, and they will not be hurt by the "second death" (see v. 14). This first resurrection had to do with those beheaded martyrs and not us today. It is similar to the resurrection pictured in Ezekiel 37, foreseeing Judah being released from Babylonian captivity.

34. **Revelation 20:7-8**—At a time unspecified and for a specific length unspecified, Satan is to be figuratively released and able to "deceive the nations" (persecuting the people of God) again (cf. 20:3) "in the four corners of the earth," perhaps signifying totality. This is some kind of last attempt to destroy the work of Christ (perhaps during a time when the influence of Scripture is limited), but his efforts will be totally in vain.

(continued on next page)

Mark Your Bible

35. **Revelation 20:8**—The terms "Gog and Magog" are found in the O.T. (ex: Gen. 10:2), especially in Ezekiel 38, where they are connected with the vicious persecutions that the Jews suffered during the intertestamental period at the hands of Antiochus IV Epiphanes. They are used symbolically in Revelation 20, just as Sodom and Egypt were in 11:8. This is not a literal battle, nor should Gog and Magog be taken literally, with attempts to identify some actual location. Here they symbolize the fierce nations of the world, in league with and under the rule of the devil, going against God and His people. They would fail!

36. **Revelation 20:9**—In 16:16, they were gathering together against the Lord at Armageddon. In 19:19, the armies are gathered together for war, and the beast and the false prophet are thrown into the lake of fire (19:20-21). Here they come from all corners of the earth to encircle and destroy God's people, and instead, they are destroyed. The Lord God delivers His people in flaming fire.

37. **Revelation 20:10**—See "Helpful Notes" on Revelation 14 for a fuller discussion of "hell." The torment is continuous and thus it is a conscious punishment (cf. 14:9-11). It is not annihilation.

38. **Revelation 20:11-15**—There is only one day of judgment, not multiple. It is on the "day" that God has "appointed" on which Jesus "will judge the world" (Acts 17:31). This will happen on that "last day" (John 6:39-40, 44; 11:24; 12:48)—"the day of judgment" (2 Pet. 2:9; 3:7; 1 John 4:17)—when "all" people (Matt. 25:31-46), without any exceptions (Rev. 20:12), "stand before the judgment seat of Christ" (Rom. 14:10; 2 Cor. 5:10; cf. Acts 10:42; 2 Tim. 4:1; 1 Pet. 4:5).

39. **Revelation 20:11**—The "great throne" symbolizes universal sovereignty and the "white throne" symbolizes the holy justice of God.

40. **Revelation 20:11**—Judgment takes place upon the end of the material universe (2 Pet. 3:10; Matt. 24:35; Heb. 1:10-11). There "was found no place for them," as they had been utterly destroyed.

41. **Revelation 20:12**—The books that are opened appear to be (1) the standard of judgment that will be executed (i.e., the will of God

Mark Your Bible

under which an individual lived—the old covenant books and the new covenant books, cf. John 12:48); (2) the book of remembrance, which contains the "works" and "deeds" and "words" of a person that are to be brought into judgment (Rom. 2:1-16; 2 Cor. 5:10; Matt. 12:36-37). Ultimately, it is the Book of Life that will determine one's eternal destiny (20:15; 21:27; 3:5; Luke 10:20; Phil. 4:3).

42. **Revelation 20:13**—There is a difference between a person's body (which is found in the grave or the sea after death) and a person's soul (which is found in Hades after death).

43. **Revelation 20:14**—Death and the state of the dead (i.e., Hades) are evidence of the power of Satan (Heb. 2:14-15), so those are cast into the same place where the devil is. The last enemy is destroyed (1 Cor. 15:26).

44. **Revelation 20:14-15**—"The second death" is found in 2:11; 20:6, 14; 21:8. The first death (although it is not mentioned or called that here) is certainly physical death which all will experience (Heb. 9:27). The "second death" is the eternal punishment of the wicked and eternal separation from God in hell. Those who die outside of Christ are "not found written in the Book of Life," and they will suffer a "second death" (separation) by being cast into hell.

45. **Revelation 21:1**—The "sea" here could be the actual seas of the earth (which may symbolize the power of evil, as they were used by the dragon and beast in this book), or it could be the "sea of glass" that was temporarily separating John from the throne in 4:6 and God's people were standing on in 15:2, but is now removed and nothing separates God's people from Him any longer.

46. **Revelation 21:2**—Jerusalem is often used as a symbol for heavenly things (Gal. 4:26; Heb. 11:10; 12:22; 13:14). It stands in bold contrast to the evil, corrupt city of Babylon/Rome (18:2).

47. **Revelation 21:2, 9**—The church is also often described with terms of a bride and wedding (21:9; 22:17; 3:12; 19:7-8; Rom. 7:4; 2 Cor. 11:2; Eph. 5:22-33). This stands in bold contrast to Rome being a drunk harlot (17:5-6).

(continued on next page)

Mark Your Bible

48. **Revelation 21:2**—The perfect passive verb "prepared" emphasizes that the preparation now stands complete and that the preparation was ultimately accomplished by another acting upon the church for the benefit of the church.
49. **Revelation 21:4**—Underline the words "passed away" in this verse and connect with "passed away" in verse 1. Every earthly sorrow associated with that old earth has "passed away" with that old earth. How miserable if heaven was just on a renovated earth!
50. **Revelation 21:4**—The "last enemy" (i.e., death) has been put down (1 Cor. 15:25-26).
51. **Revelation 21:5-6**—The things that John was writing were trustworthy and dependable because God is the author and finisher of all things. His readers could depend on every detail and promise.
52. **Revelation 21:6**—The water of life is promised to those who seek for it of their own will and yield themselves to the will of God. It is not forced or irresistible upon anyone.
53. **Revelation 21:8**—The Greek for "burns" is in the present tense, denoting ongoing, continual activity. The fires of hell will never stop burning and the torment will be eternal (not momentary).
54. **Revelation 21:9-12**—Heaven being described as a city with high walls and gates is symbolic of the security and protection associated with this eternal realm, which would be extremely meaningful to Christians who felt as if they had no security or protection in life.
55. **Revelation 21:12-14**—The mention of the "twelve tribes" and the "twelve apostles" may indicate the presence of God's redeemed from both the Old Testament and New Testament times. The number "twelve" represents the fullness of God's people, the total of 24 may be intended to remind of the 24 elders, who are representative of God's people around the throne of God. (See Revelation 4.)
56. **Revelation 21:14**—There were actually 13 faithful apostles (including Paul). The use of the number "12" here emphasizes that numbers are used symbolically in this book. That's important to know.

Mark Your Bible

57. **Revelation 21:16**—The holy of holies in the O.T. was also a cube (1 Kgs. 6:20), and it represented the dwelling place of God among His people. Heaven is perfect—perfect in size (figurative 12,000), perfect in inhabitants (figurative 144,000), with a perfect God and perfect Redeemer.

58. **Revelation 21:18-21**—The description of all of the precious metals and precious stones should not be taken literally, nor should it cause the reader to try to identify each specific stone. The purpose is to overwhelm the reader with the inexpressible beauty of our eternal home! Human language and earthly materials cannot possibly describe the glory and magnificence of this spiritual realm.

59. **Revelation 21:22**—The temple was the place where God met His people, but we will be in the presence of God and the Lamb for eternity, and we will worship them directly. The temple was also the place where sacrifice for sin and intercession for sin was made. Neither of those is needed in heaven, where there will be no sin!

60. **Revelation 21:24**—Only the "saved" are in heaven! There is only one way to be saved in the N.T. (Acts 4:12; 2:37-38; Eph. 4:5), and the saved are in Christ's church (Acts 2:41-47; Eph. 5:23). Therefore, one must be in the church to be saved and to go to heaven (Heb. 12:23).

61. **Revelation 21:25**—The gates are never shut because the enemies have all been destroyed. There is no danger for God's people anymore ever again!

62. **Revelation 21:26**—"The glory and the honor" that comes into heaven "of the nations" is the best that those nations have to offer—the redeemed of Christ of every tribe, nation and tongue (Phil. 3:20).

63. **Revelation 21:27**—Underline the word "anything." Then, tie the word "lie" back to 21:8 and then to 22:15.

64. **Revelation 22:1**—"Life" is linked to the "throne." The word "throne" emphasizes that the one upon it has the authority to bestow life—i.e., eternal life. Only deity can do that, which applies to both the Father and the Son (the Lamb). Christ has been victorious!

(continued on next page)

Mark Your Bible

65. **Revelation 22:2**—"The healing" in heaven can have many possible applications: diseases of the spirit, hurt feelings, anguish of heart, imperfections, sour attitudes, etc. God has healing, nurture and care for His people in heaven.

66. **Revelation 22:3**—The last thing that man received in the Garden of Eden was a curse (Gen. 3:16-24). In heaven, there will be "no more curse." The curse of sin that separated man from God is now gone. The curse of death that pointed to man's mortality is now gone. The curse of submission, rulership and hard labor is now gone.

67. **Revelation 22:4**—While "no one has seen God at any time" (John 1:18; 1 John 4:12), now all the redeemed will see Him, face to face, in all His glory, forever and ever.

68. **Revelation 22:4**—Having the stamp or mark of God's name emphasizes that those in heaven belong to Him. No man or nation will ever be able to "mark" them again.

69. **Revelation 22:5**—The "reign" of the redeemed is not an indication of deity. This is our ultimate salvation, when faithful Christians enjoy eternal fellowship with deity on His throne and share with Christ in the glory and triumph of His victory (3:21; 2 Tim. 2:12).

70. **Revelation 22:7**—The word "keeps" is in the present tense, denoting continuous activity necessary to obtain the eternal blessing.

71. **Revelation 22:9**—The worship of angels (or anyone or anything else, including "saints") is never acceptable (19:10; Col. 2:18; John 4:23-24). The fact that Jesus accepted worship (Matt. 14:33) and does receive worship (Rev. 5:8-14) proves that Jesus is not an angel.

72. **Revelation 22:10**—The book is not to be sealed for a distant generation, as Daniel was told to seal up his book (Dan. 8:26; 12:4, 9).

73. **Revelation 22:11-12**—Some people (i.e., the unjust and filthy) will not change their behavior regardless of the warnings that are given. They have made their decision and nothing more can be done for them. Each person (unrighteous and righteous) will bear the responsibility and judgment of his decisions and will receive their "reward." (This leaves no room for the doctrine of purgatory.)

Mark Your Bible

74. **Revelation 22:13**—These are words that only apply to and can only be stated by deity (1:8; 21:6); therefore, Jesus is deity.
75. **Revelation 22:15**—"Dogs" refers to those who are immoral and unclean in the eyes of God (Deut. 23:17-18; Phil. 3:2).
76. **Revelation 22:16**—Jesus was both "the Root" (i.e., the source of David, emphasizing His deity) and "the Offspring of David" (emphasizing His humanity). This is a fulfillment of Isaiah 11:1 and calls to mind Jesus' question to the Pharisees of how the Christ, the "son" of David could call David His "Lord" (Matt. 22:41-46).
77. **Revelation 22:16**—As "the Bright and Morning Star," Jesus is the only hope for mankind. In the world of darkness, He is the true light of the world and the herald of a new day.
78. **Revelation 22:17**—There is a "free" gift offered to "whoever" will take of it, but one must (1) "desire" or "thirst" for it, (2) "come" and (3) "take of" it. Man's free will is emphasized here, as obedience is required to partake of heaven's blessings. "The Spirit" (through His inspired Word) invites all who will come, and "the bride" (i.e., the church) is to extend that same invitation to all to come—this is the Great Commission, calling souls to Christ before it is too late.
79. **Revelation 22:18-19**—These warnings apply especially to the book of Revelation. These same principles are taught elsewhere and apply to all of Scripture (Deut. 4:2; 5:32; 12:32; Prov. 30:5-6; Gal. 1:6-9; 2 John 9).

Day of Reflection

Take time today to reflect on the five chapters that you read this week. You may choose to read all five chapters again, in one sitting, or certain parts of them. Take time today to answer at least one of these questions below. You may or may not write anything down—you can choose to write or simply reflect.

1. What personal application do I need to make from the chapters I have read this week?

2. How can these five chapters help draw me closer to Jesus?

3. What words, phrases or verses in these chapters do I want to go back and study more in depth?

4. What questions do I have about what I have read this week on which I need to do some further Biblical research?

One Final Day

December 31

Take time today to reflect on the year (the last 364 days) and all that you have read and studied in God's New Testament. You may or may not choose to write anything down here, but take time to reflect.

1. What was my favorite part of the New Testament while going through this study?
2. What did I learn that I had not realized before?
3. Which parts of the New Testament do I want to go back, dig into and become more knowledgeable about?
4. How has spending a whole year in the New Testament helped me to draw closer to Jesus?
5. What suggested prayers for each week do I need to go back and make part of my regular prayer life?
6. Starting tomorrow, with a new year, what do I need to do to maintain my spiritual stamina, excitement and continued growth?
7. Would going through this study again help me to grow even more?

Prayer for this past year:

"Heavenly Father,
thank You for Your amazing New Testament!
Thank You for ALL that You have done for me!
Please help me to conform myself to the image of Jesus!"

Appendix A

Brief Introduction to Each Book of the New Testament

Brief Introduction to the Book of

Matthew

Author:

The apostle Matthew, also called Levi
(a tax collector or publican by trade)

Recipients:

Primarily for the Jews

Date of Writing (approx.):

50-68 A.D.

Place of Writing (if known):

Likely Palestine

Theme:

Jesus is the Messiah, the King of the Jews.

Key Words:

fulfilled, kingdom, kingdom of heaven

"You are the Christ, the Son of the living God…on this rock I will build My church, and the gates of Hades shall not prevail against it. And I will give you the keys of the kingdom of heaven…"
(Matthew 16:16-19).

Brief Introduction to the Book of

Mark

Author:

John Mark

(Cousin of Barnabas [Col. 4:10] and close associate of Peter [1 Pet. 5:13])

Recipients:

Primarily for the Romans

Date of Writing (approx.):

63-68 A.D.

Place of Writing (if known):

Perhaps Rome

Theme:

Jesus is the suffering and wonderfully perfect servant of God.

Key Words:

immediately, then, and

"But whoever desires to become great among you shall be your servant. ...For even the Son of Man did not come to be served, but to serve, and to give His life a ransom for many" (Mark 10:43-45).

Brief Introduction to the Book of

Luke

Author:
Luke
(The physician [Col. 4:14], regular traveling companion of Paul and the only Gentile writer of the N.T.)

Recipients:
Primarily for the Greeks
Specifically to a man named Theophilus

Date of Writing (approx.):
60-61 A.D.

Place of Writing (if known):
Likely Rome

Theme:
Jesus is the perfect Son of Man, the ideal man, the Savior and Perfecter of all men.

Key Words:
Son of Man, kingdom, kingdom of God

"For the Son of Man has come
to seek and to save that which was lost"
(Luke 19:10).

Brief Introduction to the Book of

John

<u>Author</u>:
The apostle John
(The brother of James and son of Zebedee [Matt. 4:21],
a fisherman [Mark 1:16-20] and "the disciple
whom Jesus loved" [John 13:23; 19:26; 20:2; 21:7, 20, 24])

<u>Recipients</u>:
All Christians everywhere

<u>Date of Writing (approx.)</u>:
80-90 A.D.

<u>Place of Writing (if known)</u>:
Ephesus

<u>Theme</u>:
Jesus is the Christ, the Son of God.

<u>Key Words</u>:
believe, Father, life, love, sign

"And truly Jesus did many other signs in the presence of His disciples, which are not written in this book; but these are written that you may believe that Jesus is the Christ, the Son of God, and that believing you may have life in His name" (John 20:30-31).

Brief Introduction to the Book of

Acts

Author:
Luke
(The physician [Col. 4:14], regular traveling companion of Paul and the only Gentile writer of the N.T.)

Recipients:
A man named Theophilus
(Likely a government official—1:3; cf. 23:26; 26:25)

Date of Writing (approx.):
61-62 A.D.

Place of Writing (if known):
Likely Rome

Theme:
The origin, establishment and spread of New Testament Christianity

Key Words:
church, beginning, Christian, believe, baptize/baptism

"But in every nation
whoever fears Him and
works righteousness is accepted by Him"
(Acts 10:35).

Brief Introduction to the Book of

Romans

Author:
The apostle Paul (1:1)

Recipients:
The church ("saints") in Rome (1:7)

Date of Writing (approx.):
56-58 A.D.

Place of Writing (if known):
Corinth (Acts 20:3)

Theme:
Justification is only through obedient faith in Jesus Christ.

Key Words:
righteousness, righteous, faith, law, sin, gospel

"For I am not ashamed of the gospel of Christ, for it is the power of God to salvation for everyone who believes, for the Jew first and also for the Greek. For in it the righteousness of God is revealed from faith to faith; as it is written, 'The just shall live by faith'" (Romans 1:16-17).

Brief Introduction to the Book of

First Corinthians

Author:
The apostle Paul (1:1)

Recipients:
The church of God at Corinth (1:2)

Date of Writing (approx.):
55-56 A.D.

Place of Writing (if known):
Ephesus (Acts 19:10)

Theme:
Division in the Lord's church is unacceptable and must be resolved by devotion to Christ as Lord.

Key Words:
Lord, our Lord, wisdom

"Now I plead with you, brethren, by the name of our Lord Jesus Christ, that you all speak the same thing, and that there be no divisions among you, but that you be perfectly joined together in the same mind and in the same judgment"
(1 Corinthians 1:10).

Brief Introduction to the Book of

Second Corinthians

Author:
The apostle Paul (1:1)

Recipients:
The church of God at Corinth (1:1)

Date of Writing (approx.):
55-56 A.D.

Place of Writing (if known):
Macedonia (Acts 20:1-2)

Theme:
Paul's defense of his ministry of the gospel of Christ, of his apostleship and of his authority

Key Words:
comfort, ministry/minister, apostle(s)

"Blessed be the God and Father of our Lord Jesus Christ, the Father of mercies and God of all comfort, who comforts us in all our tribulation, that we may be able to comfort those who are in any trouble, with the comfort with which we ourselves are comforted by God" (2 Corinthians 1:3-4).

Brief Introduction to the Book of

Galatians

Author:
The apostle Paul (1:1)

Recipients:
The churches of Galatia (1:2)

Date of Writing (approx.):
53-57 A.D.

Place of Writing (if known):
Either Ephesus (Acts 19:10) or Corinth (Acts 20:3)

Theme:
True liberty is found only in Christ.

Key Words:
liberty, free, gospel, law, faith, Christ, justified, bondage

> "Stand fast therefore in the liberty
> by which Christ has made us free,
> and do not be entangled again
> with a yoke of bondage"
> (Galatians 5:1).

Brief Introduction to the Book of

Ephesians

Author:

The apostle Paul (1:1)

Recipients:

The church ("saints") in Ephesus (1:1)

Date of Writing (approx.):

60-62 A.D.

Place of Writing (if known):

Roman prison (Acts 28:30-31; Phil. 1:13; 4:22)

Theme:

God's eternal purpose is fulfilled in the church of Christ.

Key Words:

"in Christ," Christ, church, body, walk

"To the intent that now the manifold wisdom of God might be made known by the church to the principalities and powers in the heavenly places, according to the eternal purpose which He accomplished in Christ Jesus our Lord" (Ephesians 3:10-11).

Brief Introduction to the Book of

Philippians

Author:
The apostle Paul (1:1)

Recipients:
The church ("saints") in Philippi (1:1)

Date of Writing (approx.):
60-62 A.D.

Place of Writing (if known):
Roman prison (Acts 28:30-31; Phil. 1:13; 4:22)

Theme:
Christ and His gospel
are the keys to true joy as a Christian.

Key Words:
joy, rejoice, gospel, Christ

"Let nothing be done through selfish ambition or conceit, but in lowliness of mind let each esteem others better than himself. Let each of you look out not only for his own interests, but also for the interests of others" (Philippians 2:3-4).

Brief Introduction to the Book of

Colossians

Author:
The apostle Paul (1:1)

Recipients:
The church ("saints") in Colossae (1:2)

Date of Writing (approx.):
60-62 A.D.

Place of Writing (if known):
Roman prison (Acts 28:30-31; Phil. 1:13; 4:22)

Theme:
The supremacy, authority and all-sufficiency of Christ

Key Words:
Christ, know, knowledge, fullness, filled, body, all

"And whatever you do in word or deed, do all in the name of the Lord Jesus, giving thanks to God the Father through Him" (Colossians 3:17).

Brief Introduction to the Book of

First Thessalonians

Author:
The apostle Paul (1:1)

Recipients:
The church in Thessalonica (1:1)

Date of Writing (approx.):
50-51 A.D.

Place of Writing (if known):
Corinth (Acts 18:5)

Theme:
Comfort and hope for faithful Christians at the second coming of Christ

Key Words:
hope, sanctification, comfort, gospel, Lord

> "For this reason we also thank God without ceasing, because when you received the word of God which you heard from us, you welcomed it not as the word of men, but as it is in truth, the word of God, which also effectively works in you who believe"
> (1 Thessalonians 2:13).

Brief Introduction to the Book of

Second Thessalonians

Author:
The apostle Paul (1:1)

Recipients:
The church in Thessalonica (1:1)

Date of Writing (approx.):
51-52 A.D.

Place of Writing (if known):
Corinth (Acts 18:11)

Theme:
Proper and necessary preparations for the second coming of Christ

Key Words:
day, come, coming

"...In flaming fire taking vengeance on those who do not know God, and on those who do not obey the gospel of our Lord Jesus Christ. These shall be punished with everlasting destruction from the presence of the Lord and from the glory of His power" (2 Thessalonians 1:8-9).

Brief Introduction to the Book of

First Timothy

Author:
The apostle Paul (1:1)

Recipients:
Timothy, while he was in Ephesus (1:2)

Date of Writing (approx.):
62-67 A.D.

Place of Writing (if known):
Macedonia

Theme:
The conduct of the church, in its life and work, must be in accordance with sound doctrine.

Key Words:
doctrine, truth, faith, church, charge

"But if I am delayed, I write so that you may know how you ought to conduct yourself in the house of God, which is the church of the living God, the pillar and ground of the truth"
(1 Timothy 3:15).

Brief Introduction to the Book of

Second Timothy

Author:
The apostle Paul (1:1)

Recipients:
Timothy, while he was in Ephesus (1:2)

Date of Writing (approx.):
67-68 A.D.

Place of Writing (if known):
Roman prison (second imprisonment)

Theme:
A final and personal charge to remain steadfast and preach the word, as accords with sound doctrine

Key Words:
doctrine, sound, faith, faithful, truth, endure

"All Scripture is given by inspiration of God, and is profitable for doctrine, for reproof, for correction, for instruction in righteousness, that the man of God may be complete, thoroughly equipped for every good work" (2 Timothy 3:16-17).

Brief Introduction to the Book of

Titus

Author:
The apostle Paul (1:1)

Recipients:
Titus, while he was in Crete (1:4)

Date of Writing (approx.):
62-67 A.D.

Place of Writing (if known):
Macedonia

Theme:
The orderly pattern of sound doctrine
for the church and Christian lives

Key Words:
doctrine, sound, good works

"For this reason I left you in Crete, that you should set in order the things that are lacking, and appoint elders in every city as I commanded you" (Titus 1:5).

Brief Introduction to the Book of

Philemon

Author:
The apostle Paul (v. 1)

Recipients:
Philemon (v. 2)

Date of Writing (approx.):
60-62 A.D.

Place of Writing (if known):
Roman prison (Acts 28:30-31; Phil. 1:13; 4:22)

Theme:
Christian forgiveness through
the transforming power of the gospel

Key Words:
receive, brother, Christ, love

"For perhaps he departed for a while for this purpose, that you might receive him forever, no longer as a slave but more than a slave—a beloved brother, especially to me but how much more to you, both in the flesh and in the Lord" (Philemon 15-16).

Brief Introduction to the Book of

Hebrews

Author:
Unknown

Recipients:
Jewish Christians, most likely in Rome

Date of Writing (approx.):
Perhaps 64-68 A.D.

Place of Writing (if known):
Unknown

Theme:
An exhortation to faithfulness and a warning against apostasy by appealing to the superiority of Christ and His new covenant over the old covenant

Key Words:
better, Christ, "let us," priest, faith, eternal, forever

> "And for this reason He is the Mediator of the new covenant, by means of death, for the redemption of the transgressions under the first covenant, that those who are called may receive the promise of the eternal inheritance" (Hebrews 9:15).

Brief Introduction to the Book of

James

Author:

James, the half-brother of Jesus (1:1; cf. 1 Cor. 15:7; Gal. 2:9)

Recipients:

Jewish Christians, scattered due to persecution (1:1-2)

Date of Writing (approx.):

45-49 A.D.

Place of Writing (if known):

Possibly Jerusalem

Theme:

Practicing pure and undefiled religion in everyday life

Key Words:

faith, work, works, brethren

"But be doers of the word, and not hearers only, deceiving yourselves…But he who looks into the perfect law of liberty and continues in it, and is not a forgetful hearer but a doer of the work, this one will be blessed in what he does"

(James 1:22, 25).

Brief Introduction to the Book of

First Peter

Author:
The apostle Peter (1:1)

Recipients:
Christians dispersed
throughout the provinces of Asia Minor (1:1)

Date of Writing (approx.):
64-68 A.D.

Place of Writing (if known):
"Babylon" (5:13)

Theme:
Hope and grace for Christians in the midst of persecution

Key Words:
suffer, suffered, suffering, hope, grace, glory

"Blessed be the God and Father of our Lord Jesus Christ, who according to His abundant mercy has begotten us again to a living hope through the resurrection of Jesus Christ from the dead, to an inheritance incorruptible and undefiled and that does not fade away, reserved in heaven for you" (1 Peter 1:3-4).

Brief Introduction to the Book of

Second Peter

Author:

The apostle Peter (1:1)

Recipients:

Likely the same recipients as the first letter (1:1; 3:1)
Christians dispersed throughout Asia Minor (1 Pet. 1:1)

Date of Writing (approx.):

65-68 A.D.

Place of Writing (if known):

Perhaps still in "Babylon" (1 Pet. 5:13)

Theme:

Christians must grow in knowledge of Christ and His will

Key Words:

know, knowledge, remind, diligent

"...As His divine power has given to us all things that pertain to life and godliness, through the knowledge of Him who called us by glory and virtue"
(2 Peter 1:3).

Brief Introduction to the Book of

First John

Author:
The apostle John

Recipients:
A general letter to all Christians,
possibly to circulate among the churches in Asia Minor

Date of Writing (approx.):
90-95 A.D.

Place of Writing (if known):
Likely Ephesus

Theme:
The joyful assurance of eternal life
through Jesus Christ, the Son of God

Key Words:
know, love, little children, fellowship, righteousness, truth

> "These things I have written to you who believe in the name of the Son of God, that you may know that you have eternal life, and that you may continue to believe in the name of the Son of God"
> (1 John 5:13).

Brief Introduction to the Book of

Second John

Author:
The apostle John

Recipients:
The elect lady and her children (v. 1)

Date of Writing (approx.):
90-95 A.D.

Place of Writing (if known):
Likely Ephesus

Theme:
Abide in the truth and do not be led astray from it by false teachers.

Key Words:
truth, love, commandment, walk

"Whoever transgresses and does not abide in the doctrine of Christ does not have God. He who abides in the doctrine of Christ has both the Father and the Son" (2 John 9).

Brief Introduction to the Book of

Third John

Author:
The apostle John

Recipients:
Gaius (v. 1)

Date of Writing (approx.):
90-95 A.D.

Place of Writing (if known):
Likely Ephesus

Theme:
Walk in the truth and do not be diverted from it by self-centered brethren.

Key Words:
truth, love, walk, church, beloved

"Beloved, do not imitate what is evil, but what is good. He who does good is of God, but he who does evil has not seen God" (3 John 11)

Brief Introduction to the Book of

Jude

Author:

Jude, the brother of James and half-brother of Jesus (v. 1)

Recipients:

A general epistle, perhaps to Jewish Christians

Date of Writing (approx.):

66-69 A.D.

Place of Writing (if known):

Unknown, possibly Jerusalem

Theme:

Christians must contend earnestly for the faith, and in so doing, they will be kept by God.

Key Words:

keep, ungodly, beloved, contend

"Beloved, while I was very diligent to write to you concerning our common salvation, I found it necessary to write to you exhorting you to contend earnestly for the faith which was once for all delivered to the saints" (Jude 3).

Brief Introduction to the Book of

Revelation

Author:
The apostle John (1:1, 4, 9; 21:2; 22:8)

Recipients:
The seven churches of Asia (1:4)

Date of Writing (approx.):
95-96 A.D.

Place of Writing (if known):
The island of Patmos (1:9)

Theme:
Comfort and encouragement to persecuted Christians to remain faithful, knowing that the ultimate victory over evil would belong to Jesus and His people

Key Words:
overcome, church, churches, seven

"Be faithful until death,
and I will give you the crown of life"
(Revelation 2:10).

Appendix B

One Year Reading Schedule for the New Testament

One Year Reading Schedule for N.T.

❑ Jan. 1 Matthew 1
❑ Jan. 2 Matthew 2
❑ Jan. 3 Matthew 3
❑ Jan. 4 Matthew 4
❑ Jan. 5 Matthew 5
❑ Jan. 6 Mark Your Bible
❑ Jan. 7 Day of Reflection

❑ Jan. 8 Matthew 6
❑ Jan. 9 Matthew 7
❑ Jan. 10 Matthew 8
❑ Jan. 11 Matthew 9
❑ Jan. 12 Matthew 10
❑ Jan. 13 Mark Your Bible
❑ Jan. 14 Day of Reflection

❑ Jan. 15 Matthew 11
❑ Jan. 16 Matthew 12
❑ Jan. 17 Matthew 13
❑ Jan. 18 Matthew 14
❑ Jan. 19 Matthew 15
❑ Jan. 20 Mark Your Bible
❑ Jan. 21 Day of Reflection

❑ Jan. 22 Matthew 16
❑ Jan. 23 Matthew 17
❑ Jan. 24 Matthew 18
❑ Jan. 25 Matthew 19
❑ Jan. 26 Matthew 20
❑ Jan. 27 Mark Your Bible
❑ Jan. 28 Day of Reflection

❑ Jan. 29 Matthew 21
❑ Jan. 30 Matthew 22
❑ Jan. 31 Matthew 23
❑ Feb. 1 Matthew 24
❑ Feb. 2 Matthew 25
❑ Feb. 3 Mark Your Bible
❑ Feb. 4 Day of Reflection

❑ Feb. 5 Matthew 26
❑ Feb. 6 Matthew 27
❑ Feb. 7 Matthew 28
❑ Feb. 8 Mark 1
❑ Feb. 9 Mark 2
❑ Feb. 10 Mark Your Bible
❑ Feb. 11 Day of Reflection

❑ Feb. 12 Mark 3
❑ Feb. 13 Mark 4
❑ Feb. 14 Mark 5
❑ Feb. 15 Mark 6
❑ Feb. 16 Mark 7
❑ Feb. 17 Mark Your Bible
❑ Feb. 18 Day of Reflection

❑ Feb. 19 Mark 8
❑ Feb. 20 Mark 9
❑ Feb. 21 Mark 10
❑ Feb. 22 Mark 11
❑ Feb. 23 Mark 12
❑ Feb. 24 Mark Your Bible
❑ Feb. 25 Day of Reflection

One Year Reading Schedule for N.T.

- ❑ Feb. 26 Mark 13
- ❑ Feb. 27 Mark 14
- ❑ Feb. 28 Mark 15
- ❑ Mar. 1 Mark 16
- ❑ Mar. 2 Luke 1
- ❑ Mar. 3 Mark Your Bible
- ❑ Mar. 4 Day of Reflection

- ❑ Mar. 5 Luke 2
- ❑ Mar. 6 Luke 3
- ❑ Mar. 7 Luke 4
- ❑ Mar. 8 Luke 5
- ❑ Mar. 9 Luke 6
- ❑ Mar. 10 Mark Your Bible
- ❑ Mar. 11 Day of Reflection

- ❑ Mar. 12 Luke 7
- ❑ Mar. 13 Luke 8
- ❑ Mar. 14 Luke 9
- ❑ Mar. 15 Luke 10
- ❑ Mar. 16 Luke 11
- ❑ Mar. 17 Mark Your Bible
- ❑ Mar. 18 Day of Reflection

- ❑ Mar. 19 Luke 12
- ❑ Mar. 20 Luke 13
- ❑ Mar. 21 Luke 14
- ❑ Mar. 22 Luke 15
- ❑ Mar. 23 Luke 16
- ❑ Mar. 24 Mark Your Bible
- ❑ Mar. 25 Day of Reflection

- ❑ Mar. 26 Luke 17
- ❑ Mar. 27 Luke 18
- ❑ Mar. 28 Luke 19
- ❑ Mar. 29 Luke 20
- ❑ Mar. 30 Luke 21
- ❑ Mar. 31 Mark Your Bible
- ❑ Apr. 1 Day of Reflection

- ❑ Apr. 2 Luke 22
- ❑ Apr. 3 Luke 23
- ❑ Apr. 4 Luke 24
- ❑ Apr. 5 John 1
- ❑ Apr. 6 John 2
- ❑ Apr. 7 Mark Your Bible
- ❑ Apr. 8 Day of Reflection

- ❑ Apr. 9 John 3
- ❑ Apr. 10 John 4
- ❑ Apr. 11 John 5
- ❑ Apr. 12 John 6
- ❑ Apr. 13 John 7
- ❑ Apr. 14 Mark Your Bible
- ❑ Apr. 15 Day of Reflection

- ❑ Apr. 16 John 8
- ❑ Apr. 17 John 9
- ❑ Apr. 18 John 10
- ❑ Apr. 19 John 11
- ❑ Apr. 20 John 12
- ❑ Apr. 21 Mark Your Bible
- ❑ Apr. 22 Day of Reflection

One Year Reading Schedule for N.T.

- ❑ Apr. 23 John 13
- ❑ Apr. 24 John 14
- ❑ Apr. 25 John 15
- ❑ Apr. 26 John 16
- ❑ Apr. 27 John 17
- ❑ Apr. 28 Mark Your Bible
- ❑ Apr. 29 Day of Reflection

- ❑ Apr. 30 John 18
- ❑ May 1 John 19
- ❑ May 2 John 20
- ❑ May 3 John 21
- ❑ May 4 Acts 1
- ❑ May 5 Mark Your Bible
- ❑ May 6 Day of Reflection

- ❑ May 7 Acts 2
- ❑ May 8 Acts 3
- ❑ May 9 Acts 4
- ❑ May 10 Acts 5
- ❑ May 11 Acts 6
- ❑ May 12 Mark Your Bible
- ❑ May 13 Day of Reflection

- ❑ May 14 Acts 7
- ❑ May 15 Acts 8
- ❑ May 16 Acts 9
- ❑ May 17 Acts 10
- ❑ May 18 Acts 11
- ❑ May 19 Mark Your Bible
- ❑ May 20 Day of Reflection

- ❑ May 21 Acts 12
- ❑ May 22 Acts 13
- ❑ May 23 Acts 14
- ❑ May 24 Acts 15
- ❑ May 25 Acts 16
- ❑ May 26 Mark Your Bible
- ❑ May 27 Day of Reflection

- ❑ May 28 Acts 17
- ❑ May 29 Acts 18
- ❑ May 30 Acts 19
- ❑ May 31 Acts 20
- ❑ June 1 Acts 21
- ❑ June 2 Mark Your Bible
- ❑ June 3 Day of Reflection

- ❑ June 4 Acts 22
- ❑ June 5 Acts 23
- ❑ June 6 Acts 24
- ❑ June 7 Acts 25
- ❑ June 8 Acts 26
- ❑ June 9 Mark Your Bible
- ❑ June 10 Day of Reflection

- ❑ June 11 Acts 27
- ❑ June 12 Acts 28
- ❑ June 13 Romans 1
- ❑ June 14 Romans 2
- ❑ June 15 Romans 3
- ❑ June 16 Mark Your Bible
- ❑ June 17 Day of Reflection

One Year Reading Schedule for N.T.

- ❑ June 18 Romans 4
- ❑ June 19 Romans 5
- ❑ June 20 Romans 6
- ❑ June 21 Romans 7
- ❑ June 22 Romans 8
- ❑ June 23 Mark Your Bible
- ❑ June 24 Day of Reflection

- ❑ June 25 Romans 9
- ❑ June 26 Romans 10
- ❑ June 27 Romans 11
- ❑ June 28 Romans 12
- ❑ June 29 Romans 13
- ❑ June 30 Mark Your Bible
- ❑ July 1 Day of Reflection

- ❑ July 2 Romans 14
- ❑ July 3 Romans 15
- ❑ July 4 Romans 16
- ❑ July 5 1 Corinthians 1
- ❑ July 6 1 Corinthians 2
- ❑ July 7 Mark Your Bible
- ❑ July 8 Day of Reflection

- ❑ July 9 1 Corinthians 3
- ❑ July 10 1 Corinthians 4
- ❑ July 11 1 Corinthians 5
- ❑ July 12 1 Corinthians 6
- ❑ July 13 1 Corinthians 7
- ❑ July 14 Mark Your Bible
- ❑ July 15 Day of Reflection

- ❑ July 16 1 Corinthians 8
- ❑ July 17 1 Corinthians 9
- ❑ July 18 1 Corinthians 10
- ❑ July 19 1 Corinthians 11
- ❑ July 20 1 Corinthians 12
- ❑ July 21 Mark Your Bible
- ❑ July 22 Day of Reflection

- ❑ July 23 1 Corinthians 13
- ❑ July 24 1 Corinthians 14
- ❑ July 25 1 Corinthians 15
- ❑ July 26 1 Corinthians 16
- ❑ July 27 2 Corinthians 1
- ❑ July 28 Mark Your Bible
- ❑ July 29 Day of Reflection

- ❑ July 30 2 Corinthians 2
- ❑ July 31 2 Corinthians 3
- ❑ Aug. 1 2 Corinthians 4
- ❑ Aug. 2 2 Corinthians 5
- ❑ Aug. 3 2 Corinthians 6
- ❑ Aug. 4 Mark Your Bible
- ❑ Aug. 5 Day of Reflection

- ❑ Aug. 6 2 Corinthians 7
- ❑ Aug. 7 2 Corinthians 8
- ❑ Aug. 8 2 Corinthians 9
- ❑ Aug. 9 2 Corinthians 10
- ❑ Aug. 10 2 Corinthians 11
- ❑ Aug. 11 Mark Your Bible
- ❑ Aug. 12 Day of Reflection

One Year Reading Schedule for N.T.

- ❑ Aug. 13 2 Corinthians 12
- ❑ Aug. 14 2 Corinthians 13
- ❑ Aug. 15 Galatians 1
- ❑ Aug. 16 Galatians 2
- ❑ Aug. 17 Galatians 3
- ❑ Aug. 18 Mark Your Bible
- ❑ Aug. 19 Day of Reflection

- ❑ Aug. 20 Galatians 4
- ❑ Aug. 21 Galatians 5
- ❑ Aug. 22 Galatians 6
- ❑ Aug. 23 Ephesians 1
- ❑ Aug. 24 Ephesians 2
- ❑ Aug. 25 Mark Your Bible
- ❑ Aug. 26 Day of Reflection

- ❑ Aug. 27 Ephesians 3
- ❑ Aug. 28 Ephesians 4
- ❑ Aug. 29 Ephesians 5
- ❑ Aug. 30 Ephesians 6
- ❑ Aug. 31 Philippians 1
- ❑ Sept. 1 Mark Your Bible
- ❑ Sept. 2 Day of Reflection

- ❑ Sept. 3 Philippians 2
- ❑ Sept. 4 Philippians 3
- ❑ Sept. 5 Philippians 4
- ❑ Sept. 6 Colossians 1
- ❑ Sept. 7 Colossians 2
- ❑ Sept. 8 Mark Your Bible
- ❑ Sept. 9 Day of Reflection

- ❑ Sept. 10 Colossians 3
- ❑ Sept. 11 Colossians 4
- ❑ Sept. 12 1 Thessalonians 1
- ❑ Sept. 13 1 Thessalonians 2
- ❑ Sept. 14 1 Thessalonians 3
- ❑ Sept. 15 Mark Your Bible
- ❑ Sept. 16 Day of Reflection

- ❑ Sept. 17 1 Thessalonians 4
- ❑ Sept. 18 1 Thessalonians 5
- ❑ Sept. 19 2 Thessalonians 1
- ❑ Sept. 20 2 Thessalonians 2
- ❑ Sept. 21 2 Thessalonians 3
- ❑ Sept. 22 Mark Your Bible
- ❑ Sept. 23 Day of Reflection

- ❑ Sept. 24 1 Timothy 1
- ❑ Sept. 25 1 Timothy 2
- ❑ Sept. 26 1 Timothy 3
- ❑ Sept. 27 1 Timothy 4
- ❑ Sept. 28 1 Timothy 5
- ❑ Sept. 29 Mark Your Bible
- ❑ Sept. 30 Day of Reflection

- ❑ Oct. 1 1 Timothy 6
- ❑ Oct. 2 2 Timothy 1
- ❑ Oct. 3 2 Timothy 2
- ❑ Oct. 4 2 Timothy 3
- ❑ Oct. 5 2 Timothy 4
- ❑ Oct. 6 Mark Your Bible
- ❑ Oct. 7 Day of Reflection

One Year Reading Schedule for N.T.

- ❑ Oct. 8 Titus 1
- ❑ Oct. 9 Titus 2
- ❑ Oct. 10 Titus 3
- ❑ Oct. 11 Philemon
- ❑ Oct. 12 Hebrews 1
- ❑ Oct. 13 Mark Your Bible
- ❑ Oct. 14 Day of Reflection

- ❑ Oct. 15 Hebrews 2
- ❑ Oct. 16 Hebrews 3
- ❑ Oct. 17 Hebrews 4
- ❑ Oct. 18 Hebrews 5
- ❑ Oct. 19 Hebrews 6
- ❑ Oct. 20 Mark Your Bible
- ❑ Oct. 21 Day of Reflection

- ❑ Oct. 22 Hebrews 7
- ❑ Oct. 23 Hebrews 8
- ❑ Oct. 24 Hebrews 9
- ❑ Oct. 25 Hebrews 10
- ❑ Oct. 26 Hebrews 11
- ❑ Oct. 27 Mark Your Bible
- ❑ Oct. 28 Day of Reflection

- ❑ Oct. 29 Hebrews 12
- ❑ Oct. 30 Hebrews 13
- ❑ Oct. 31 James 1
- ❑ Nov. 1 James 2
- ❑ Nov. 2 James 3
- ❑ Nov. 3 Mark Your Bible
- ❑ Nov. 4 Day of Reflection

- ❑ Nov. 5 James 4
- ❑ Nov. 6 James 5
- ❑ Nov. 7 1 Peter 1
- ❑ Nov. 8 1 Peter 2
- ❑ Nov. 9 1 Peter 3
- ❑ Nov. 10 Mark Your Bible
- ❑ Nov. 11 Day of Reflection

- ❑ Nov. 12 1 Peter 4
- ❑ Nov. 13 1 Peter 5
- ❑ Nov. 14 2 Peter 1
- ❑ Nov. 15 2 Peter 2
- ❑ Nov. 16 2 Peter 3
- ❑ Nov. 17 Mark Your Bible
- ❑ Nov. 18 Day of Reflection

- ❑ Nov. 19 1 John 1
- ❑ Nov. 20 1 John 2
- ❑ Nov. 21 1 John 3
- ❑ Nov. 22 1 John 4
- ❑ Nov. 23 1 John 5
- ❑ Nov. 24 Mark Your Bible
- ❑ Nov. 25 Day of Reflection

- ❑ Nov. 26 2 John
- ❑ Nov. 27 3 John
- ❑ Nov. 28 Jude
- ❑ Nov. 29 Revelation 1
- ❑ Nov. 30 Revelation 2
- ❑ Dec. 1 Mark Your Bible
- ❑ Dec. 2 Day of Reflection

One Year Reading Schedule for N.T.

- ❑ Dec. 3 Revelation 3
- ❑ Dec. 4 Revelation 4
- ❑ Dec. 5 Revelation 5
- ❑ Dec. 6 Revelation 6
- ❑ Dec. 7 Revelation 7
- ❑ Dec. 8 Mark Your Bible
- ❑ Dec. 9 Day of Reflection

- ❑ Dec. 10 Revelation 8
- ❑ Dec. 11 Revelation 9
- ❑ Dec. 12 Revelation 10
- ❑ Dec. 13 Revelation 11
- ❑ Dec. 14 Revelation 12
- ❑ Dec. 15 Mark Your Bible
- ❑ Dec. 16 Day of Reflection

- ❑ Dec. 17 Revelation 13
- ❑ Dec. 18 Revelation 14
- ❑ Dec. 19 Revelation 15
- ❑ Dec. 20 Revelation 16
- ❑ Dec. 21 Revelation 17
- ❑ Dec. 22 Mark Your Bible
- ❑ Dec. 23 Day of Reflection

- ❑ Dec. 24 Revelation 18
- ❑ Dec. 25 Revelation 19
- ❑ Dec. 26 Revelation 20
- ❑ Dec. 27 Revelation 21
- ❑ Dec. 28 Revelation 22
- ❑ Dec. 29 Mark Your Bible
- ❑ Dec. 30 Day of Reflection

- ❑ Dec. 31 One Final Day

Appendix C

Index of Helpful Notes & Terms

("Symbolism in Revelation" listed together)

Index of Helpful Notes & Terms

Symbolism in Revelation:

Symbolism in Revelation (cont.):

Symbolism in Revelation (cont.):

Symbolism in Revelation (cont.):

Alphabetized Index (cont.)

Made in the USA
Middletown, DE
22 August 2024